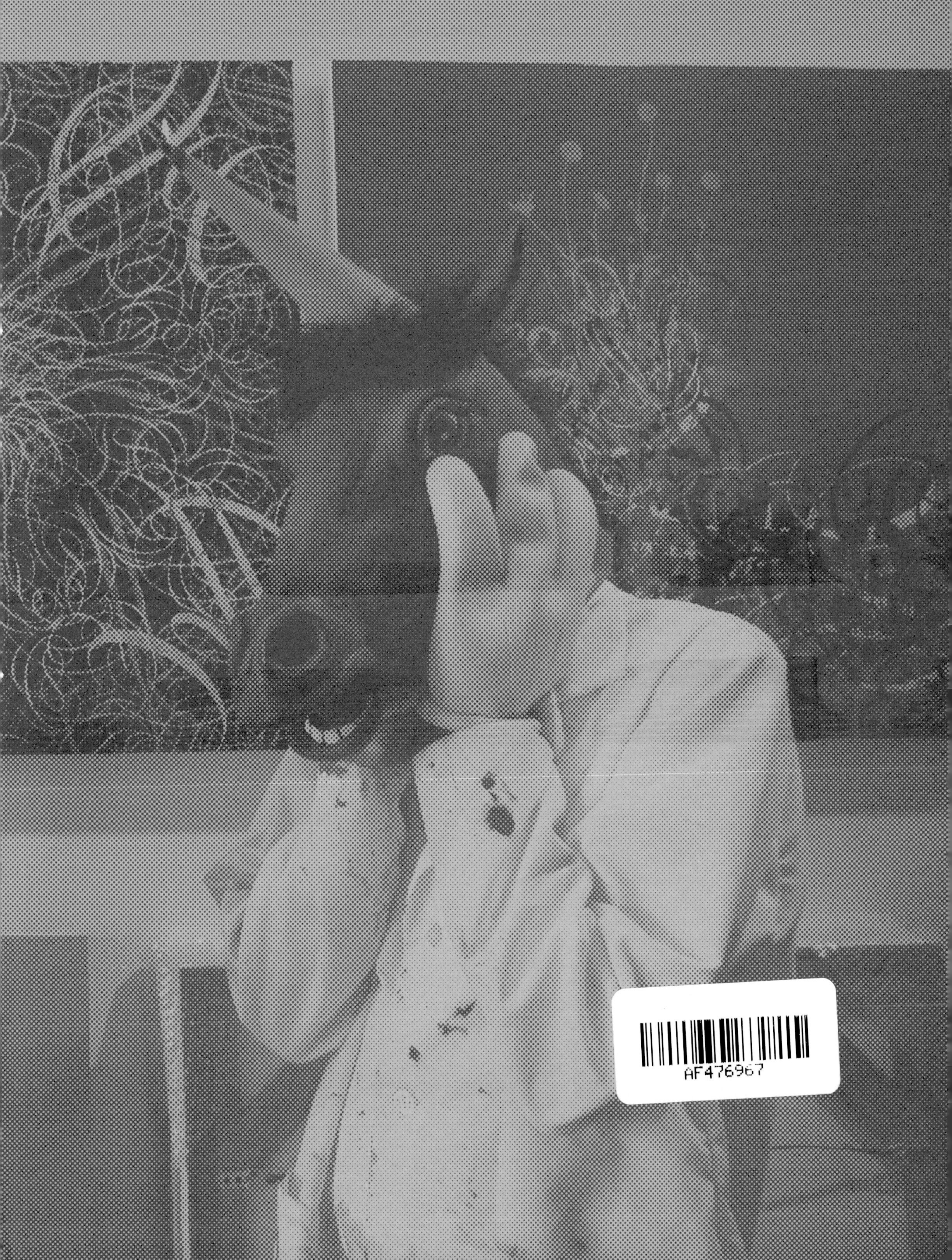

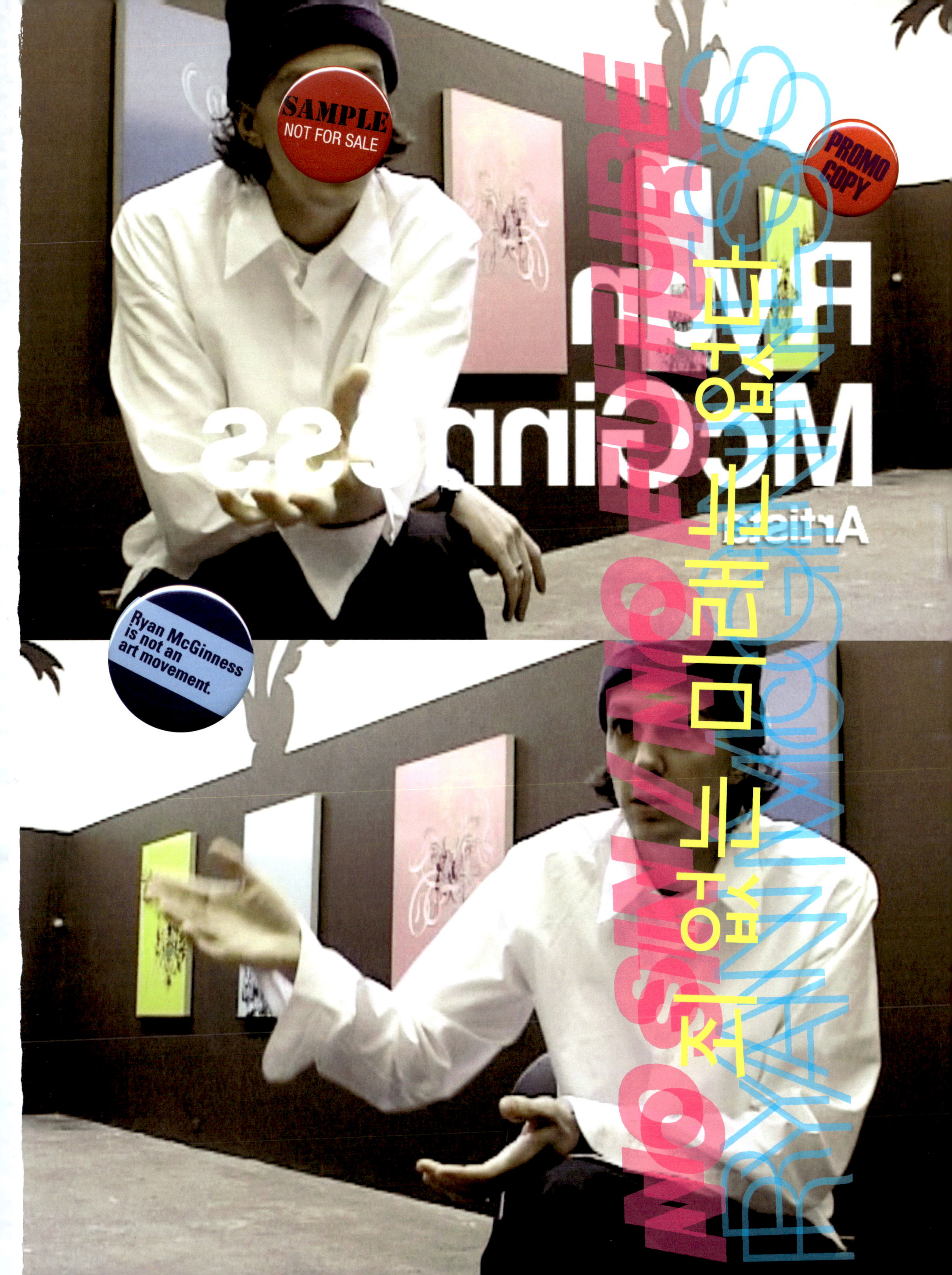
SAMPLE
NOT FOR SALE
PROMO
COPY
Ryan McGinness
is not an
art movement.

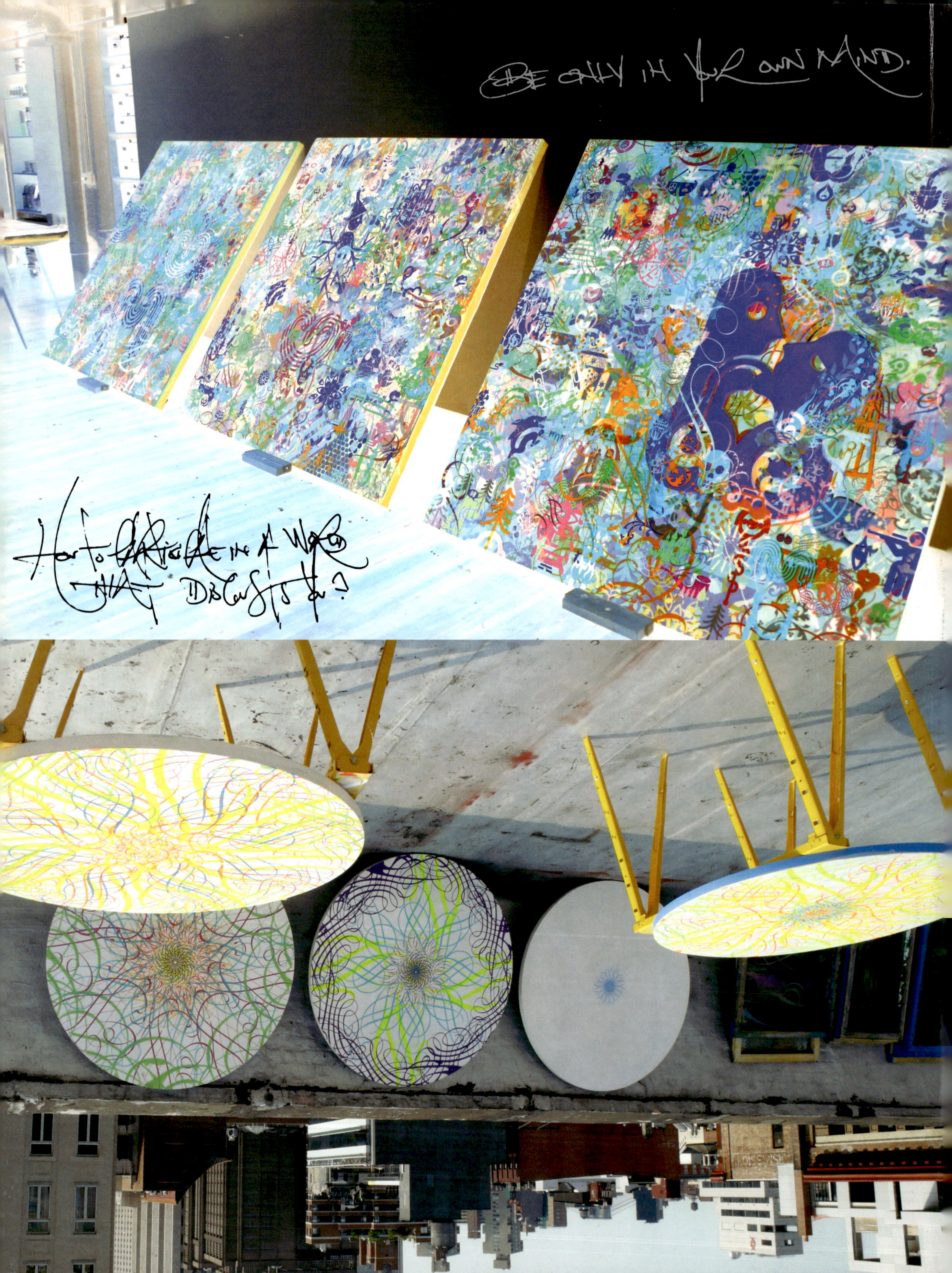
BE ONLY IN YOUR OWN MIND.

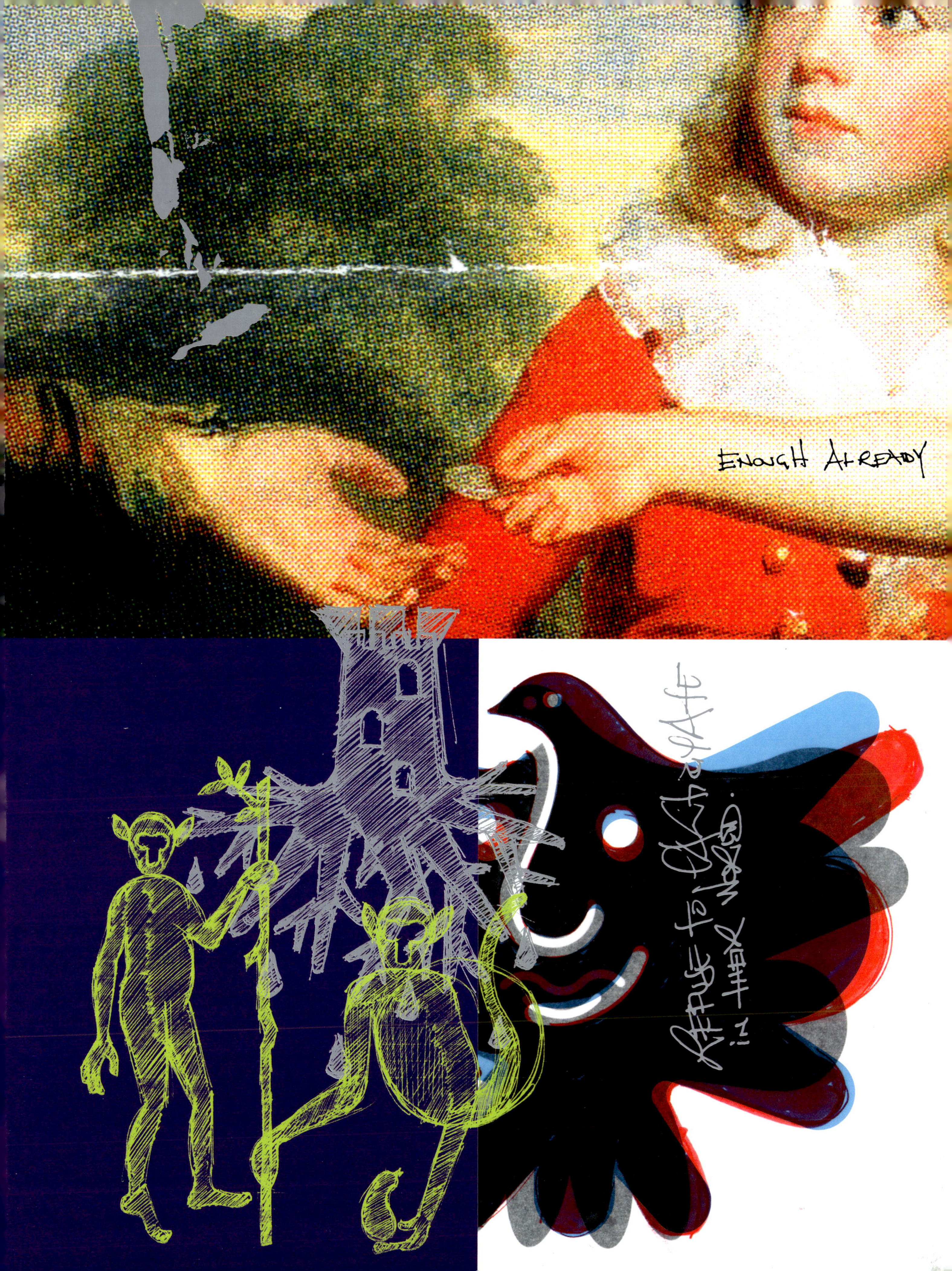
ENOUGH ALREADY
REFUSE to PARTICIPATE in their world.

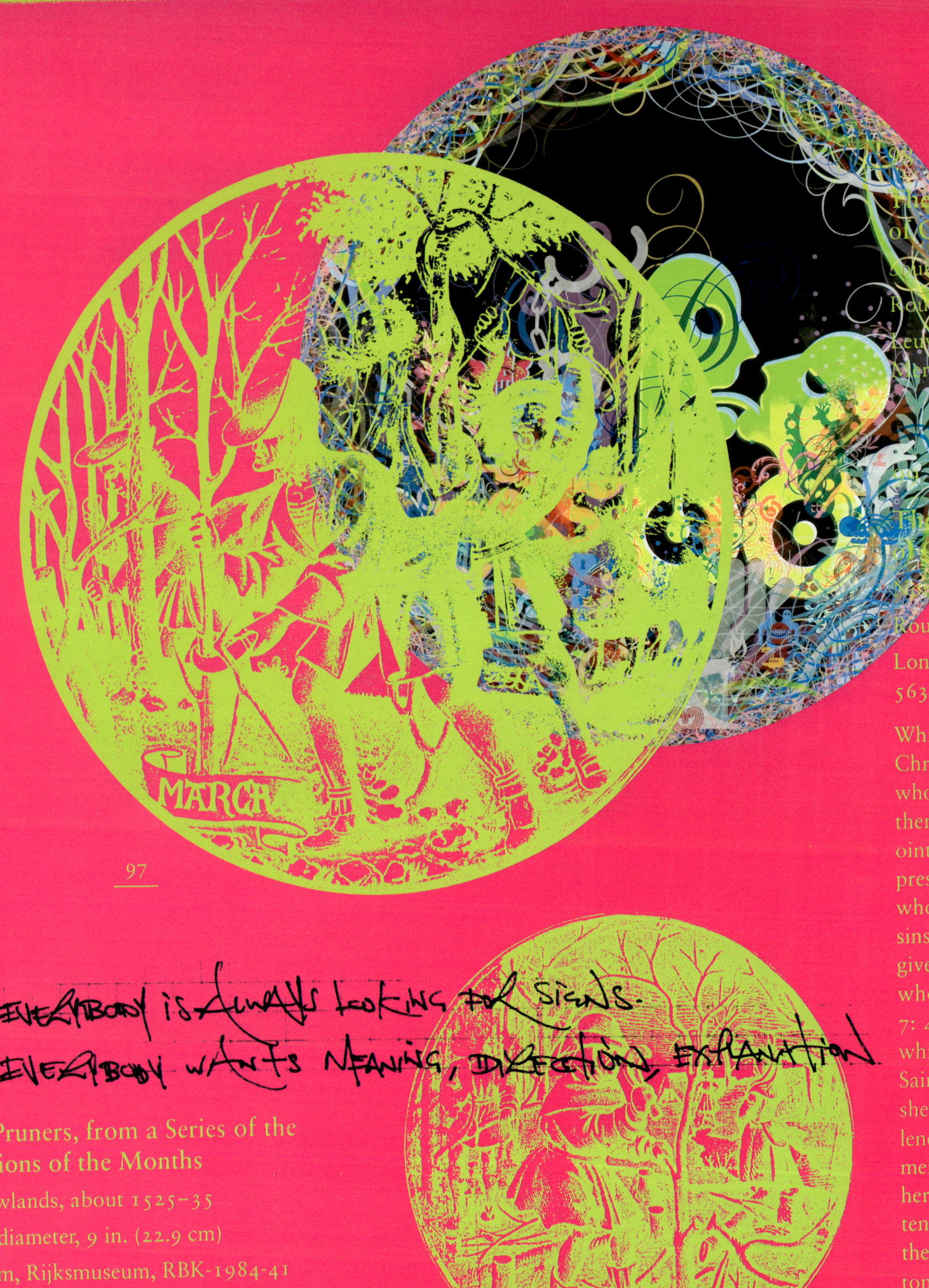

97

h: Pruners, from a Series of the
pations of the Months

Lowlands, about 1525–35
lel: diameter, 9 in. (22.9 cm)
rdam, Rijksmuseum, RBK-1984-41
bed (on the banderole): MARCIVS

onservative nature of the subject matter is ed by that of the style. The stocky figures ng stylized trees and vines have much in ion with those in an analogous composition e Master of the Death of Absalom some es earlier in date (fig. 1; see also cat. no. 20); he costumes indicate a date well into the sec- uarter of the sixteenth century. The ram, the cal sign for Aries, is seen not in its usual air-

FIG. 1 Master of the Death of Absalom. *March: Pruners*, from a series of the Occupations of the Months. Brush and black ink, with light blue highlights, on gray prepared paper. 1500–1510. London, British Museum

The Adulterous Woman
of Christ

South Lowlands, Leuven, a
Roundel: diameter, 9 in. (2
Leuven, Stedelijk Museum
Mertens, VIII/13

The Adulterous Woman
of Christ

South Lowlands, about 15
Roundel: diameter, 9 in. (2
London, Victoria and Albe
5634-1859

While a guest at the table
Christ was approached by
who proceeded to wash his
them with her hair, and t
ointment she had brough
pressed dismay that Christ
whose reputation had bee
sins. In response Christ sai
given her, because she ha
whom less is forgiven, h
7: 47). Although the recou
which appears only in th
Saint Luke (7: 36–50), doe
she is traditionally believe
lene, recognizable by her a
ment. The Leuven roundel
her identity, as three princ
tent saint's life are depicte
the far right, an angel tells
tomb that Christ has risen
the near background, M
returned to the tomb aft
what had transpired, sees
takes to be a gardener, bu
he is Christ and reaches o
ished not to touch him (
20: 14–17); and in the
Maries on their way to f
by the resurrected Christ
The Leuven roundel i

II. The Symbol

1. What is symbolic?

In looking at pictures, sculptures, architecture, and all kinds of ornamentation, including ornaments on objects of daily use, from whatever period, ranging from Stone Age discoveries to modern paintings, we are constantly faced with the question: What does it mean? What is hidden in this thing? Pictures and ornamentation are, in fact, seldom unequivocal in their statements or easily "readable." The viewer infers an underlying meaning and looks for an interpretation. This often undefinable capacity of a representation to make a statement is also denoted by the term "symbolic content." This symbolic element in pictures is an implied value, a mediator between recognizable reality and the mystical, invisible realm of religion, philosophy, and

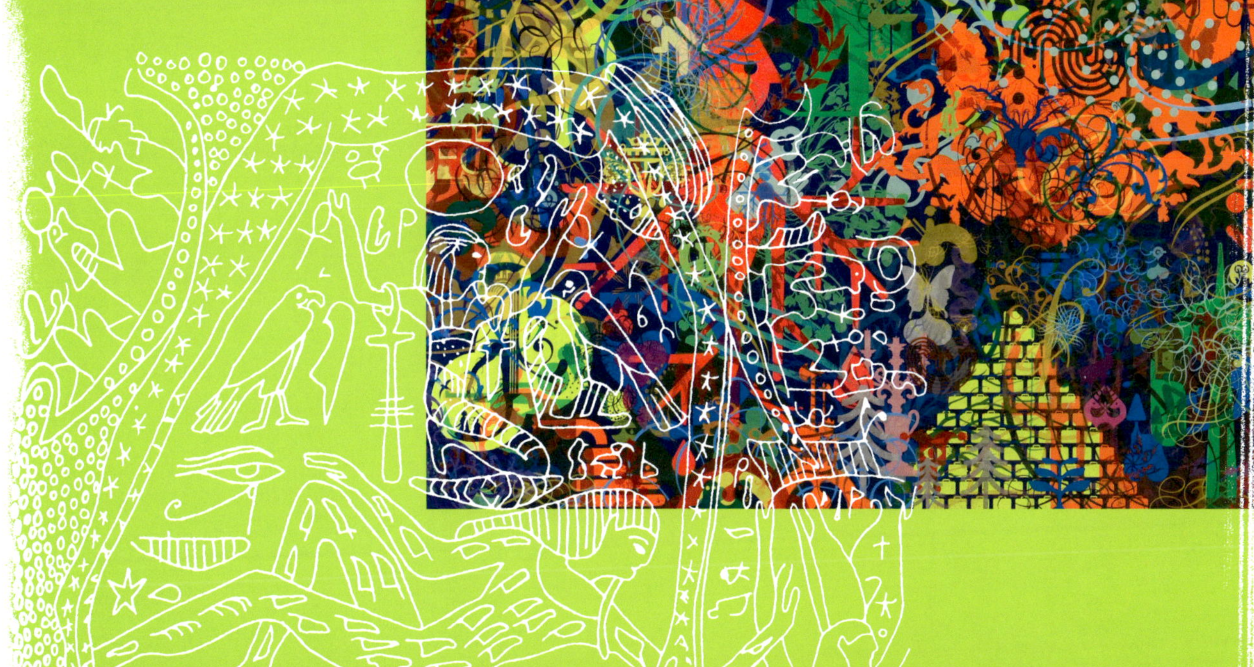

Painting on an Egyptian coffin

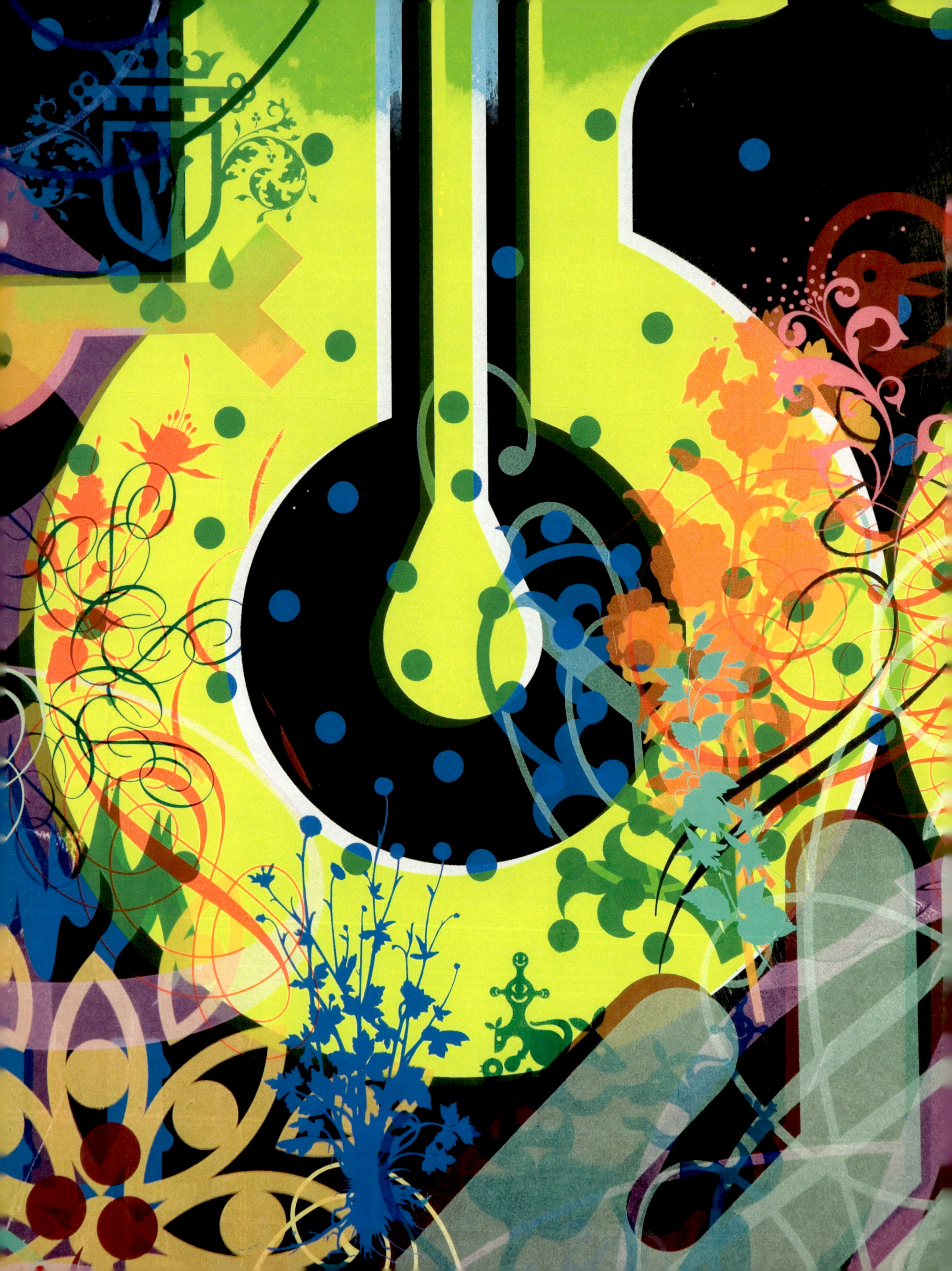

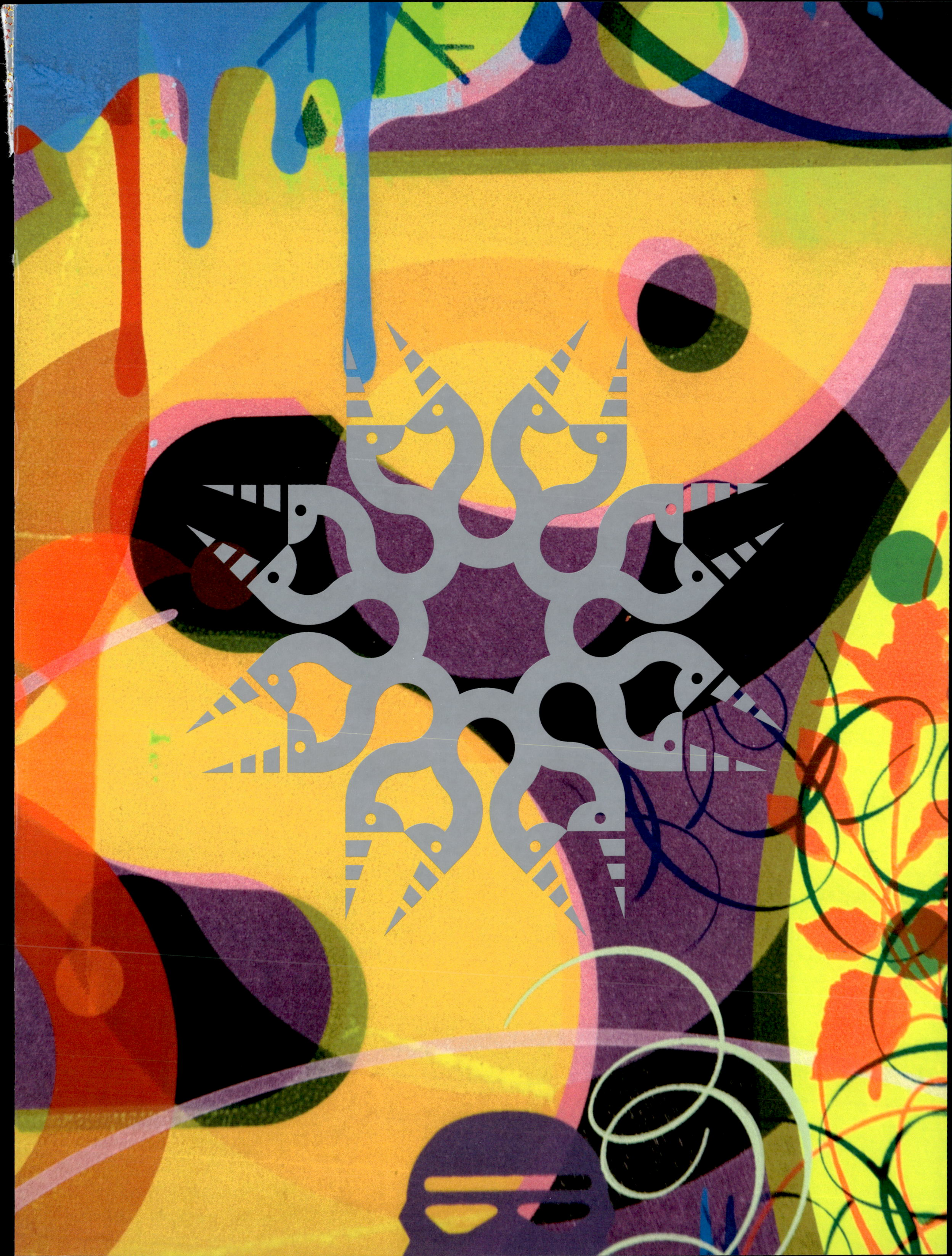

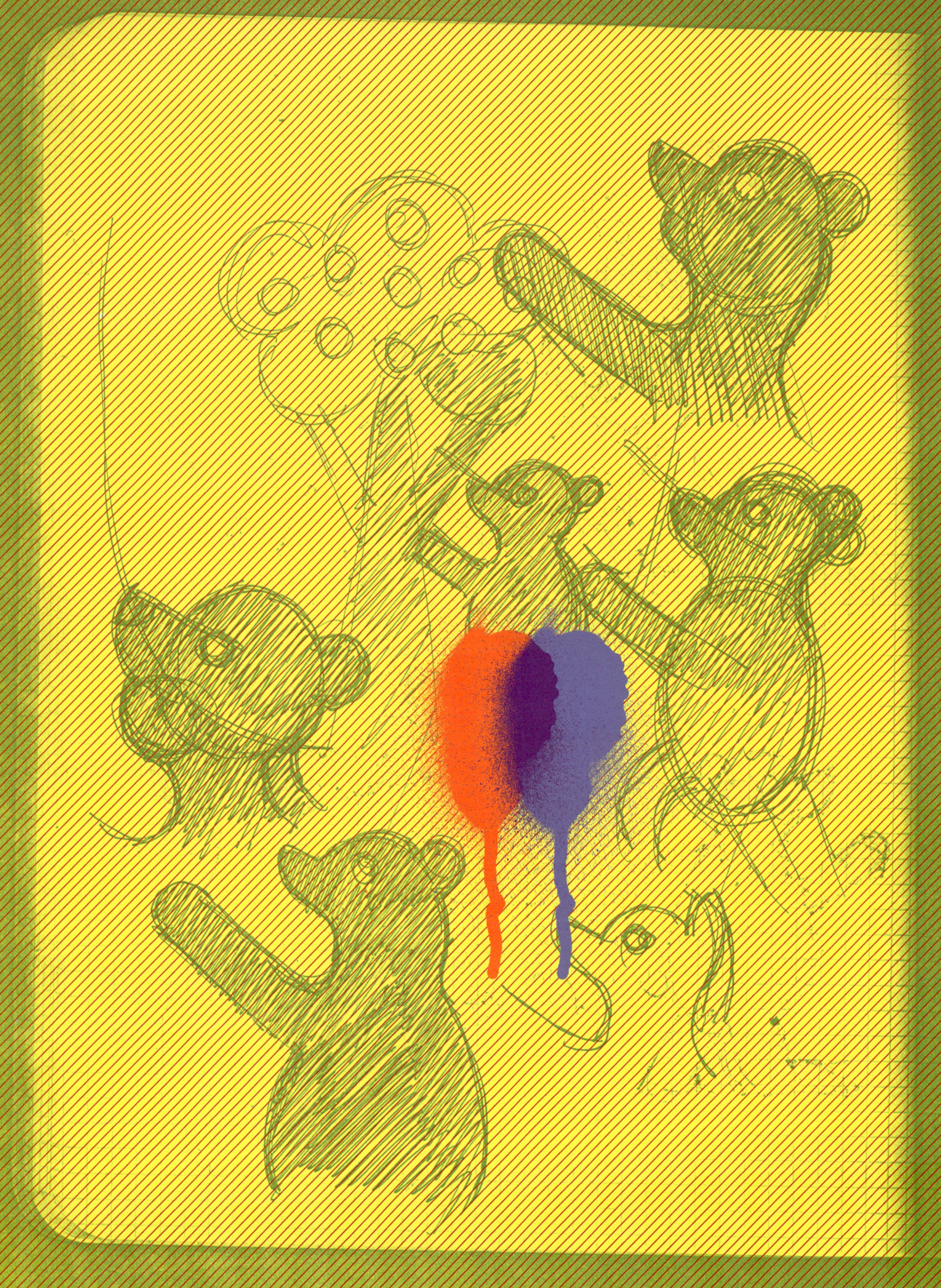

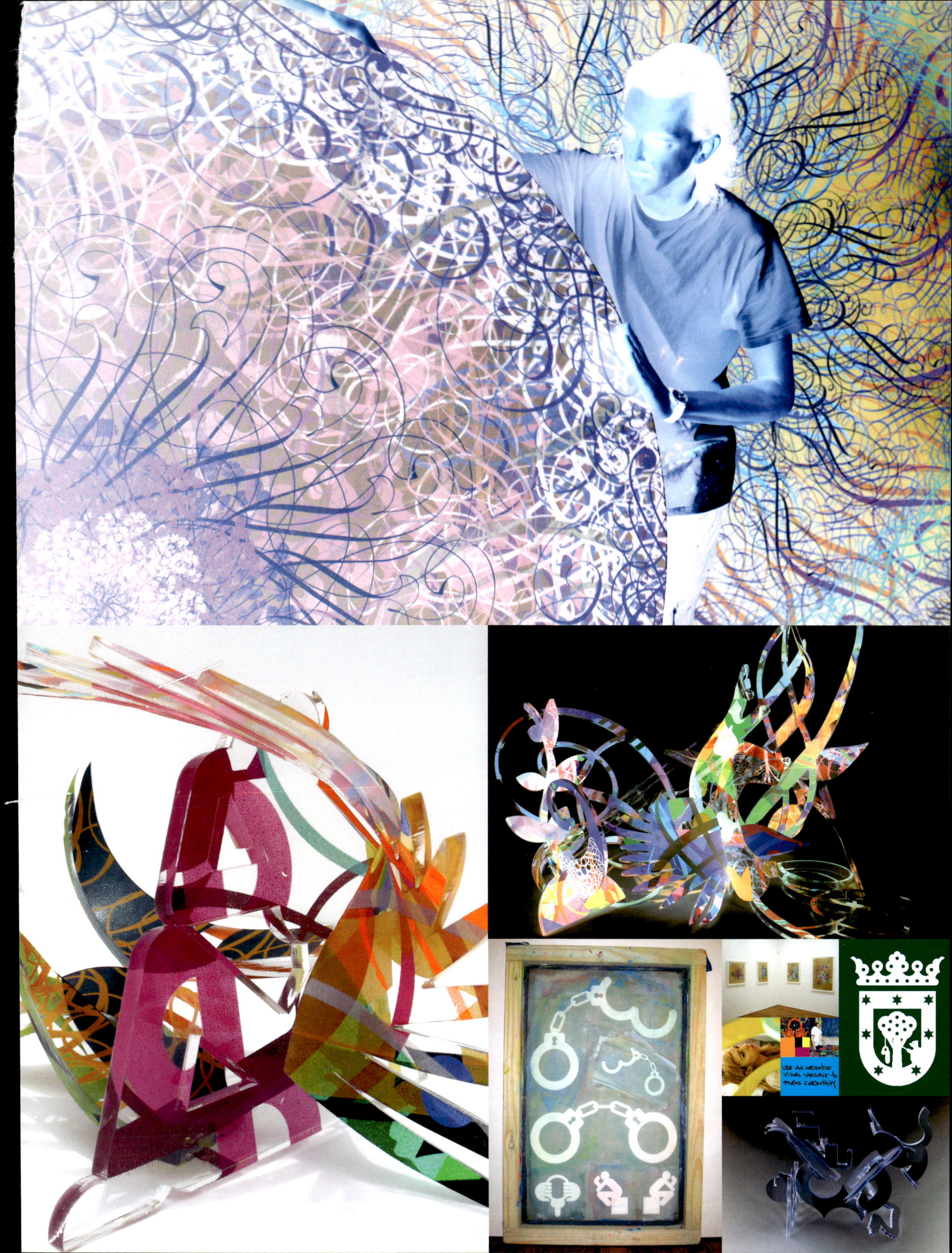
USE AN OBJECTIVE
VISUAL LANGUAGE to
FORCE SUBJECTIVITY

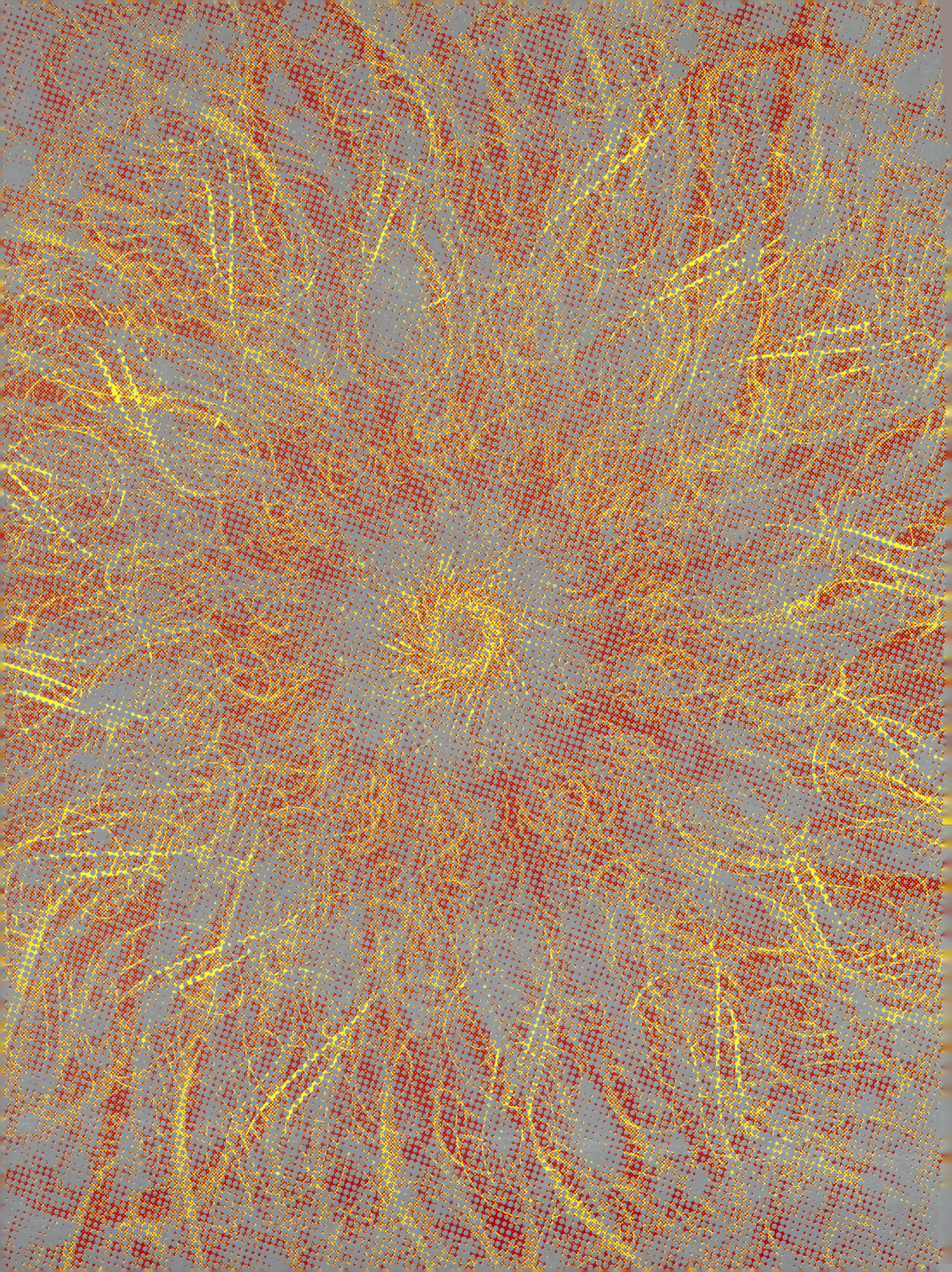

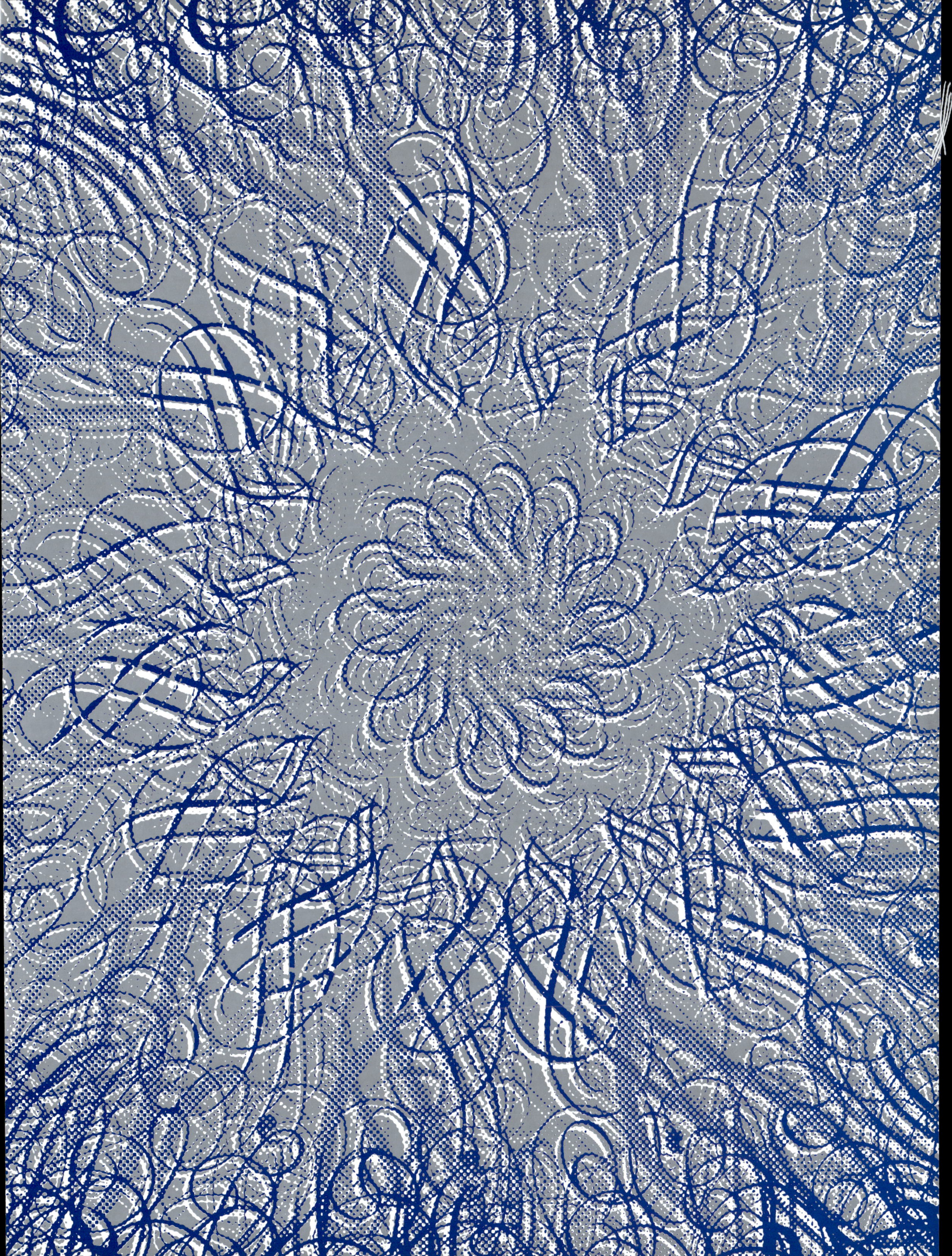

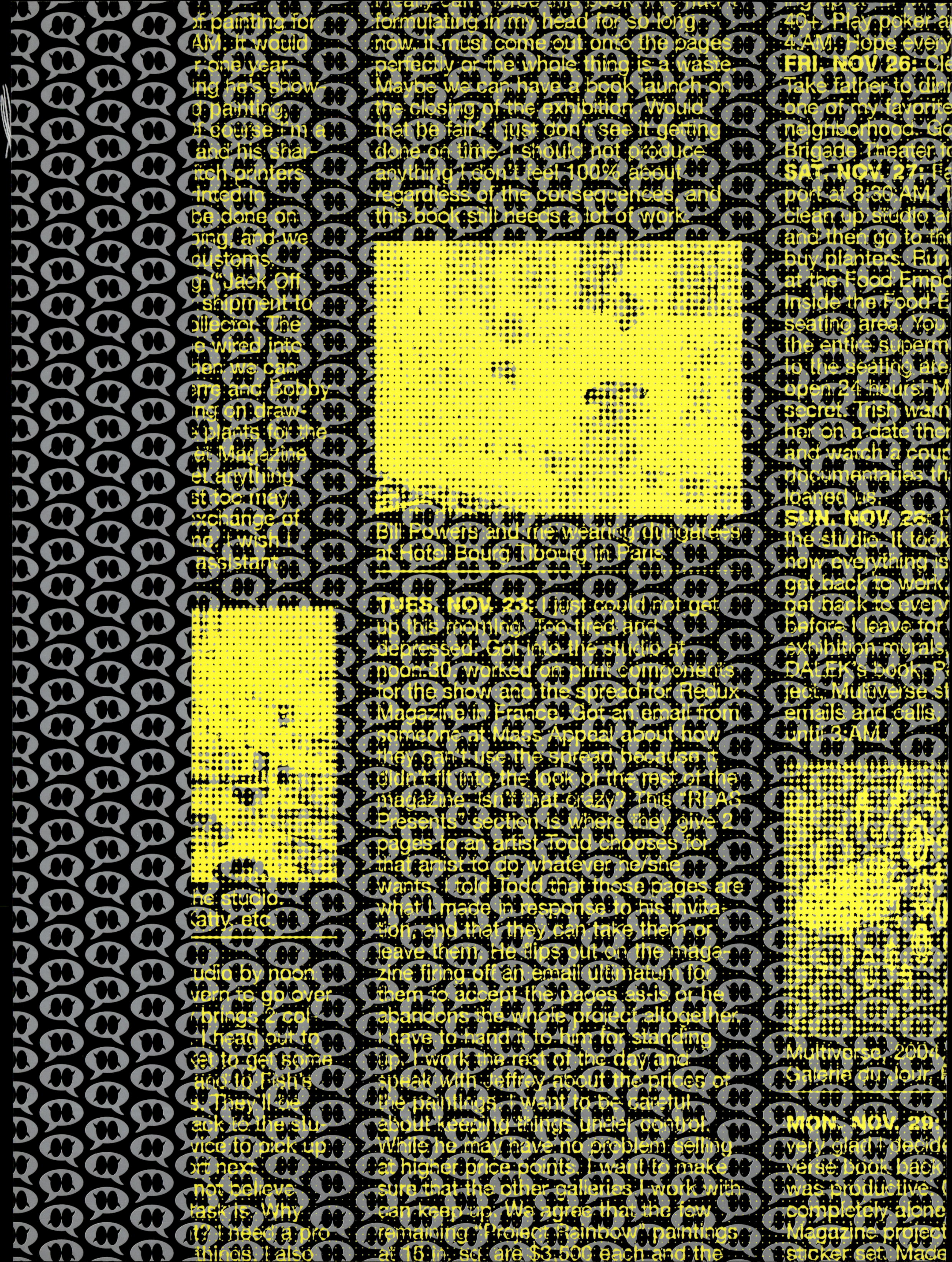

formulating in my head for so long now, it must come out onto the pages perfectly or the whole thing is a waste. Maybe we can have a book launch on the closing of the exhibition. Would that be fair? I just don't see it getting done on time. I should not produce anything I don't feel 100% about regardless of the consequences, and this book still needs a lot of work.

Bill Powers and me wearing dungarees at Hotel Bourg Tibourg in Paris.

TUES, NOV. 23: I just could not get up this morning. Too tired and depressed. Got into the studio at noon:30, worked on print components for the show and the spread for Redux Magazine in France. Got an email from someone at Mass Appeal about how they can't use the spread because it didn't fit into the look of the rest of the magazine. Isn't that crazy? This "REAS Presents" section is where they give 2 pages to an artist Todd chooses for that artist to do whatever he/she wants. I told Todd that those pages are what I made in response to his invitation, and that they can take them or leave them. He flips out on the magazine firing off an email ultimatum for them to accept the pages as-is or he abandons the whole project altogether. I have to hand it to him for standing up. I work the rest of the day and speak with Jeffrey about the prices of the paintings. I want to be careful about keeping things under control. While he may have no problem selling at higher price points, I want to make sure that the other galleries I work with can keep up. We agree that the few remaining "Project Rainbow" paintings at 16 in. sq. are $3,500 each and the

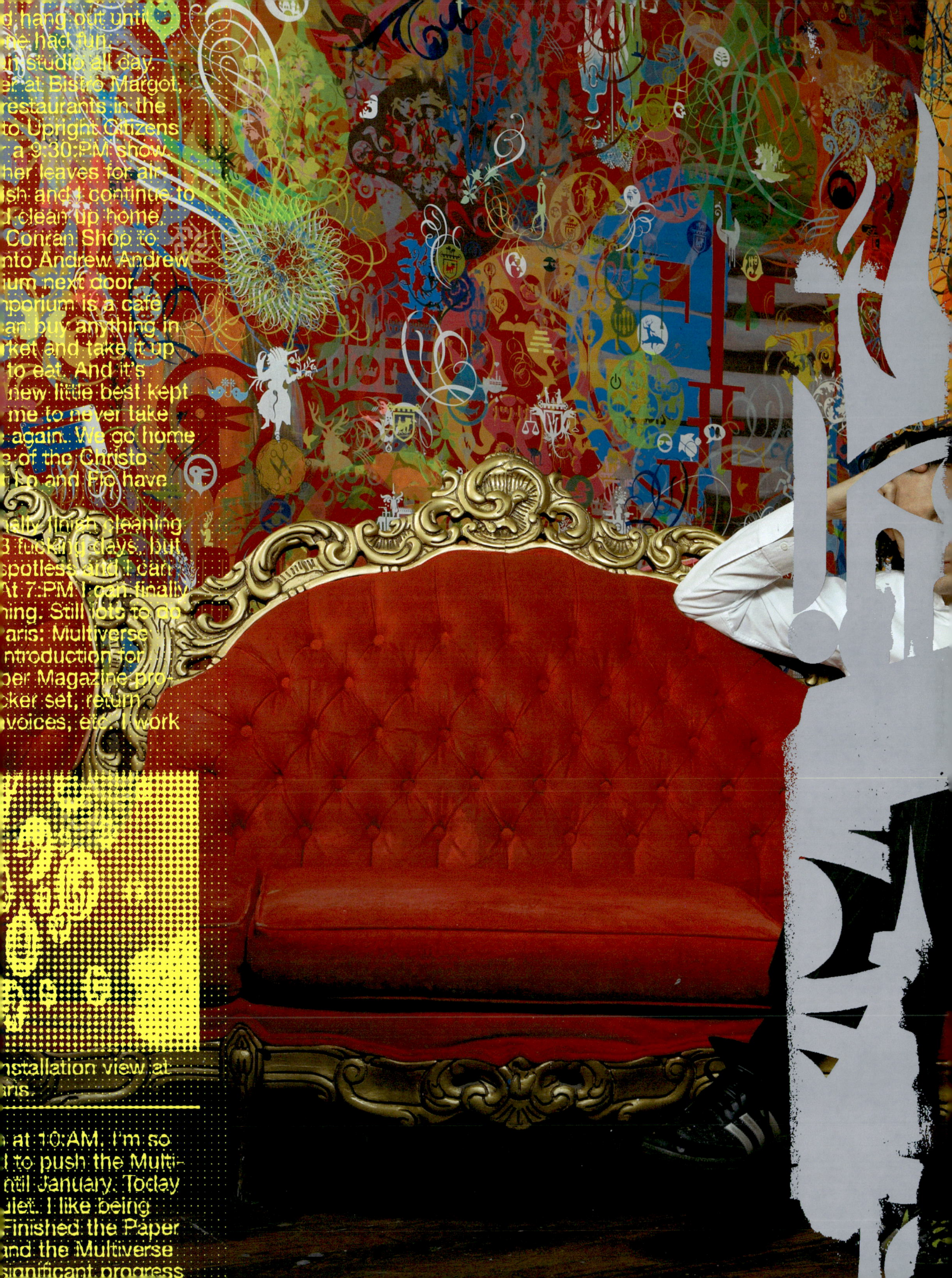

g hang out until
he had fun.
in studio all day.
er at Bistro Margot,
restaurants in the
to Upright Citizens
a 9:30 PM show.
her leaves for an-
ish and I continue to
d clean up home.
Conran Shop to
nto Andrew Andrew
ium next door.
nporium is a café
an buy anything in
rket and take it up
to eat. And it's
new little best kept
me to never take
again. We go home
e of the Christo
Lo and Flo have

ally finish cleaning
3 fucking days, but
spotless and I can
At 7 PM I can finally
hing. Still lots to do
aris: Multiverse
ntroduction for
per Magazine pro-
cker set, return
voices, etc. I work

nstallation view at
aris.

at 10 AM. I'm so
l to push the Multi-
ntil January. Today
uiet. I like being
Finished the Paper
and the Multiverse
significant progress

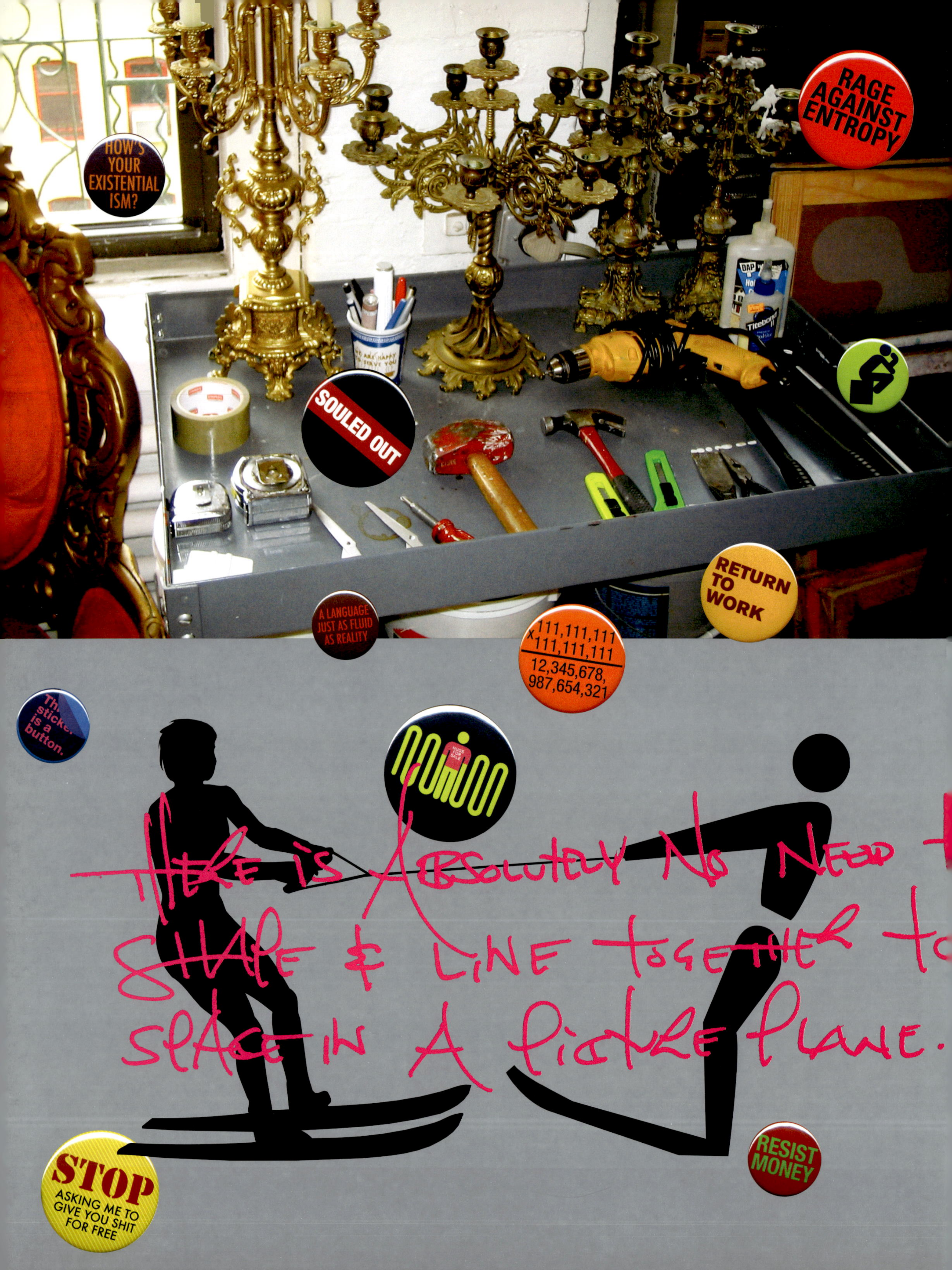
HOW'S YOUR EXISTENTIAL ISM?
RAGE AGAINST ENTROPY
SOULED OUT
RETURN TO WORK
A LANGUAGE JUST AS FLUID AS REALITY
x111,111,111
111,111,111
12,345,678,
987,654,321
WE ARE HAPPY TO SERVE YOU
Titebond
STOP
ASKING ME TO GIVE YOU SHIT FOR FREE
RESIST MONEY
THERE IS ABSOLUTELY NO NEED
SHAPE & LINE TOGETHER
SPACE IN A PICTURE PLANE.

SURVIVE SOCIETY
FUCK OFF
TREND FORECASTERS
The weather will be sponsored.
PACK YELLOW ON RED GROUND.
MOST PEOPLE JUST STEAL YOUR TIME
1 EXPAND (FILL)
2 CLIPPING MASK RELEASE
3 UNGROUP
4 CLIPPING MASK RELEASE
5 UNGROUP
6 SELECT ALL
7 FILL A COLOR
8 DELETE BOUNDING BOXES
9 GROUP
10 PATHFINDER—ADD TO SHAPE
FUCK OFF
COOL HUNTERS

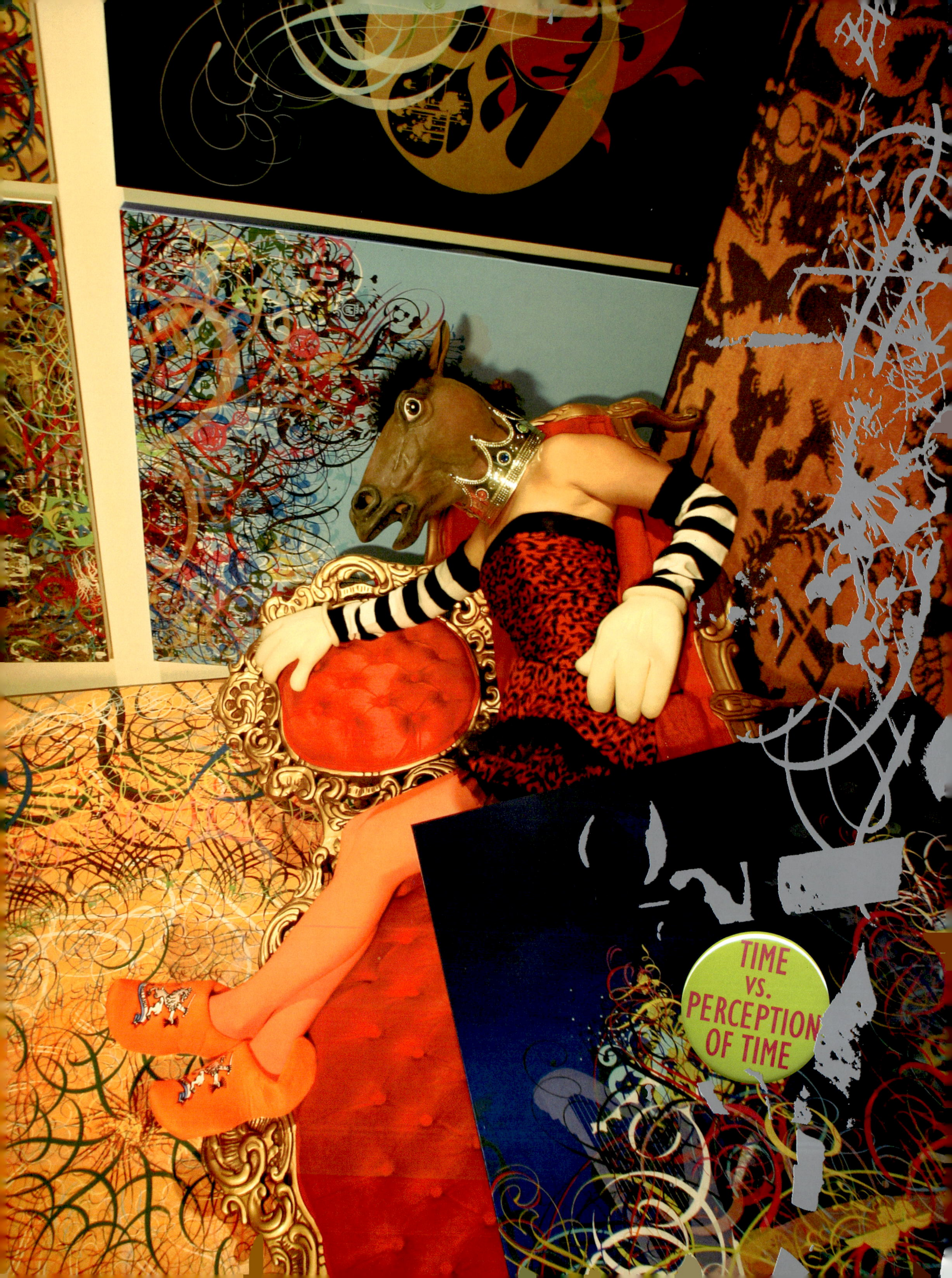
TIME
vs.
PERCEPTION
OF TIME

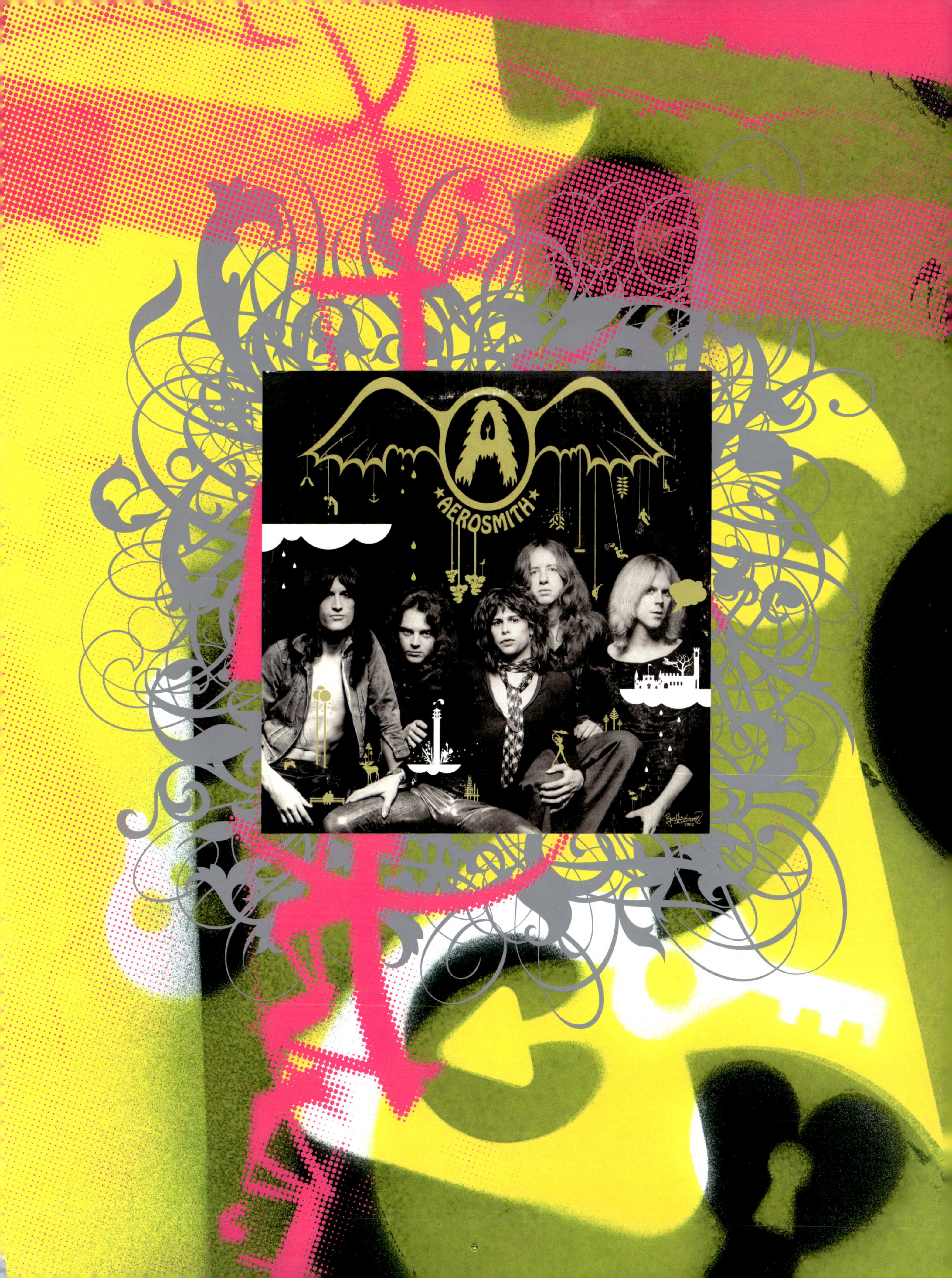
AEROSMITH

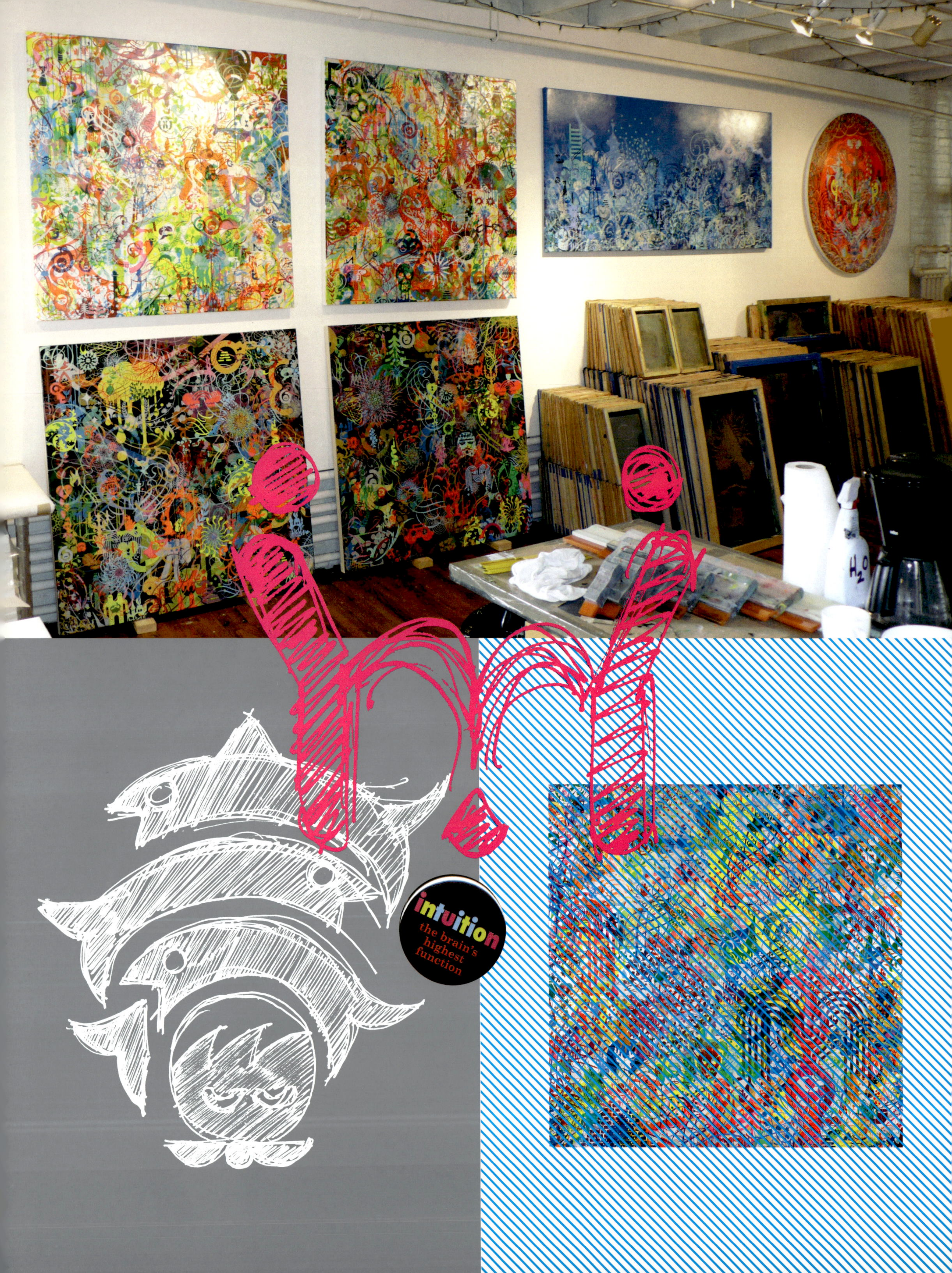
intuition
the brain's
highest
function

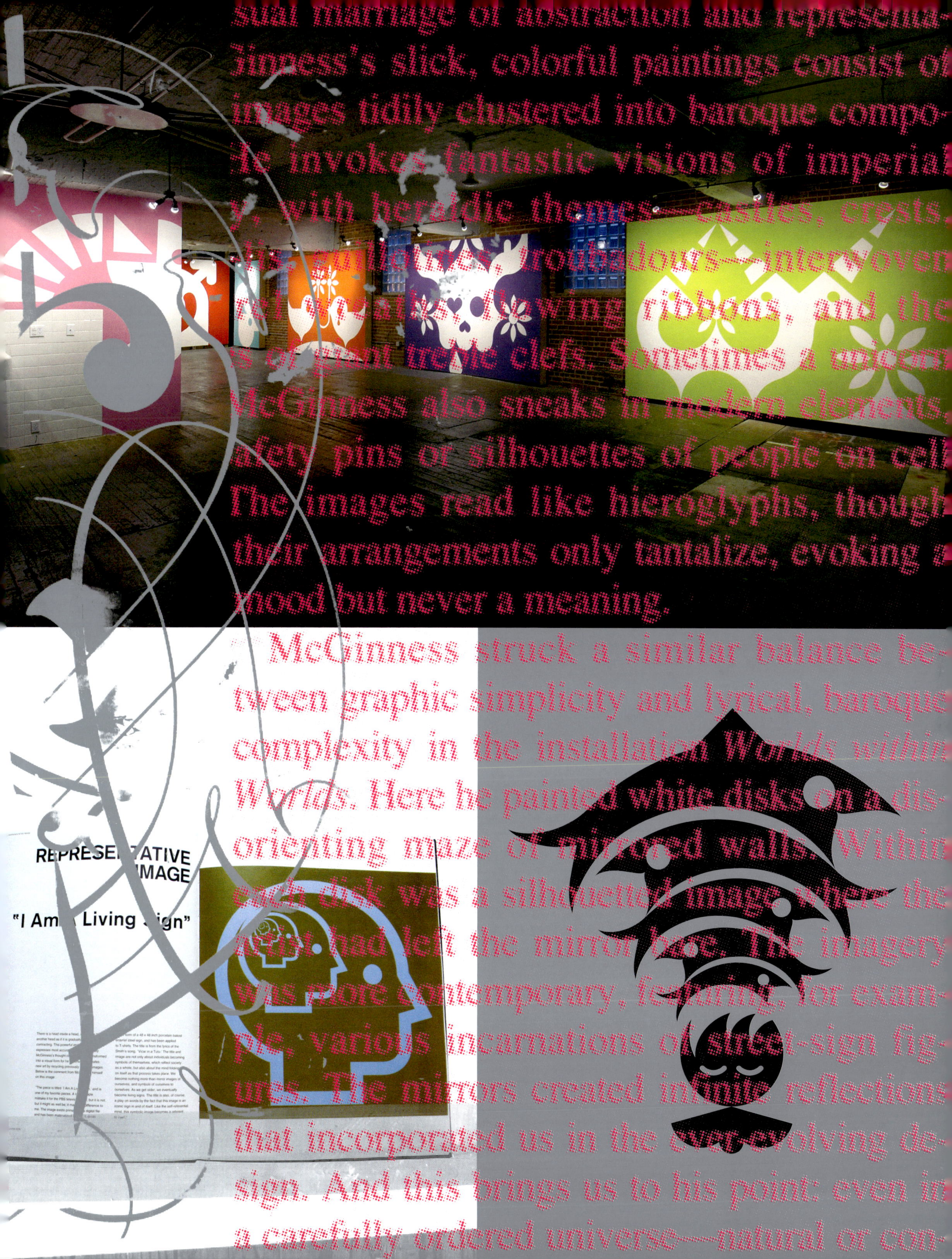

sual marriage of abstraction and representa- Ginness's slick, colorful paintings consist of images tidily clustered into baroque compo- He invokes fantastic visions of imperial y, with heraldic themes—castles, crests, lis, gauntlets, troubadours—interwoven rel wreaths, flowing ribbons, and the s of giant treble clefs. Sometimes a unicorn McGinness also sneaks in modern elements, afety pins or silhouettes of people on cell The images read like hieroglyphs, though their arrangements only tantalize, evoking a mood but never a meaning.

McGinness struck a similar balance between graphic simplicity and lyrical, baroque complexity in the installation *Worlds within Worlds*. Here he painted white disks on a disorienting maze of mirrored walls. Within each disk was a silhouetted image where the artist had left the mirror bare. The imagery was more contemporary, featuring, for example, various incarnations of street-sign figures. The mirrors created infinite reflections that incorporated us in the ever-evolving design. And this brings us to his point: even in a carefully ordered universe—natural or con-

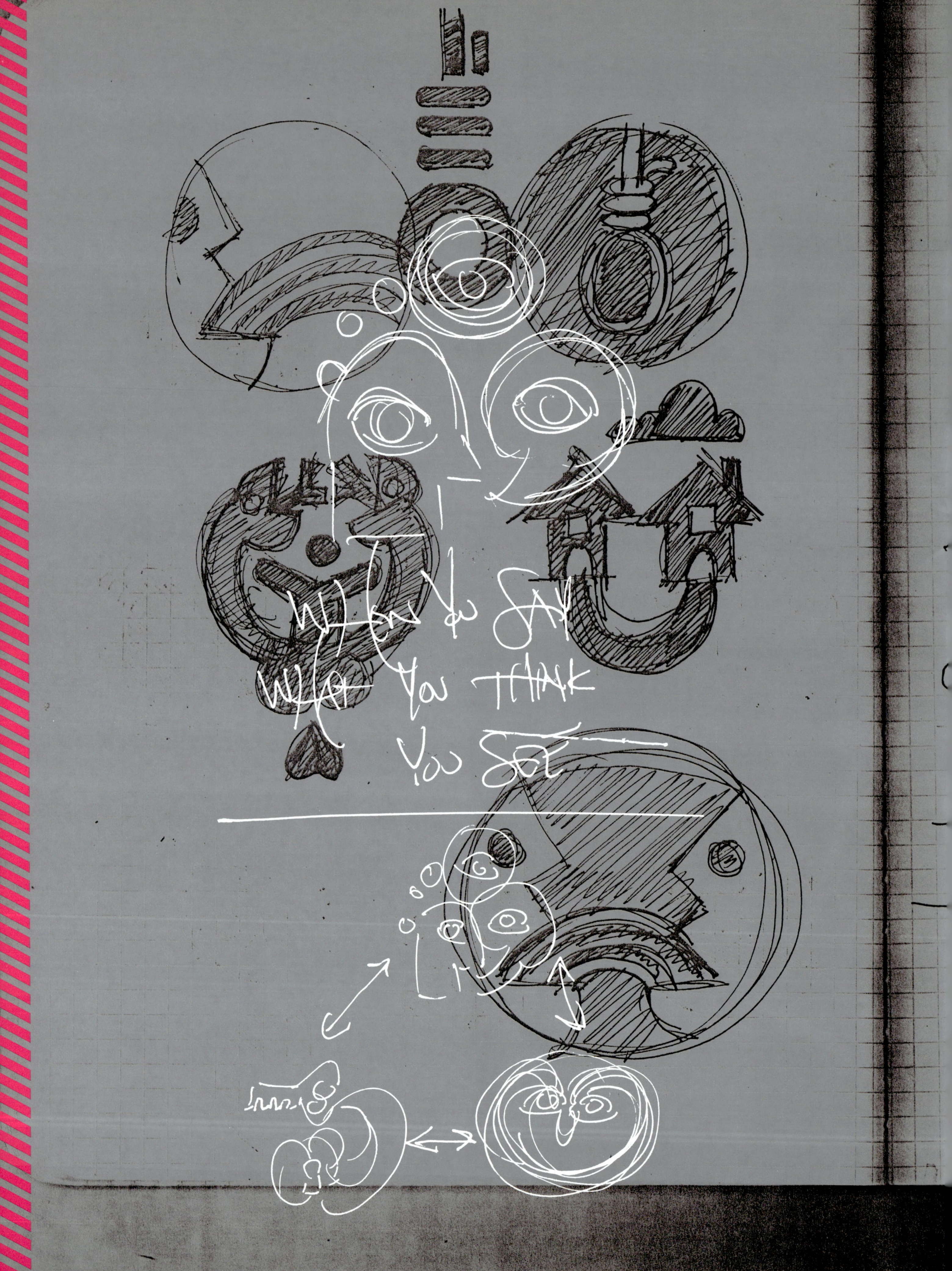
WHEN YOU SAY
WHAT YOU THINK
YOU SEE

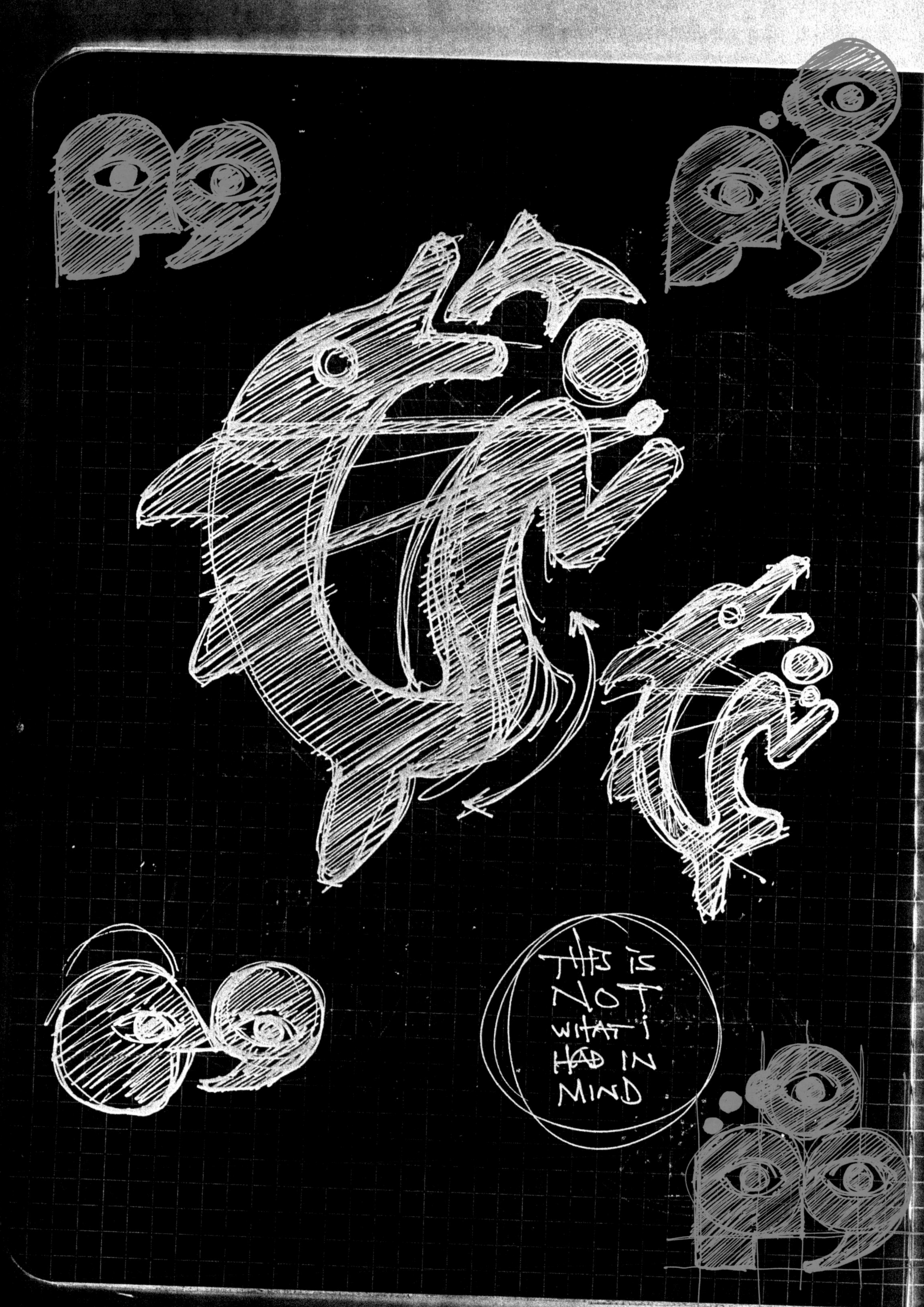
THIS IS
NOT
WHAT I
HAD IN
MIND

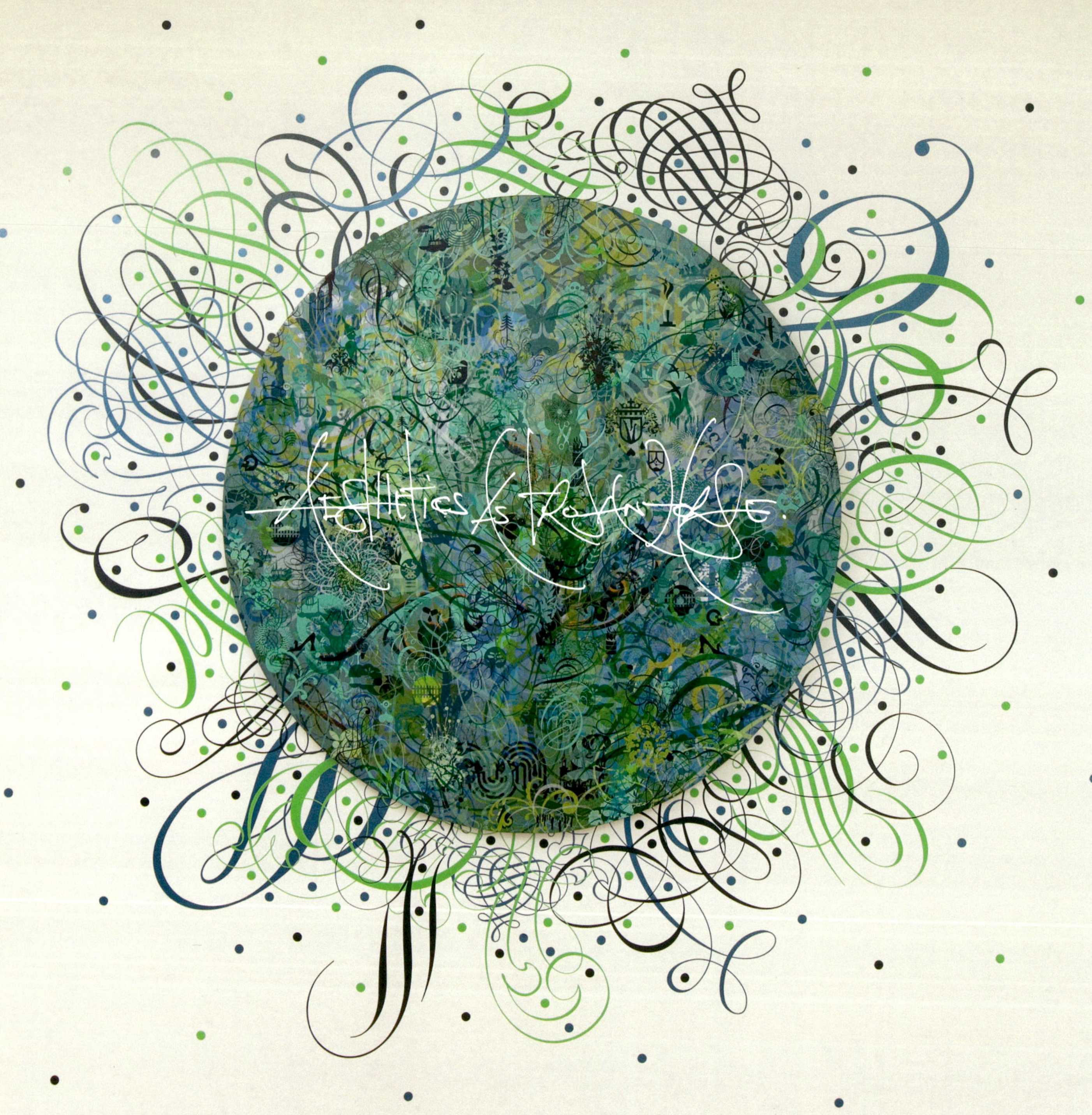
Aesthetics As Trojan Horse.

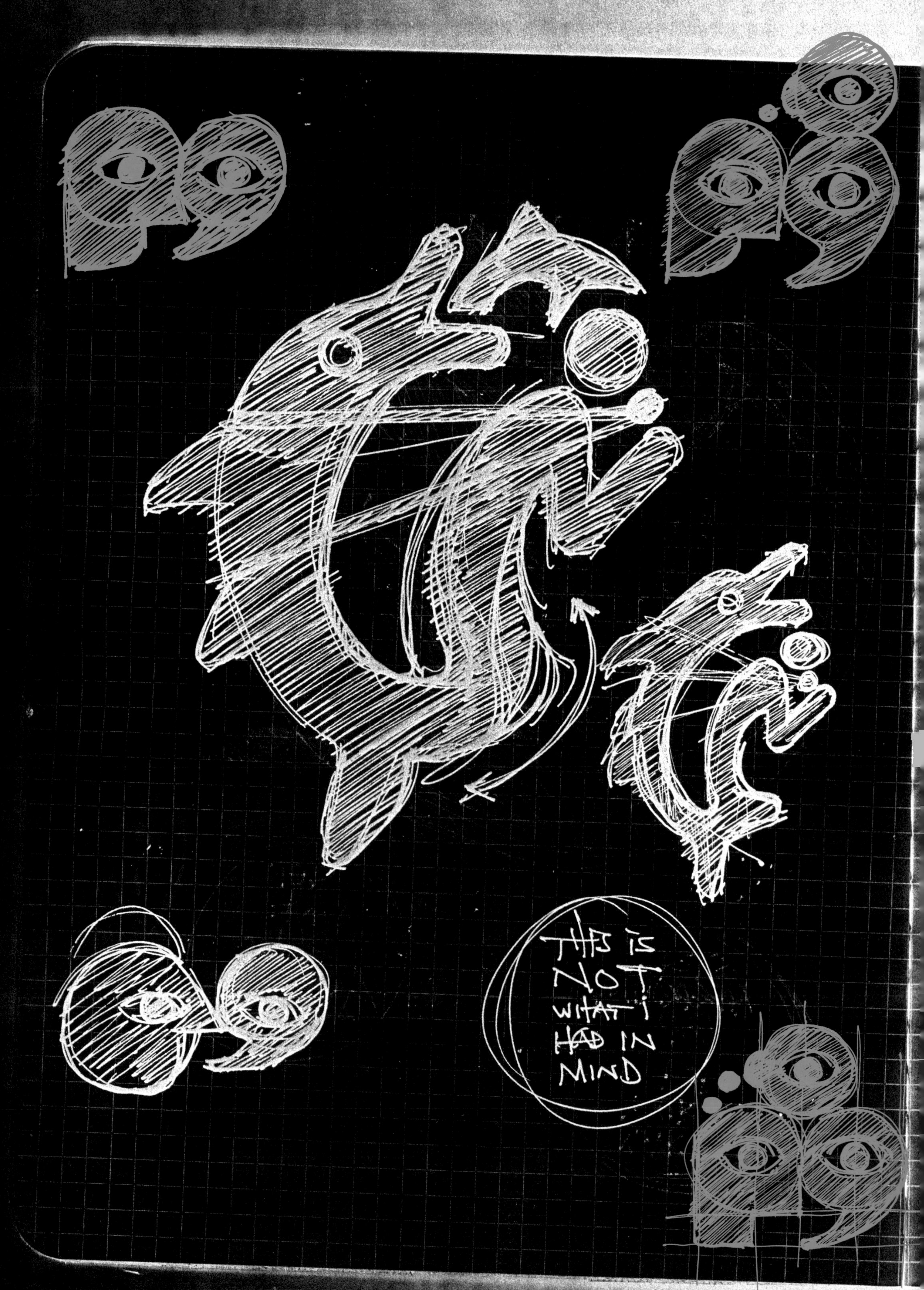
THIS IS
NOT
WHAT I
HAD IN
MIND

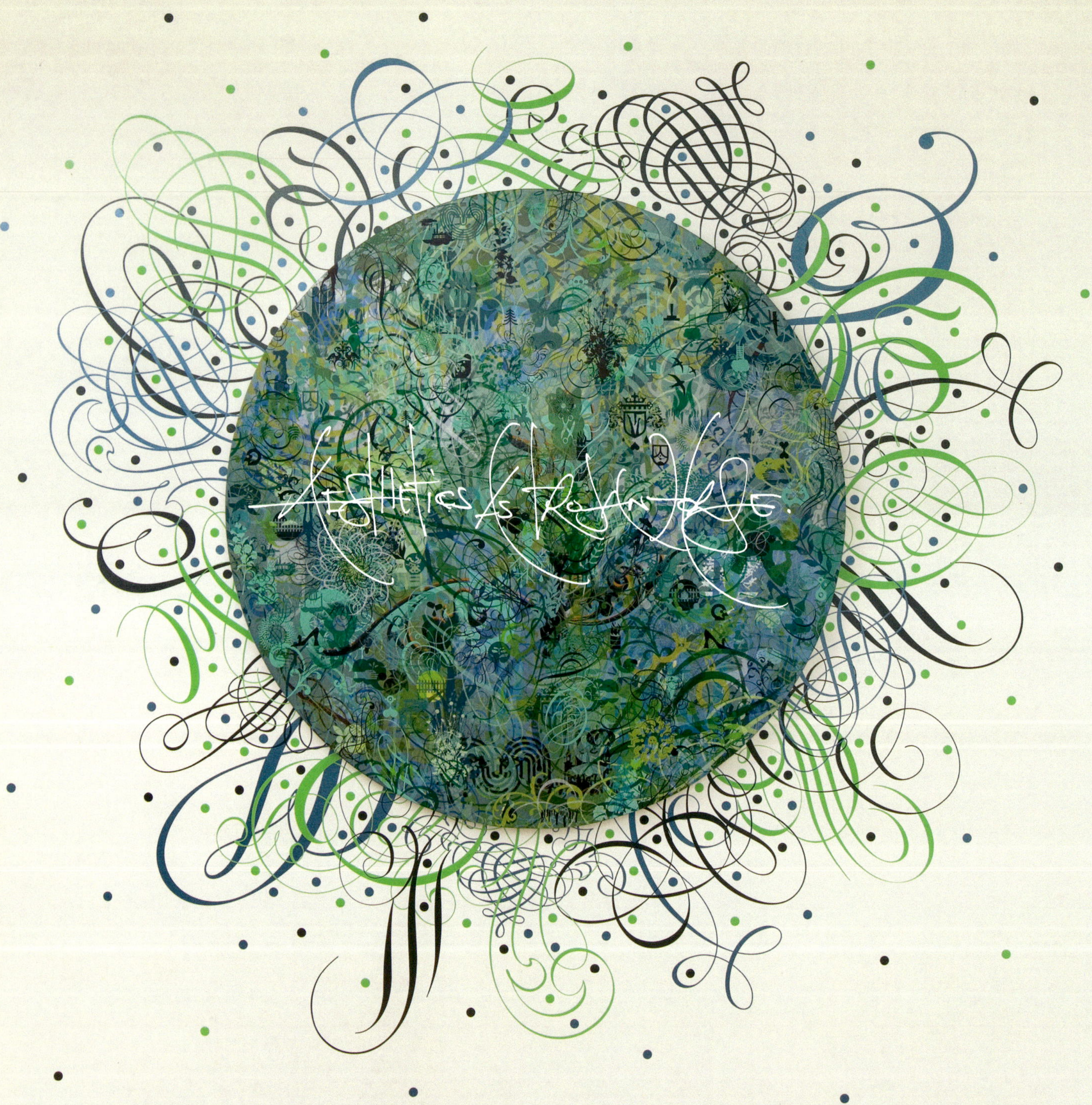
AESTHETICS AS

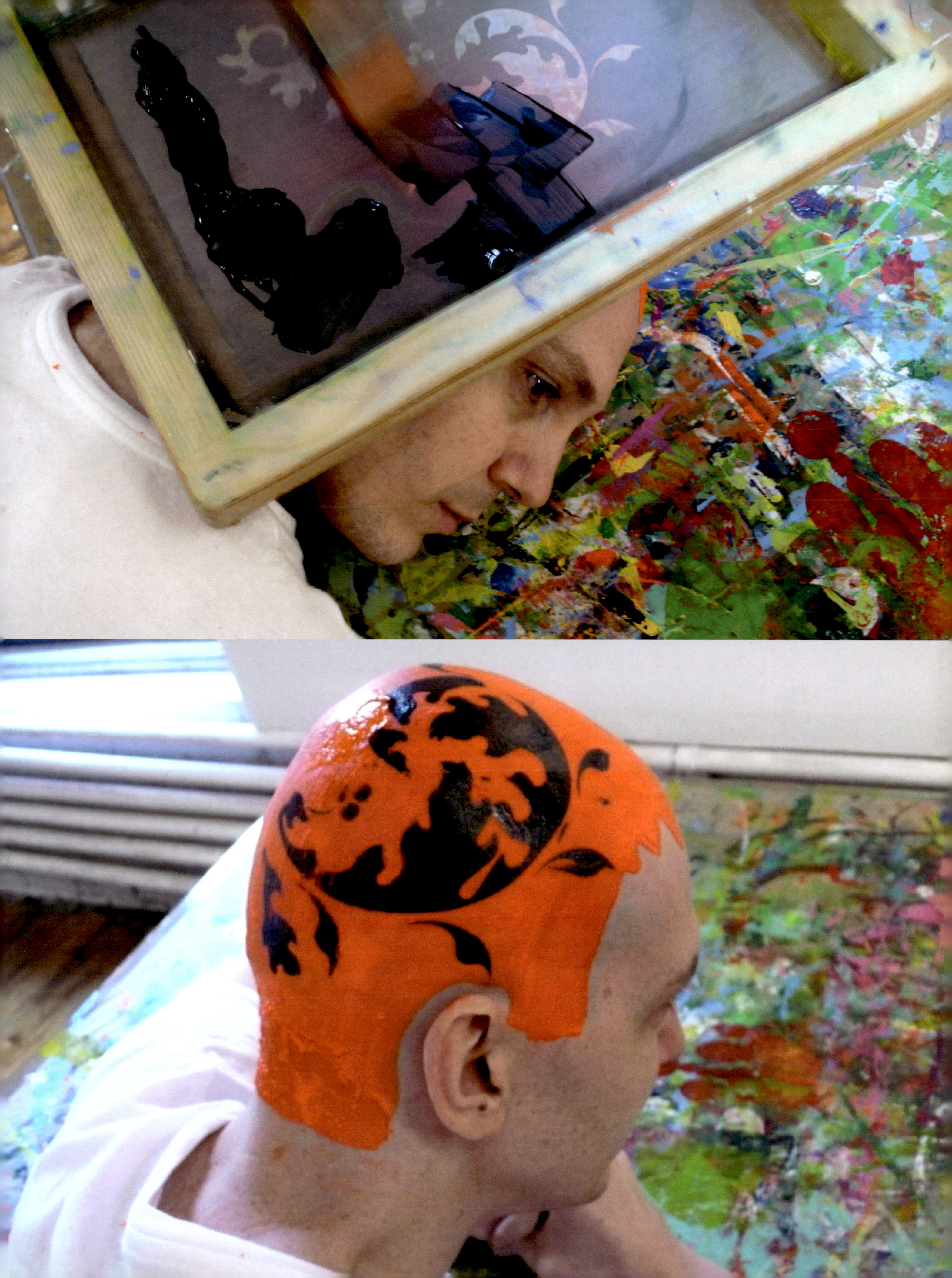

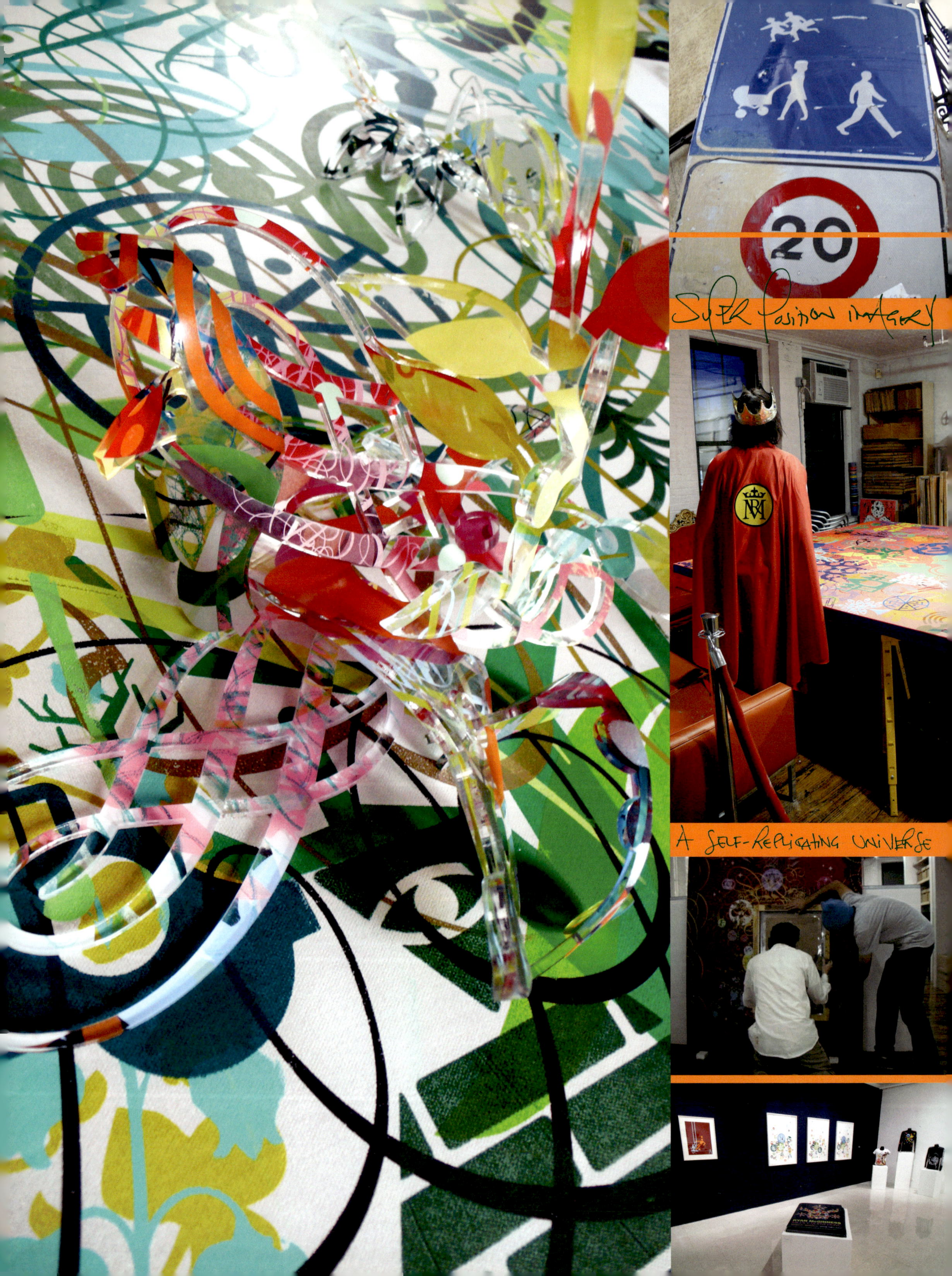
20
SUPER POSITION IMAGERY
A SELF-REPLICATING UNIVERSE

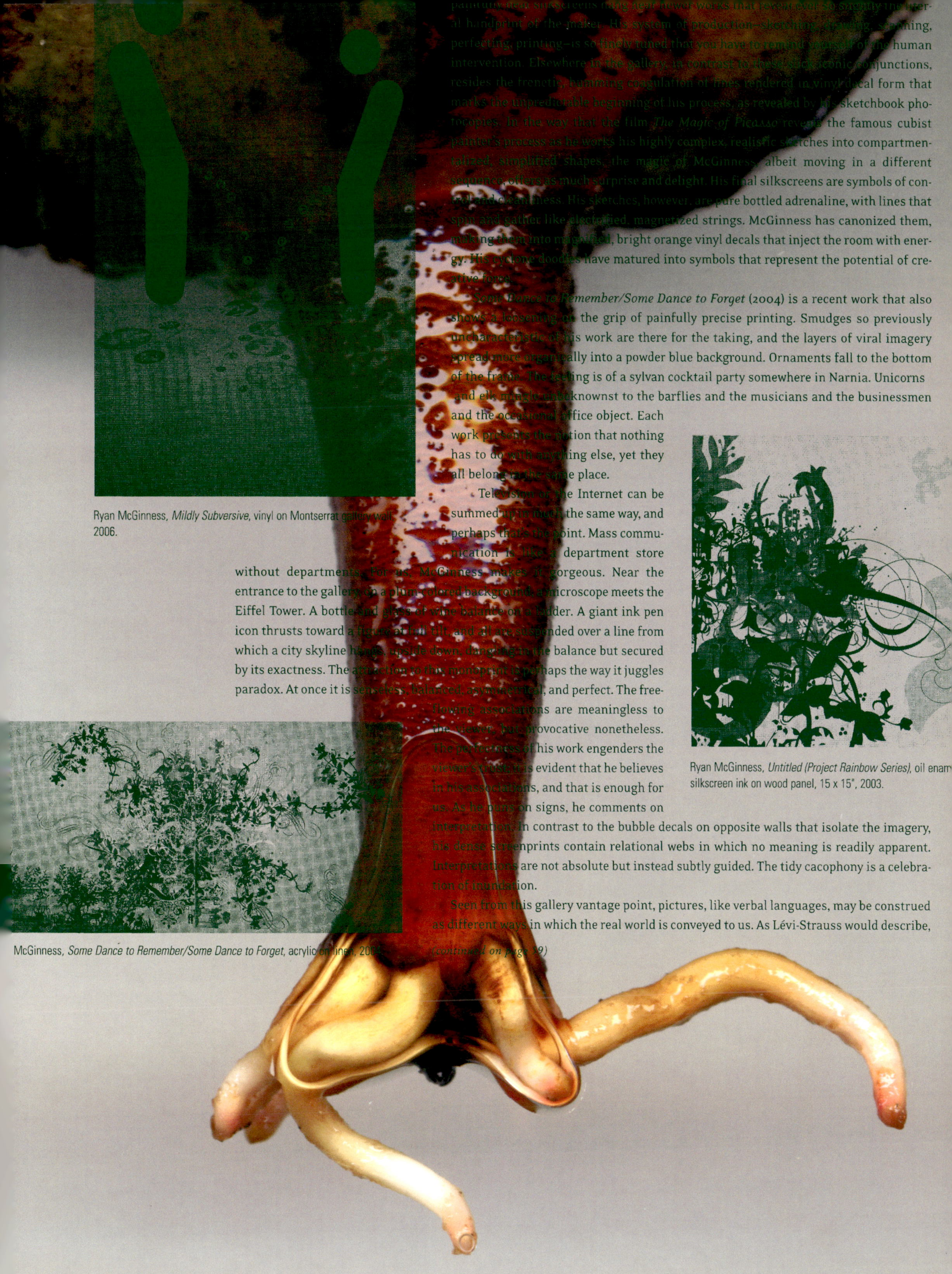

painfully neat silkscreens hang near newer works that reveal ever so slightly the literal handprint of the maker. His system of production—sketching, drawing, scanning, perfecting, printing—is so finely tuned that you have to remind yourself of the human intervention. Elsewhere in the gallery, in contrast to these slick iconic conjunctions, resides the frenetic, humming coagulation of lines rendered in vinyl decal form that marks the unpredictable beginning of his process, as revealed by his sketchbook photocopies. In the way that the film *The Magic of Picasso* reveals the famous cubist painter's process as he works his highly complex, realistic sketches into compartmentalized, simplified shapes, the magic of McGinness, albeit moving in a different sequence, offers as much surprise and delight. His final silkscreens are symbols of control and cleanliness. His sketches, however, are pure bottled adrenaline, with lines that spin and gather like electrified, magnetized strings. McGinness has canonized them, making them into magnified, bright orange vinyl decals that inject the room with energy. His cyclone doodles have matured into symbols that represent the potential of creative force.

Some Dance to Remember/Some Dance to Forget (2004) is a recent work that also shows a loosening of the grip of painfully precise printing. Smudges so previously uncharacteristic of his work are there for the taking, and the layers of viral imagery spread more organically into a powder blue background. Ornaments fall to the bottom of the frame. The feeling is of a sylvan cocktail party somewhere in Narnia. Unicorns and elk mingle unbeknownst to the barflies and the musicians and the businessmen and the occasional office object. Each work presents the notion that nothing has to do with anything else, yet they all belong in the same place.

Ryan McGinness, *Mildly Subversive*, vinyl on Montserrat gallery wall, 2006.

Television or the Internet can be summed up in much the same way, and perhaps that's the point. Mass communication is like a department store without departments. For us, McGinness makes it gorgeous. Near the entrance to the gallery, on a plum-colored background, a microscope meets the Eiffel Tower. A bottle and glass of wine balance on a ladder. A giant ink pen icon thrusts toward a figure at full tilt, and all are suspended over a line from which a city skyline hangs, upside down, dangling in the balance but secured by its exactness. The attraction to this monoprint is perhaps the way it juggles paradox. At once it is senseless, balanced, asymmetrical, and perfect. The free-flowing associations are meaningless to the viewer, but provocative nonetheless. The perfectness of his work engenders the viewer's trust; it is evident that he believes in his associations, and that is enough for us. As he puns on signs, he comments on interpretation. In contrast to the bubble decals on opposite walls that isolate the imagery, his dense screenprints contain relational webs in which no meaning is readily apparent. Interpretations are not absolute but instead subtly guided. The tidy cacophony is a celebration of inundation.

Ryan McGinness, *Untitled (Project Rainbow Series)*, oil enam silkscreen ink on wood panel, 15 x 15", 2003.

Seen from this gallery vantage point, pictures, like verbal languages, may be construed as different ways in which the real world is conveyed to us. As Lévi-Strauss would describe,

McGinness, *Some Dance to Remember/Some Dance to Forget*, acrylic on linen, 2004.

(continued on page 59)

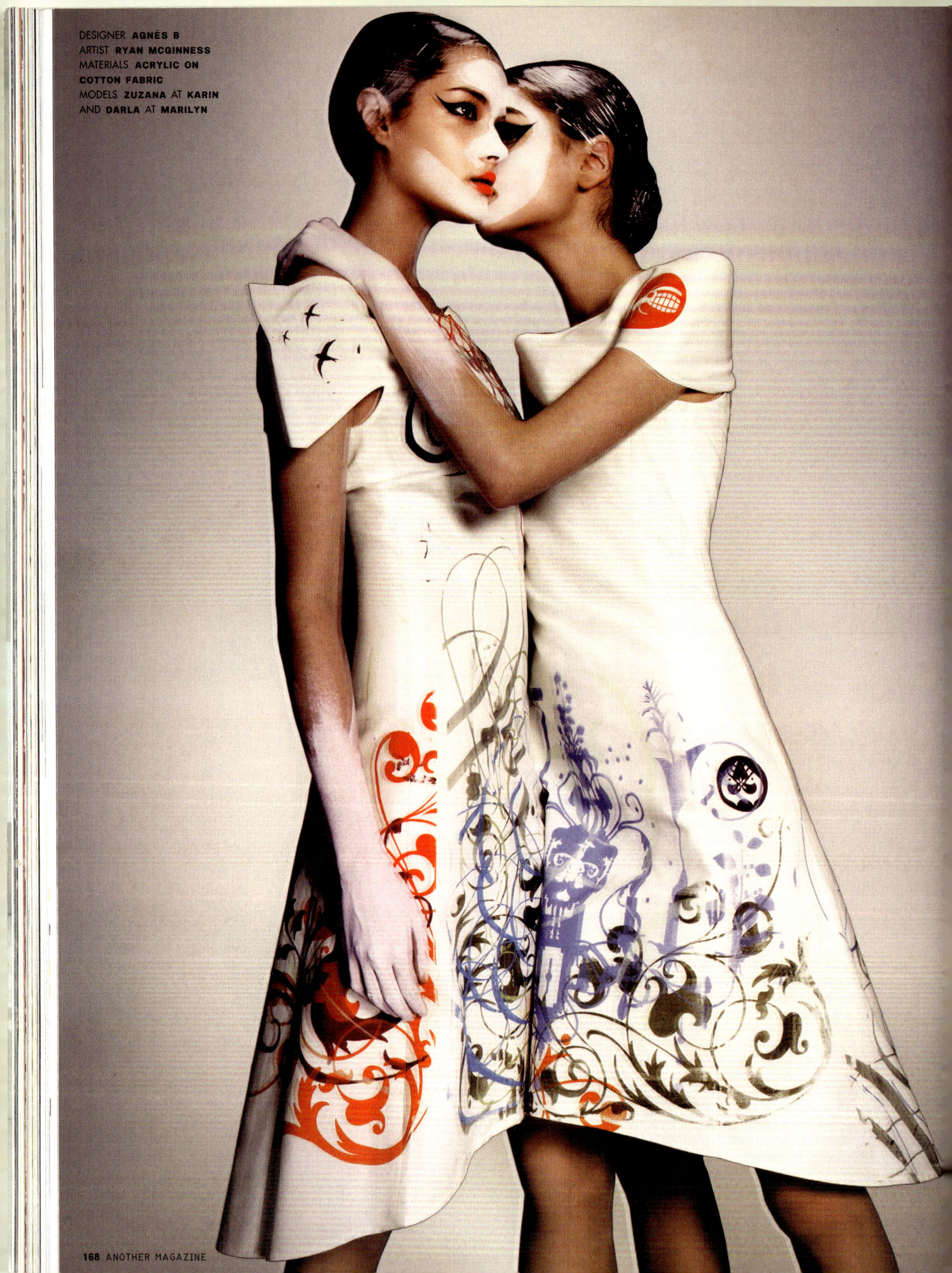

DESIGNER **AGNÈS B**
ARTIST **RYAN MCGINNESS**
MATERIALS **ACRYLIC ON COTTON FABRIC**
MODELS **ZUZANA** AT **KARIN** AND **DARLA** AT **MARILYN**

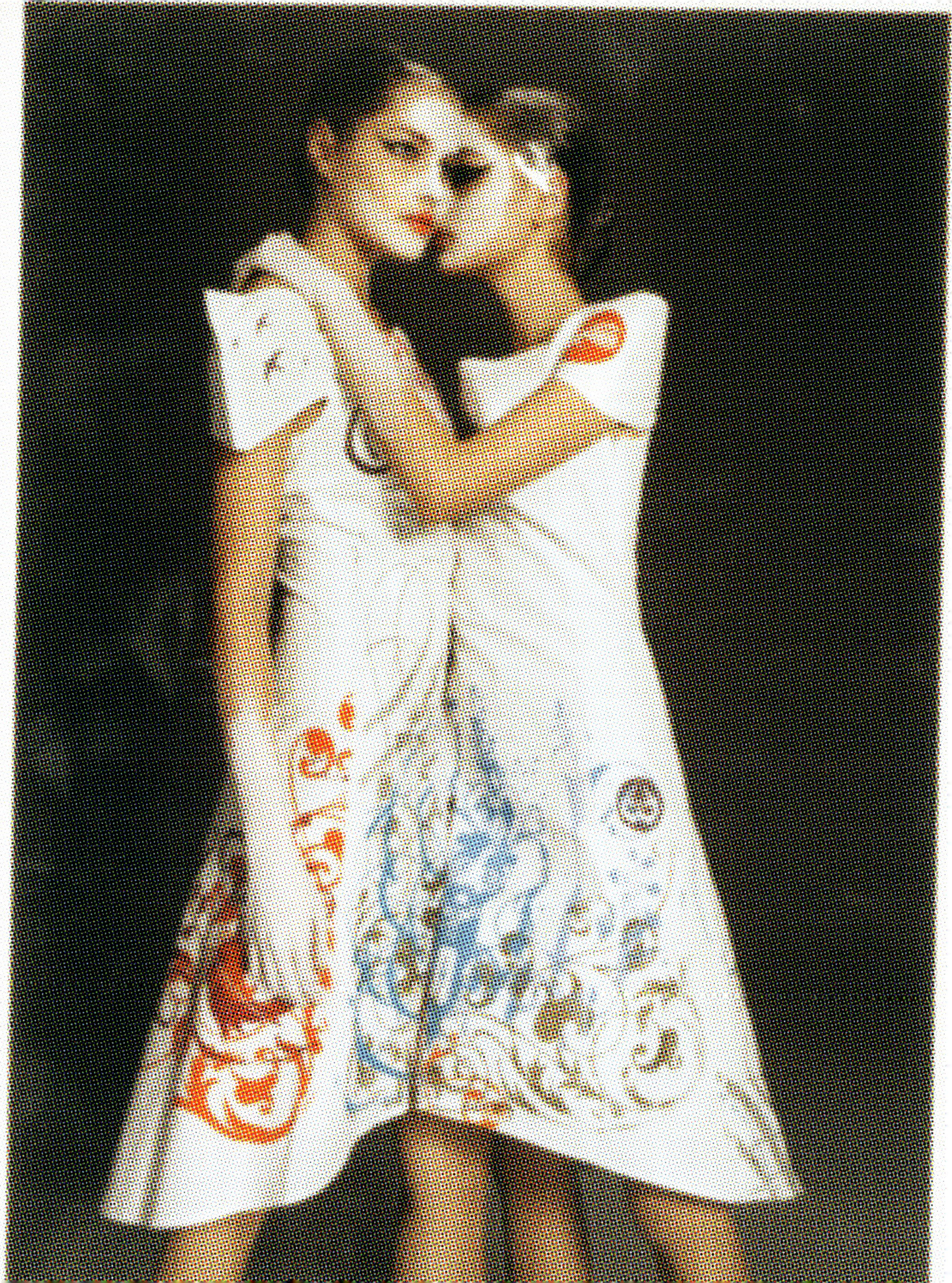

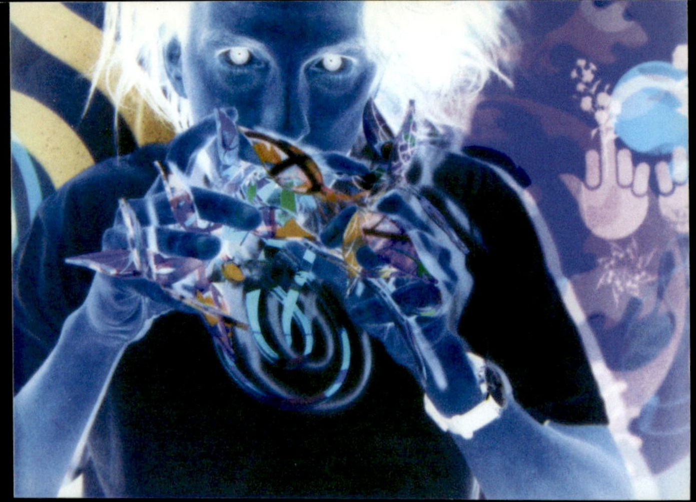

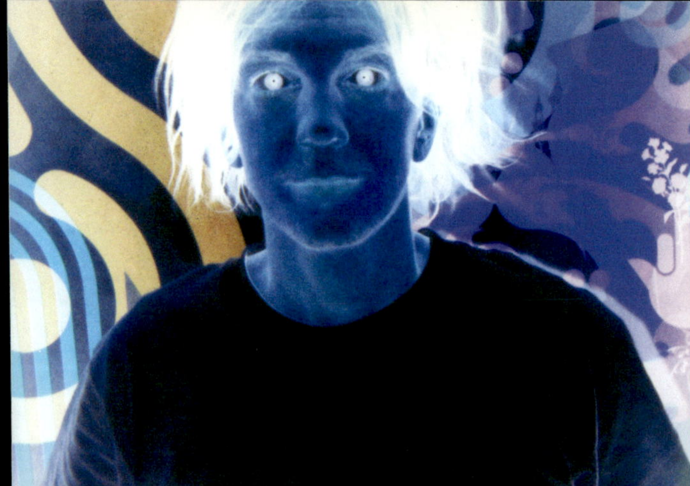

MY LIFE IS YOUR HOBBY.

A GOOD PAINTING IS NOT SIMPLY AN EXECUTED PRE-DESIGNED PLAN

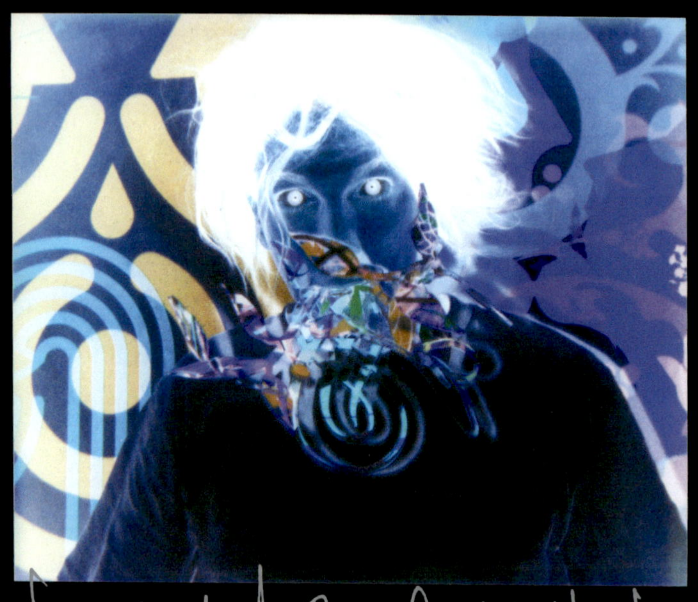

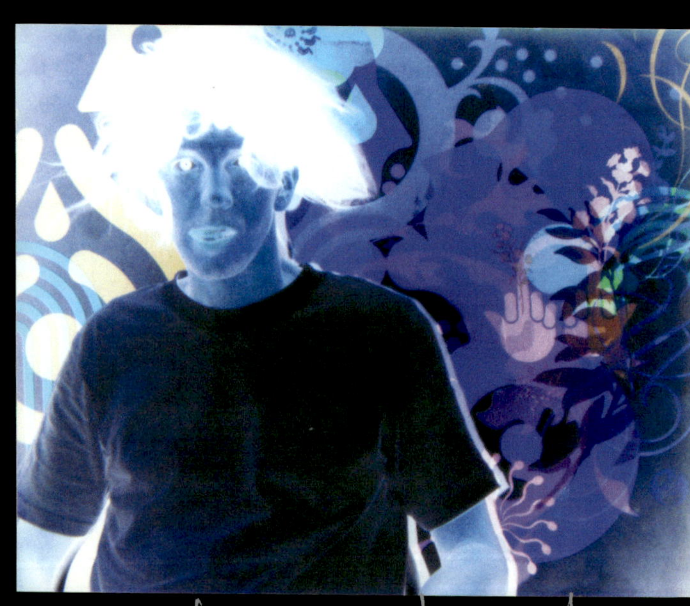

IT'S MUCH MORE IMPORTANT FOR ME TO MAKE WORK THAN TO MAKE SMALL TALK

I DO NOT WANT TO BE A MACHINE. I BELIEVE HUMANS ARE MORE VALUABLE.

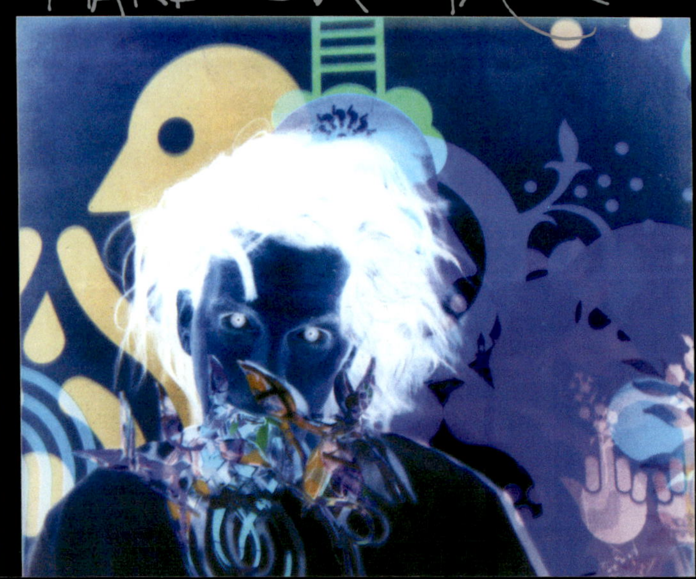

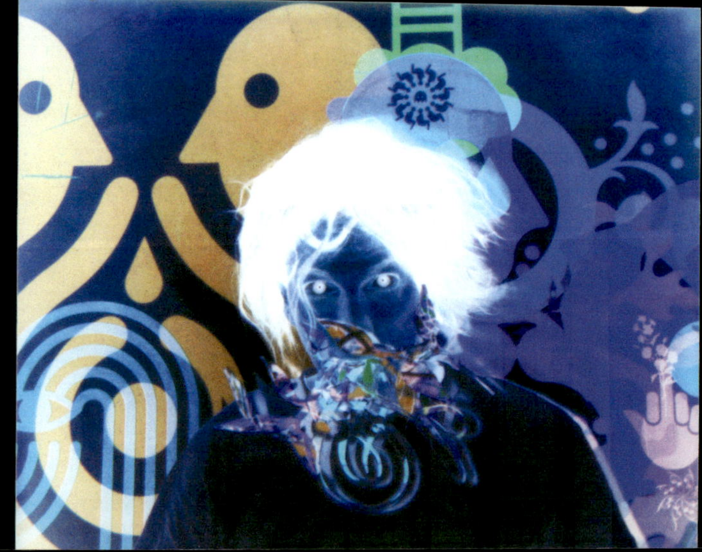

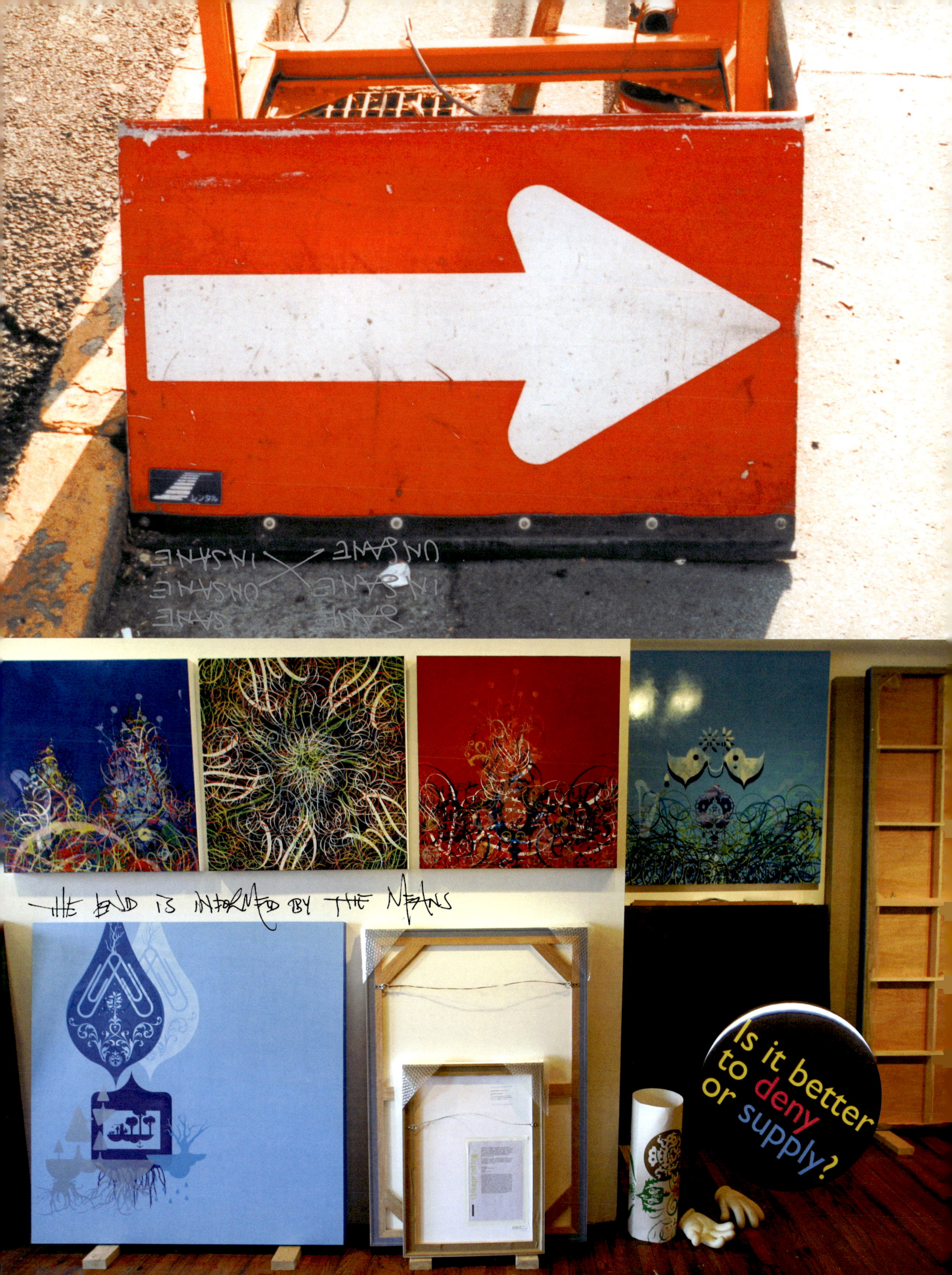
THE END IS INFORMED BY THE MEANS
Is it better to deny or supply?

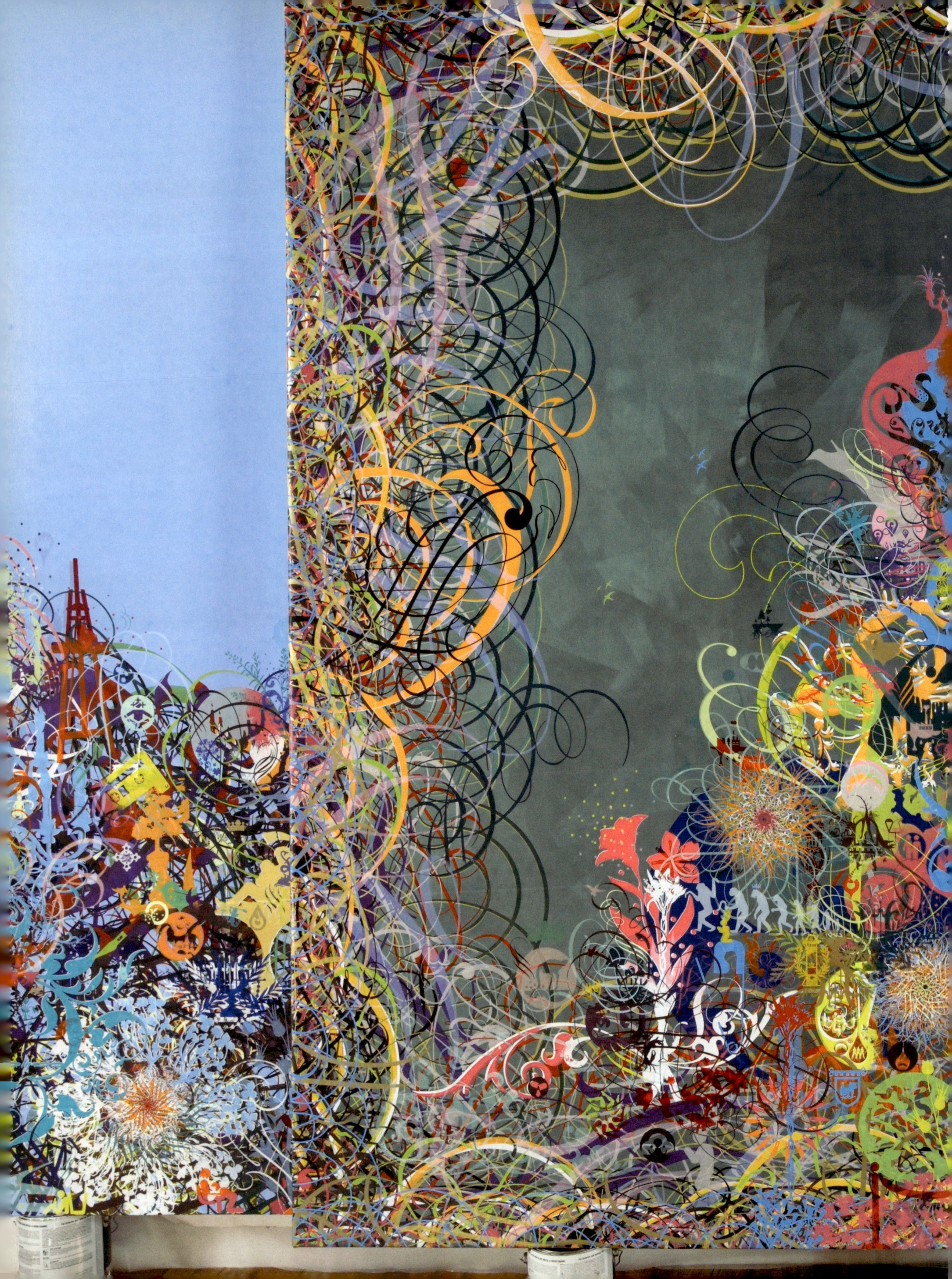

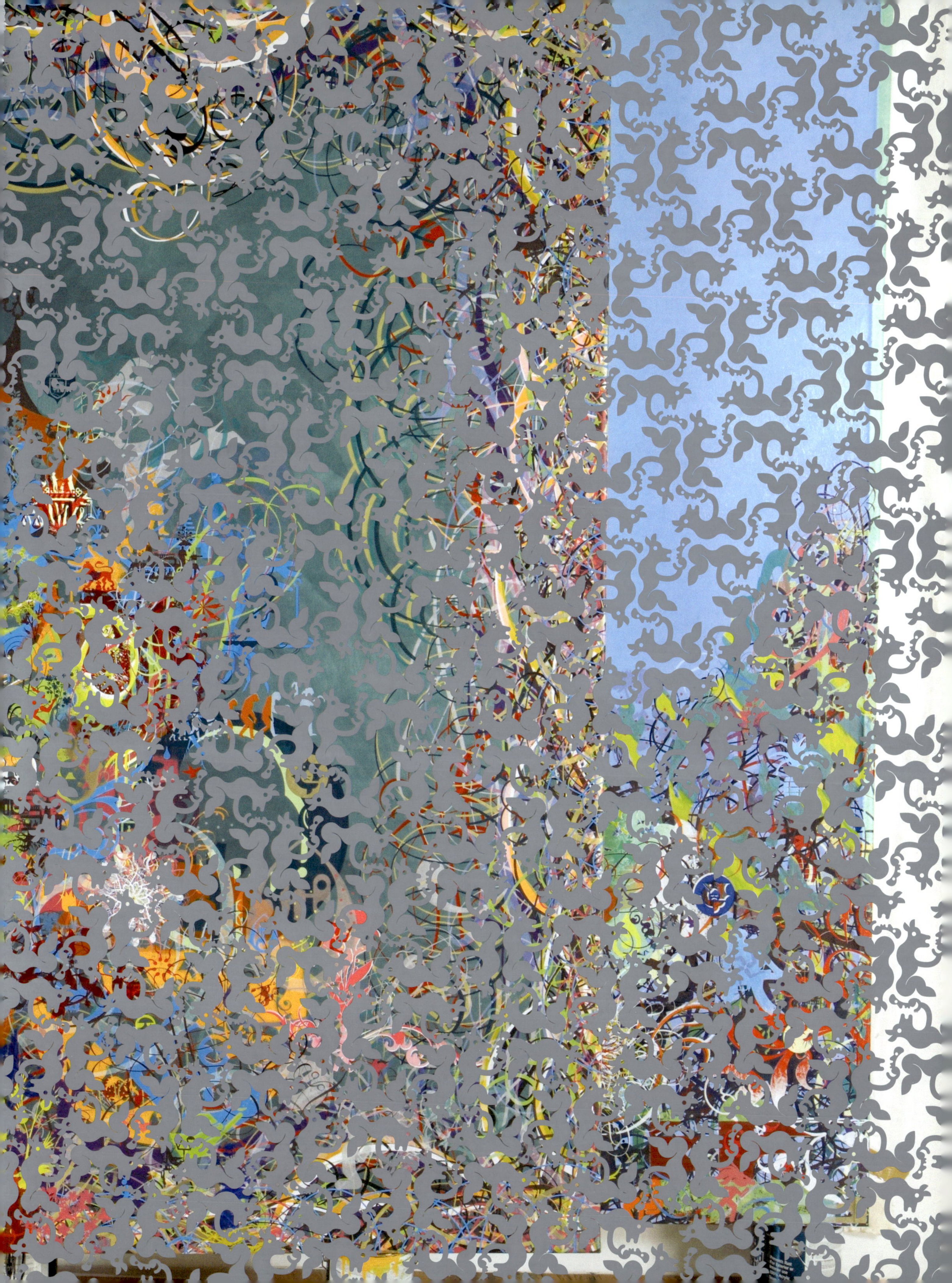

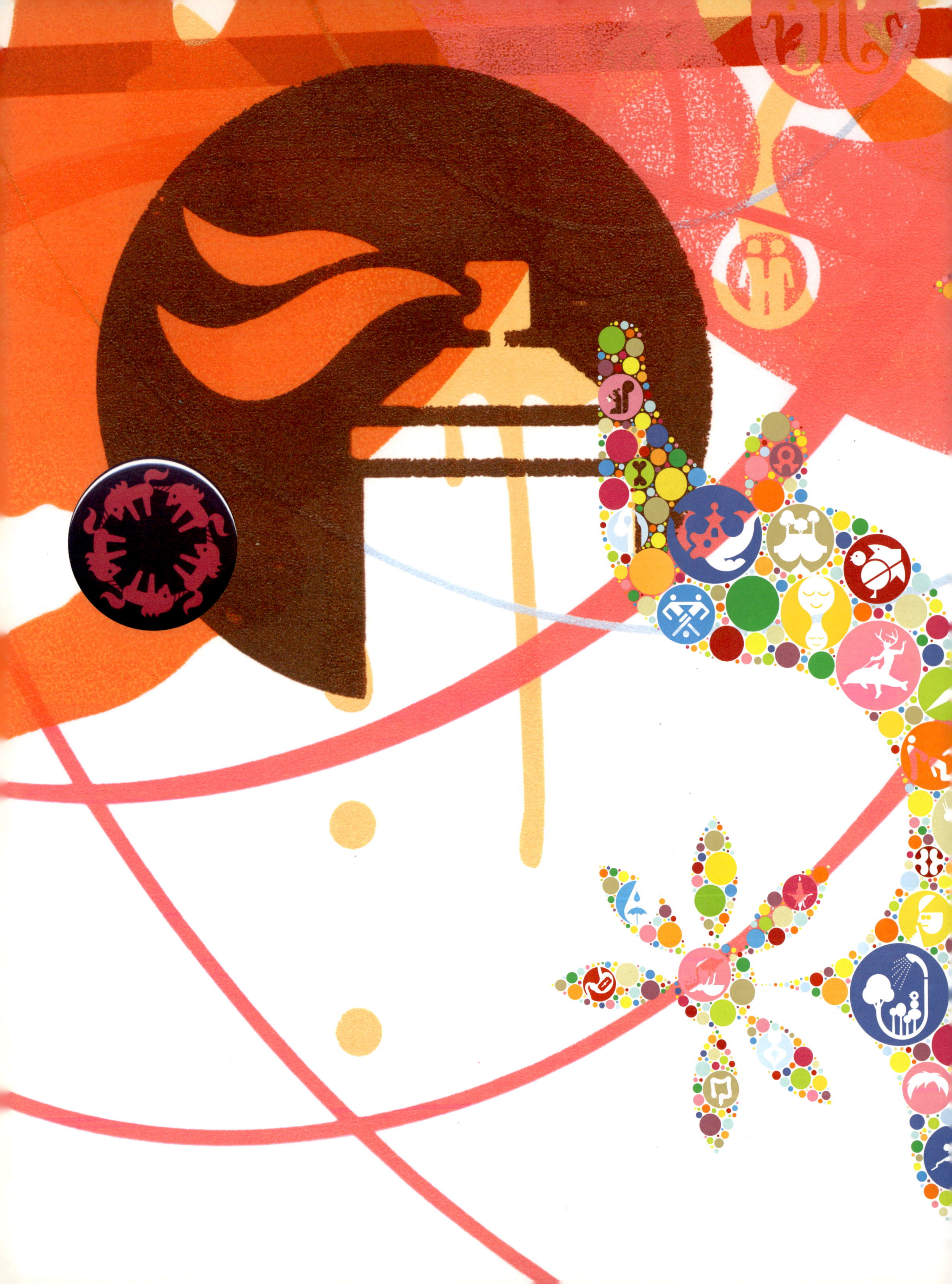

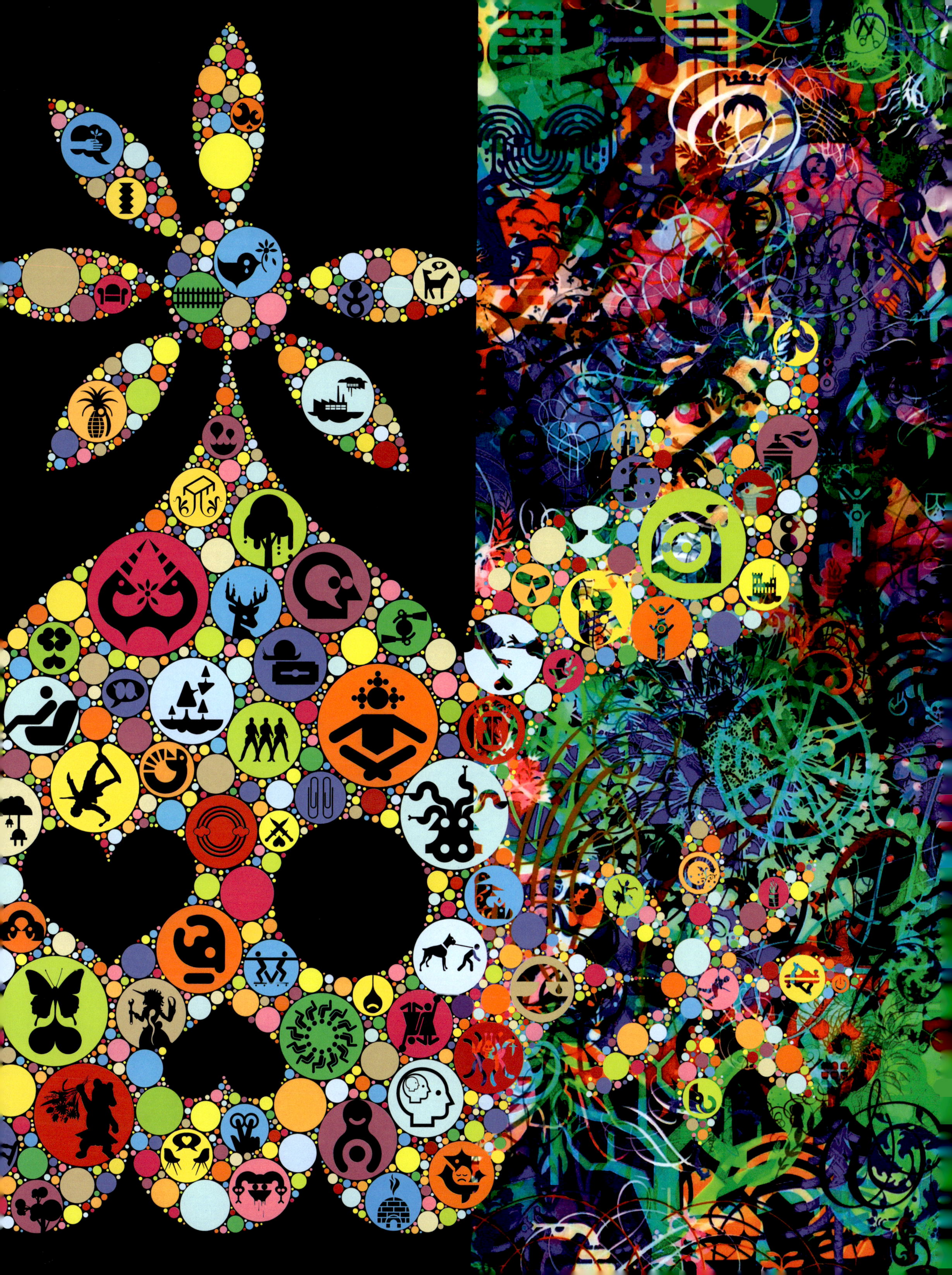

Waves & Particles

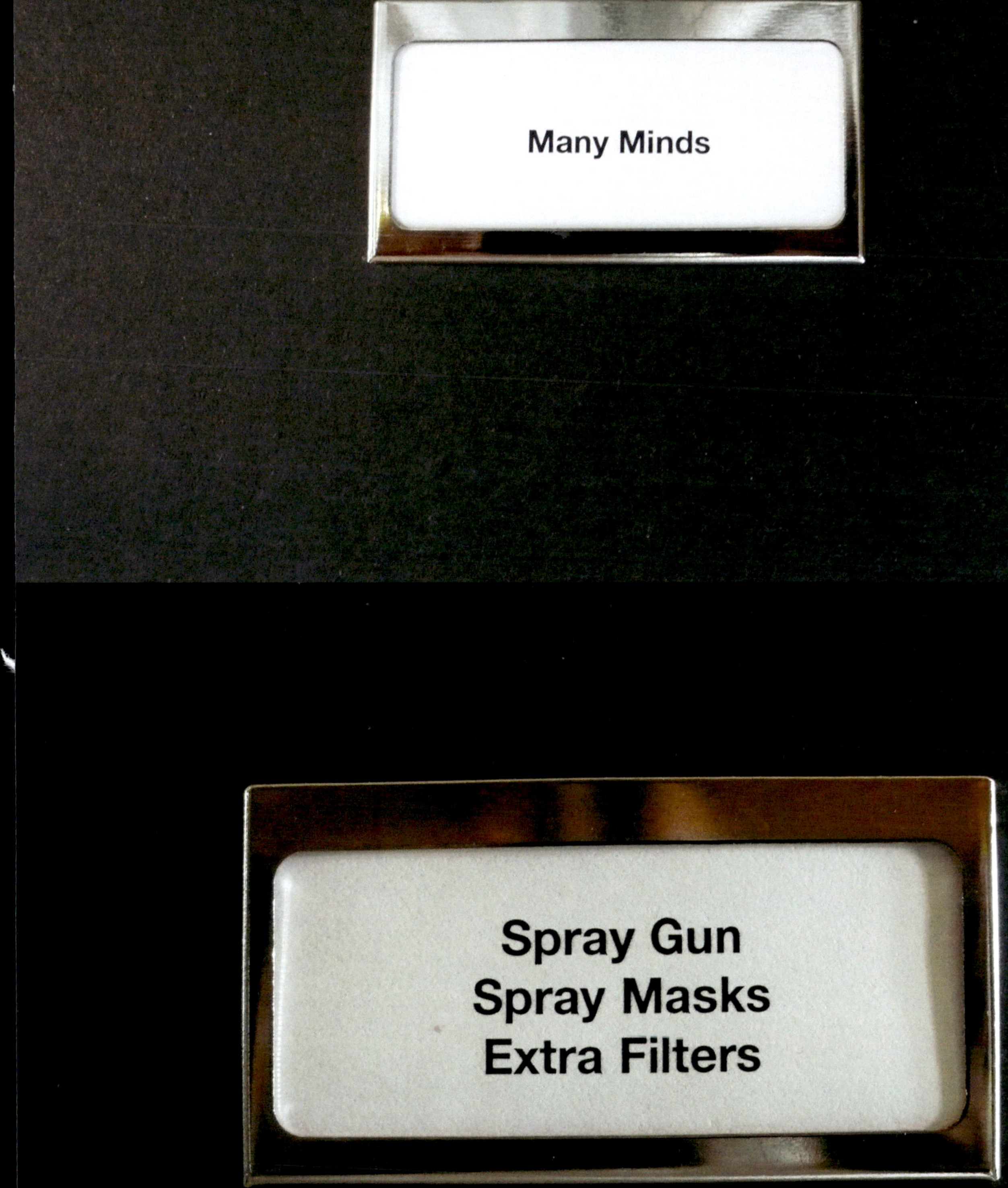

Many Minds

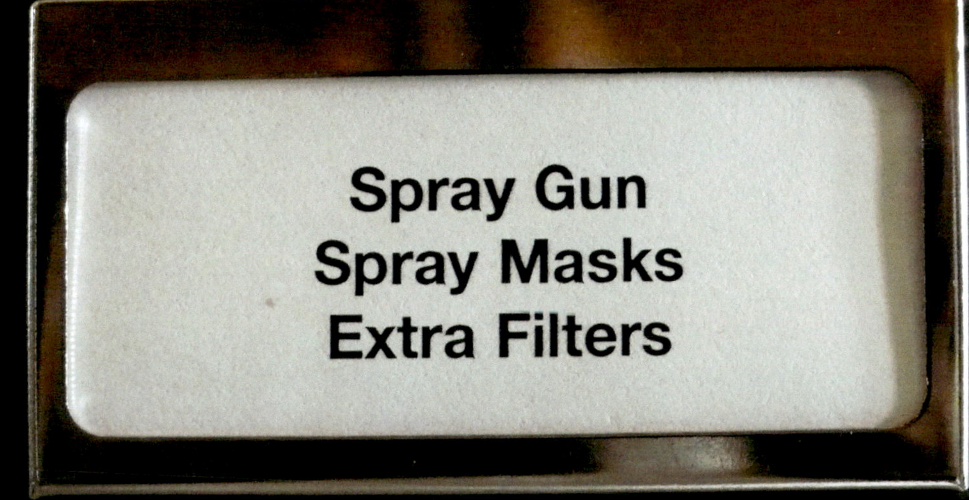

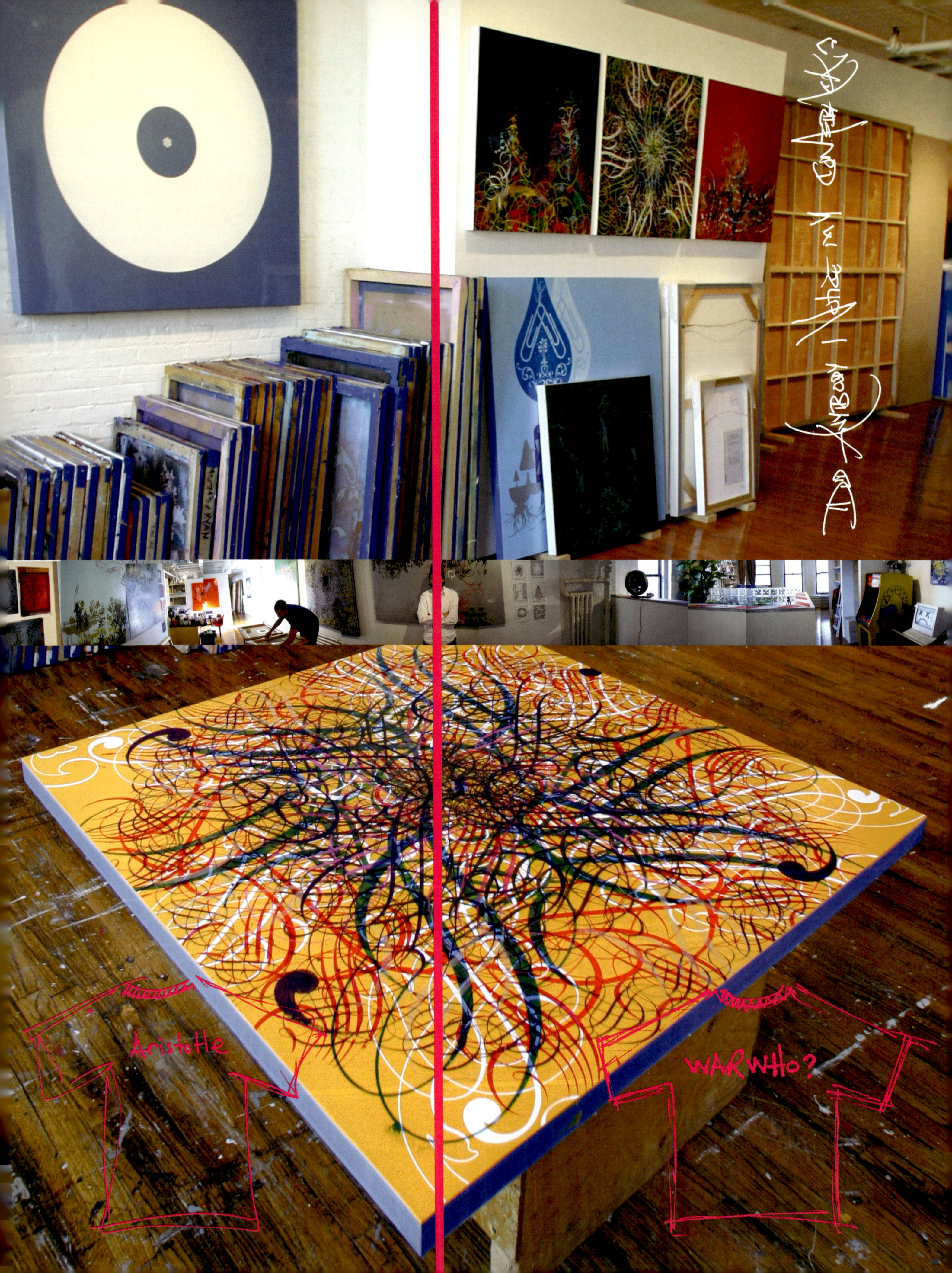
Aristotle
WARWHO?

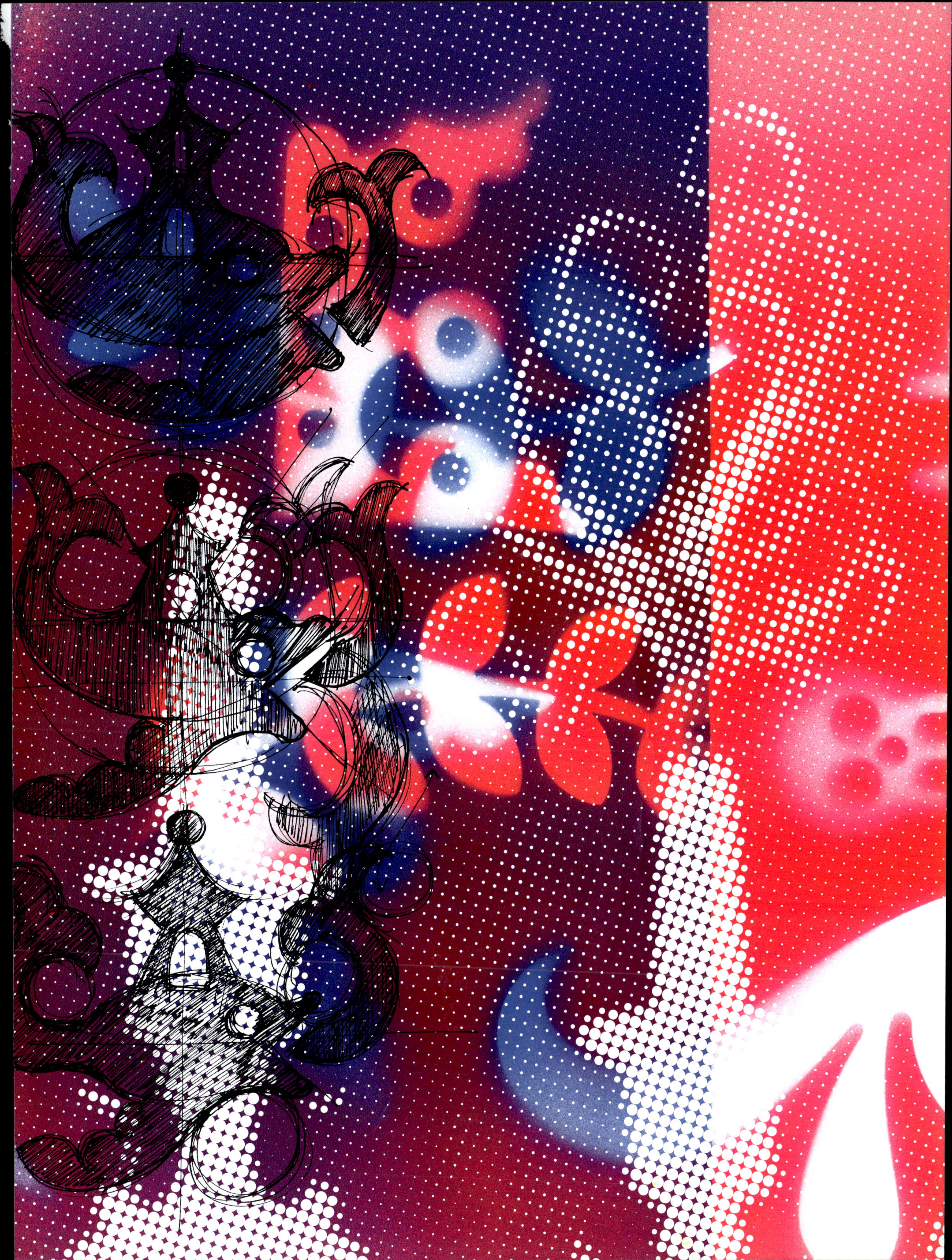

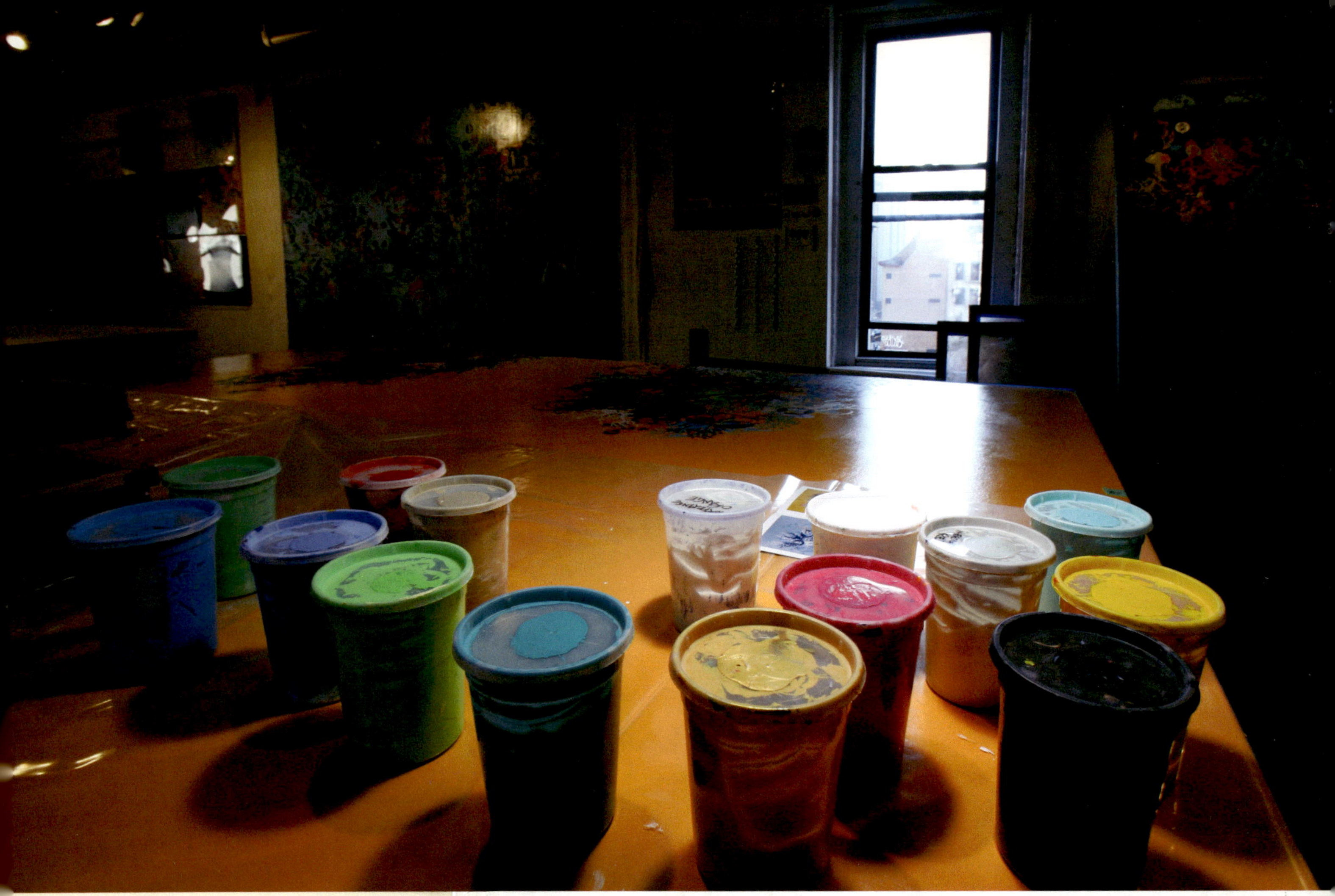

ation:
ly of action

BASIC CONCEPTS
IN PSYCHOLOGY
SERIES

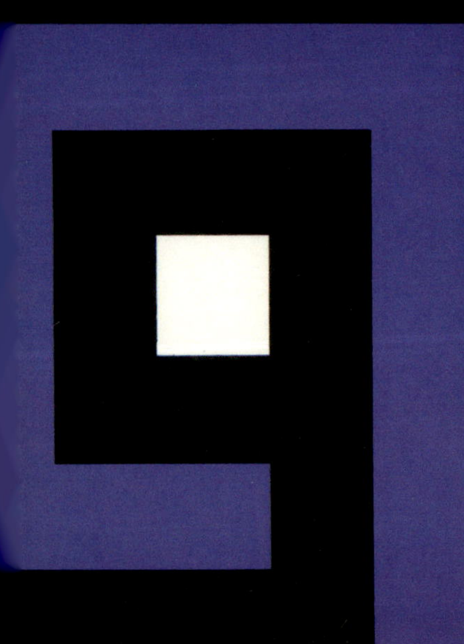

graphis diagrams

THE GRAPHIC
VISUALIZATION
OF ABSTRACT
DATA

DIE GRAPHISCHE
VISUALISIERUNG
ABSTRAKTER
GEGEBENHEITEN

LA VISUALISATION
GRAPHIQUE
DE DONNEES
ABSTRAITES

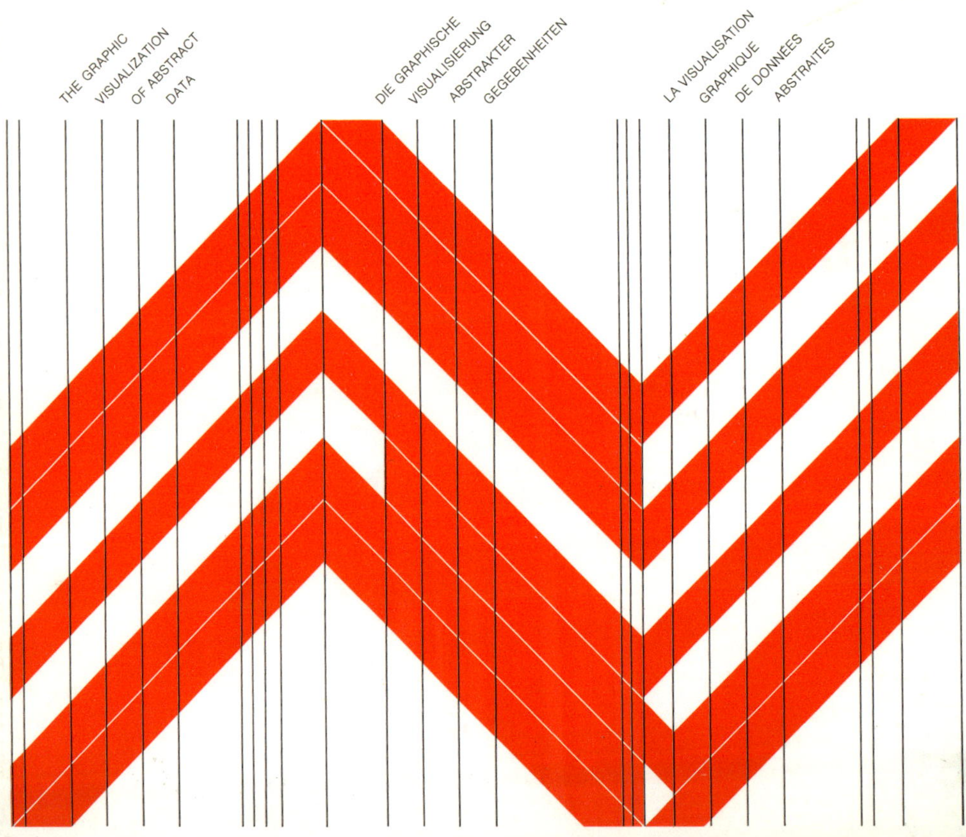

"The Warholian strategy of incorporating methods of mass-production into art is now being flipped: artists are incorporating art into methods of mass-production."

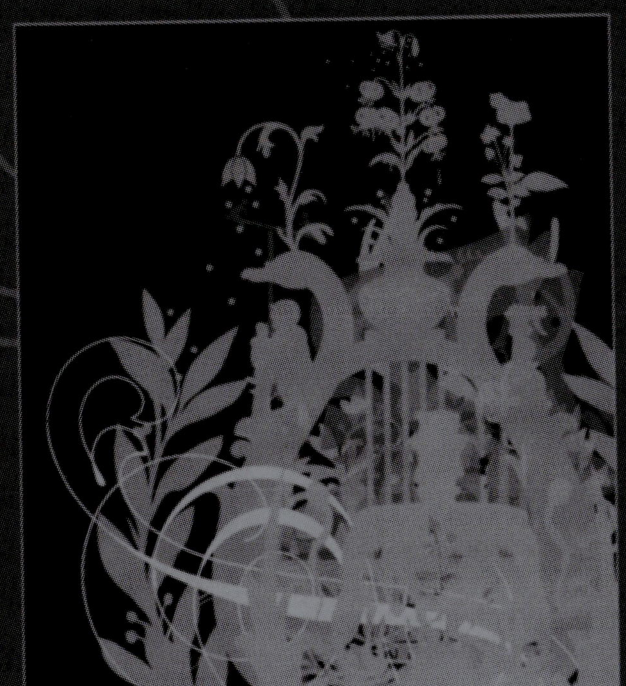

Besides the overall strangeness of it, how do you feel about your work being so widely imitated?
Children learn through imitation, and I accept the role of being a teacher.

You were quoted as saying, "I believe real culture involves a back and forth between producers and consumers with everyone playing both roles." What do you feel your obligation is as a prominent producer of signals? How does this effect your role as a consumer?
I feel my obligation is to produce and share honest messages that reflect my unique human experience. As a consumer, I am often angered and disgusted at the numerous false and deceitful messages being sent. I get depressed seeing an Abercrombie and Fitch monoculture emerging in America's middle-class as a result of mainstream media corporations broadcasting and publishing unintelligent crap and creating their own self-reflective superficial histories. Of course, we're all past the point of recognizing and complaining that our culture is consumer-driven. What's frustrating to see now is that what's being produced and consumed for the masses is so lame. The future of culture depends on art competing directly

Frank Stella

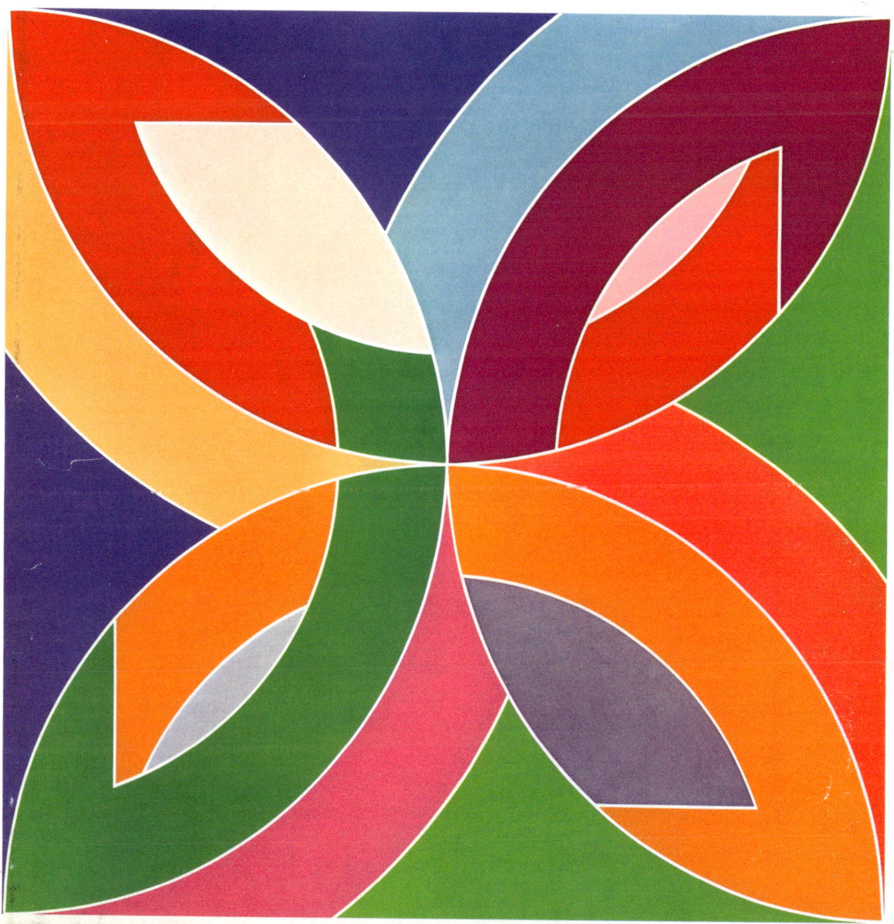

motivation: a study of action

BIRCH AND VEROFF

BASIC CONCEPTS IN PSYCHOLOGY SERIES

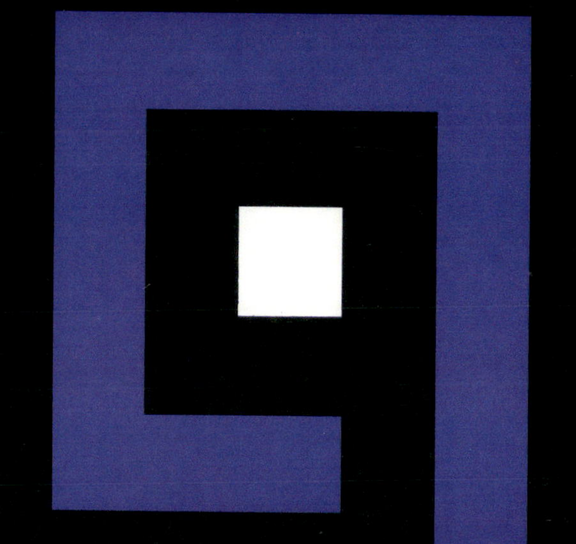

grasping out into the air toward the screen and asking "But is it real? Is it real?"

H- Because of your background in graphic design, aspects of two-dimensional space, iconography and symbols have been prominent alongside painterly swirls in your fine art pieces. Did you ever hesitate to blend these two traditionally separated concepts?

RM- No, they're all symbols. The more baroque elements are just symbols for fanciness.

H- A lot of people assume that you cut and paste clip art when in reality you change the designs to your satisfaction. Do you think you are influencing the new clip art being produced?

RM- I actually do a lot of drawing, which is more process-oriented. It takes me quite some time to get a drawing exactly right. I don't know if I am influencing new clip art being produced.

H- The swirls, layers and icons of your style have found their way into American culture; I see evidence of your impact everywhere from printed media to television. Do you have a sense of your own influence? Do you think one aspect of your art has had more influence than others?

RM- I'd be careful about including the advertising and entertainment industries in "culture." Work produced with a corporate agenda behind it is not the kind of culture I want to celebrate: But yes, I also see my influence everywhere. It's very strange for me, because my work comes from a very personal place with a deep history behind it. When the spirit of my work is co-opted by corporations and a sales agenda is attached to it, the work is emptied of absolutely everything meaningful. I know that art directors and advertising schmucks come to my shows and buy my books. Those people are in the business of raping. But it's hard to blame people for being themselves. There will always be that element in society.

H- As technology and computer programs become more popular among artists, do you think art and graphic design will become one and the same?

RM- Art and graphic design are two completely separate things. Technology

Photo by Dirk Westphal

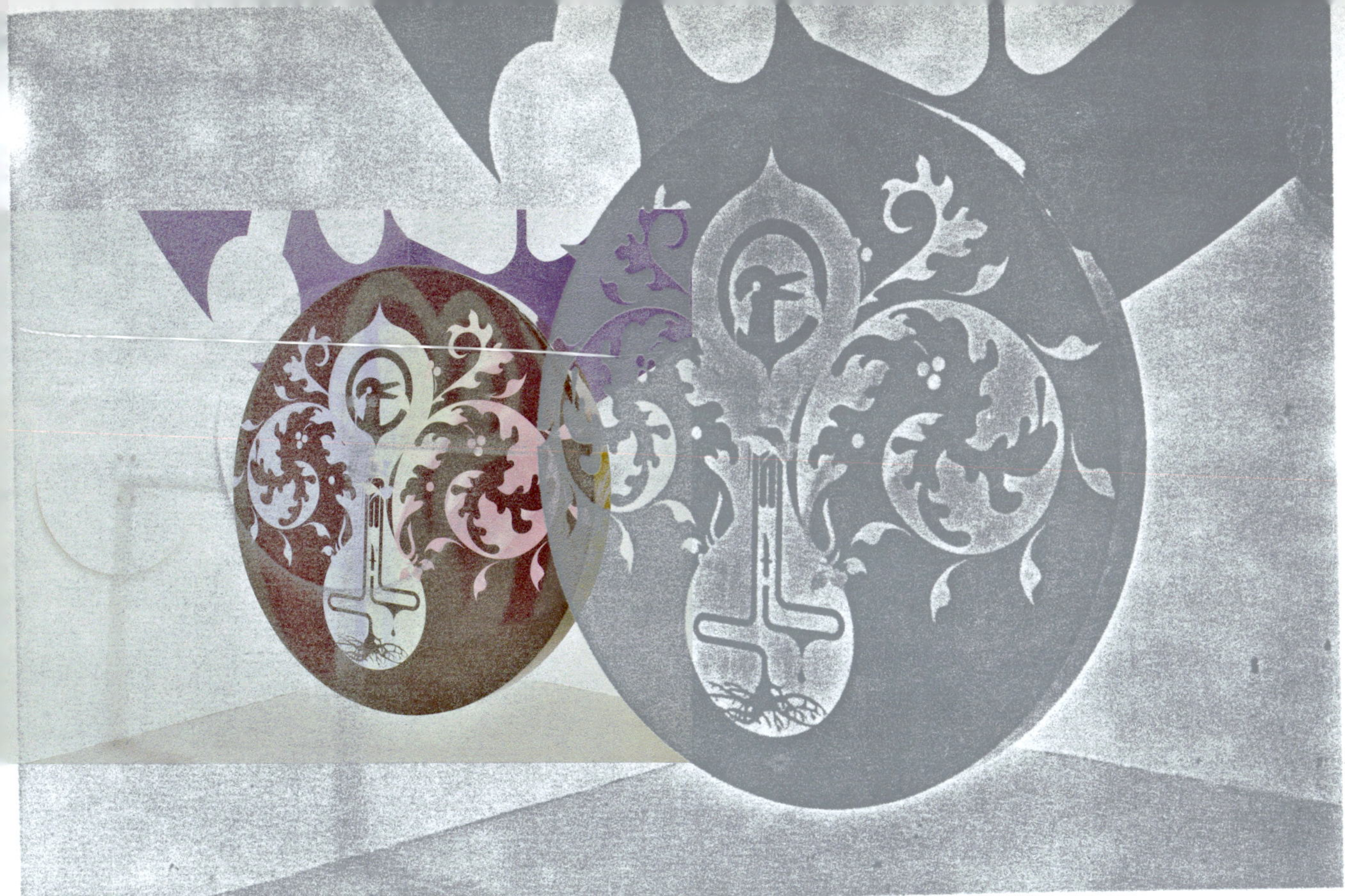

Universal (48d, No. 6),
2005, polyesterurethane on fiberglass with aluminum and wood armature, 48 in dia. x 4 in., armature: 30 in. x 3 in. dia., Photo by Tom Powel, Courtesy Deitch Projects

is just a tool. It cannot change, conceptually, the two professions any more than a microphone will make news reporting and singing the same.

H- It seems that as critics are trying to define the art movement you are a part of, they keep using terms like, "street art", "graffiti art", "skater art" and so on. Do you think it's a strategy to withhold fine art credibility?

RM- I think that they think it just sounds cool. Those kinds of terms are usually used to relate the work to a target audience – 18 to 30 year olds with disposable income. The targets usually include those who fetishize coveted objects from childhood like toys and sneakers and those who tend to believe in empty brand names, which cast only the shadows of something meaningful.

H- What do you think about all of the artist-designed toys/figures/urban-vinyl etc.?

RM- I don't think much of it. Some of my friends make those things, and I like my friends, but I am curious about fueling that market. However, it really isn't much different than making expensive art and having it purchased by rich people. "Toys/figures/urban-vinyl" is just a smaller game.

H- Are there any that you personally like or dislike?

RM- It's all so wonderful.

H- In your book, Sponsorship, the catalogue to accompany your exhibition, you interviewed many artists on the subject of corporate sponsors, commissions and collaborations. Do you see the increase of this practice as a positive turn in an art movement? Or do you feel that it has spawned imitators who oversaturate and weaken your personal visual language?

RM- It is not positive. Corporations are not positive entities.

H- What I meant was, do you and your peers feel validated that everyone is seeking out your art because they find it cool? And/or also, do you worry that it is

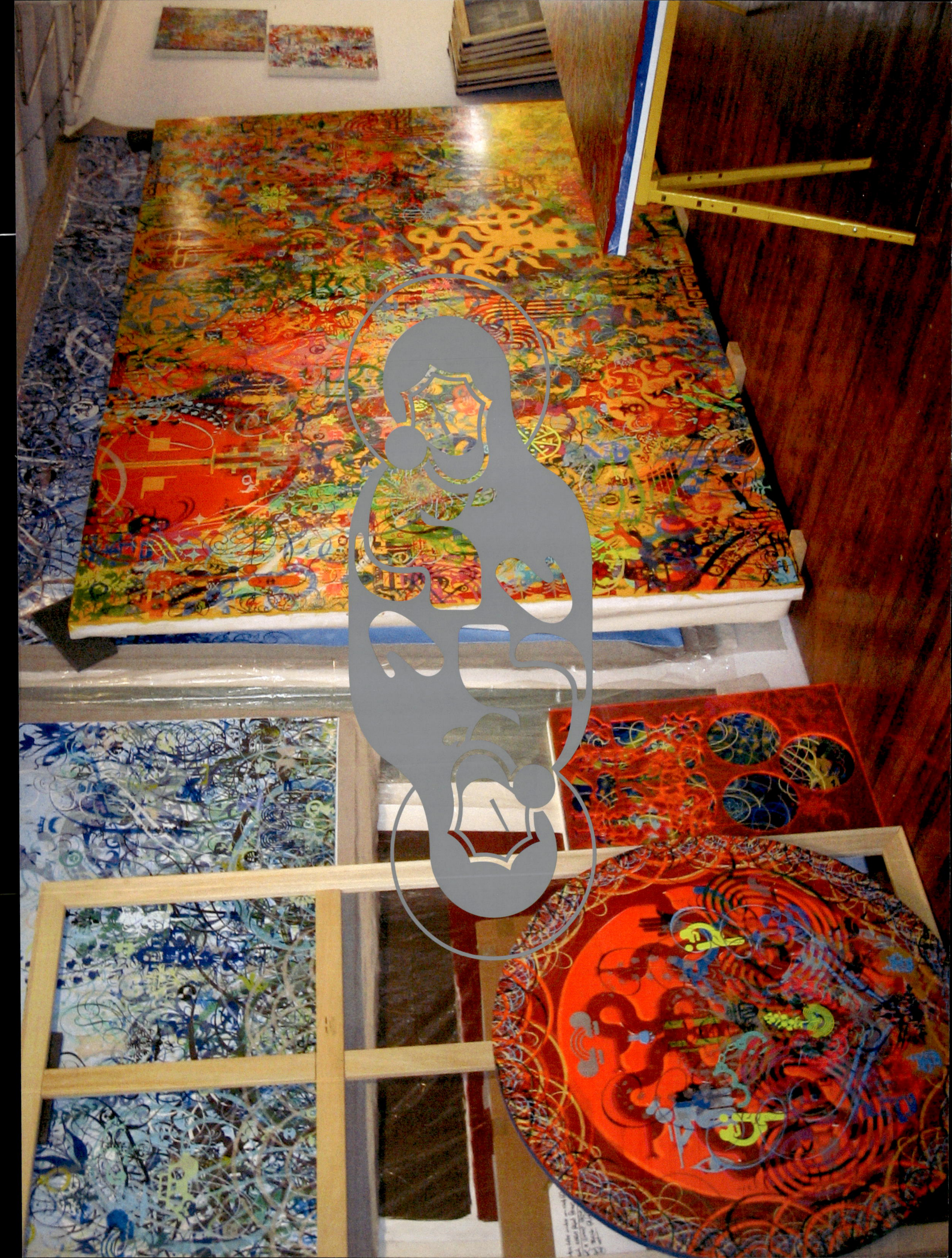

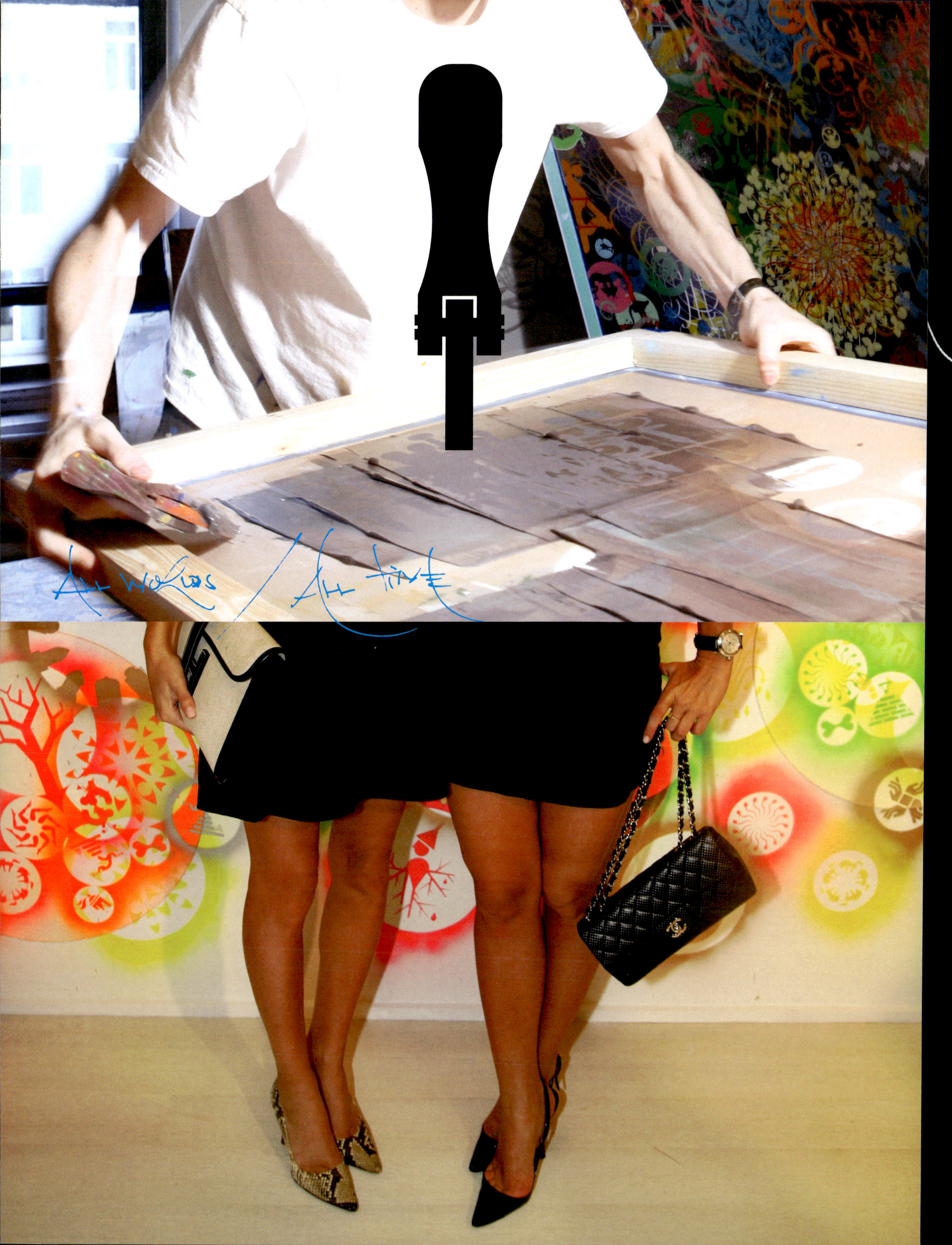
ALL WORLDS / ALL TIME

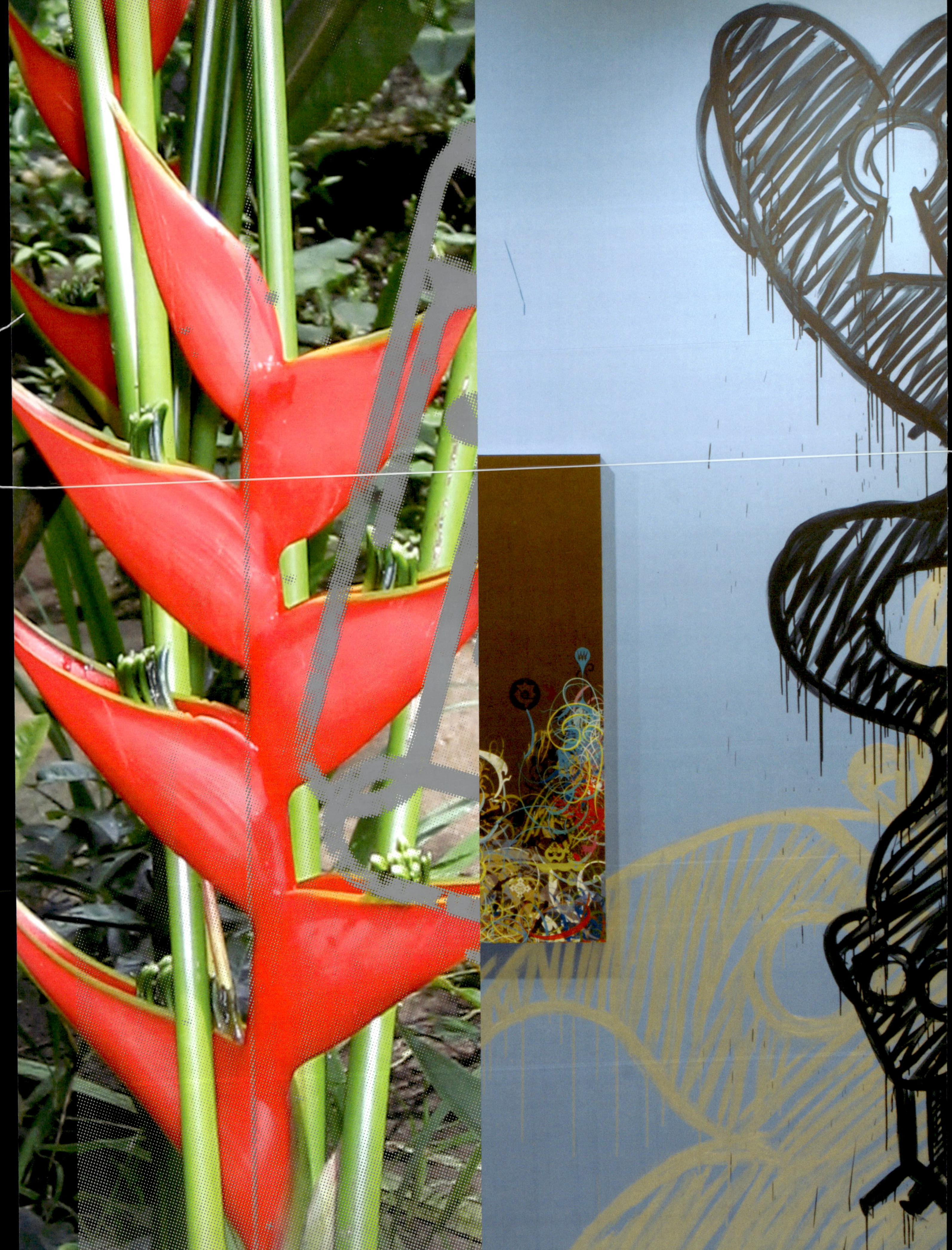

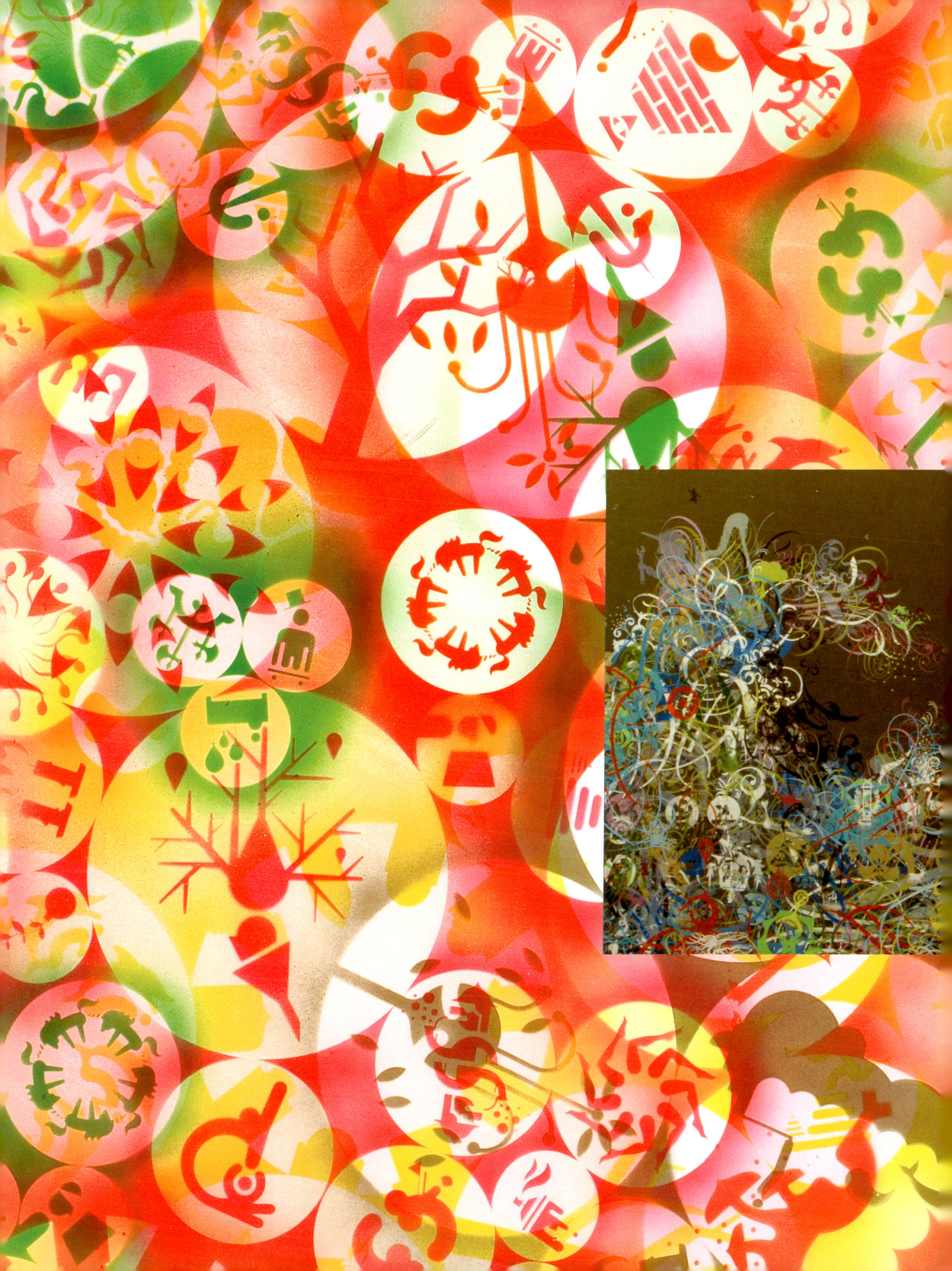

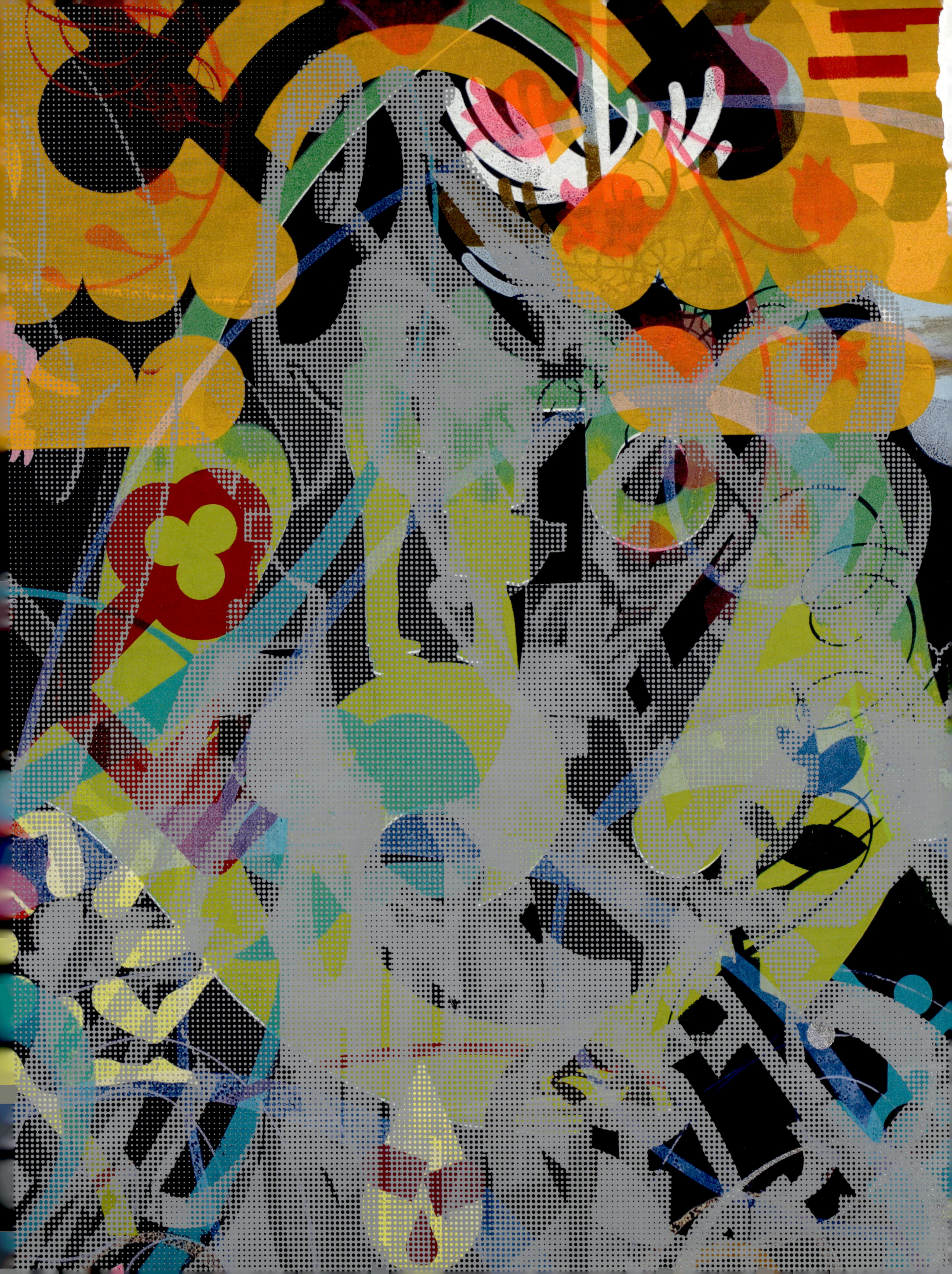

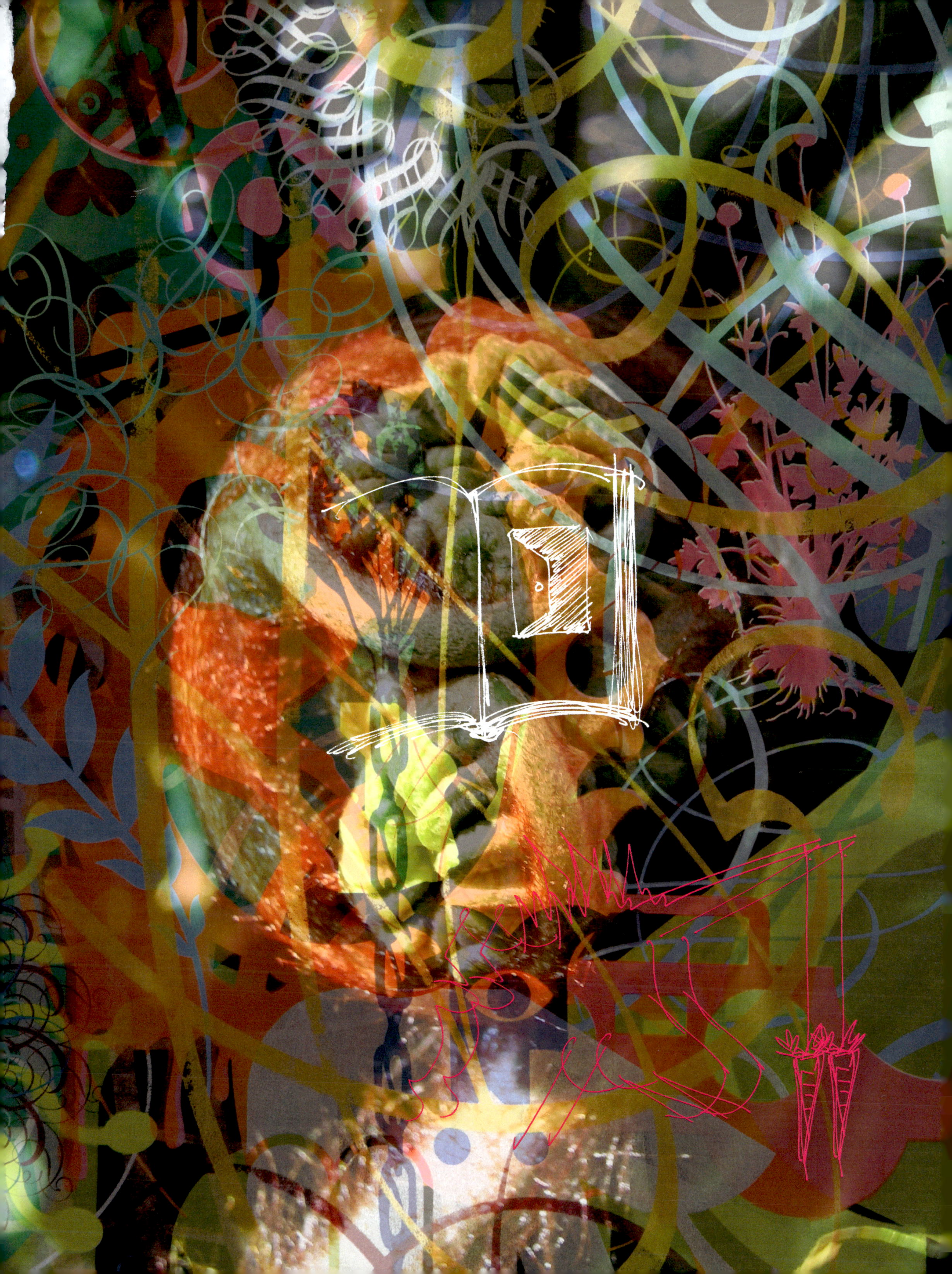

Style as signifying practice

> We are surrounded by emptiness but it is an emptiness filled with signs. (Lefebvre, 1971)

It would seem that those approaches to subculture based upon a traditional semiotics (a semiotics which begins with some notion of the 'message' – of a combination of elements referring unanimously to a fixed number of signifieds) fail to provide us with a 'way in' to the difficult and contradictory text of punk style. Any attempt at extracting a final set of meanings from the seemingly endless, often apparently random, play of signifiers in evidence here seems doomed to failure.

And yet, over the years, a branch of semiotics has emerged which deals precisely with this problem. Here the simple

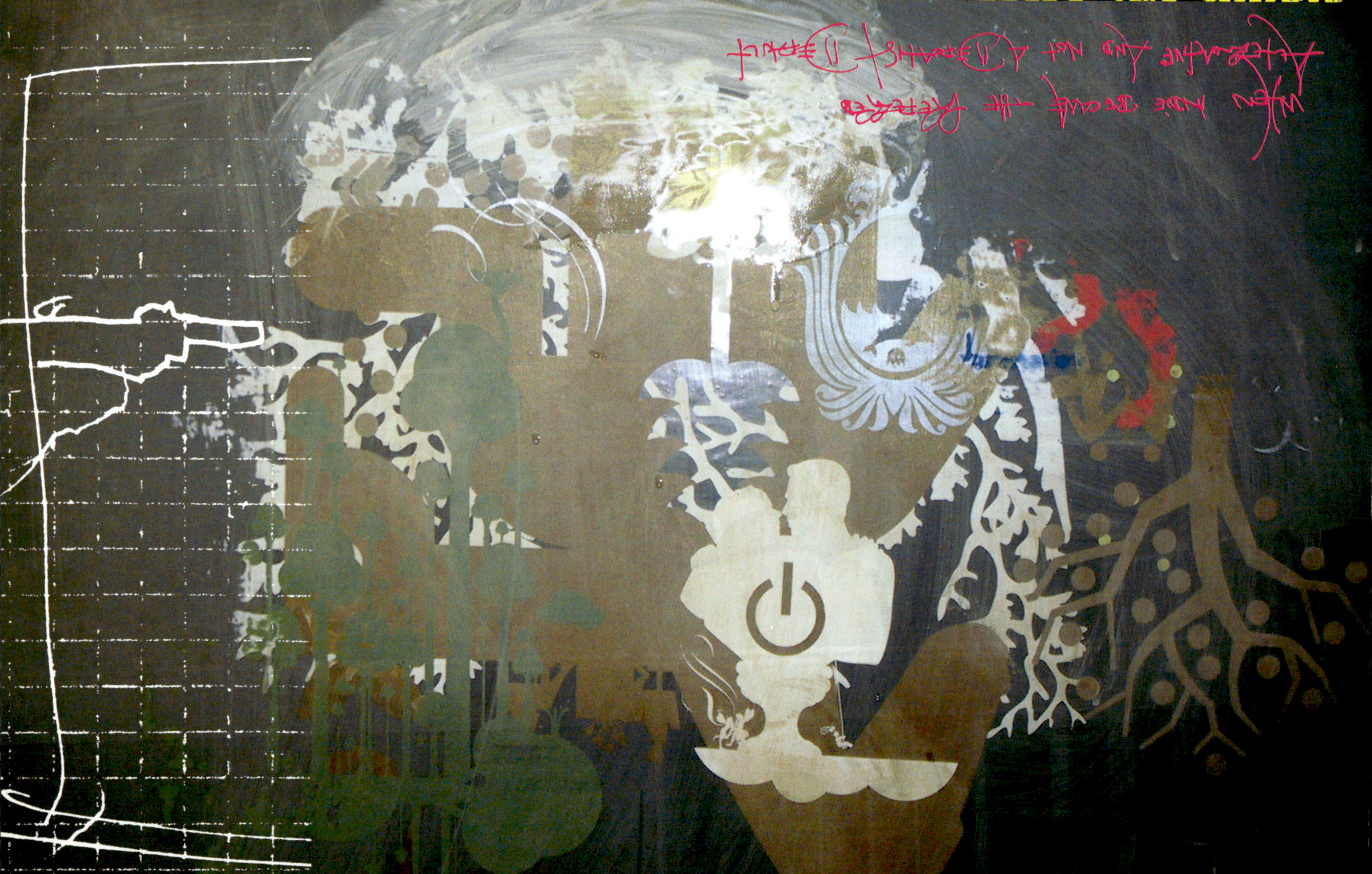

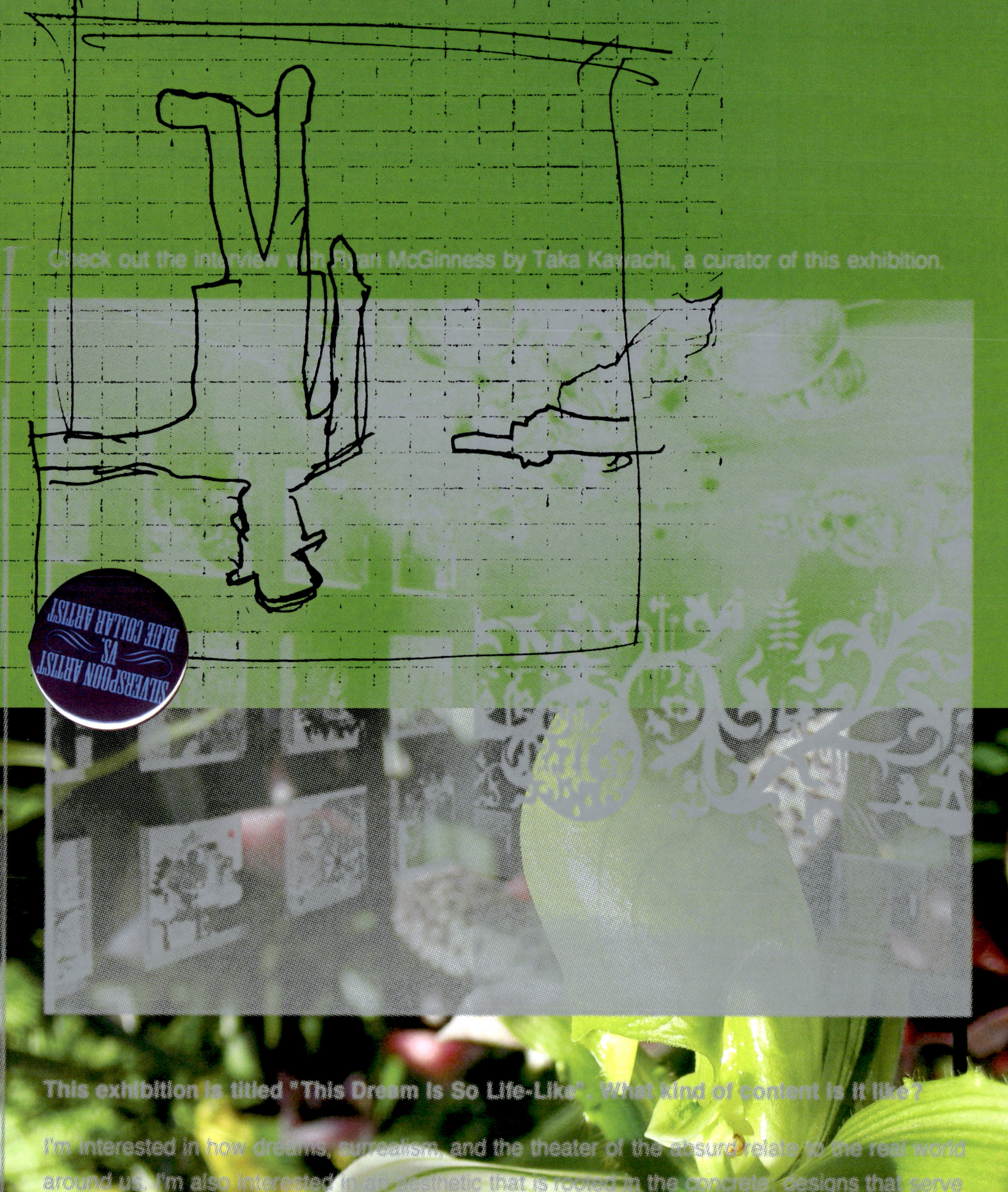

Check out the interview with Ryan McGinness by Taka Kawachi, a curator of this exhibition.

This exhibition is titled "This Dream Is So Life-Like". What kind of content is it like?

I'm interested in how dreams, surrealism, and the theater of the absurd relate to the real world around us. I'm also interested in an aesthetic that is rooted in the concrete: designs that serve to communicate clearly with an efficient use of form. These two interests are inherently at odds with each other as the former lends itself to more of a poetic and subjective interpretation of life and the latter strives to be as direct and objective as possible in describing life. "This Dream Is So Life-Like" assumes that what we know as reality has been flipped with what we consider the dream-world. I am declaring that this world around us is actually the dream, and I'm recognizing that it seems so much like the "real" world.

HOW TO RIP A HOLE IN THE SPACE-TIME CONTINUUM

2 BOX FANS BACK-TO-BACK FACING AWAY FROM EACH OTHER.

TURN BOTH ON AT THE SAME TIME. THEY WILL BOTH PULL AIR FROM THE SPACE BETWEEN THEM.

IMPORTANT: BOTH FANS MUST BE ON HIGH.

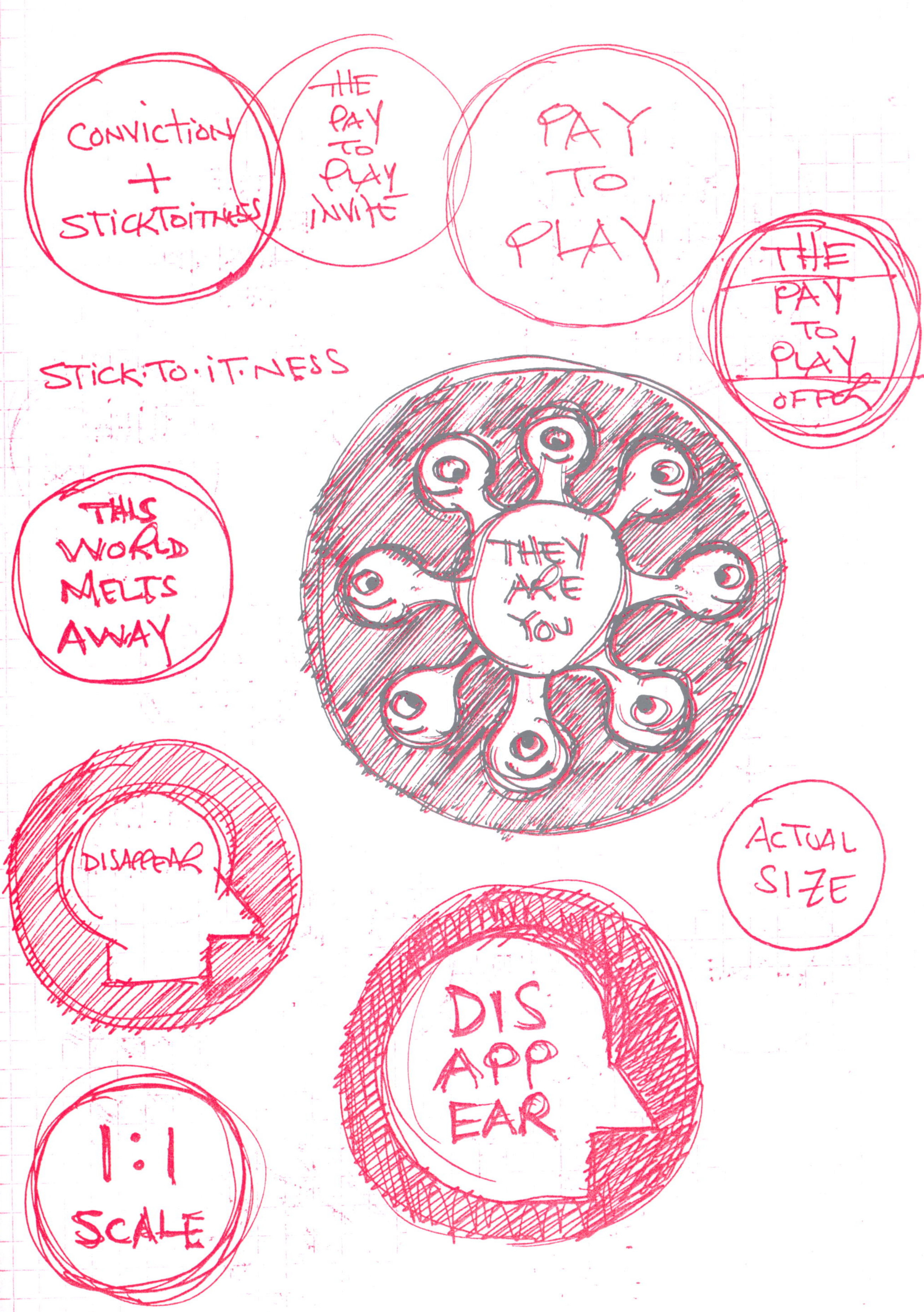

CONVICTION
+
STICKTOITNESS
THE
PAY
TO
PLAY
INVITE
PAY
TO
PLAY
THE
PAY
TO
PLAY
OFFER
STICK·TO·IT·NESS
THIS
WORLD
MELTS
AWAY
THEY
ARE
YOU
DISAPPEAR
ACTUAL
SIZE
DIS
APP
EAR
1:1
SCALE

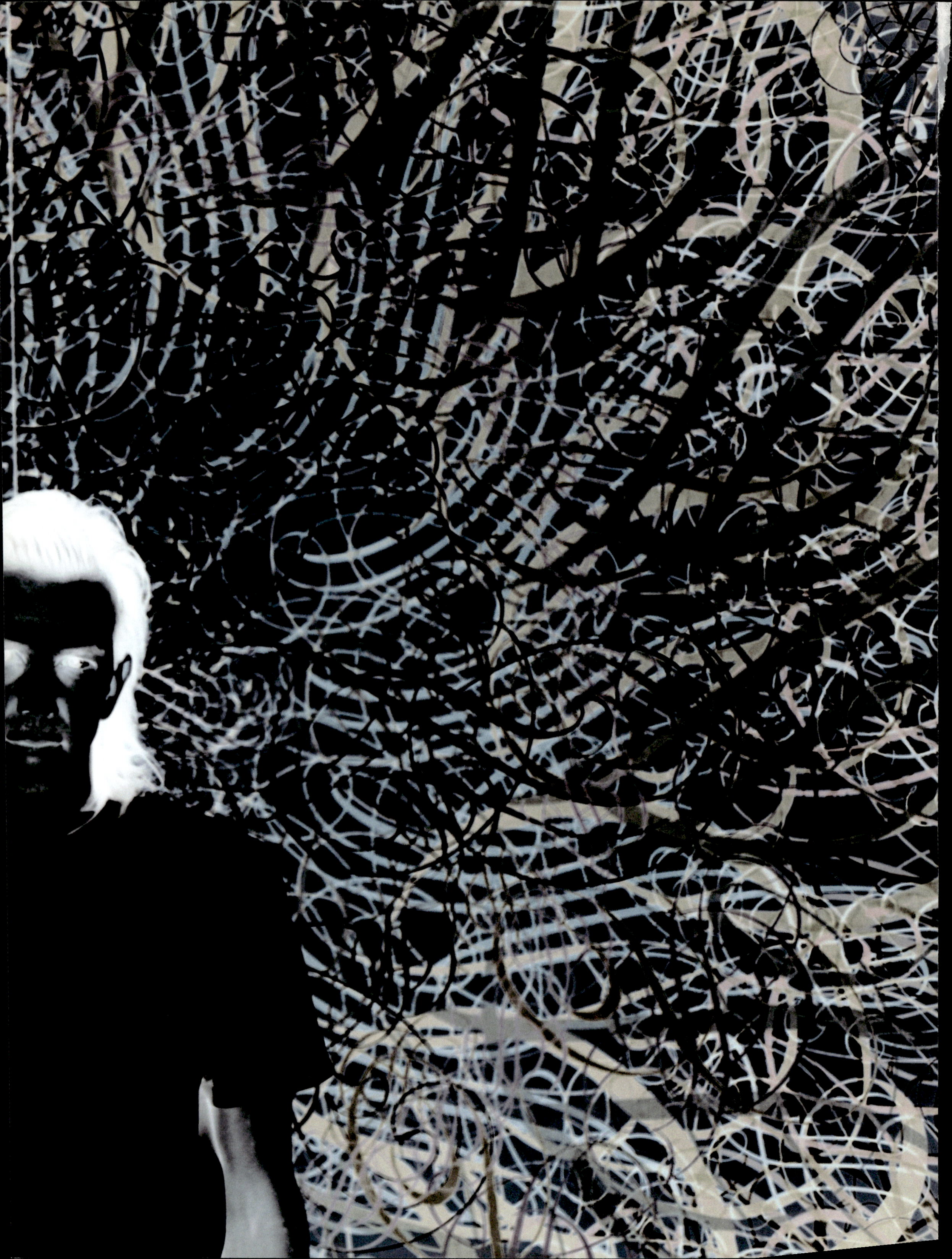

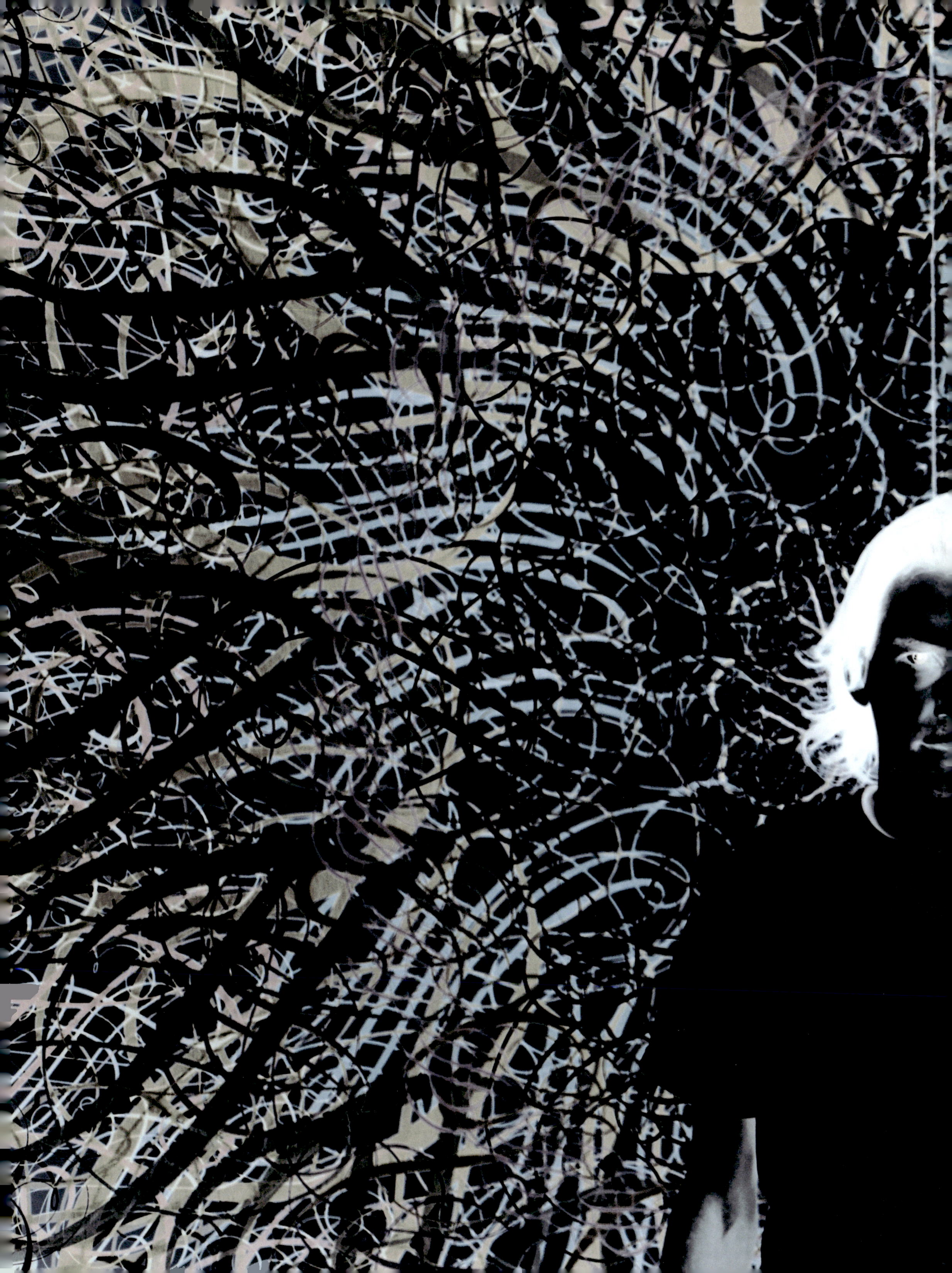

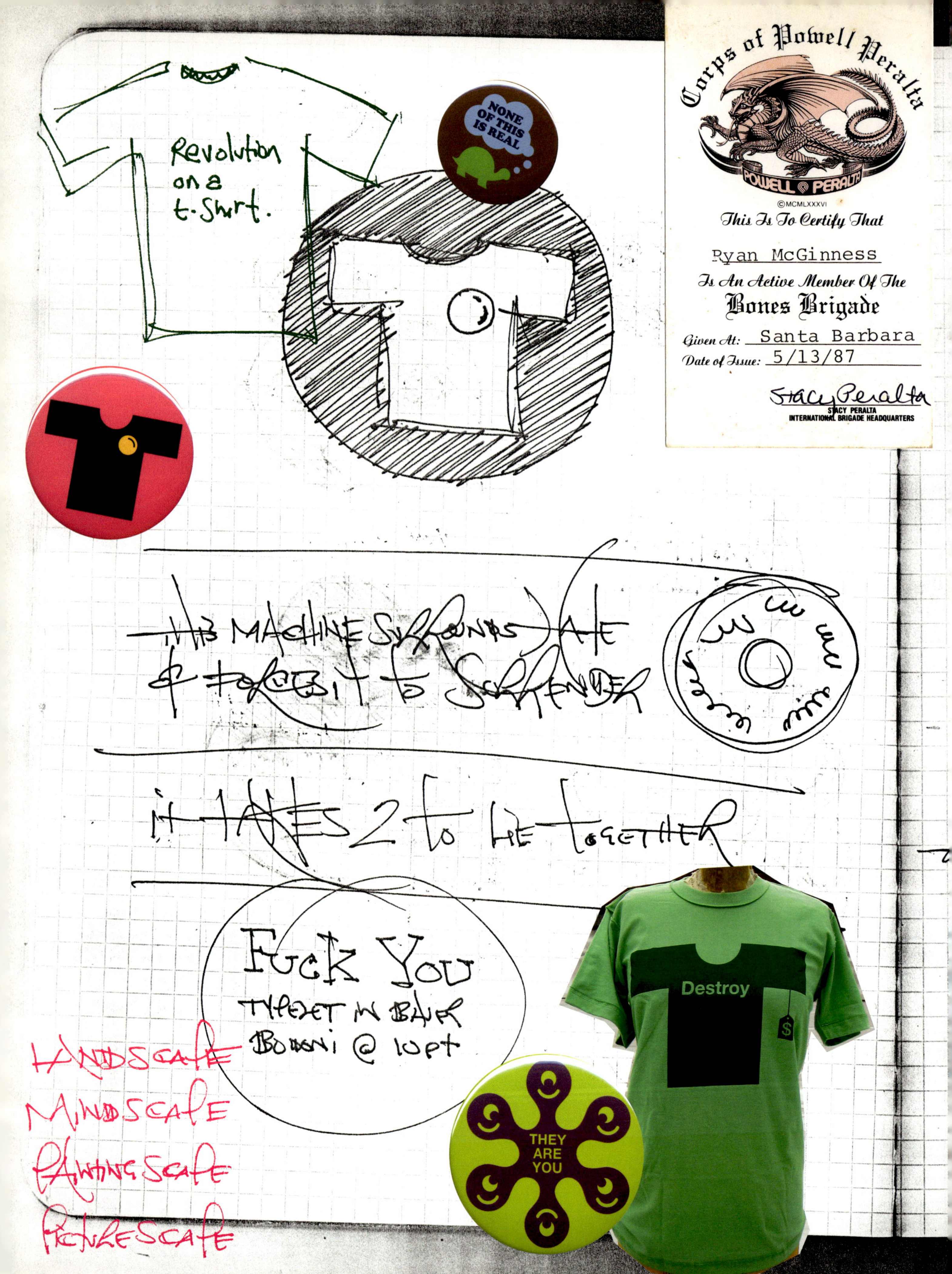
Revolution on a t-shirt.
NONE OF THIS IS REAL
Corps of Powell Peralta
POWELL PERALTA
©MCMLXXXVI
This Is To Certify That
Ryan McGinness
Is An Active Member Of The
Bones Brigade
Given At: Santa Barbara
Date of Issue: 5/13/87
Stacy Peralta
STACY PERALTA
INTERNATIONAL BRIGADE HEADQUARTERS
IT TAKES 2 TO LIE TOGETHER
FUCK YOU
TYPESET IN BAUER BODONI @ 10pt
LANDSCAPE
MINDSCAPE
Destroy
$
THEY ARE YOU

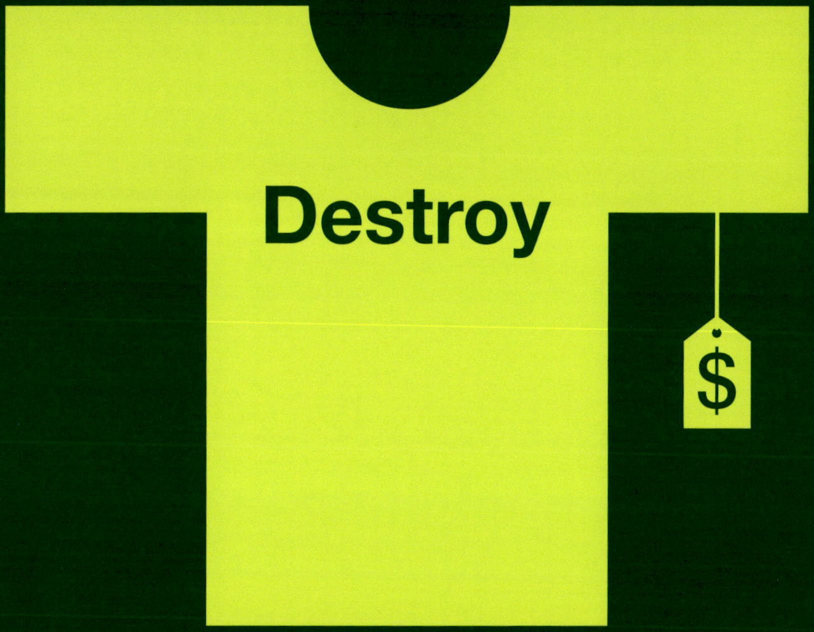

Destroy

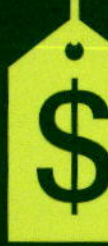

in A Position to favor my Position

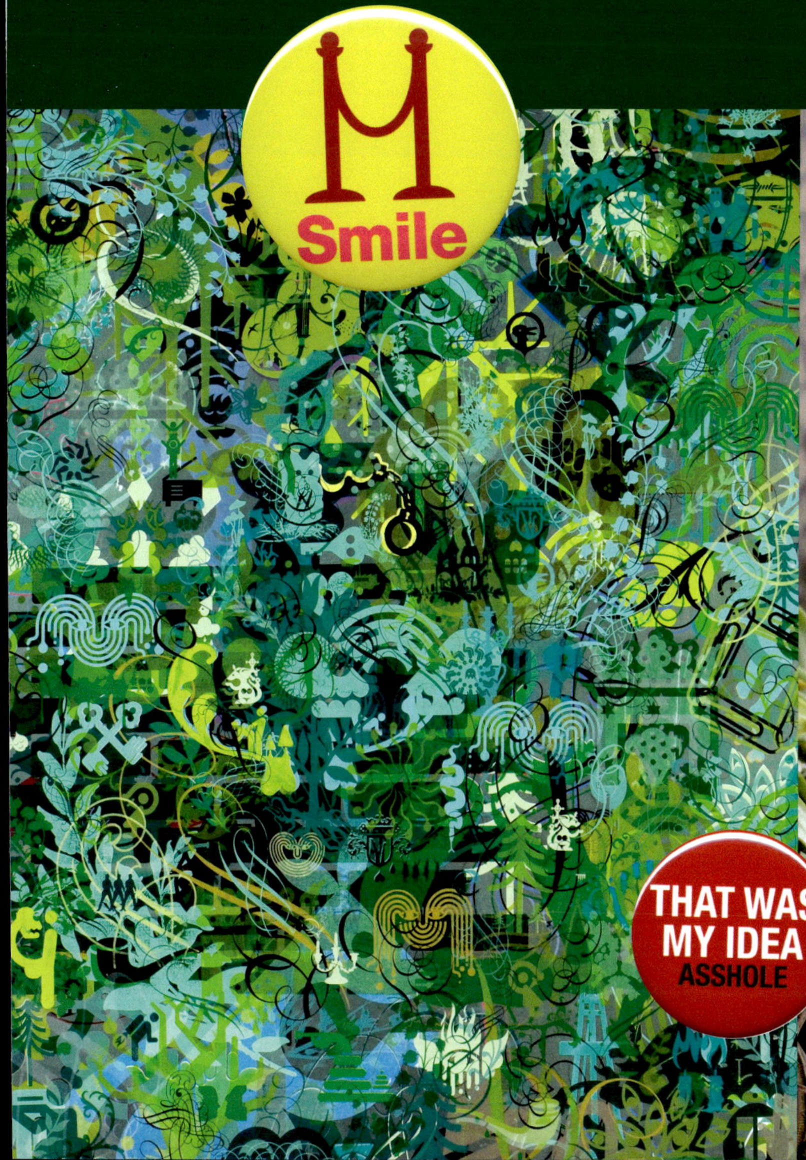

Smile

THAT WAS MY IDEA ASSHOLE

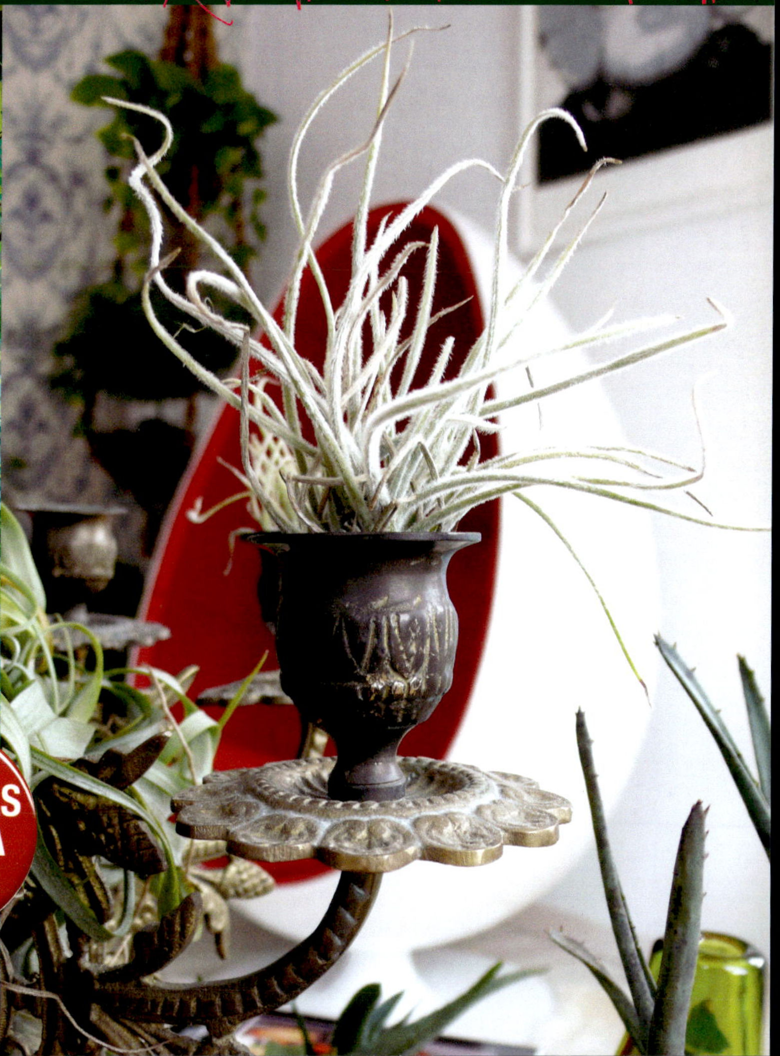

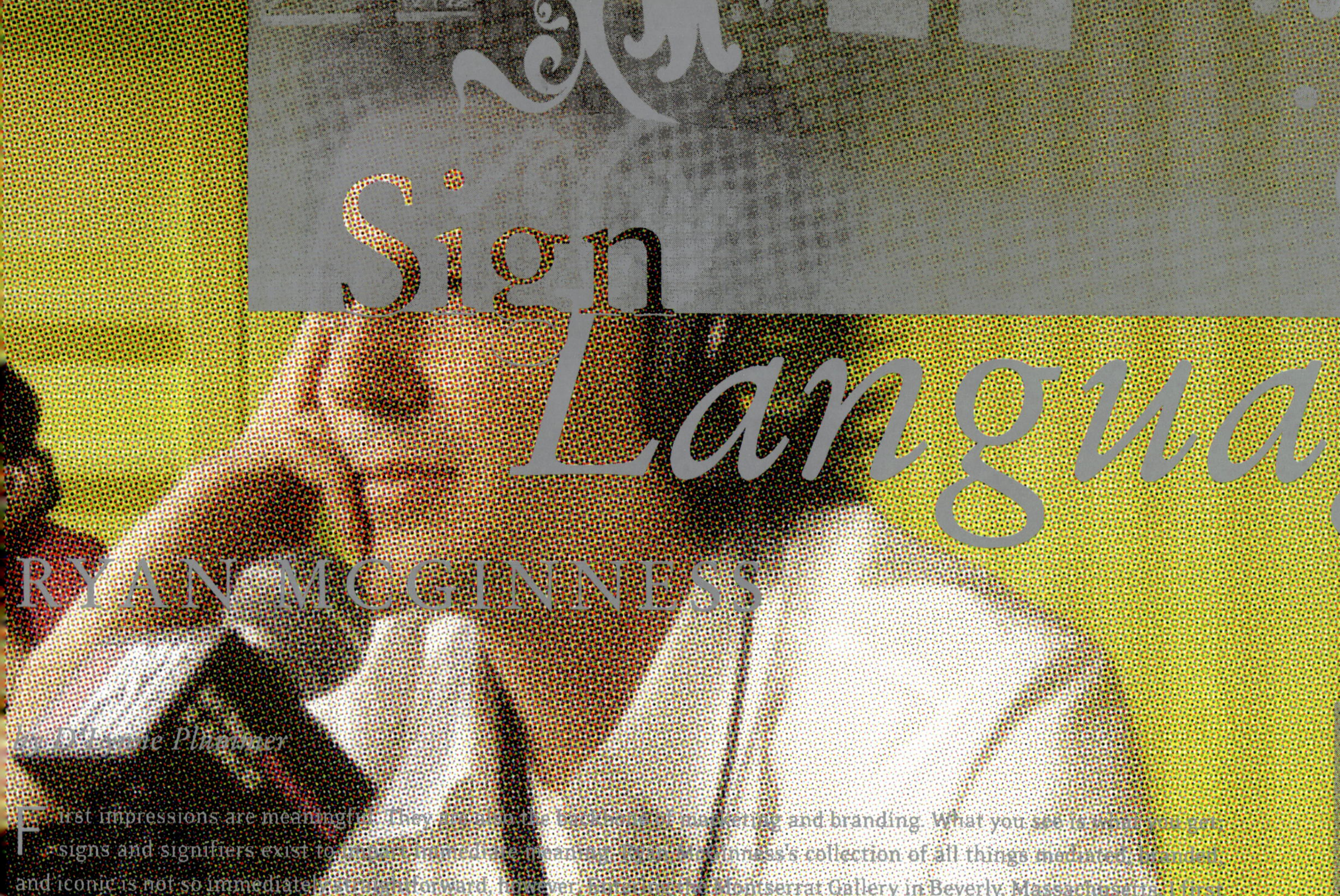

Sign Langua

RYAN MCGINNESS

by D'Lynne Plummer

First impressions are meaningful. They are also the backbone of marketing and branding. What you see is what you get: signs and signifiers exist to impart immediate meaning. Ryan McGinness's collection of all things mediated, branded and iconic is not so immediately straightforward, however. Entering the Montserrat Gallery in Beverly, Massachusetts, I first felt distrust at the walls loaded with perfect propaganda and what might come across as work firmly planted in the realm of graphic design. The gallery was a flatland of signs and an explosion of semiotics that seemed to include a vinyl decal parade.

But first impressions can be junked for the occasional epiphany. Here, distrust was eclipsed with genuine affection for this overmediated world in which we live. McGinness's youth on Virginia Beach saw many a silkscreened T-shirt, and he more than embraced the trend. McGinness took on product and emblem design as a challenge, making his own designs for T-shirts at a tender age, planting a seed that would grow into his immense success as a graphic designer and eventually as a New York artist whose works currently hang in MoMA's rotunda. If his graphic design work of the '90s was seen as some of New York's freshest, his work of the new millennium pushes the definition of the artist outward in all directions. By definition, graphic design is a form of visual communication that aims to clearly convey concepts and ideas. McGinness's work, however, does not clearly convey anything. Decorative aspects of design combine with signs and signifiers to make hilarious and often beautiful collisions of digital dissention. The line between graphic design and fine art is obliterated by the artist's own immense language of mass communication. The distinction is lost beneath a ten-layer silkscreen of perfectly viral shapes that are part of a seemingly endless worldwide web.

McGinness's consumer-culture-inspired motifs have made their way from the corporate office to skateboards and coffee mugs to the image-heavy mandalalike paintings and prints currently circulating museums and galleries. Moving from context to context, he has kept the concepts of marketing and branding as a launch pad for endless permutations of a consistent vision—simulacrums of the consumer environment. McGinness speaks volumes without words. He communicates at length through the squeegee and a limitless well of icons—little universes of meaning—serving up a lengthier conversation than most abstract paintings. While McGinness allows us to translate the aggregate of imagery for ourselves, he simultaneously relays that our systems of beliefs not only evolve but accumulate, almost to the point of incoherence. Images stacked upon images speak to this idea literally, while his appropriation of images from the public realm more subtly adds to the various meanings we ascribe to them. The head of a person is a fire symbol; conveniently, the head of the person beside him is the symbol for a fire extinguisher. Simple, and happily replicated on the

McGinness's consumer-culture-inspired mo… way from the corporate office to skateboar… the image-heavy mandalalike painting an…

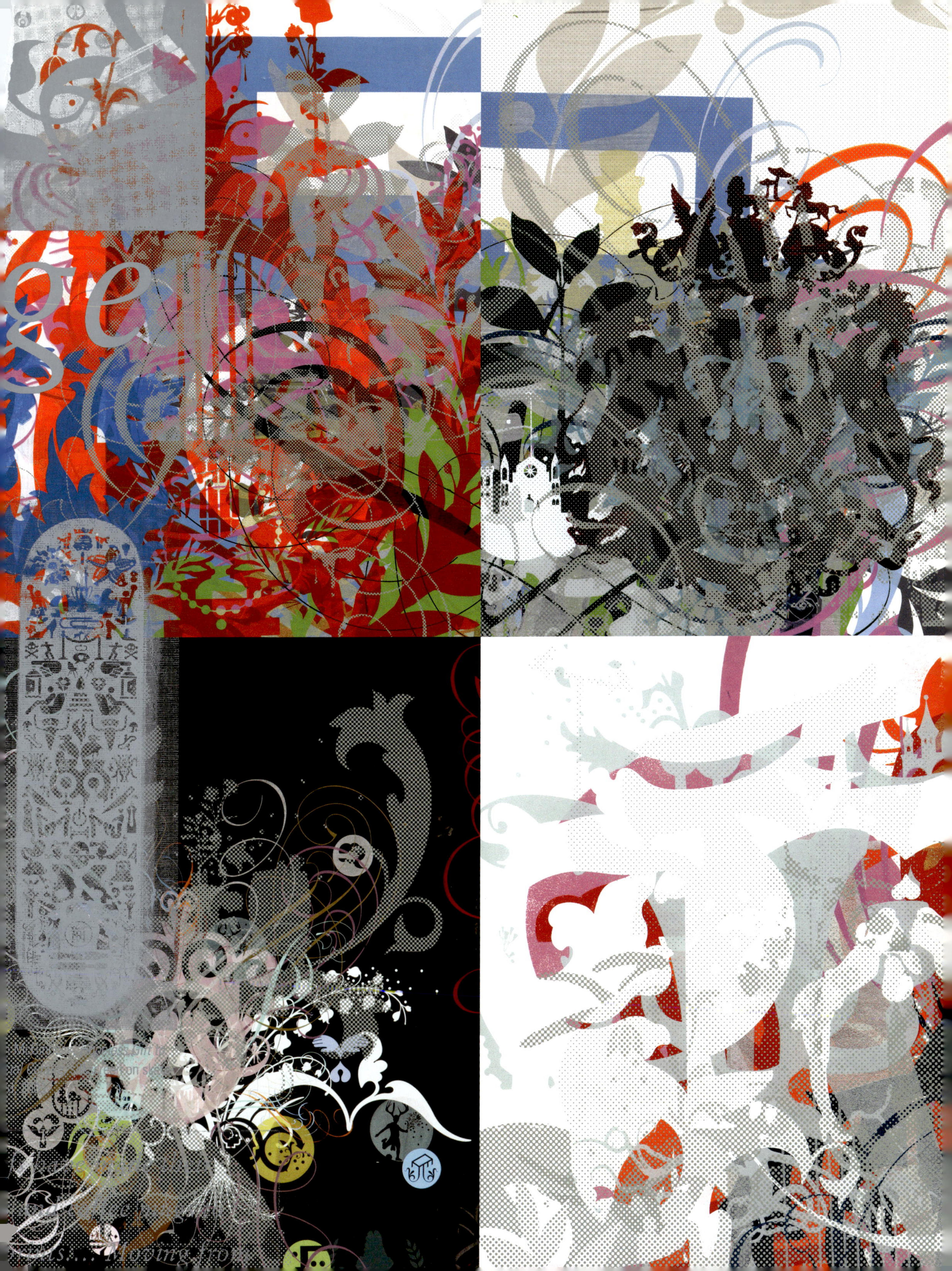

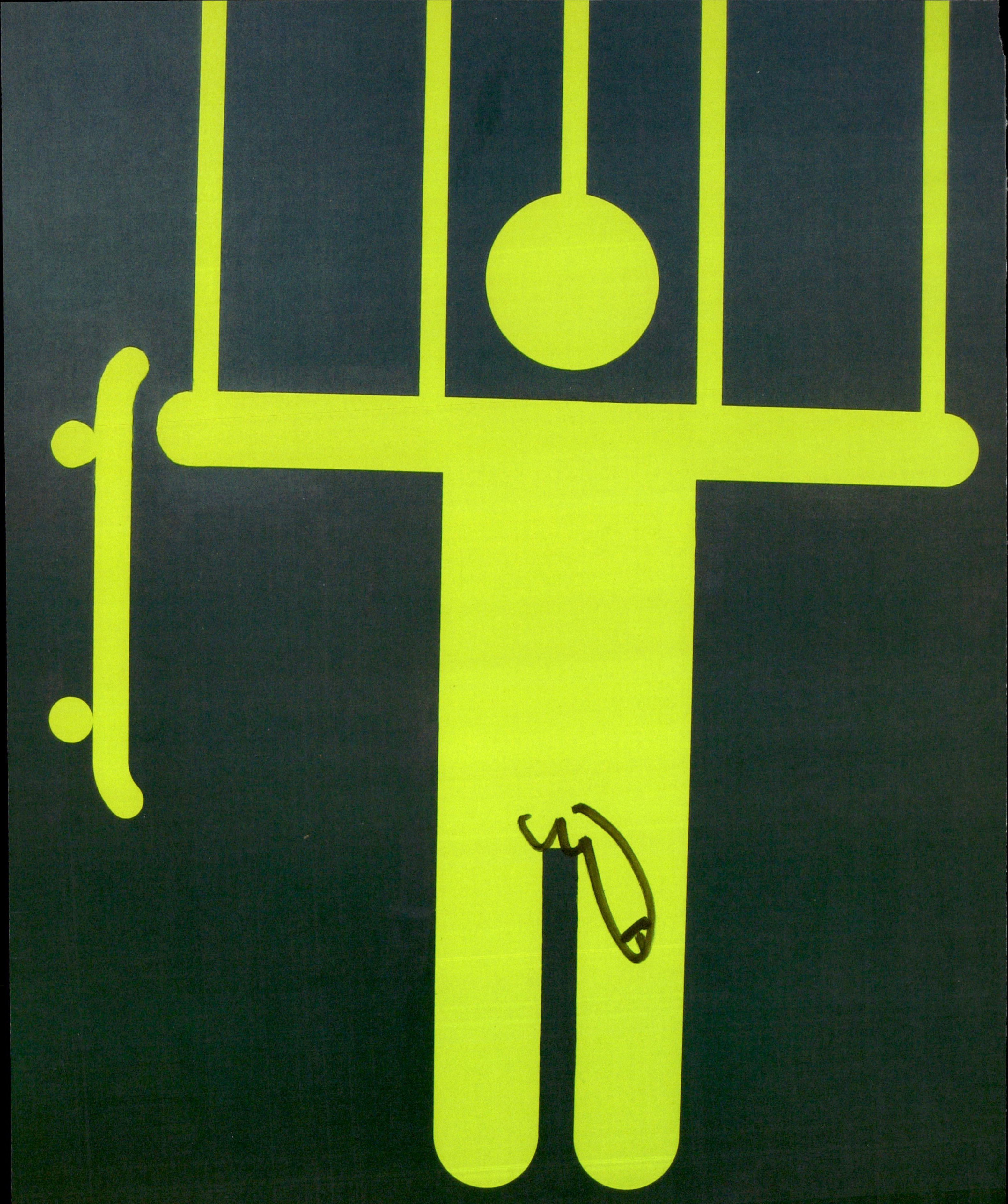

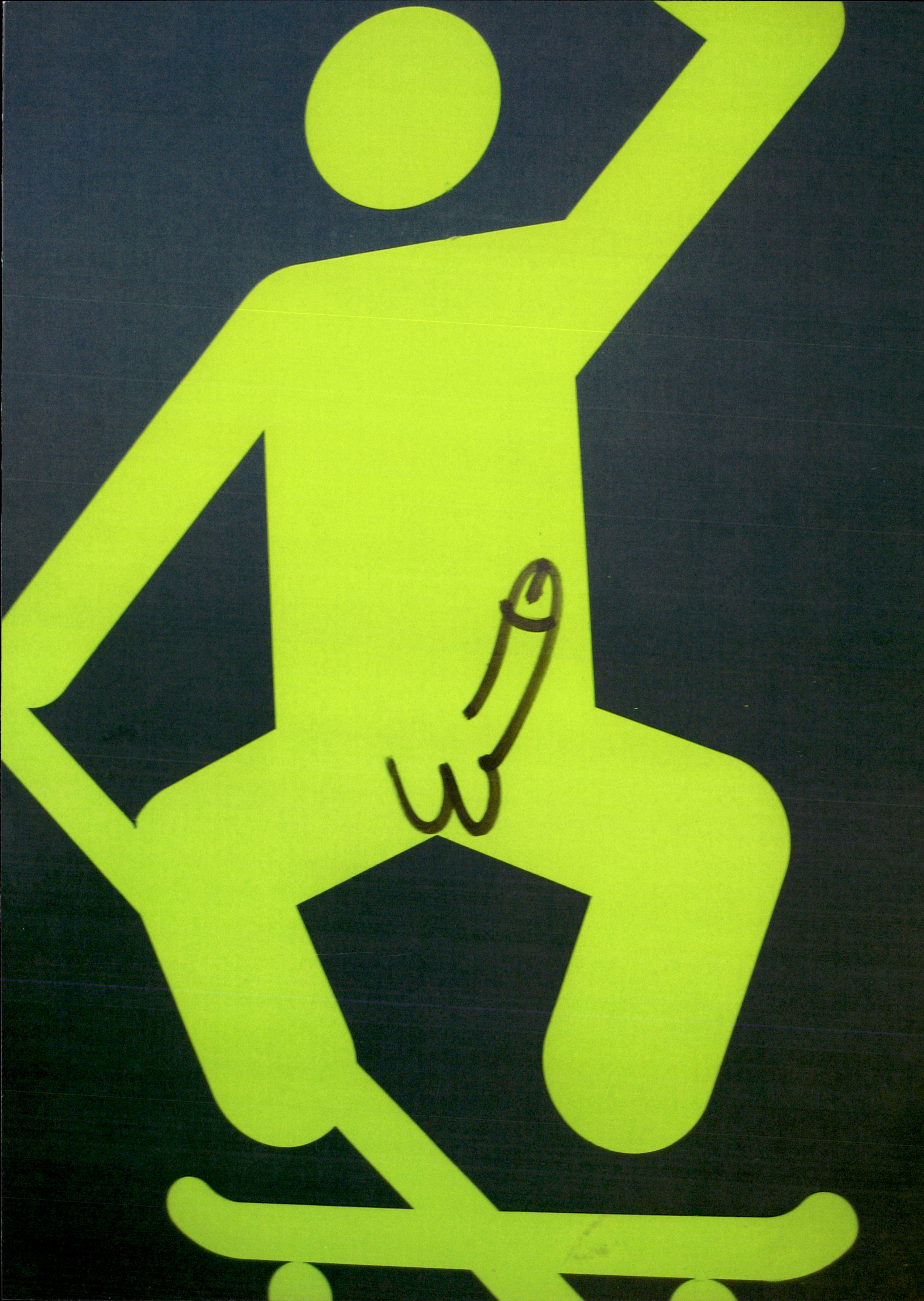

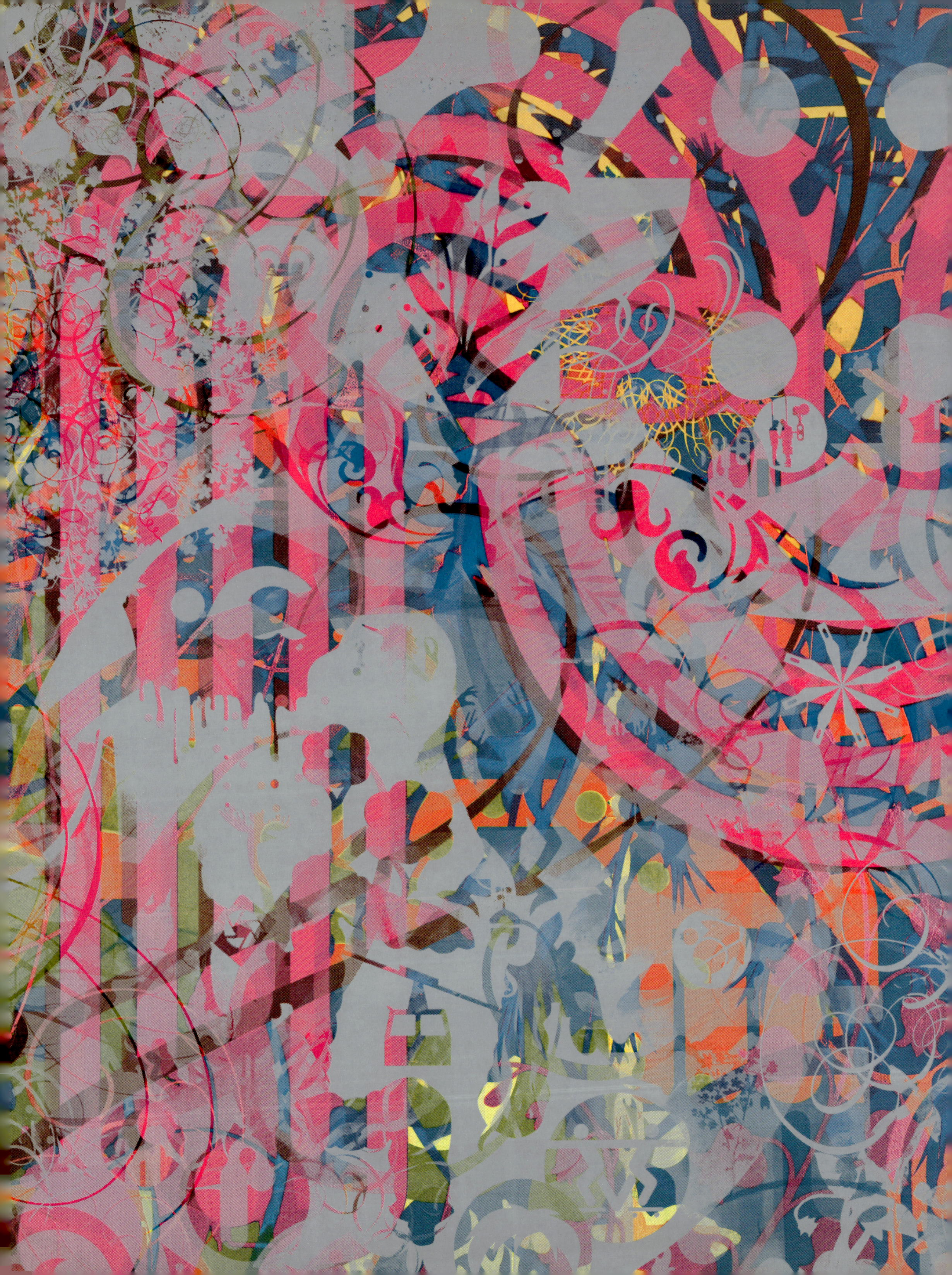

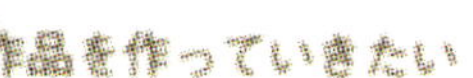

作品を作っていきたい

をデジタル化して、そ
を作りたいんだ。ペイ
として、コンピュータ
マウスパッドにしたり
ザインを学んでいたと
影響してか、昔からア
よく加工して違う形に
があるんだ。またアー
になって自分の好きな
いつまでも忘れずにい
ると、本当に大切なも
あるからさ。
教えてください。
のミュンヘンのショー

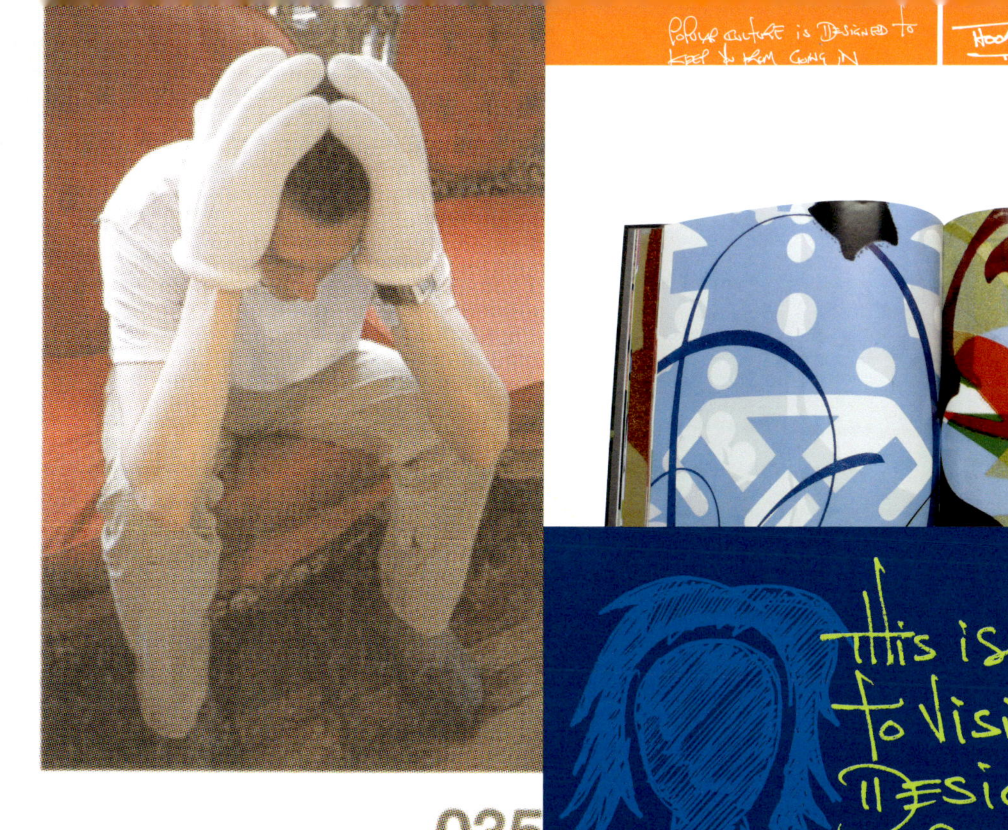

HOORAY FOR THE

035

THIS IS A PLACE TO VISIT THAT IS DESIGNED TO BE A PLACE TO VISIT

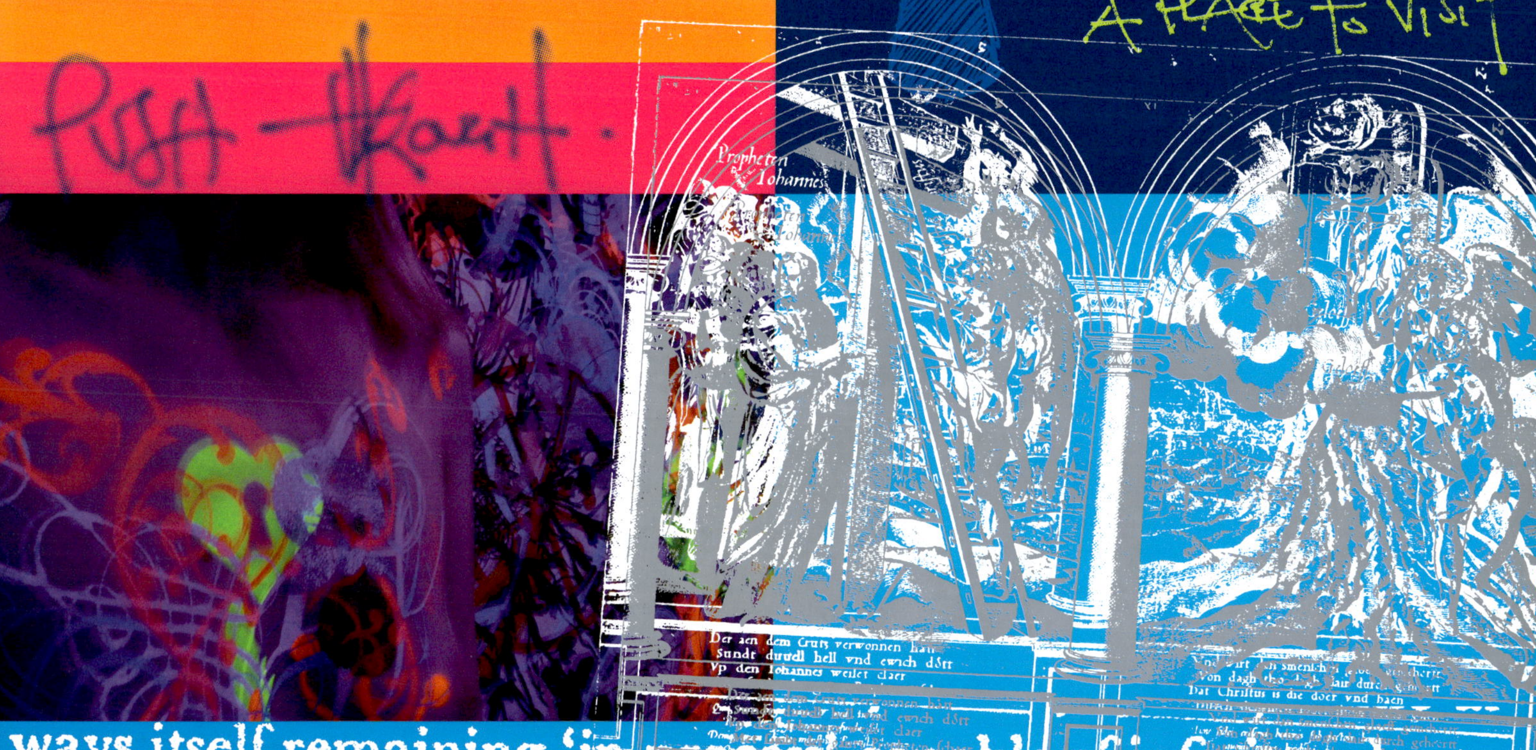

ways itself remaining 'in process' capable of infinite adaptation. This emphasis on signifying practice is accompanied by a polemical insistence that art represents the triumph of process over fixity, disruption over unity, 'collision' over 'linkage'[4] – the triumph, that is, of the signifier over the signified. It should be seen as part of the group's attempt to substitute the values of 'fissure' and contradiction for the

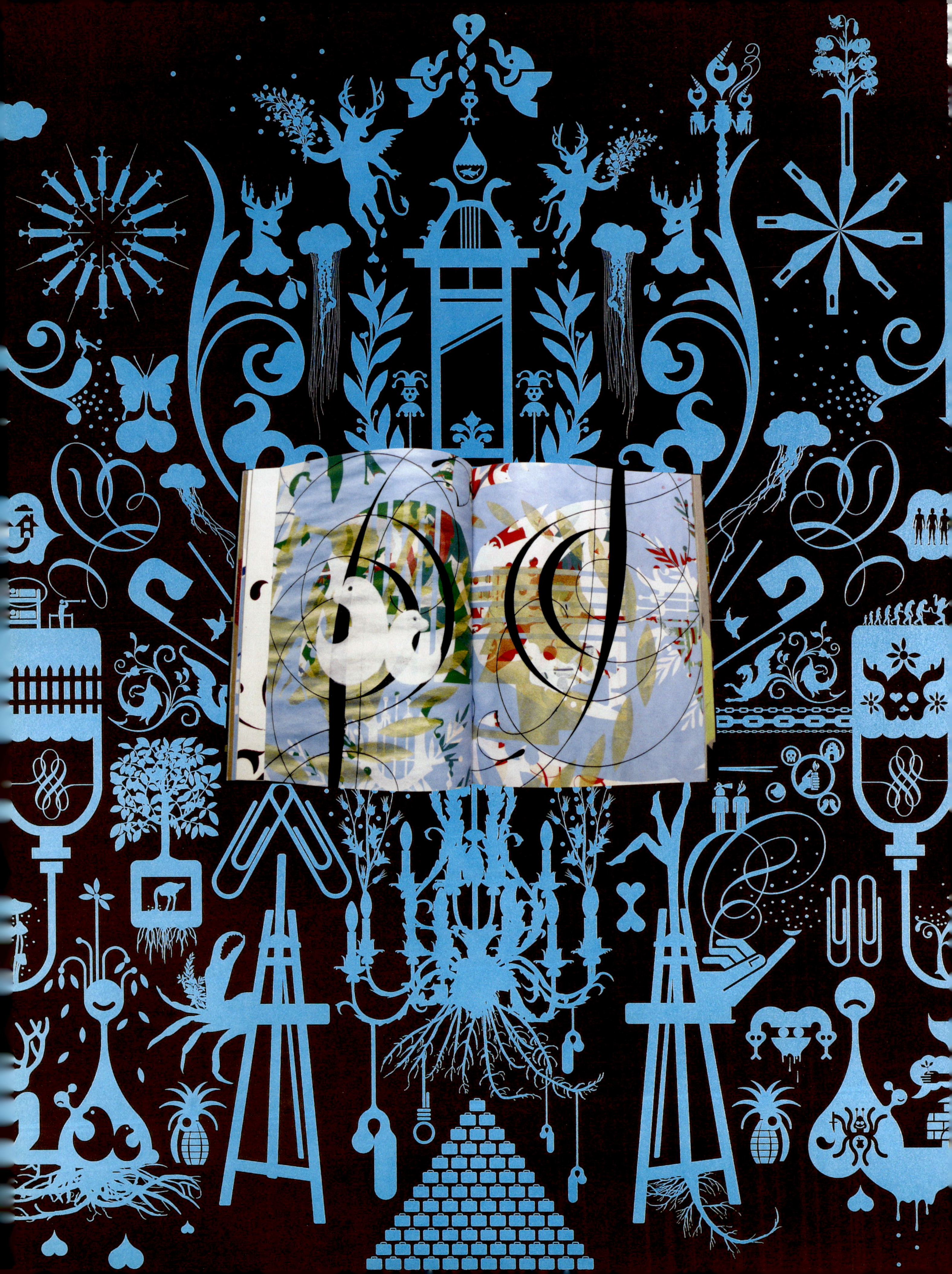

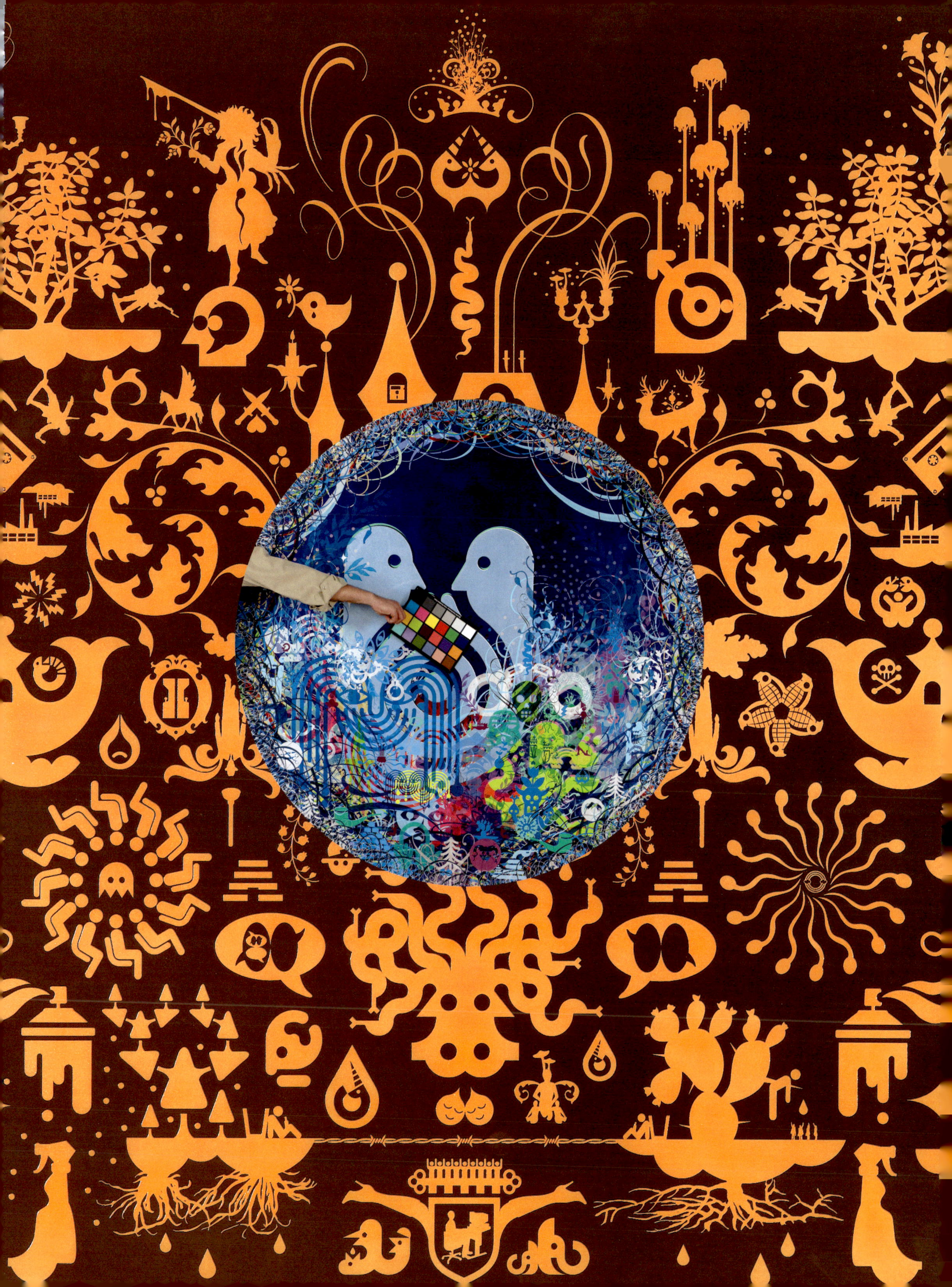

When you use signs and icons, or combine those for your work, do you always think of some stories or themes first?

No. I will usually pull together elements and allow the narrative to unfold. In doing so, I am allowing for the unconscious (and perhaps, by default, a collective unconscious) to come through in the work. The individual elements are carefully considered in their design and content, but a more free-fom approach is taken when the juxtapositions are made. The associations within the work are often unconsciously made, and often people will interpret the work differently than I do. Of course, this is more than fine with me, and in fact, multiple interpretations are encouraged. I believe for me to state "this is what the work means..." is pompous and old-fashioned. We live in a multi-cultural and multi-perspective fluid world where all voices are equal. My goal is to create work that is just as fluid and amorphous in exact interpretation. However, I do hope to hint at universal themes that relate to everyone through the experience of simply being human. These themes emerge by allowing the unconscious or subconscious to contribute to the work.

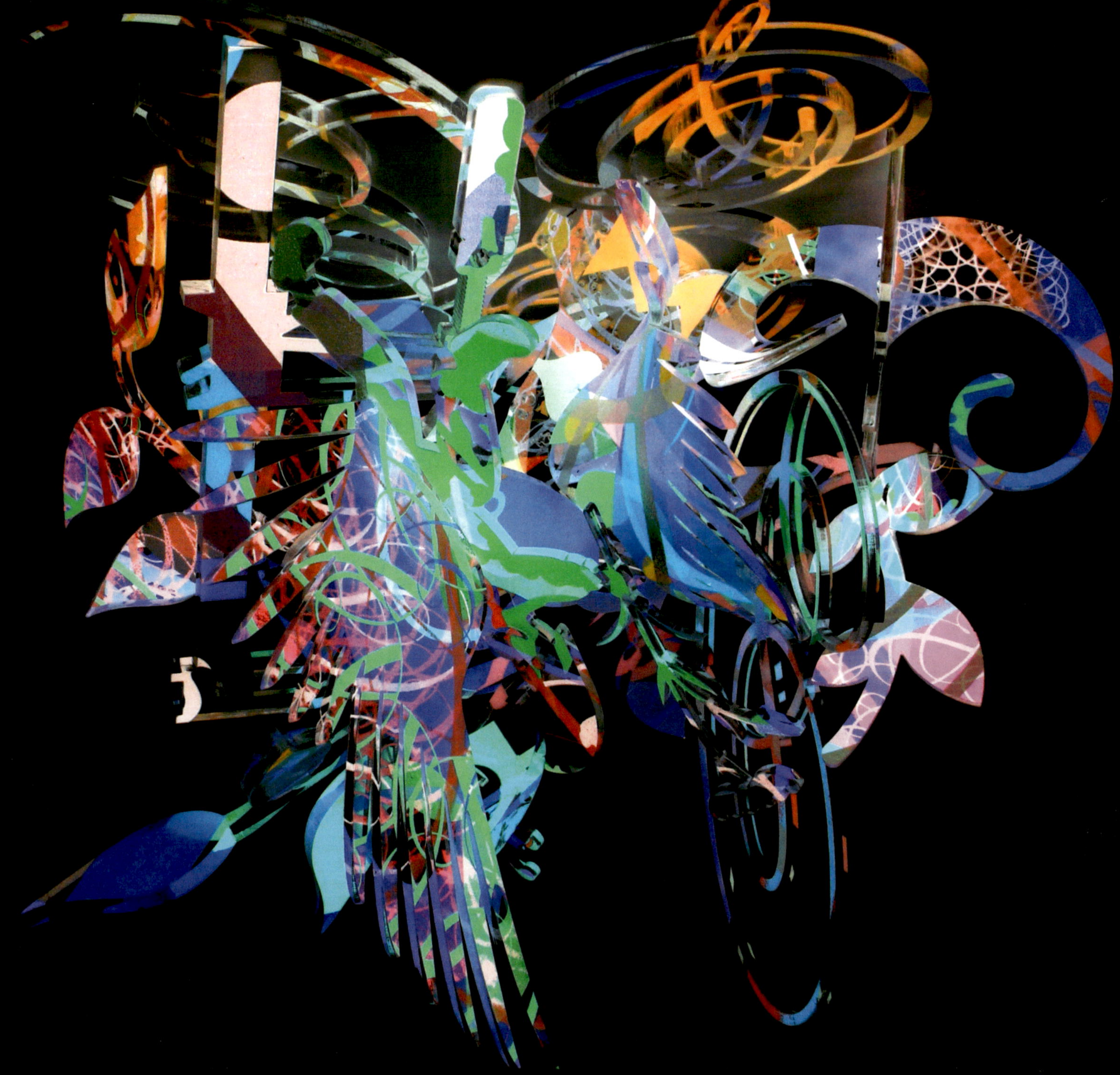

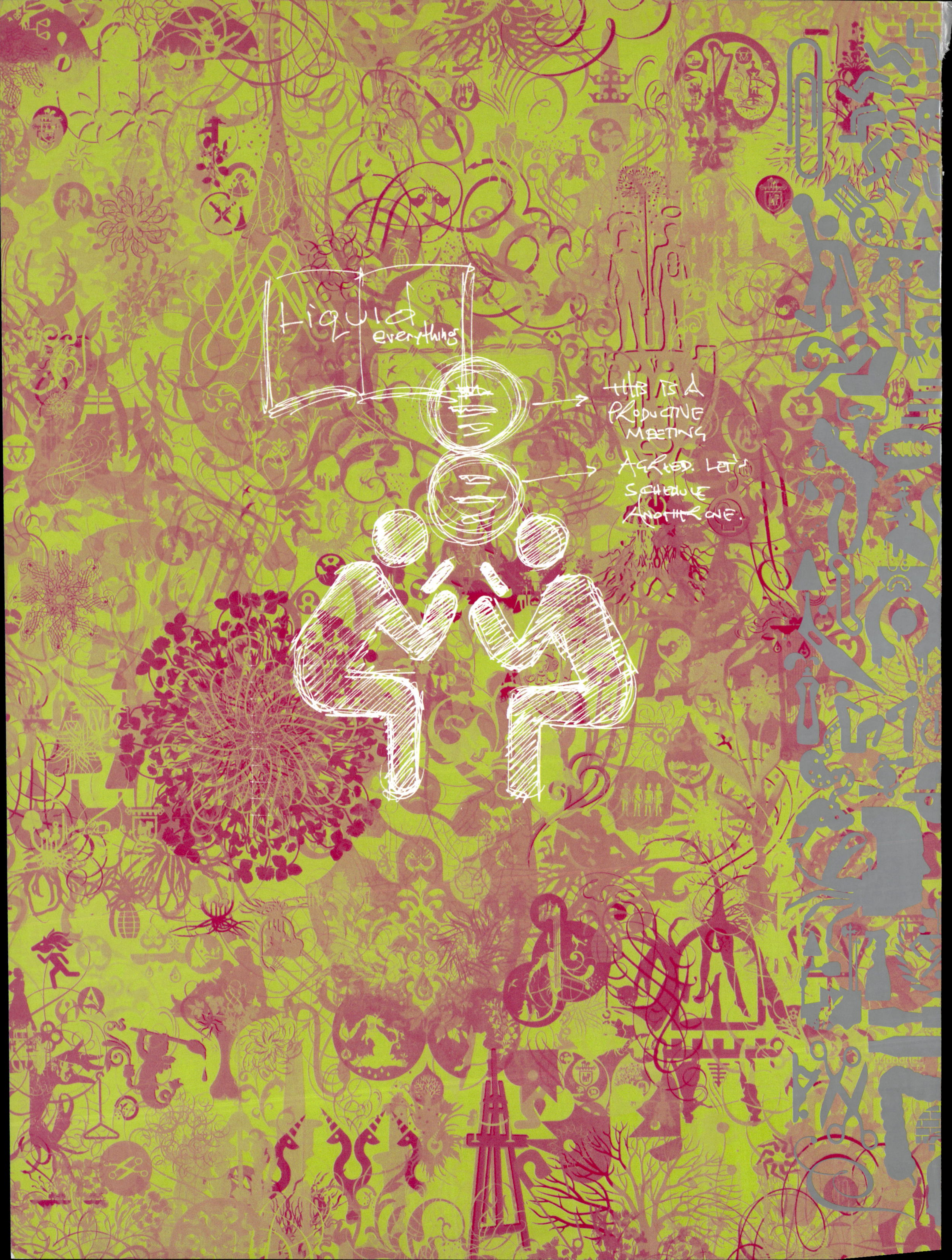
Liquid
everything
THIS IS A
PRODUCTIVE
MEETING
AGREED. LET'S
SCHEDULE
ANOTHER ONE.

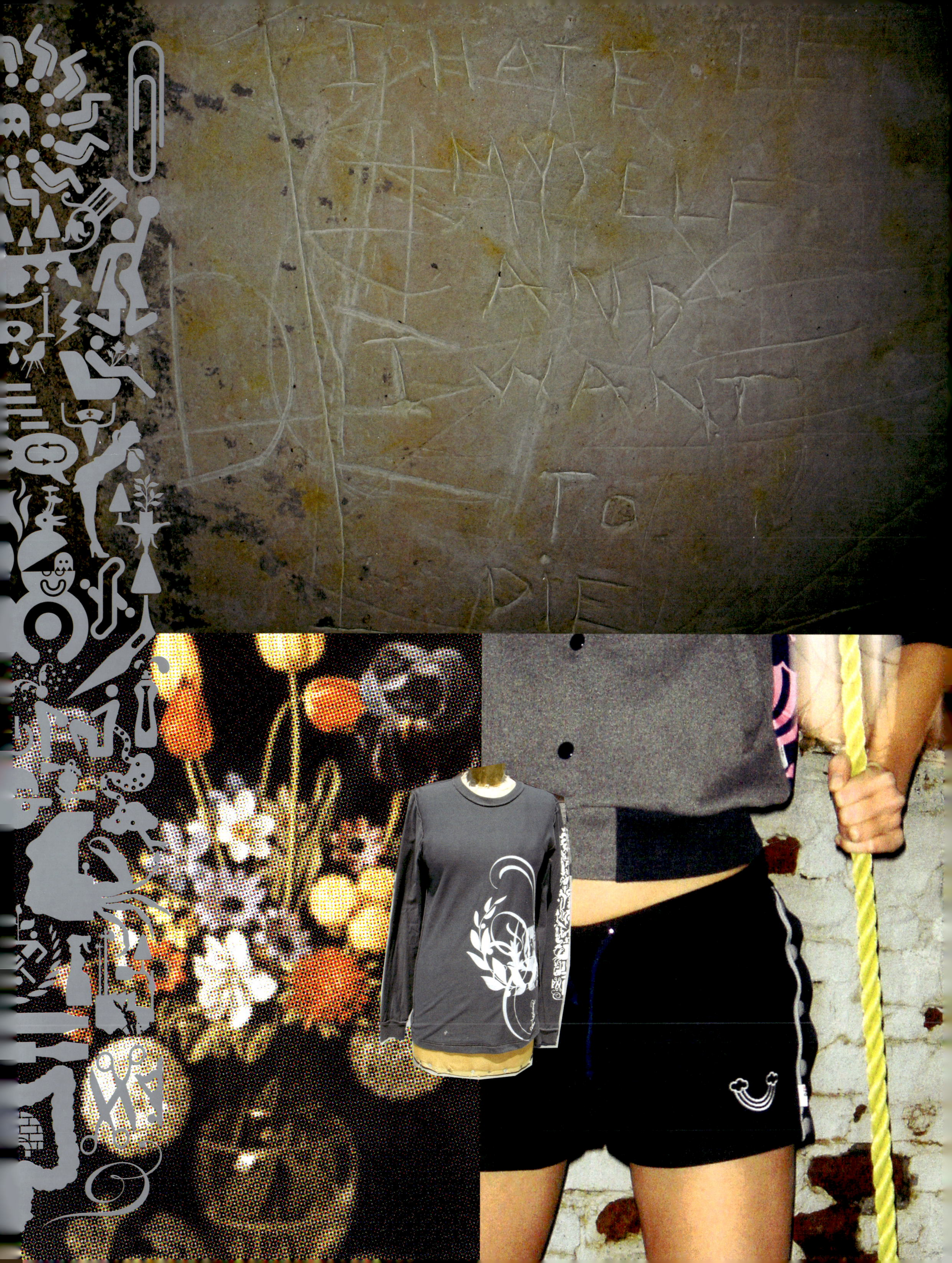
I HATE
MYSELF
AND
I WANT
TO
DIE

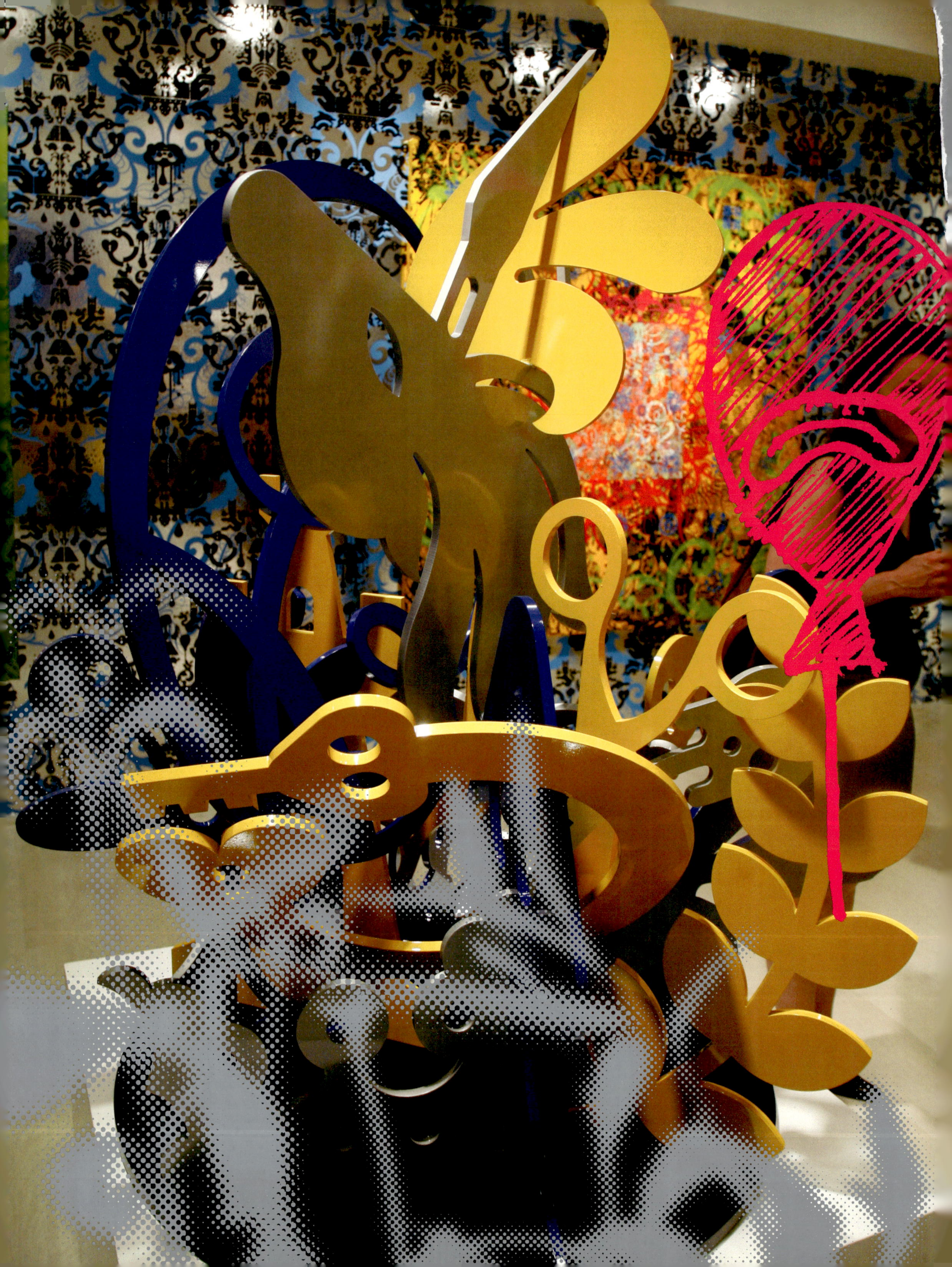

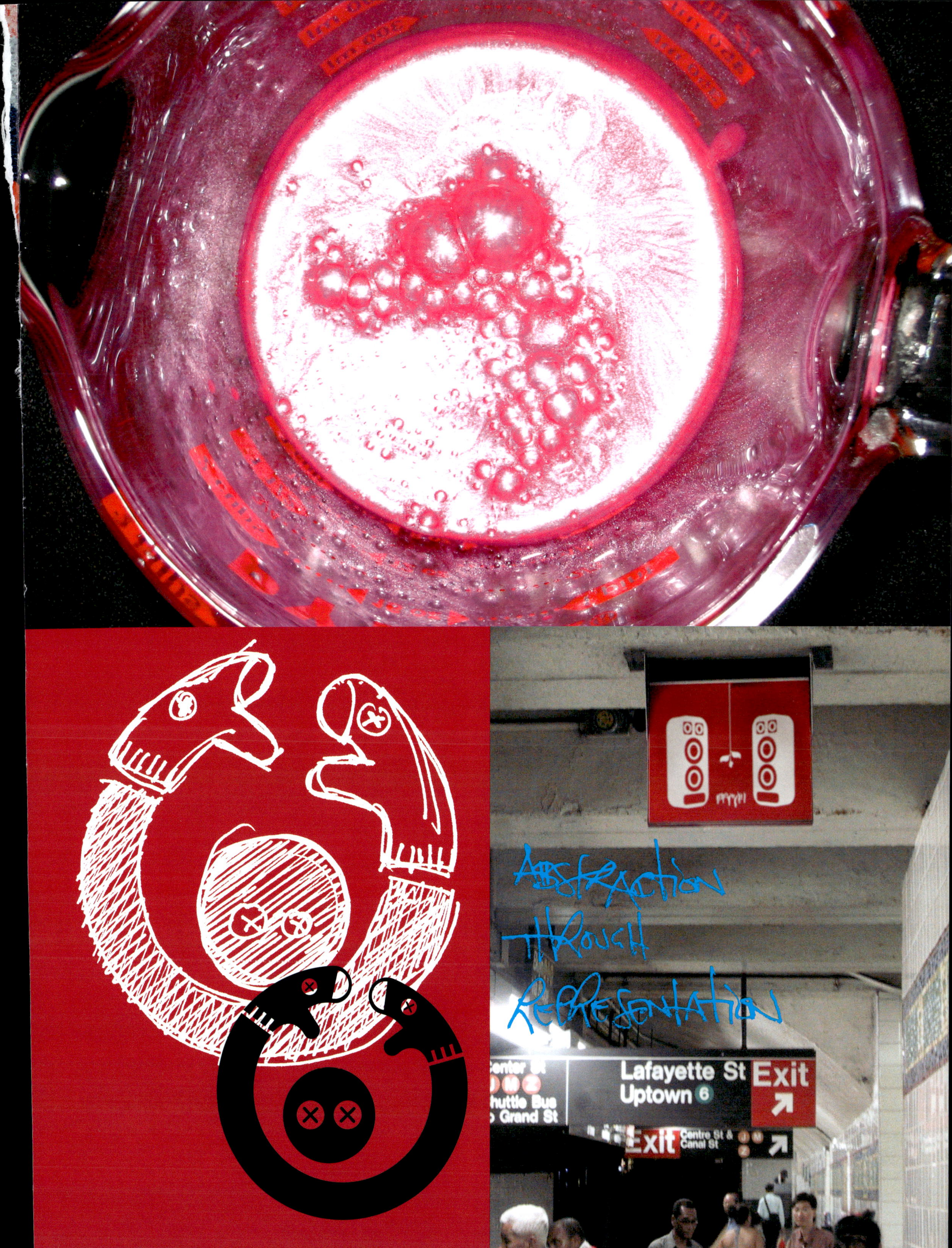
ABSTRACTION
THROUGH
REPRESENTATION
Lafayette St
Uptown 6
Exit
Exit
Centre St &
Canal St

Imagine insects with a life-span of two weeks, and then imagine further that they are trying to build up a science about the nature of time and history. Clearly, they cannot build a model on the basis of a few days in summer. So let us endow them with a language and a culture through which they can pass on their knowledge to future generations. Summer passes, then autumn; finally it is winter. The winter insects are a whole new breed, and they perfect a new and revolutionary science on the basis of the "hard facts" of their perceptions of snow. As for the myths and legends of summer: certainly the intelligent insects are not going to believe the superstitions of their primitive ancestors.

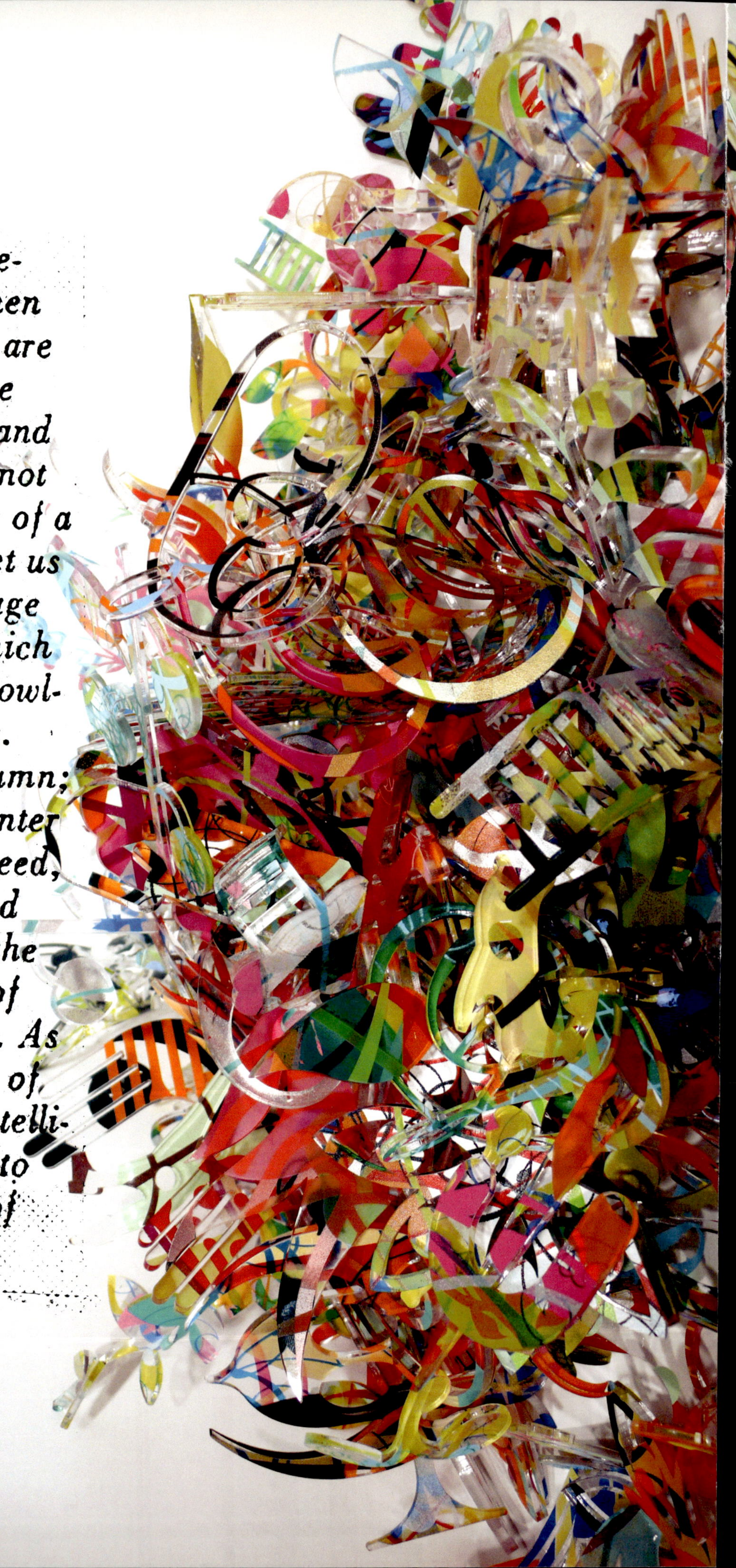

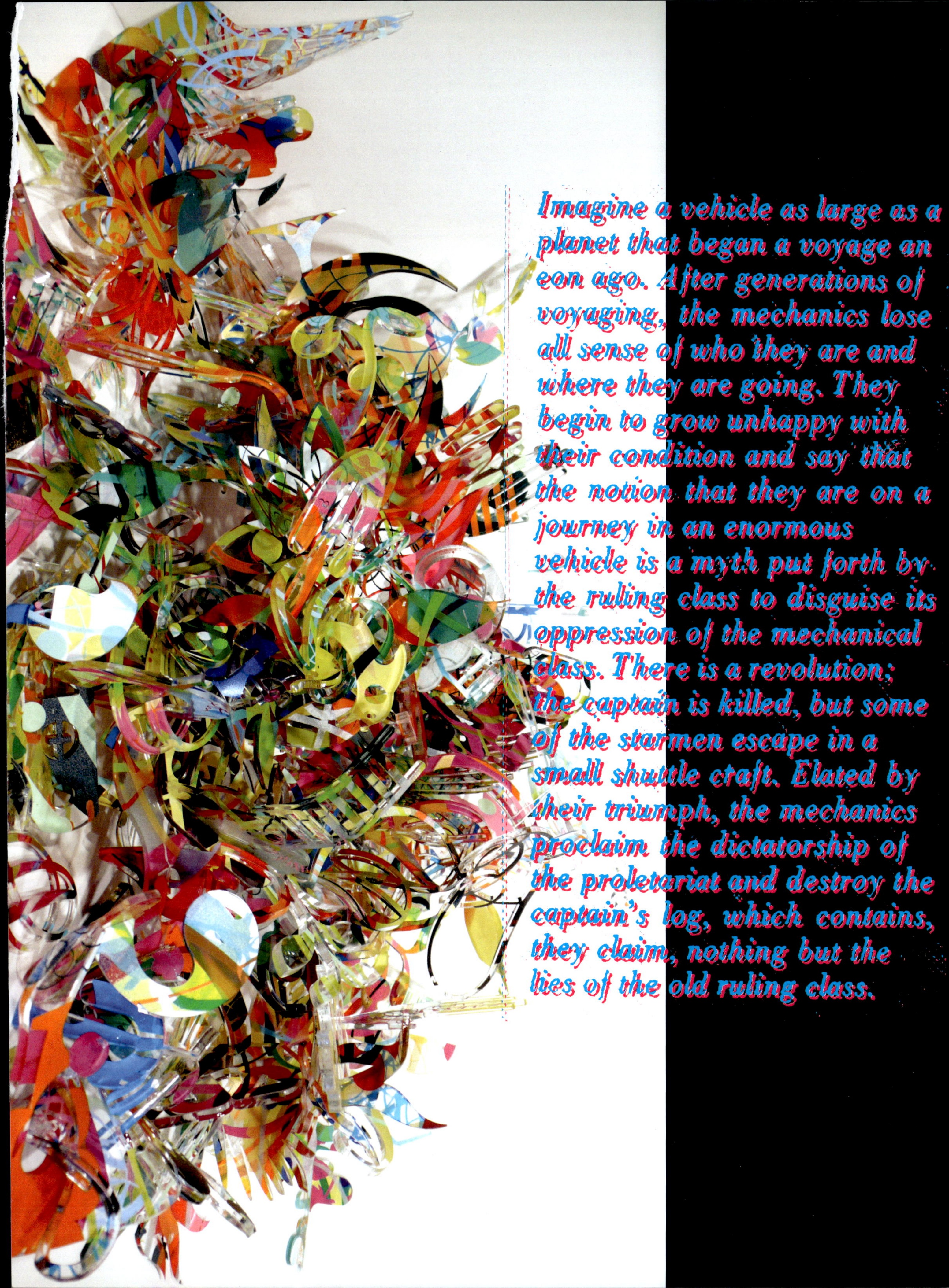

Imagine a vehicle as large as a planet that began a voyage an eon ago. After generations of voyaging, the mechanics lose all sense of who they are and where they are going. They begin to grow unhappy with their condition and say that the notion that they are on a journey in an enormous vehicle is a myth put forth by the ruling class to disguise its oppression of the mechanical class. There is a revolution; the captain is killed, but some of the starmen escape in a small shuttle craft. Elated by their triumph, the mechanics proclaim the dictatorship of the proletariat and destroy the captain's log, which contains, they claim, nothing but the lies of the old ruling class.

Imagine that you have just discovered a civilization as small as a DNA molecule. You want to establish contact, but since your own dimensions prevent you from entering the same space-time envelope, you must search for other means of communication. From observing the civilization closely, you find that there is an informational class that seems to carry messages back and forth among parts of the society, and you observe further that these messengers are actually enzymes of a kind you are familiar with. Since you cannot talk directly to the members of the civilization, you decide to talk through the events of their own society. Unfortunately, there are only certain times when the enzymes are in a position to carry your new information, and that is at the times when the structure is either breaking apart or about to come together again. Choosing your opening and closing epochs carefully, you begin to carry on an extended communication with the civilization.

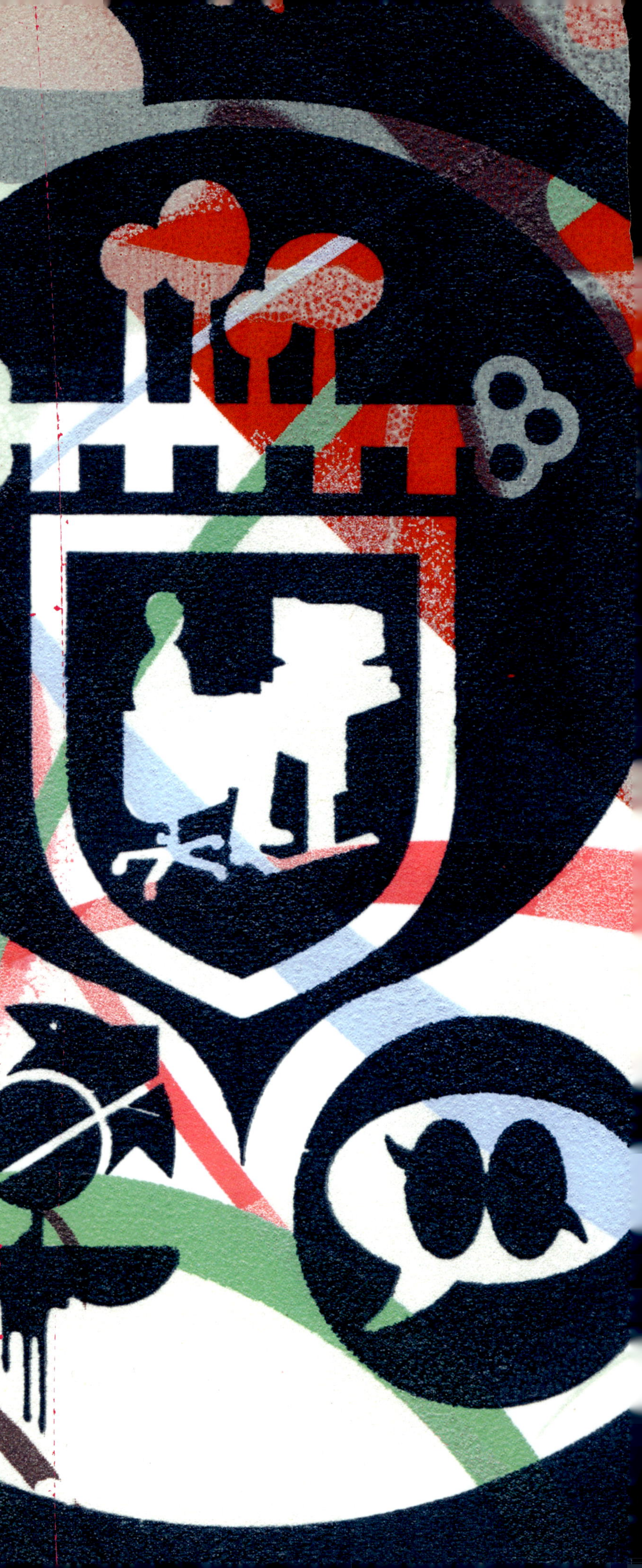

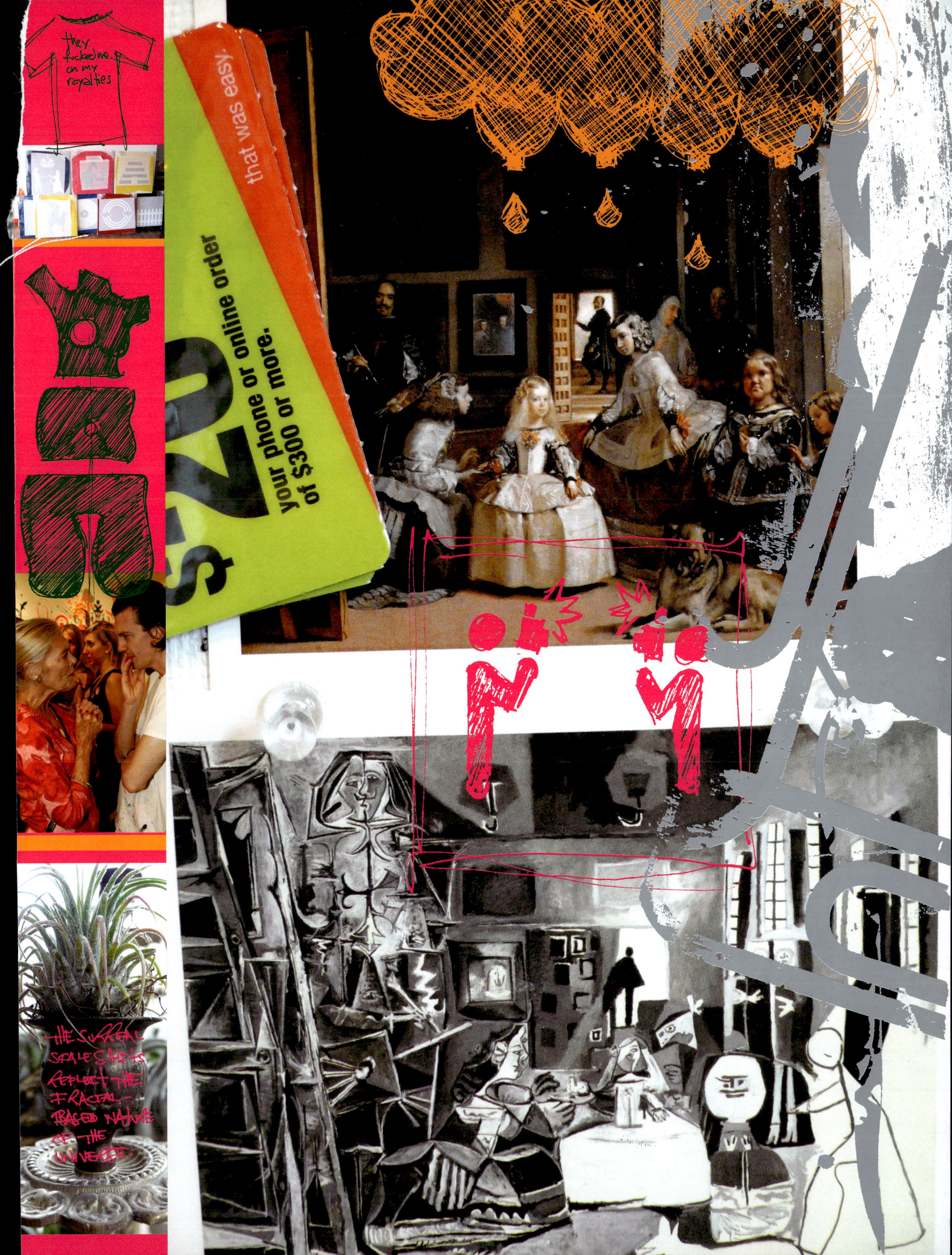
they fucked me on my royalties
that was easy.
$20
your phone or online order
of $300 or more.
THE SURREAL SCALE SHIFTS REFLECT THE FRACTAL-BASED NATURE OF THE UNIVERSE.

adrenals? It would be rash and premature to affirm it. The most we can say is that some kind of a *prima facie* case has been made out. Meanwhile the clue is being systematically followed, the sleuths—biochemists, psychiatrists, psychologists—are on the trail.

By a series of, for me, extremely fortunate circumstances I found myself, in the spring of 1953, squarely athwart that trail. One of the sleuths had come on business to California. In spite of seventy years of mescalin research, the psychological material at his disposal was still absurdly inadequate, and he was anxious to add to it. I was on the spot and willing, indeed eager, to be a guinea pig. Thus it came about that, one bright May morning, I swallowed four-tenths of a gram of mescalin dissolved in half a glass of water and sat down to wait for the results.

We live together, we act on, and react to, one another; but always and in all circumstances we are by ourselves. The martyrs go hand in hand into the arena; they are crucified alone. Embraced, the lovers desperately try to fuse their insulated ecstasies into a single self-transcendence; in vain. By its very nature every embodied spirit is doomed to suffer and enjoy in solitude. Sensations, feelings, insights, fancies—all these are private and, except through symbols and at second hand, incommunicable. We can pool information about experiences, but

d premature to affirm it.
me kind of a *prima facie*
nwhile the clue is being
euths—biochemists, psy-
ı the trail.
remely fortunate circum-
spring of 1953, squarely
leuths had come on busi-
seventy years of mescalin
terial at his disposal was
ne was anxious to add to
ng, indeed eager, to be a
ut that, one bright May
hs of a gram of mescalin
ter and sat down to wait

and react to, one another;
nces we are by ourselves.
into the arena; they are
lovers desperately try to
to a single self-transcend-
ıre every embodied spirit
y in solitude. Sensations,
these are private and, ex-
econd hand, incommuni-
n about experiences, but

never the experiences themselves. From family to nation, every human group is a society of island universes.

Most island universes are sufficiently like one another to permit of inferential understanding or even of mutual empathy or "feeling into." Thus, remembering our own bereavements and humiliations, we can condole with others in analogous circumstances, can put ourselves (always, of course, in a slightly Pickwickian sense) in their places. But in certain cases communication between universes is incomplete or even nonexistent. The mind is its own place, and the places inhabited by the insane and the exceptionally gifted are so different from the places where ordinary men and women live, that there is little or no common ground of memory to serve as a basis for understanding or fellow feeling. Words are uttered, but fail to enlighten. The things and events to which the symbols refer belong to mutually exclusive realms of experience.

To see ourselves as others see us is a most salutary gift. Hardly less important is the capacity to see others as they see themselves. But what if these others belong to a different species and inhabit a radically alien universe? For example, how can the sane get to know what it actually feels like to be mad? Or, short of being born again as a visionary, a medium, or a musical genius, how can we ever visit the worlds which, to Blake, to Sweden-

tle pissed off by the glut
lacking imagination.
her off constantly. Right
ng Ryan McGinness hard-
an't believe people
u feel good as an artist
a poor man's version of
Yankovic.

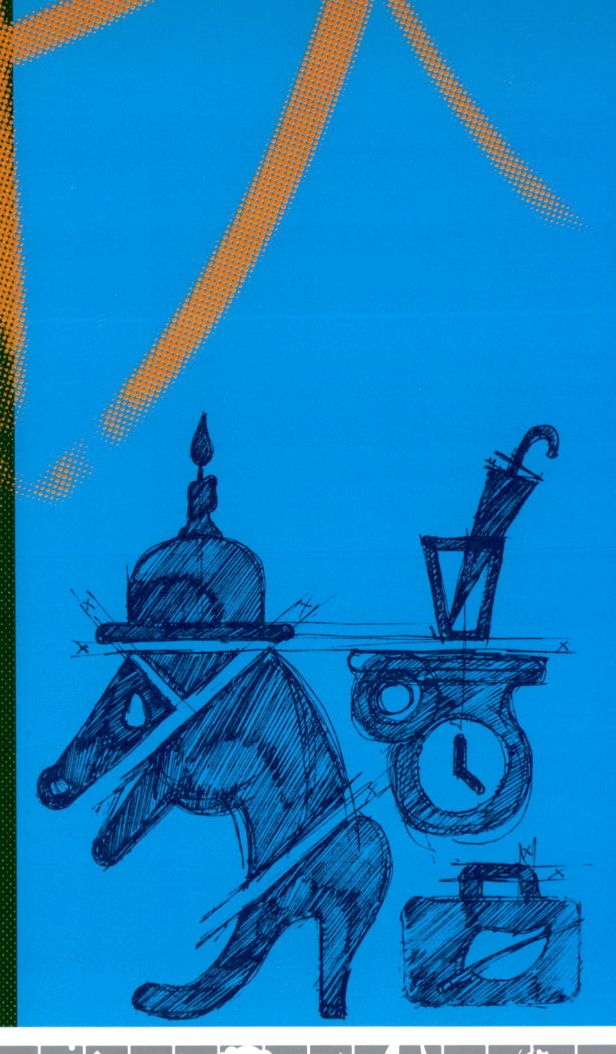

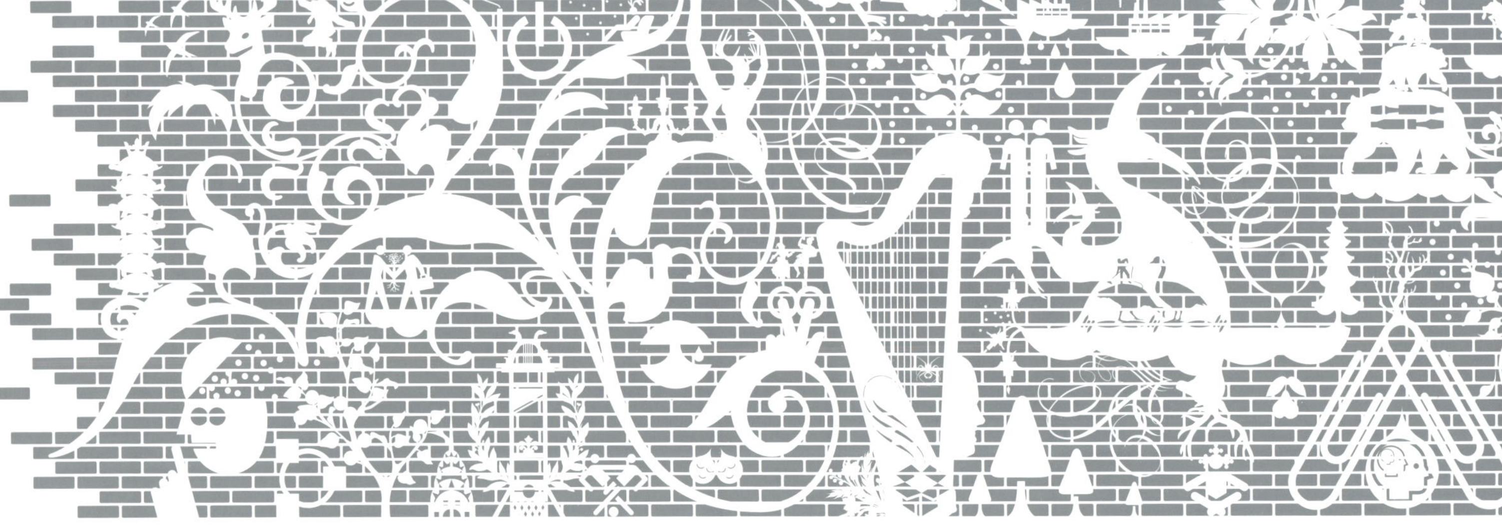

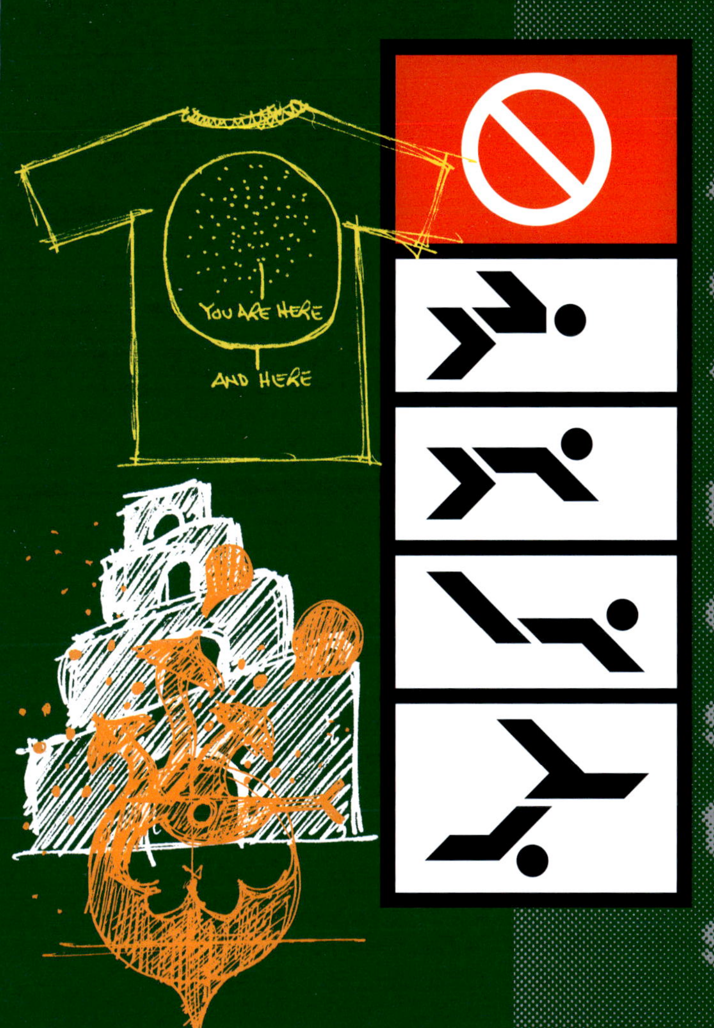

Anthony Yankovic is a li
of artists and designers
"People just rip each ot
now, 'designers' are bit
core. It's pathetic. I just
sometimes. How can yo
to know that you're just
someone else." Opines

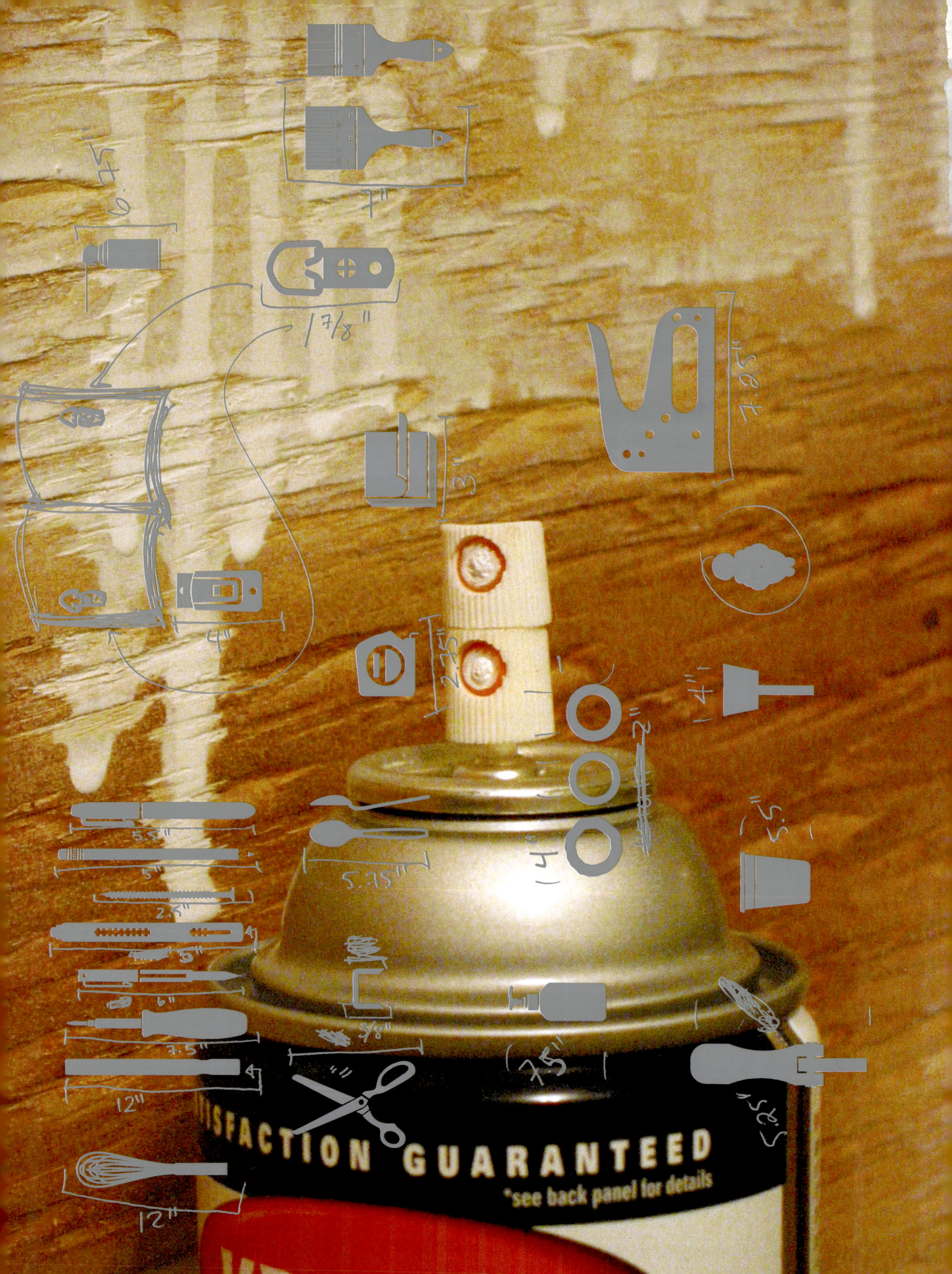
ISFACTION GUARANTEED
*see back panel for details
7"
1 7/8"
4"
3"
12"
12"

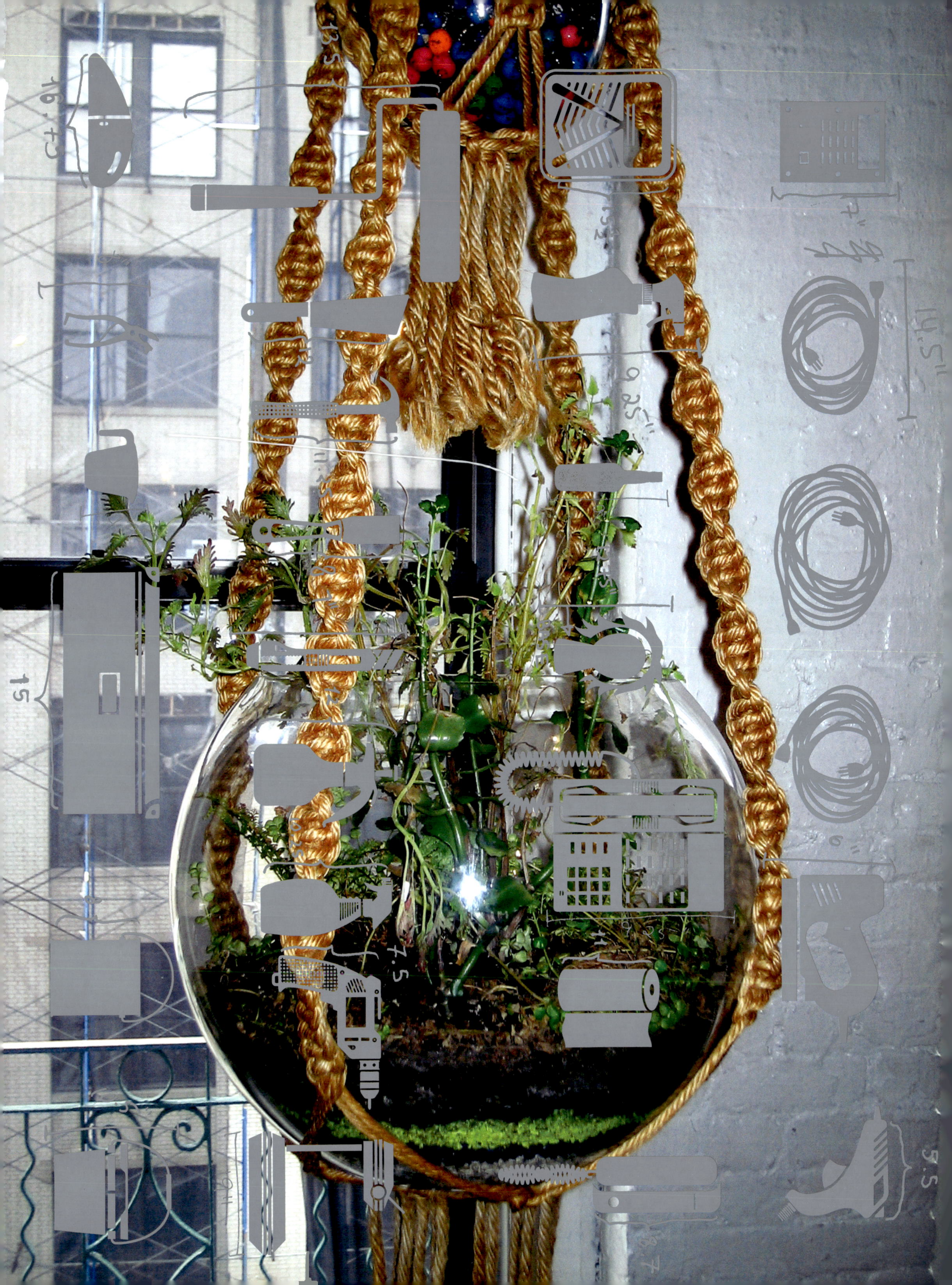

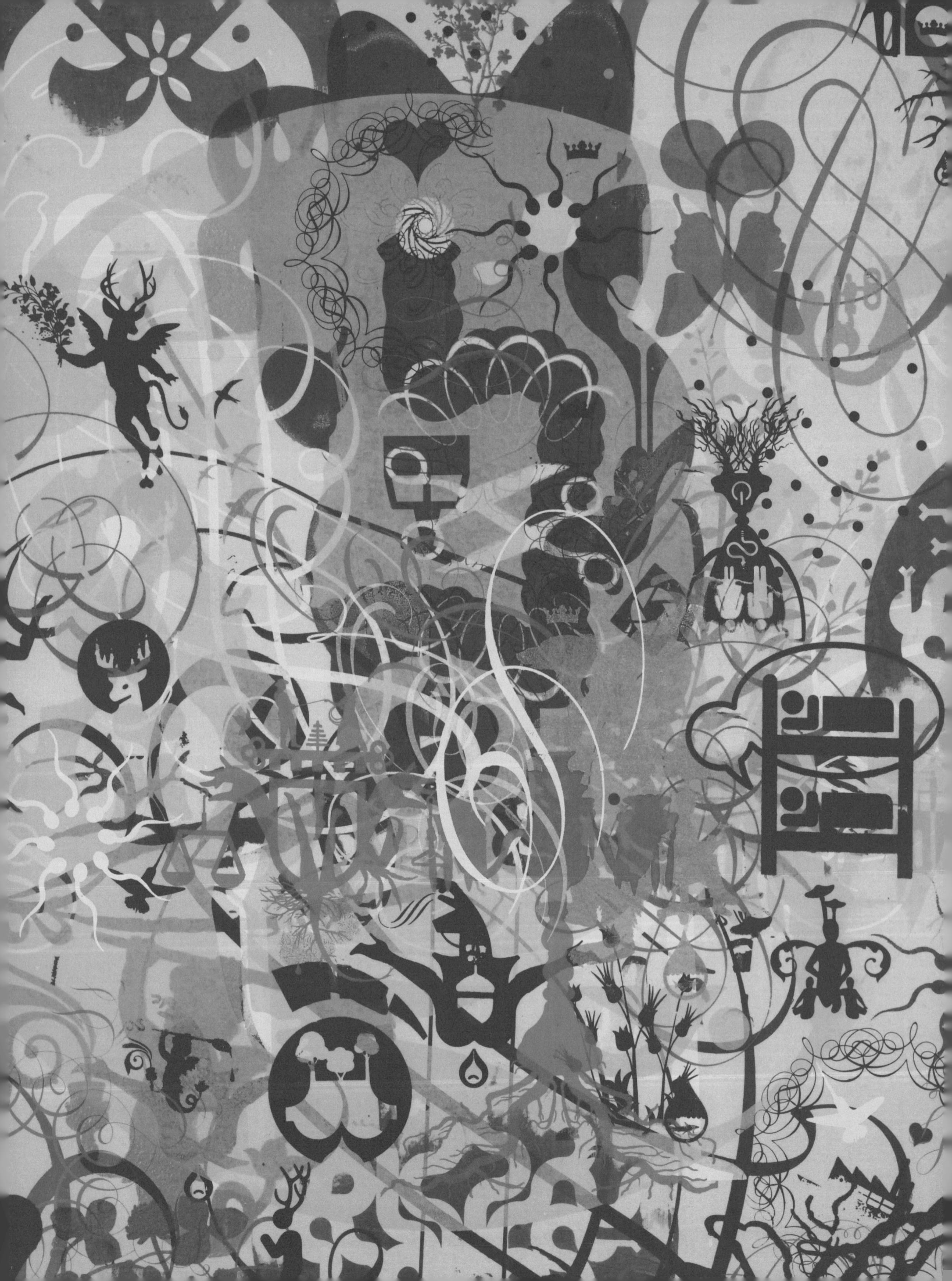

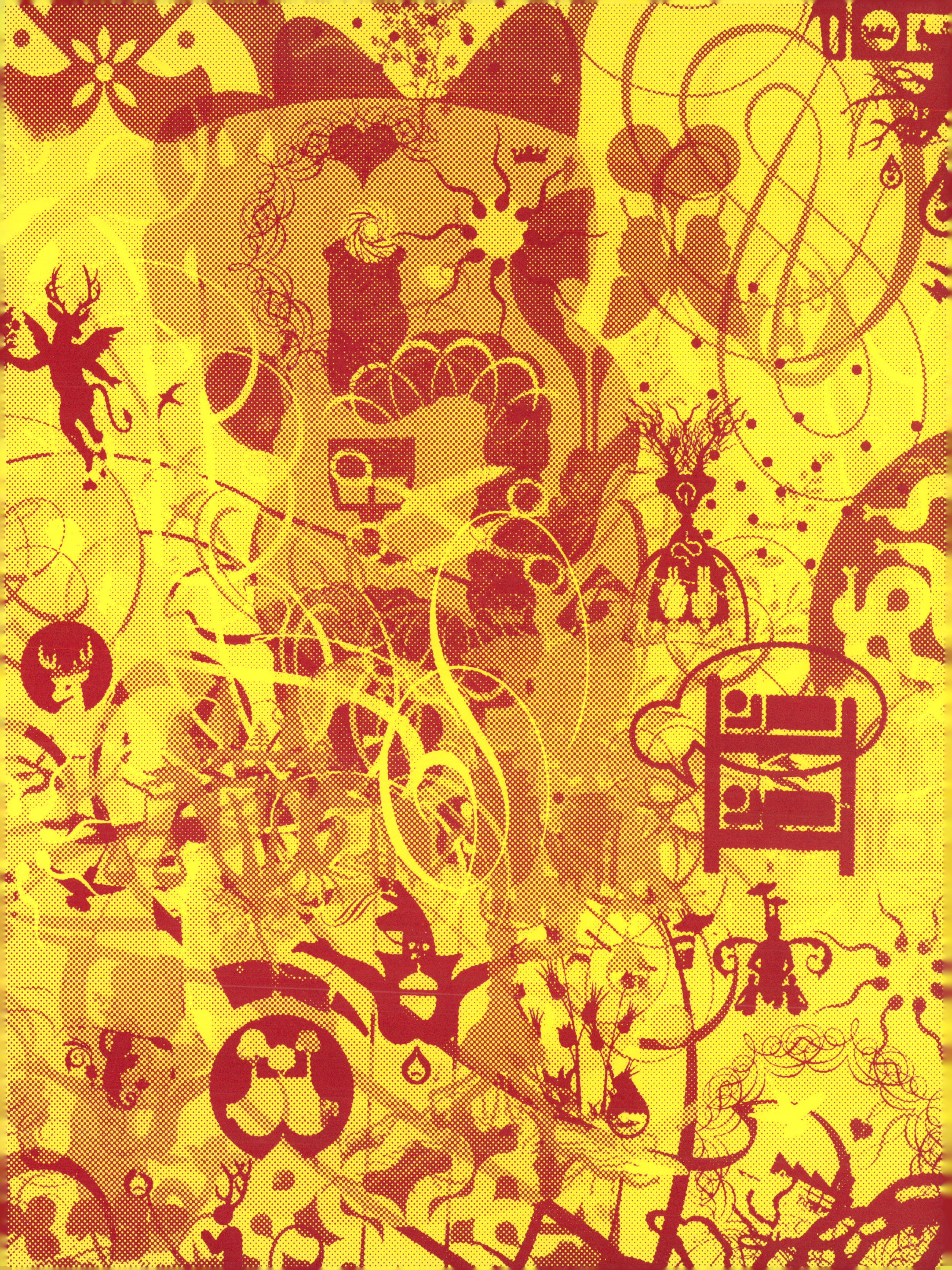

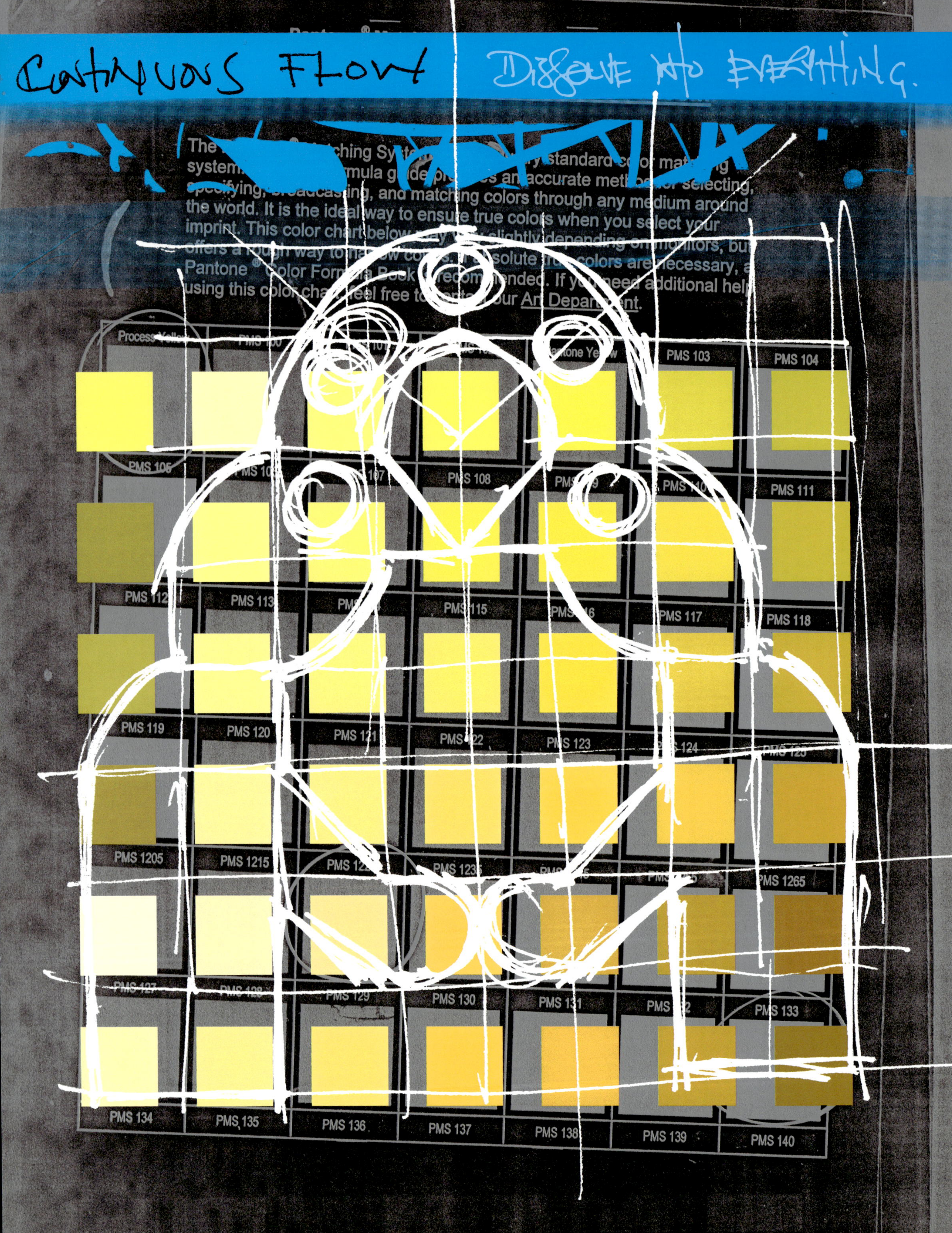
CONTINUOUS FLOW
DISSOLVE INTO EVERYTHING.

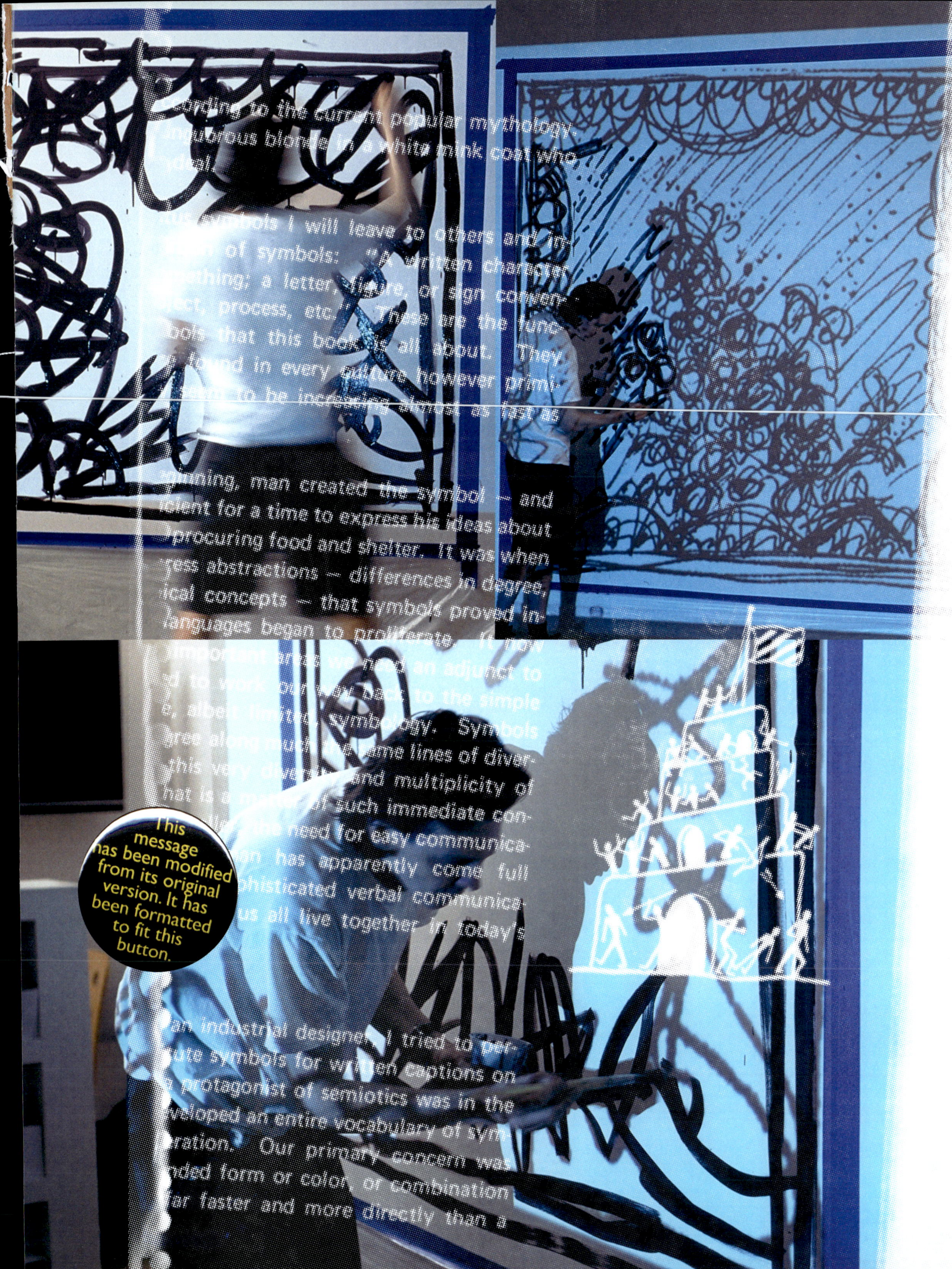

to the current popular mythology
blonde in a white mink coat who
symbols I will leave to others and in
of symbols: a written character
thing; a letter, figure, or sign conven
process, etc. These are the func
that this book is all about. They
found in every culture however primi
to be increasing almost as fast as
ning, man created the symbol — and
for a time to express his ideas about
procuring food and shelter. It was when
abstractions — differences in degree
concepts — that symbols proved in
languages began to proliferate. It now
we need an adjunct to
to work our way back to the simple
symbology. Symbols
along much the same lines of diver
this very diversity and multiplicity of
such immediate con
the need for easy communica
has apparently come full
sophisticated verbal communica
us all live together in today's
an industrial designer, I tried to per
symbols for written captions on
protagonist of semiotics was in the
developed an entire vocabulary of sym
Our primary concern was
form or color, or combination
far faster and more directly than a
This message has been modified from its original version. It has been formatted to fit this button.

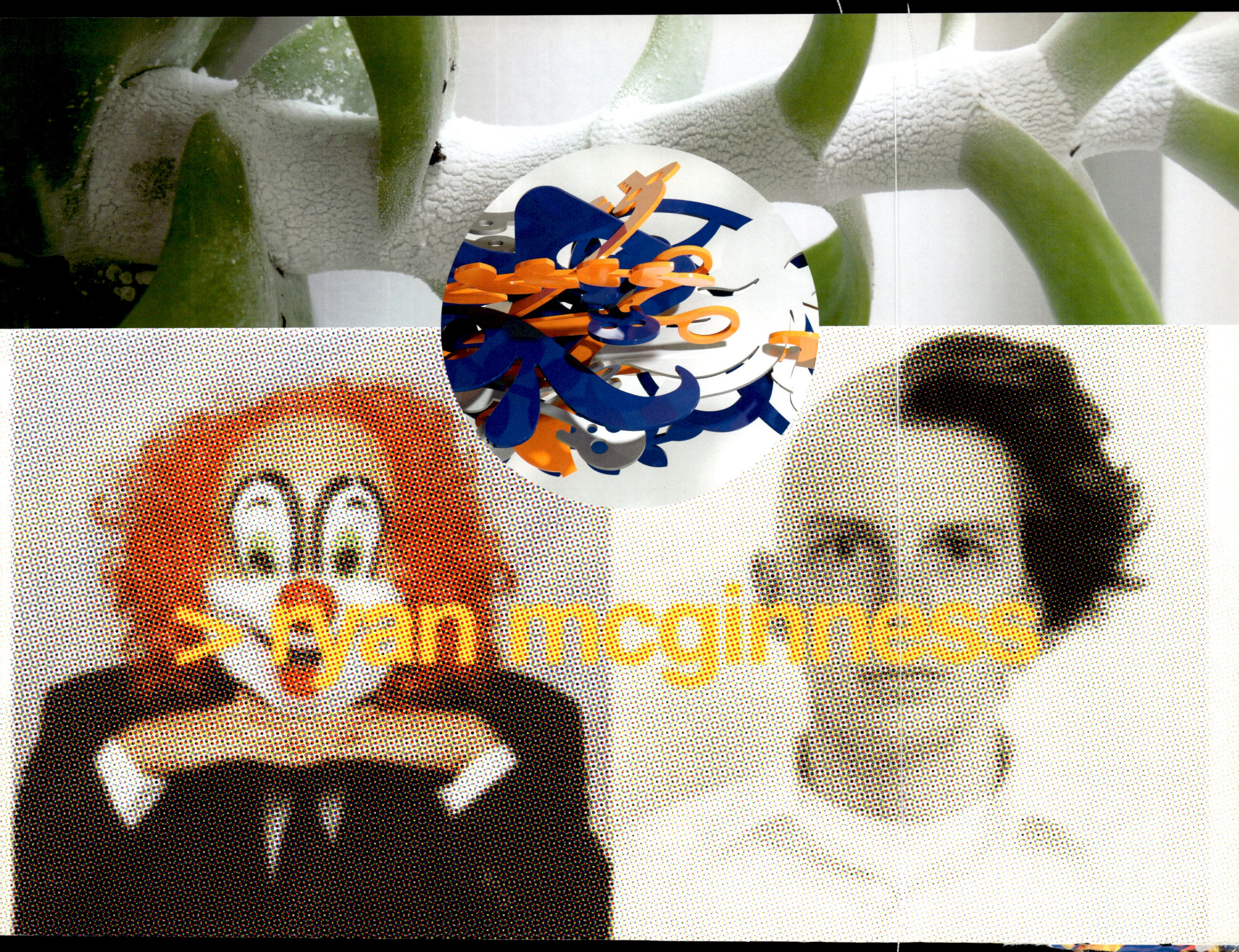
>ryan mcginness

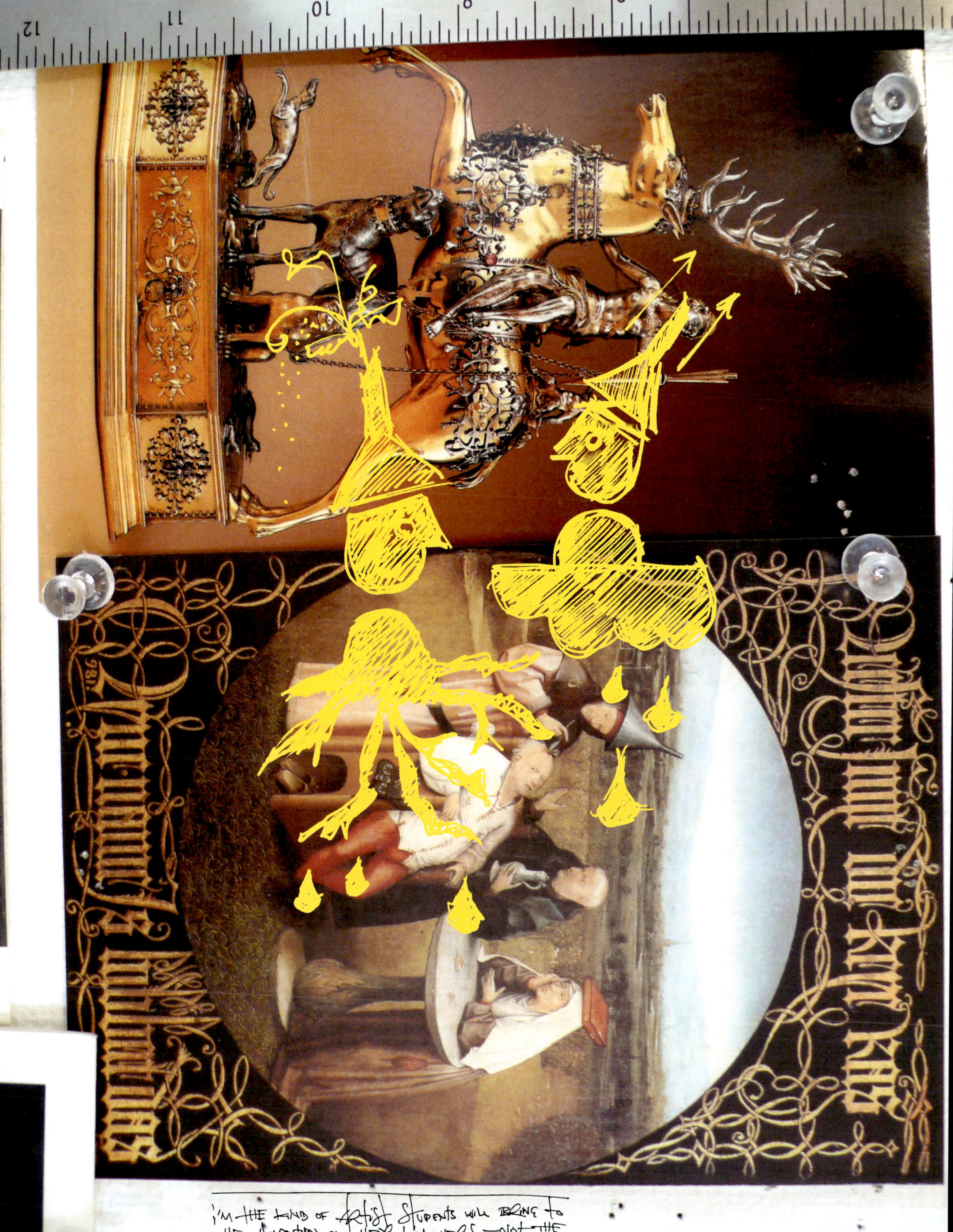

I'M THE KIND OF ARTIST STUDENTS WILL BRING TO THE ATTENTION OF THEIR TEACHERS —NOT THE OTHER WAY AROUND.

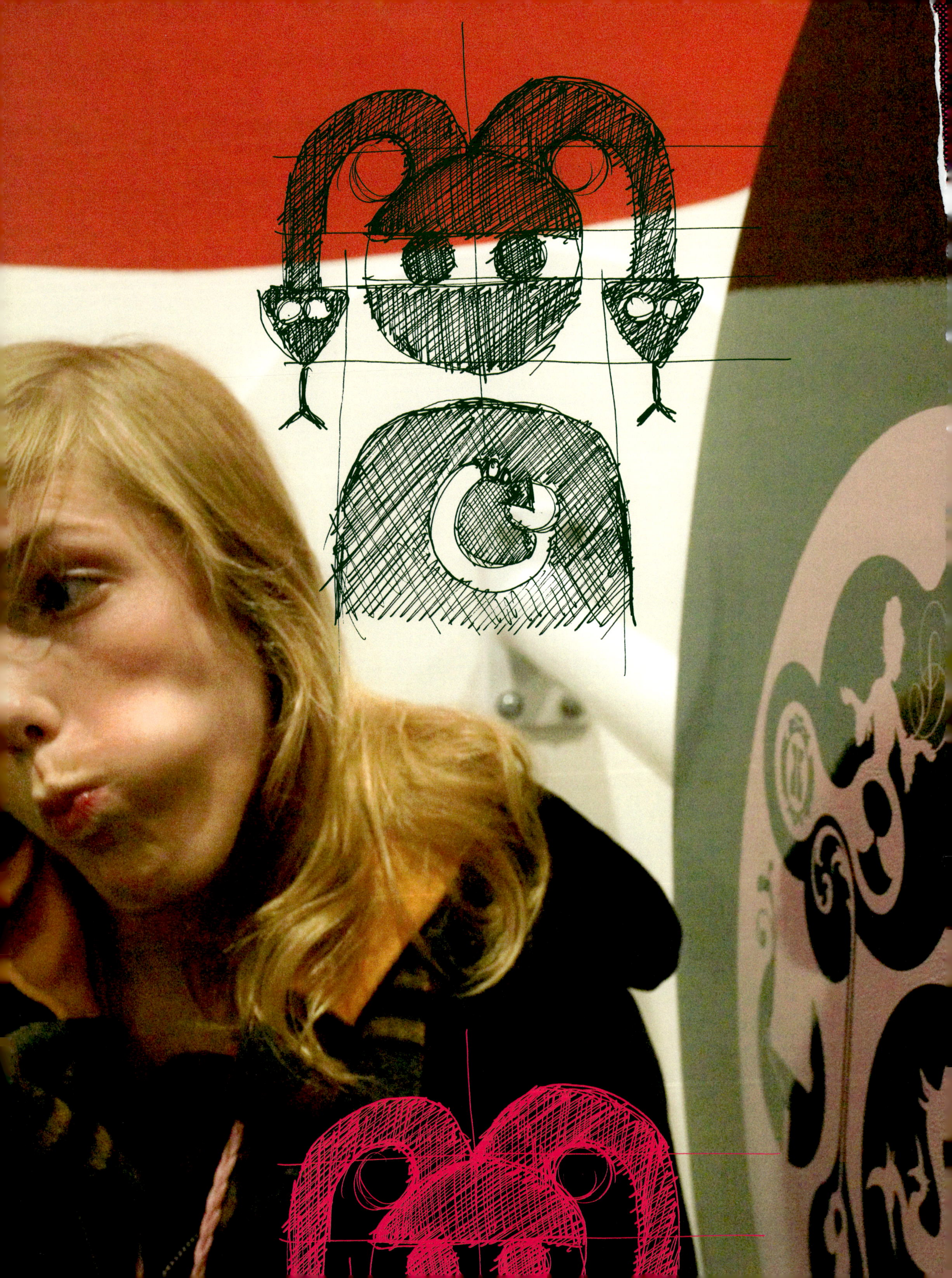

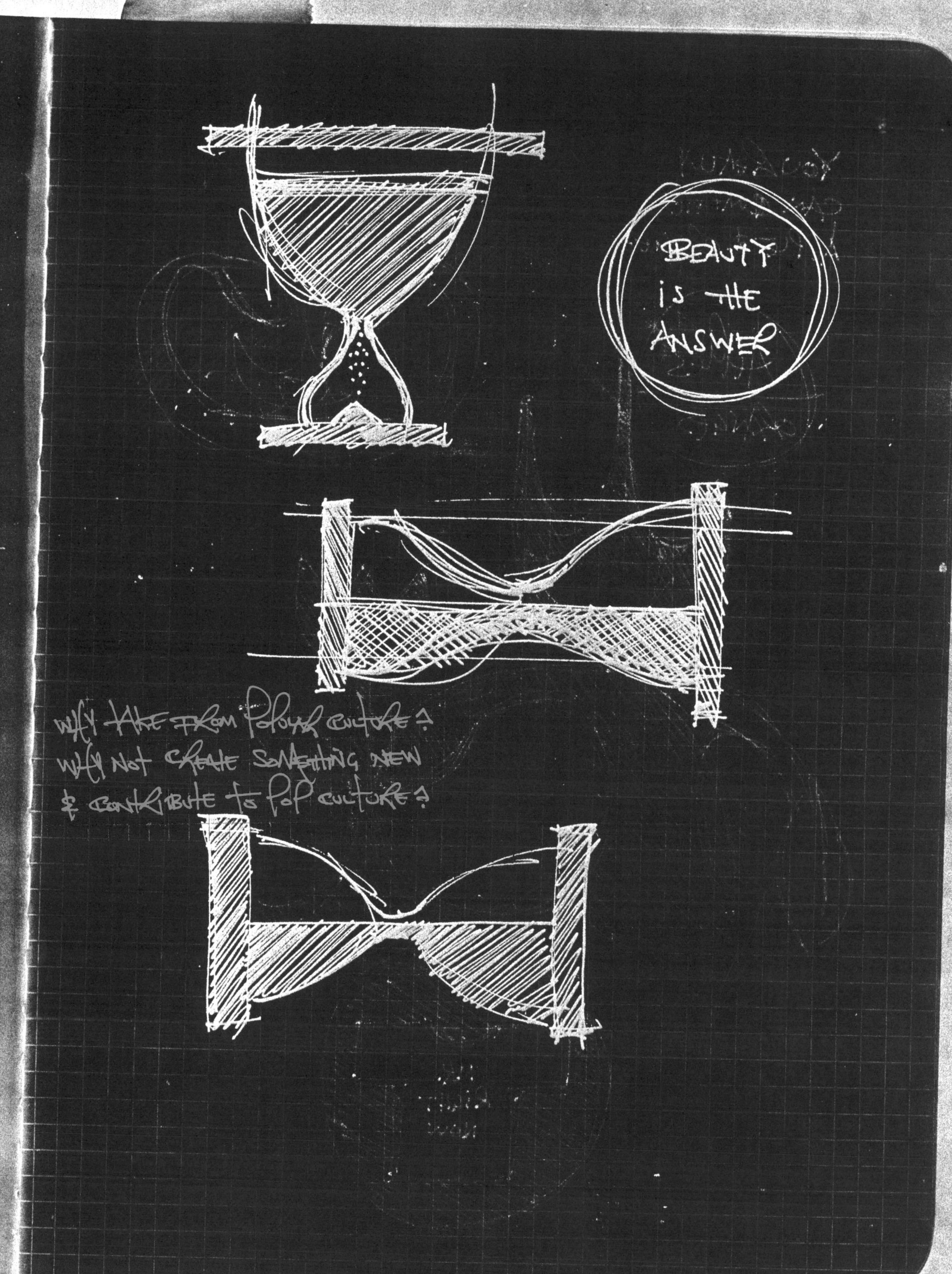
BEAUTY
IS THE
ANSWER
WHY TAKE FROM POPULAR CULTURE?
WHY NOT CREATE SOMETHING NEW
& CONTRIBUTE TO POP CULTURE?

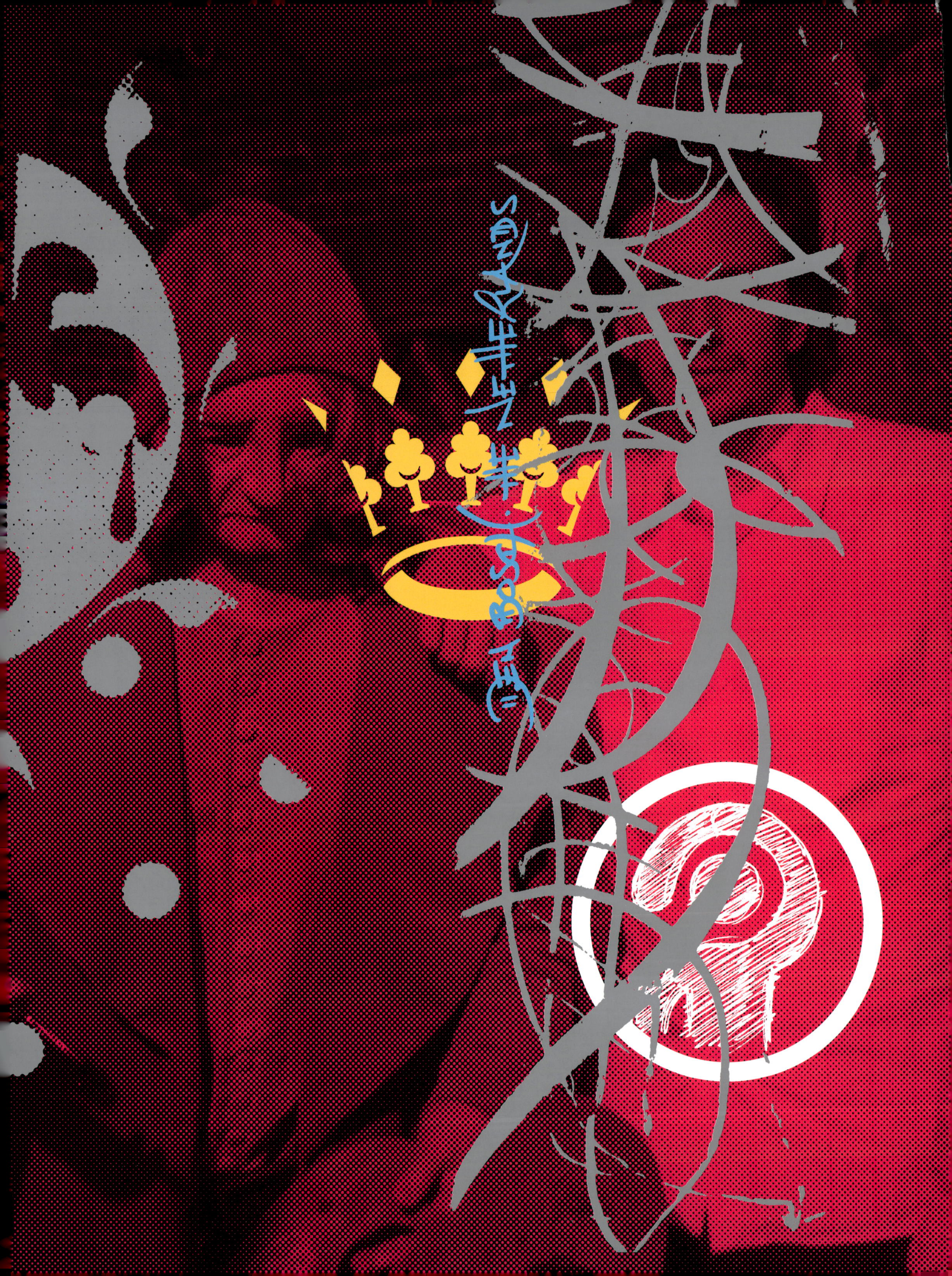
JAN BOSCH · THE NETHERLANDS

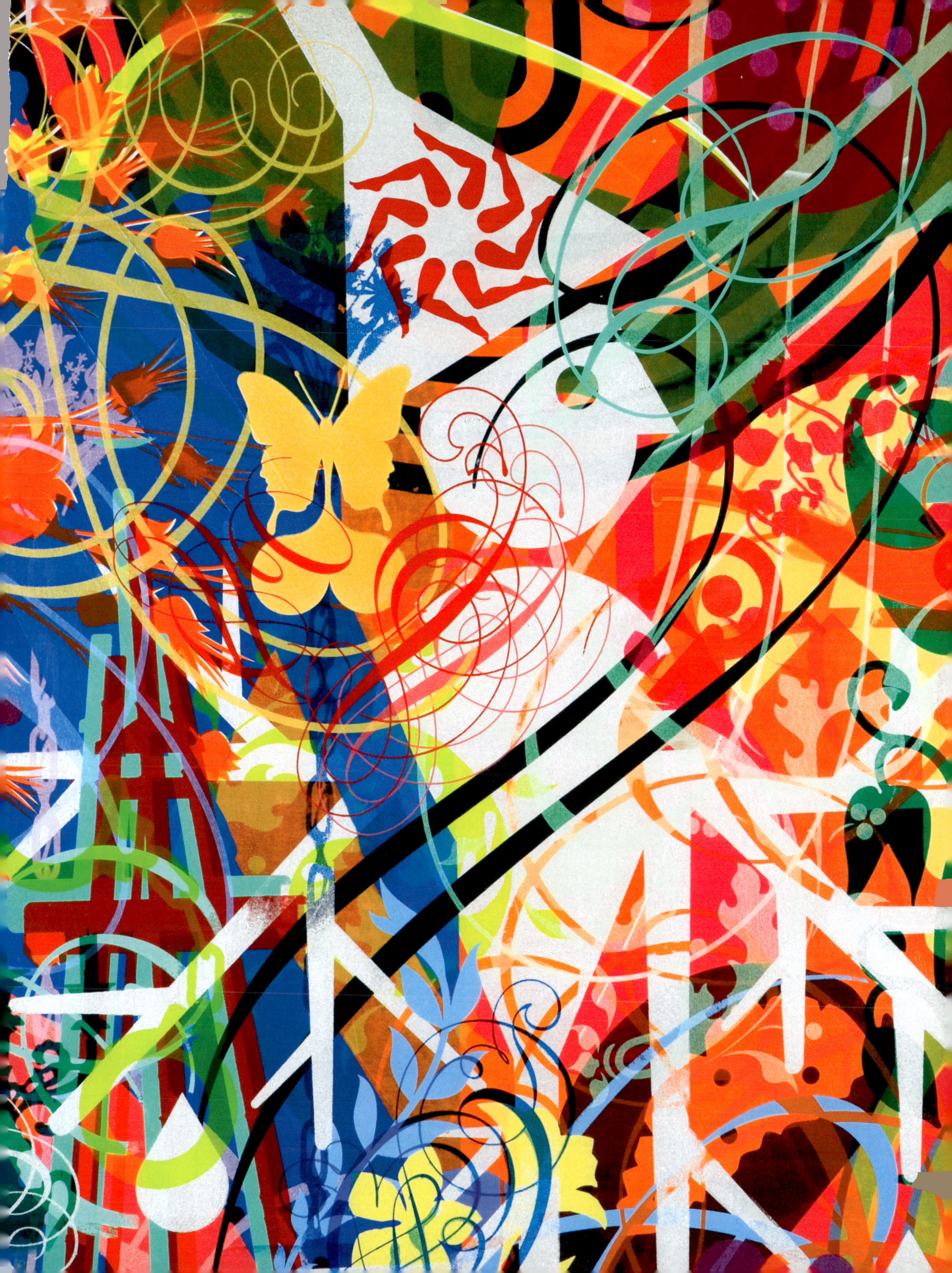

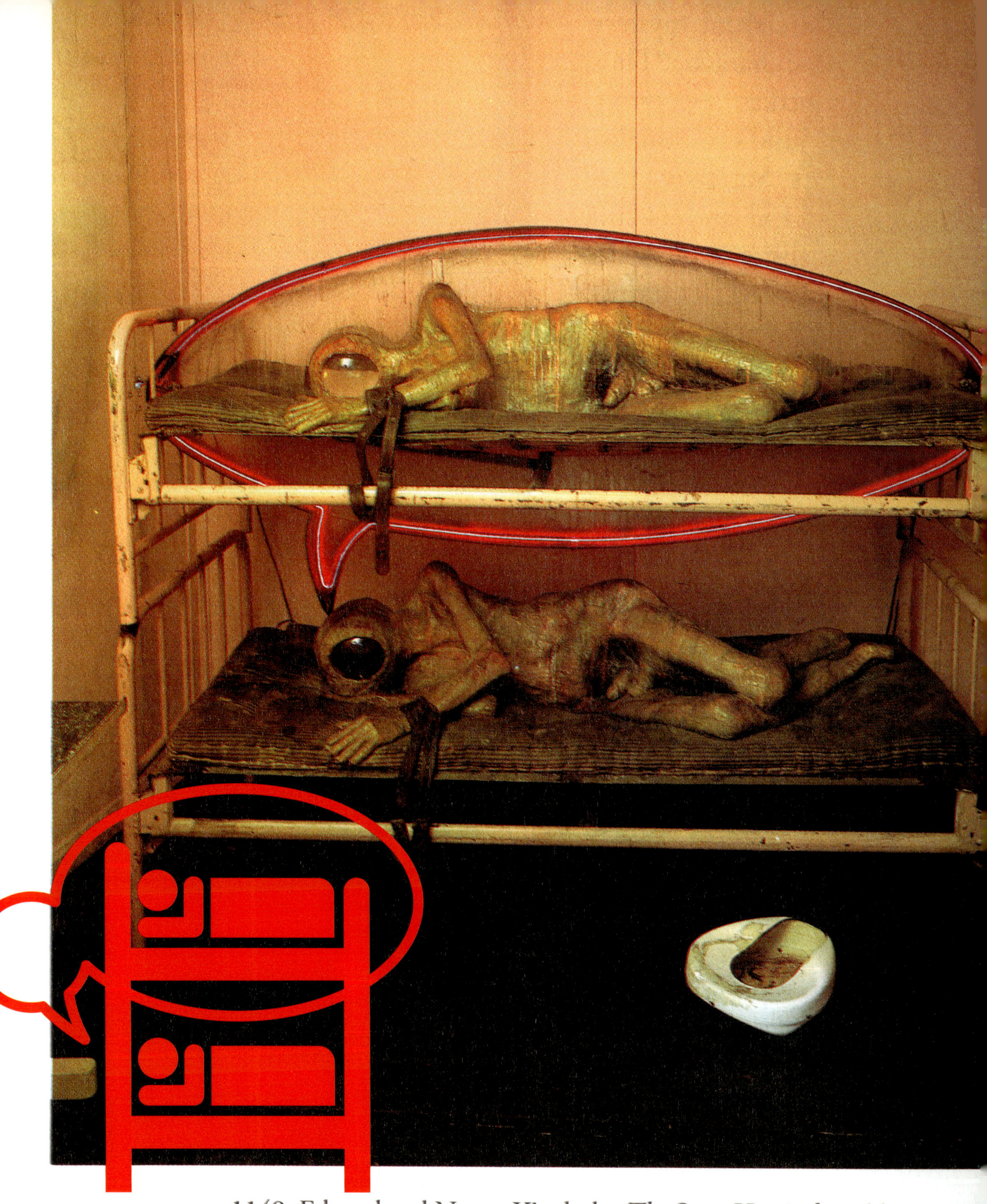

1149. Edward and Nancy Kienholz. *The State Hospital.* 1966.
Mixed mediums, 8 x 12 x 10' (2.4 x 3.7 x 3.1 m). Moderna Museet, Stockholm

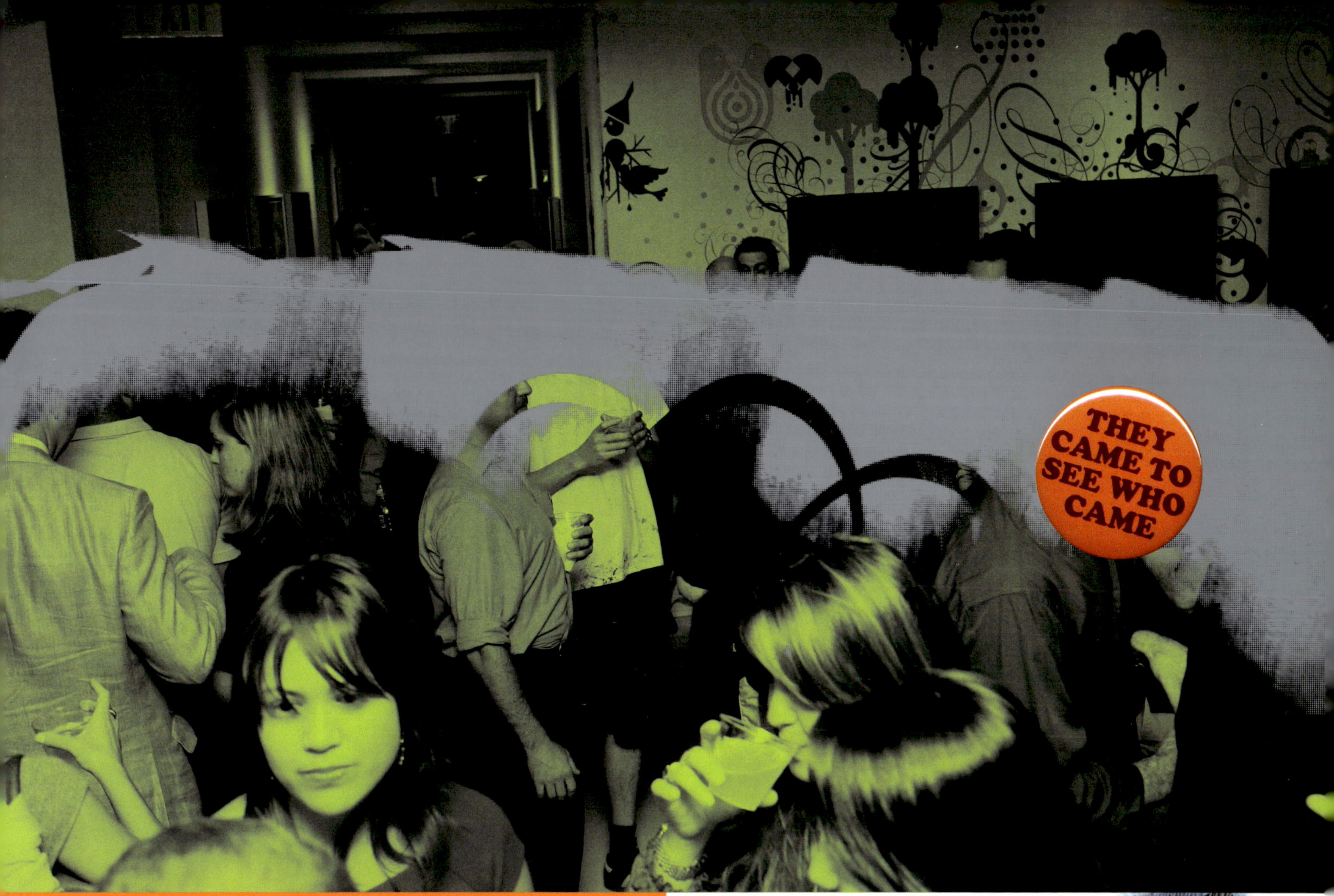

THEY CAME TO SEE WHO CAME

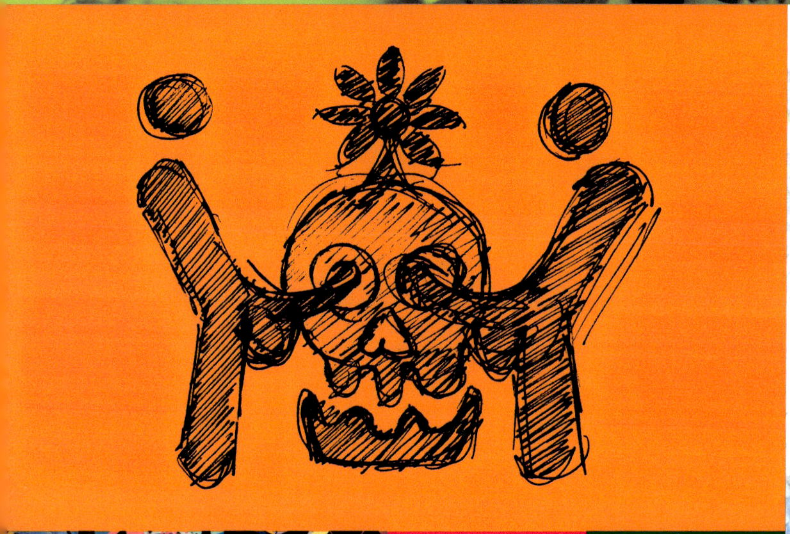

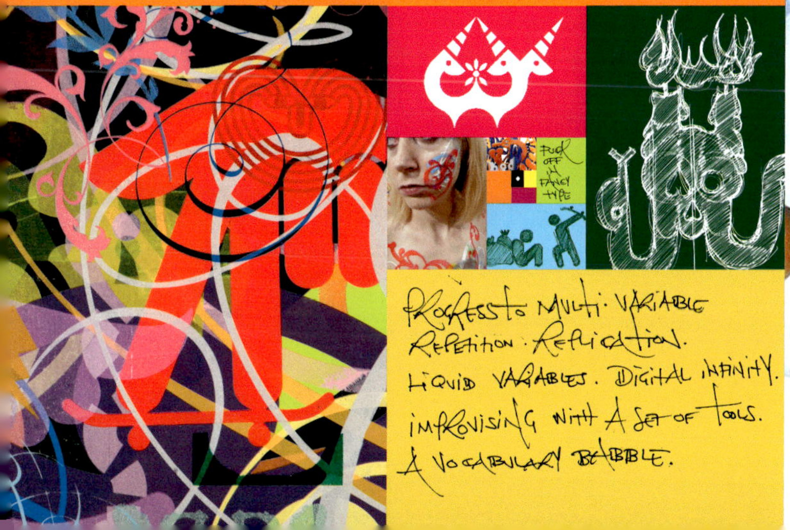

FUCK OFF IN FANCY TYPE

PROGRESS TO MULTI-VARIABLE REPETITION. REPLICATION. LIQUID VARIABLES. DIGITAL INFINITY. IMPROVISING WITH A SET OF TOOLS. A VOCABULARY BABBLE.

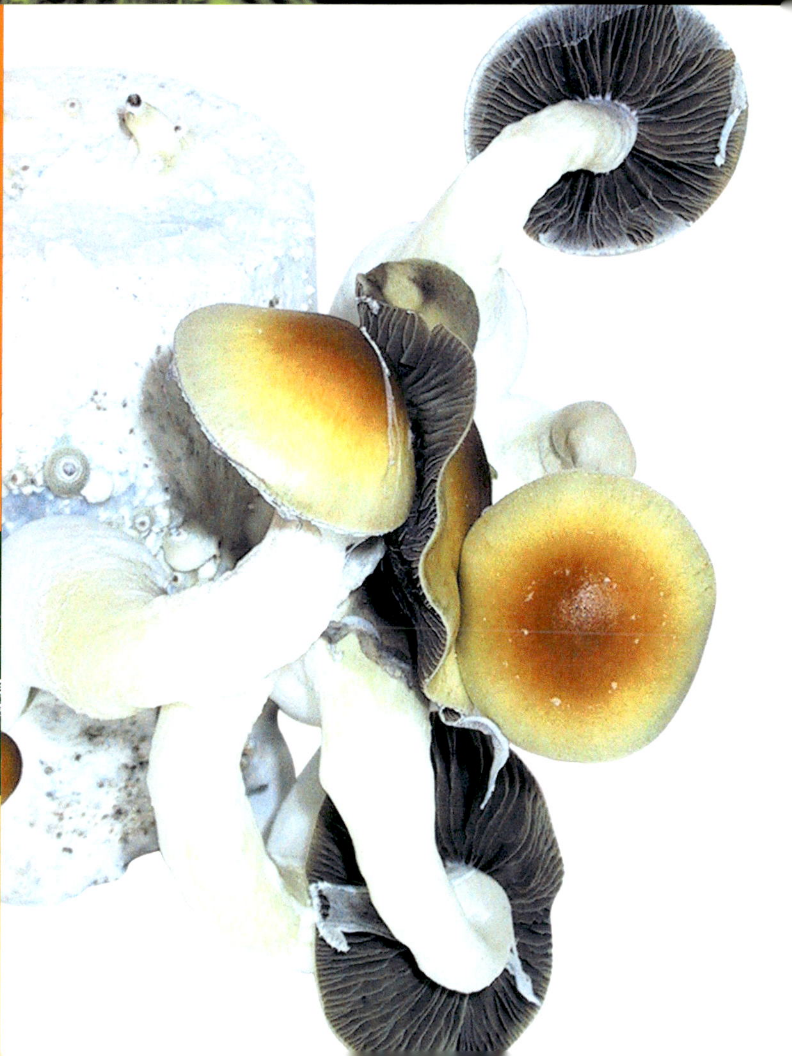

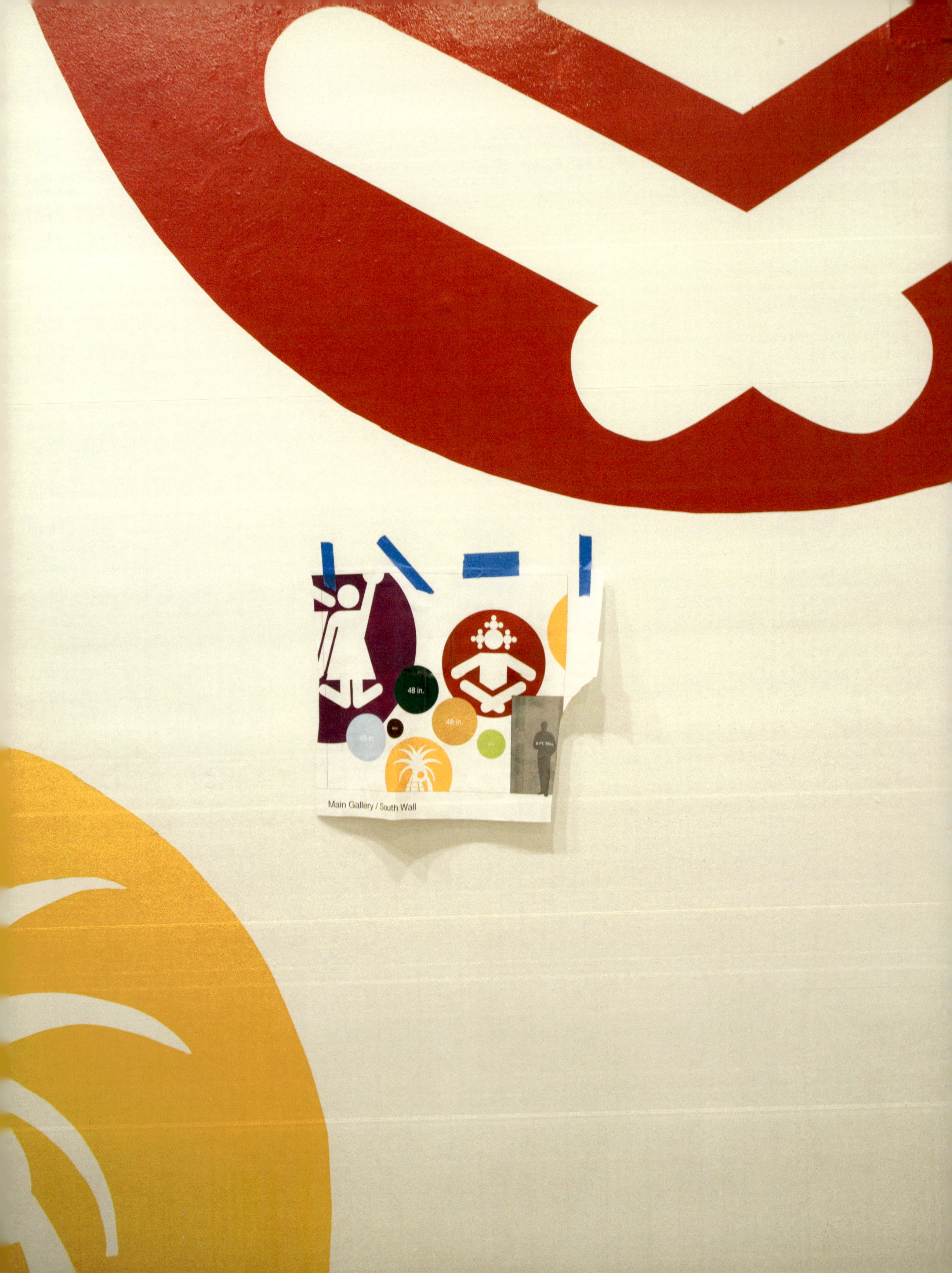
48 in.
48 in.
48 in.
Main Gallery / South Wall

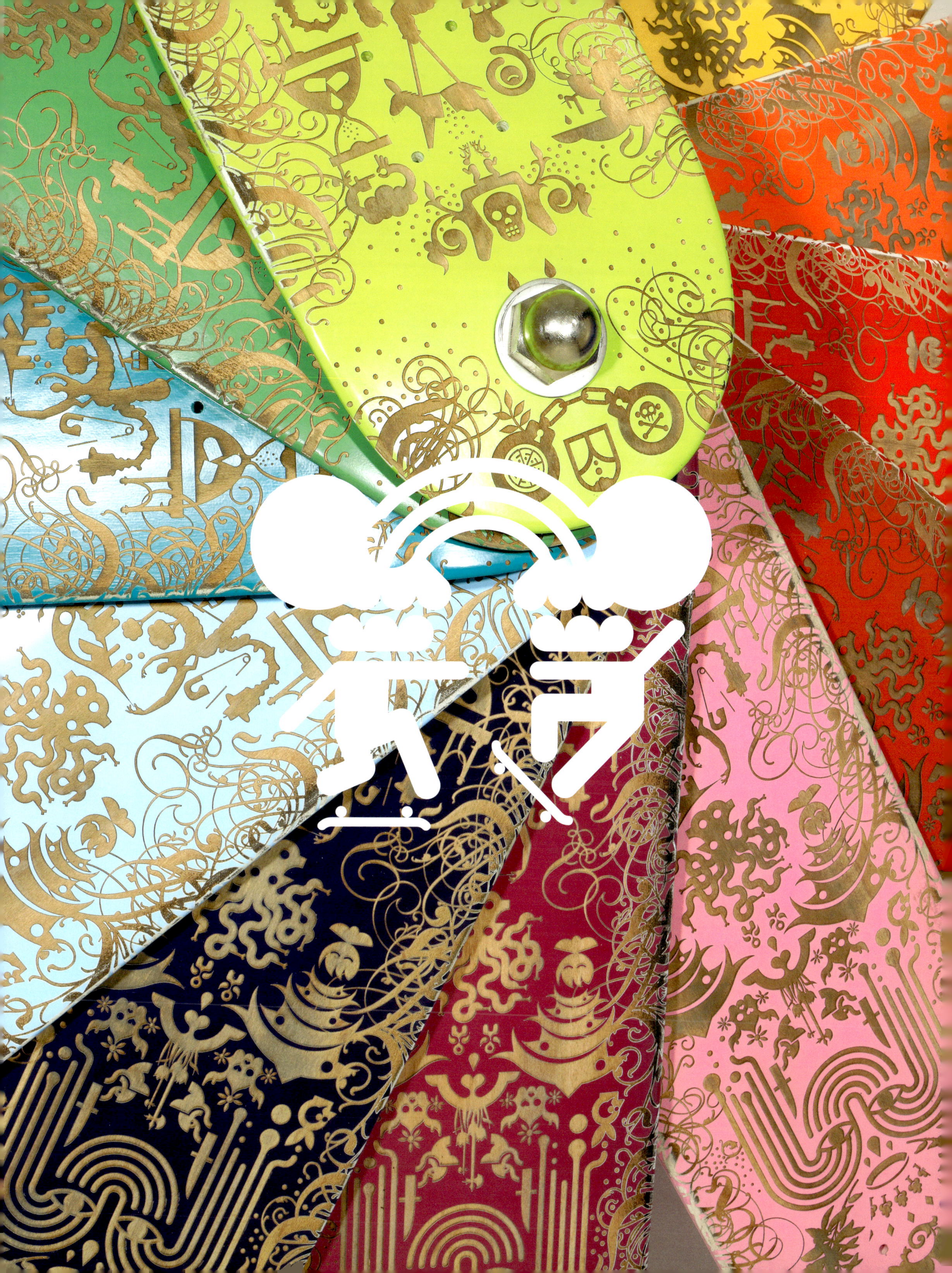

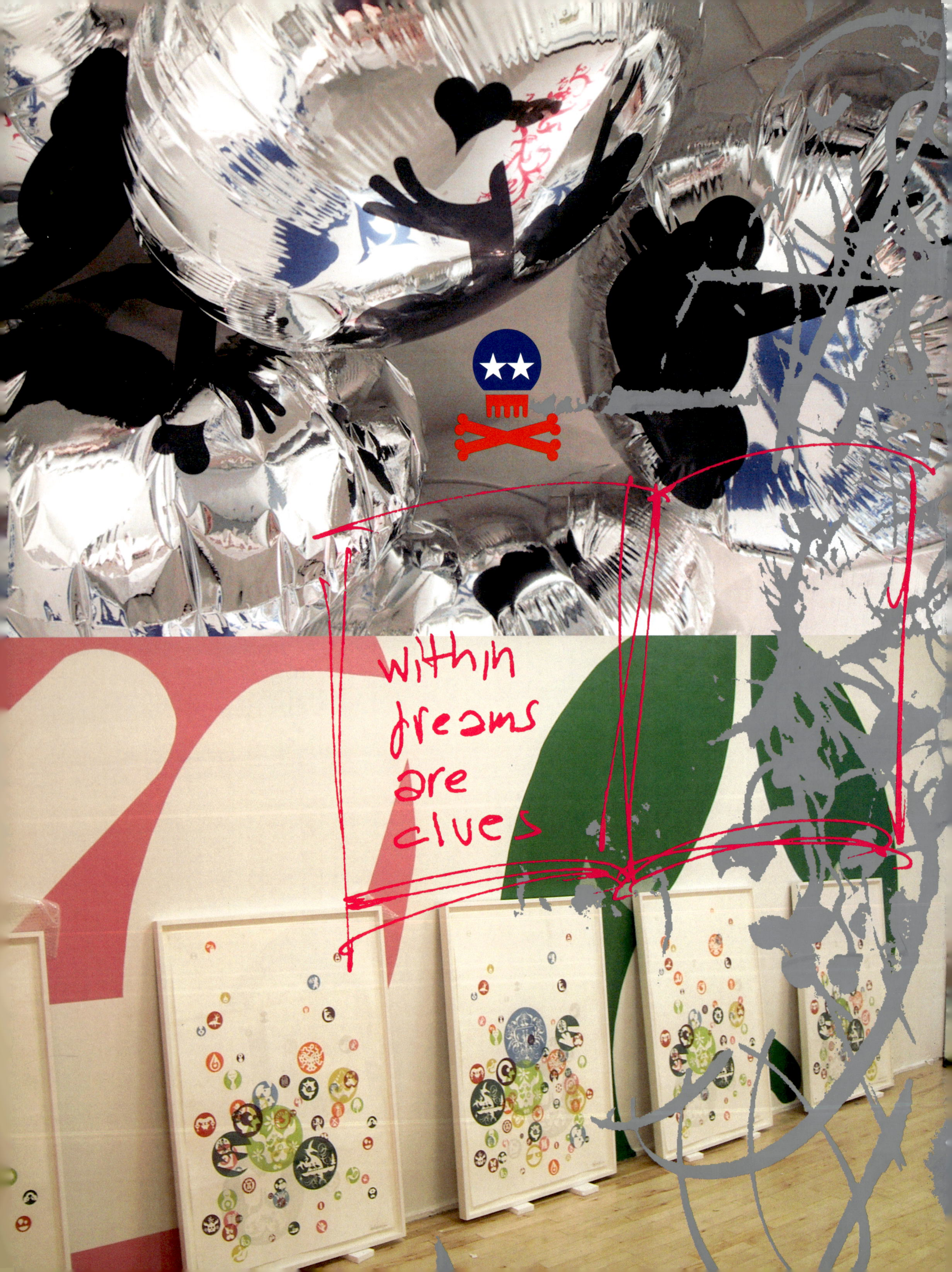
within
dreams
are
clues

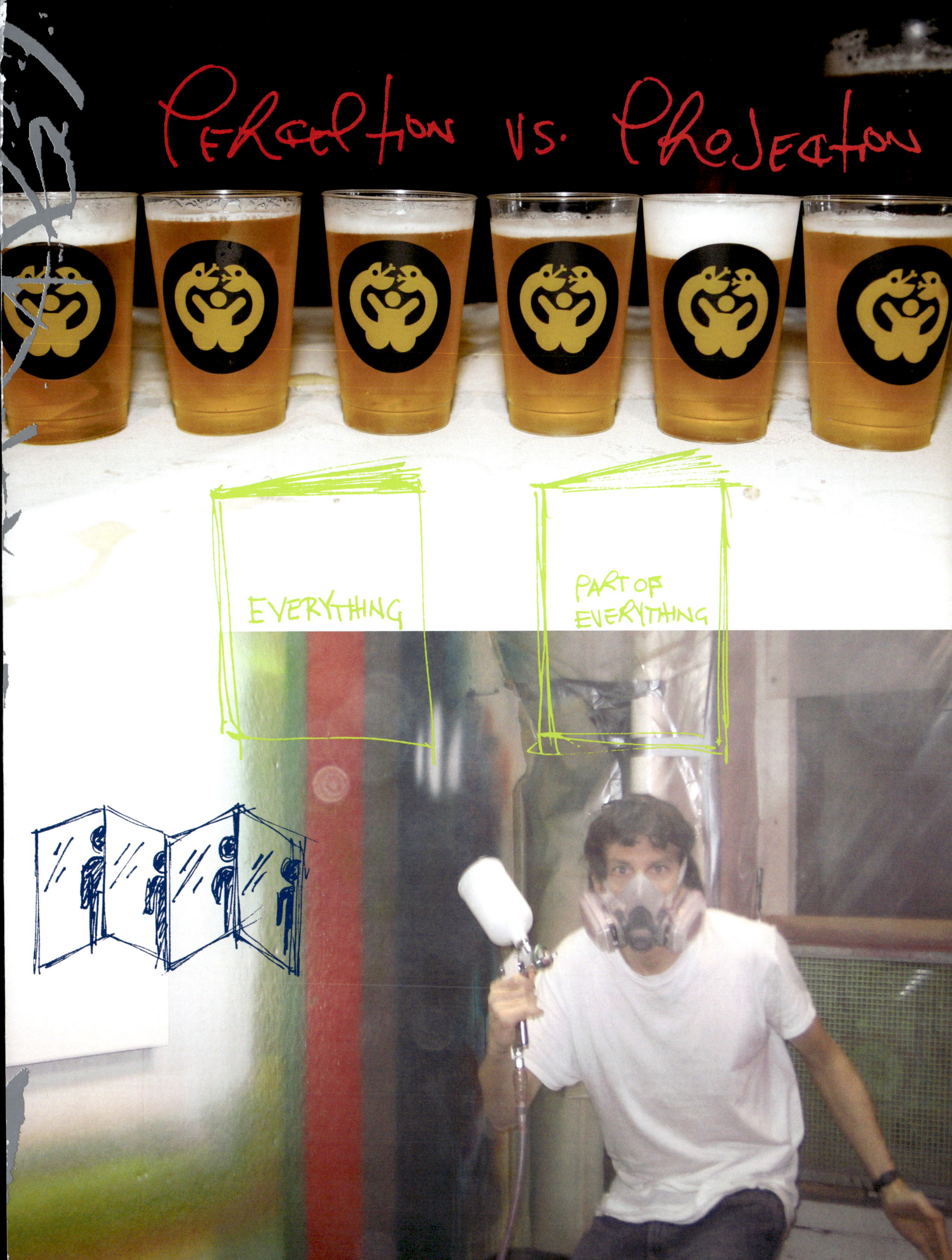
PERCEPTION VS. PROJECTION
EVERYTHING
PART OF
EVERYTHING

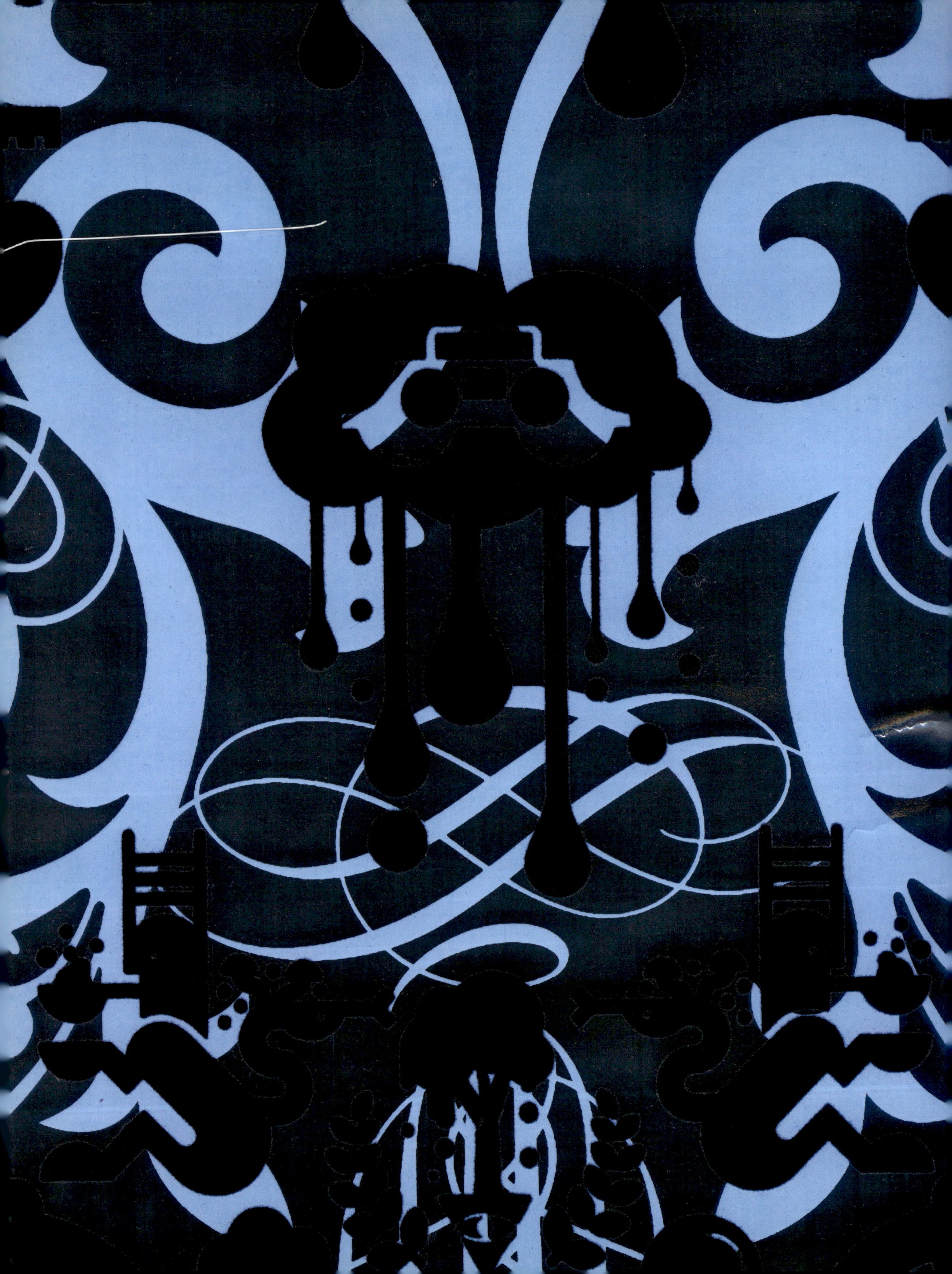

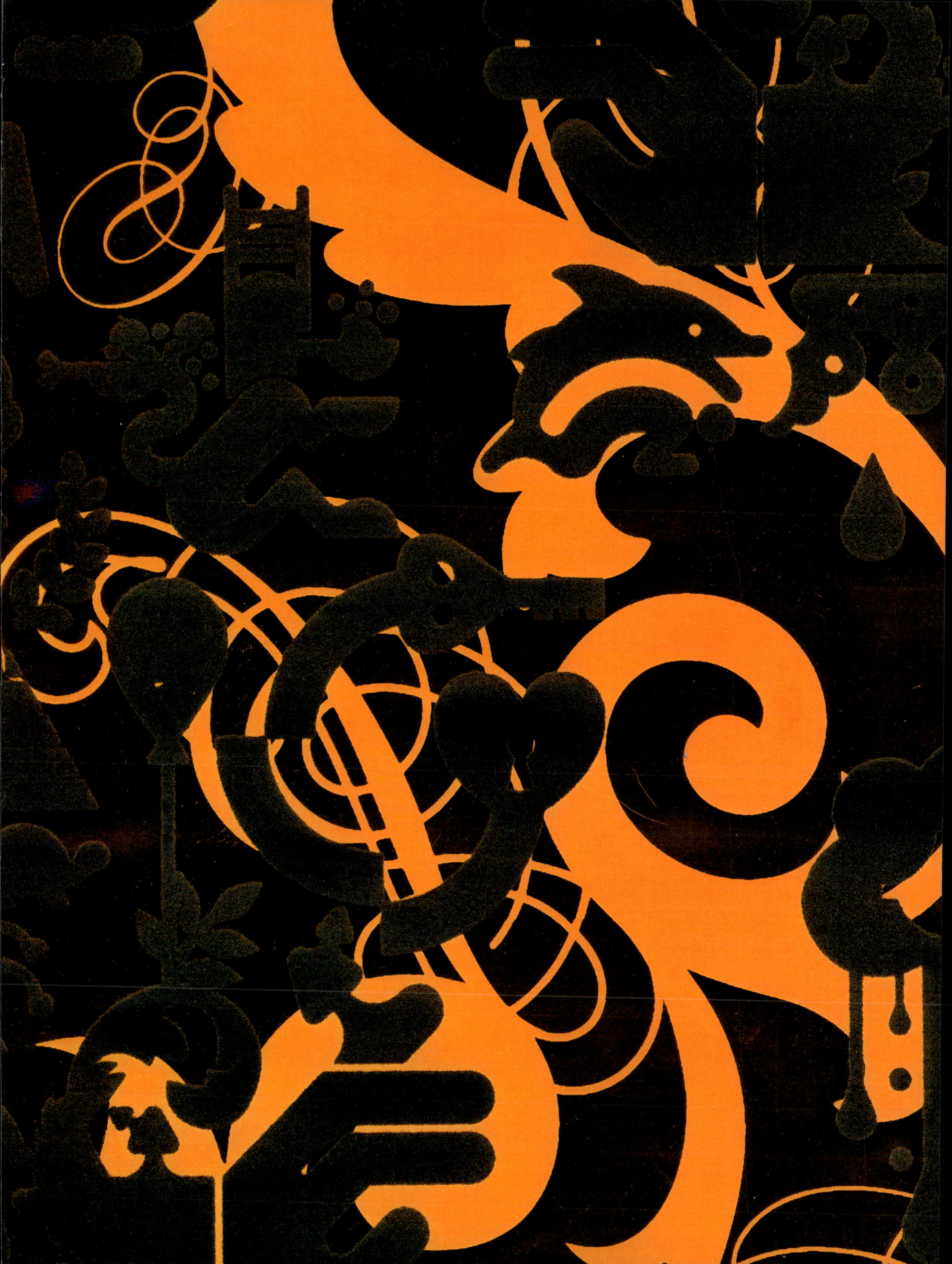

The price of this piece (p) shall be determined according to the following equation: $p = d((x-y)/f)$, where x = the price of the most expensive unsold piece in the exhibition rounded to the closest whole U.S. dollar; y = the price of the least expensive unsold piece in the exhibition rounded to the closest whole U.S. dollar; d = the number of full days in the duration of the exhibition that have passed; and f = the number of full days remaining in the duration of the exhibition.

Note that d+f will equal one less than the total number of days in the exhibition, as the current day is not included in the calculation. When f=0 (the last day of an exhibition), use f=1. The total number of days of the exhibition are calendar days and shall include days the gallery is closed.

Example 1: On the 6th day of a 30-day exhibition, where the most expensive unsold piece in the exhibition is $10,000, and the least expensive unsold piece in the exhibition is $500, the price of this piece is $1,979.16, because p = 5((10,000-500)/24).

Example 2: On the last day of a 28-day exhibition, where the most expensive unsold piece in the exhibition is $400, and the least expensive unsold piece in the exhibition is $30, the price of this piece is $9,990, because p = 27((400-30)/1).

Example 3: On the 2nd day of a 30-day exhibition, where the most expensive unsold piece in the exhibition is $600, and the least expensive unsold piece in the exhibition is $75, the price of this piece is $18.75, because p=1((600-75)/28).

It is therefore in the interest of a prospective buyer to purchase this piece as soon as possible. The price of this piece is further reduced as the difference between the most expensive unsold piece in the exhibition and the least expensive piece in the exhibition approaches zero. In the rare instance that all the unsold pieces in the exhibition are the same price, this piece is free regardless of when during the exhibition it is sold (p = d((0-0)/f)).

Upon conclusion of the exhibition, this piece is no longer for sale, and the rights to ownership revert to the artist.

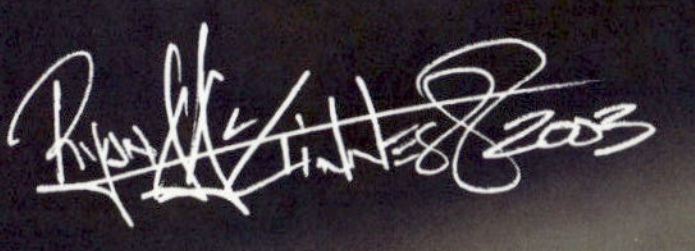

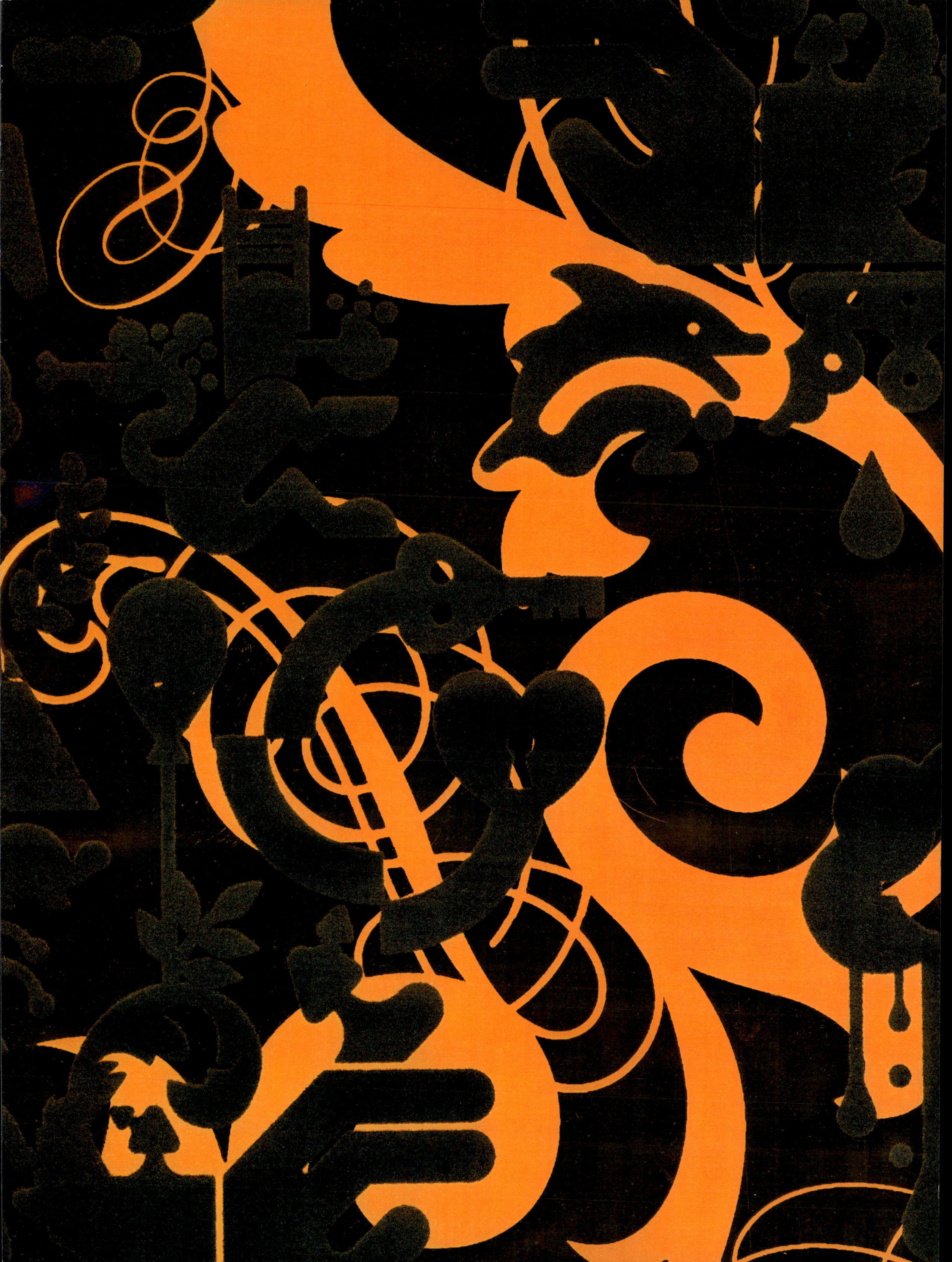

The price of this piece (p) shall be determined according to the following equation: $p = d((x-y)/f)$, where x = the price of the most expensive unsold piece in the exhibition rounded to the closest whole U.S. dollar; y = the price of the least expensive unsold piece in the exhibition rounded to the closest whole U.S. dollar; d = the number of full days in the duration of the exhibition that have passed; and f = the number of full days remaining in the duration of the exhibition.

Note that d+f will equal one less than the total number of days in the exhibition, as the current day is not included in the calculation. When f=0 (the last day of an exhibition), use f=1. The total number of days of the exhibition are calendar days and shall include days the gallery is closed.

Example 1: On the 6th day of a 30-day exhibition, where the most expensive unsold piece in the exhibition is $10,000, and the least expensive unsold piece in the exhibition is $500, the price of this piece is $1,979.16, because $p = 5((10,000-500)/24)$.

Example 2: On the last day of a 28-day exhibition, where the most expensive unsold piece in the exhibi- s $400, and the least expensive unsold piece in xhibition is $30, the price of this piece is $9,990, ase $p = 27((400-30)/1)$.

Example 3: On the 2nd day of a 30-day exhibition, where the most expensive unsold piece in the exhibition is $600, and the least expensive unsold piece in the exhibition is $75, the price of this piece is $18.75, because $p=1((600-75)/28)$.

It is therefore in the interest of a prospective buyer to chase this piece as soon as possible. The price of is piece is further reduced as the difference between the most expensive unsold piece in the exhibition and the least expensive piece in the exhibition approaches zero. In the rare instance that all the unsold pieces in the exhibition are the same price, this piece is free regardless of when during the exhibition it is sold ($p = d((0-0)/f)$).

Upon conclusion of the exhibition, this piece is no longer for sale, and the rights to ownership revert to the artist.

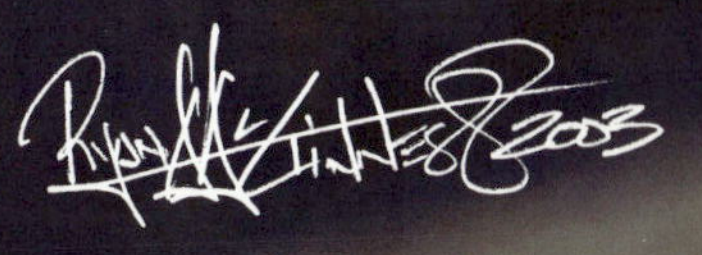

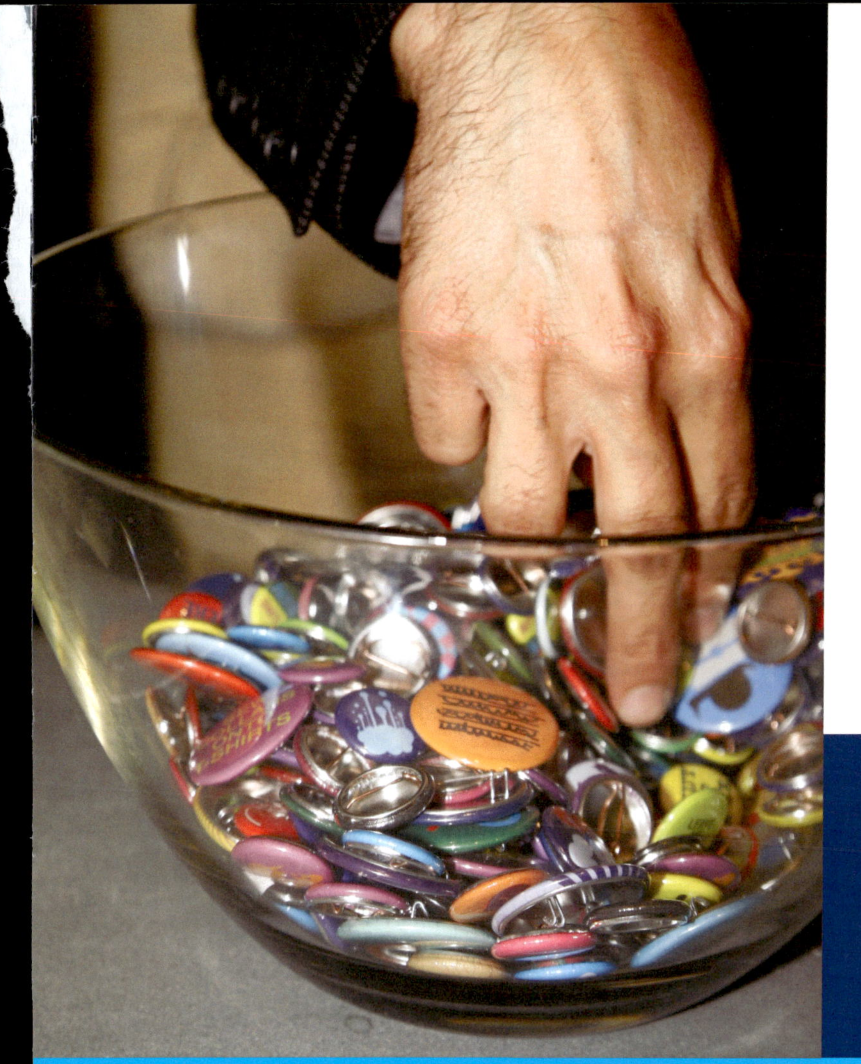

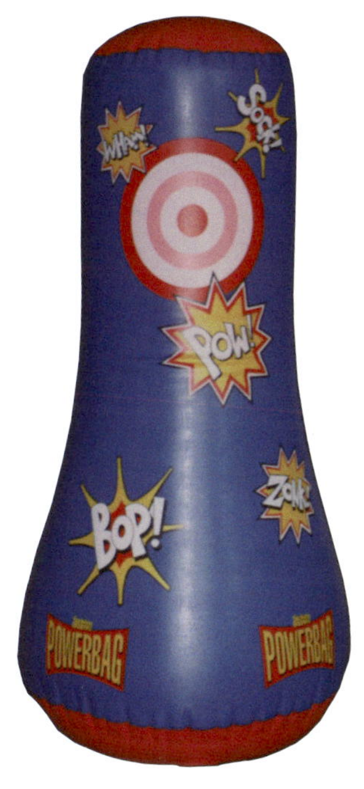

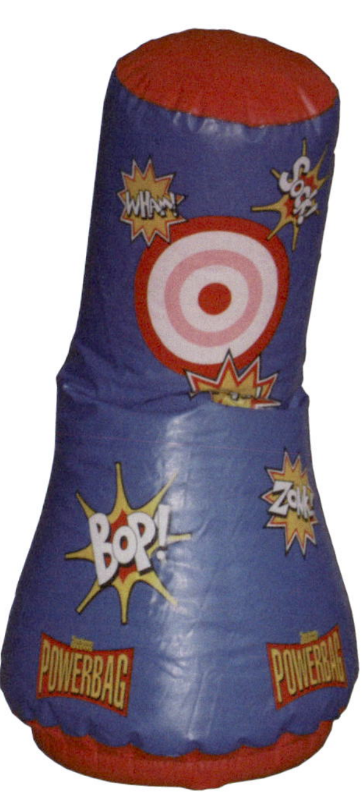

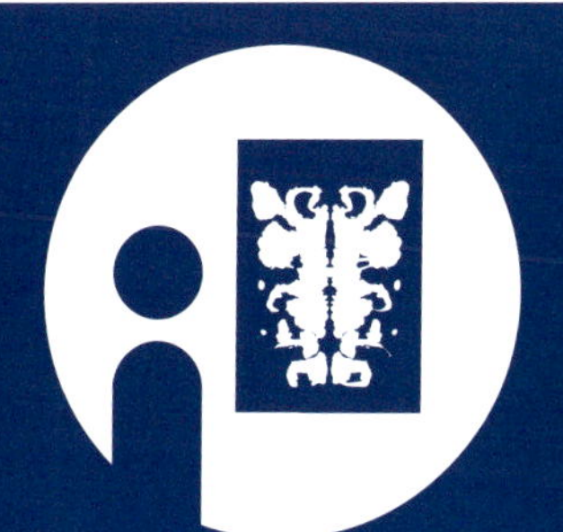

I USE THE VISUAL LANGUAGE OF CORPORATE LOGOS & ICONIC SIGNAGE. I WAS TRAINED IN MAKING THOSE KINDS OF DRAWINGS. I USE THAT POWER & EXERCISE MY SKILLS AT CREATING GEOMETRICALLY LOGICAL IMAGES TO SUBVERT THAT AESTHETIC & UNDERMINE THE ASSUMPTIONS PEOPLE HAVE ABOUT THOSE ANONYMOUS FORMS.

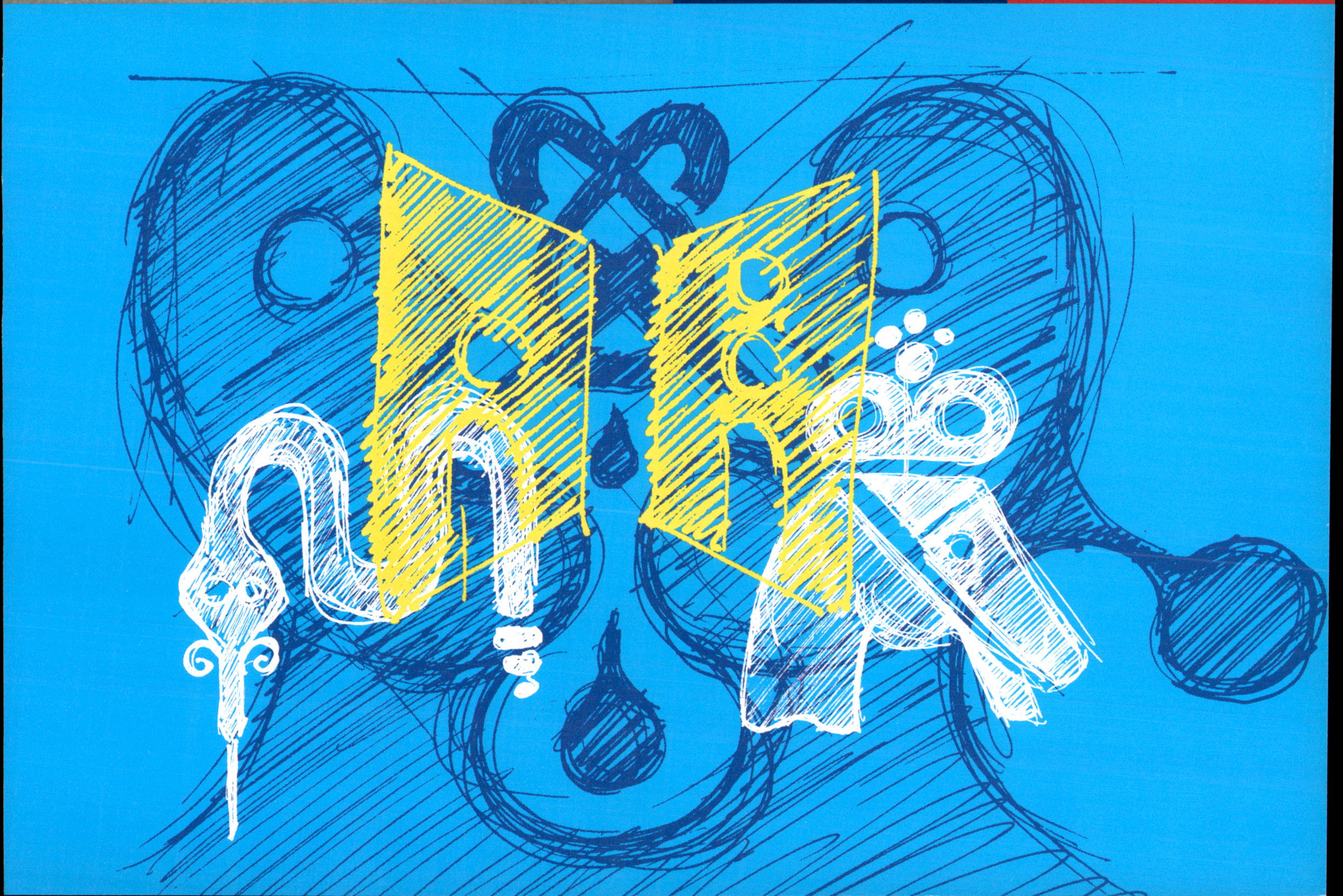

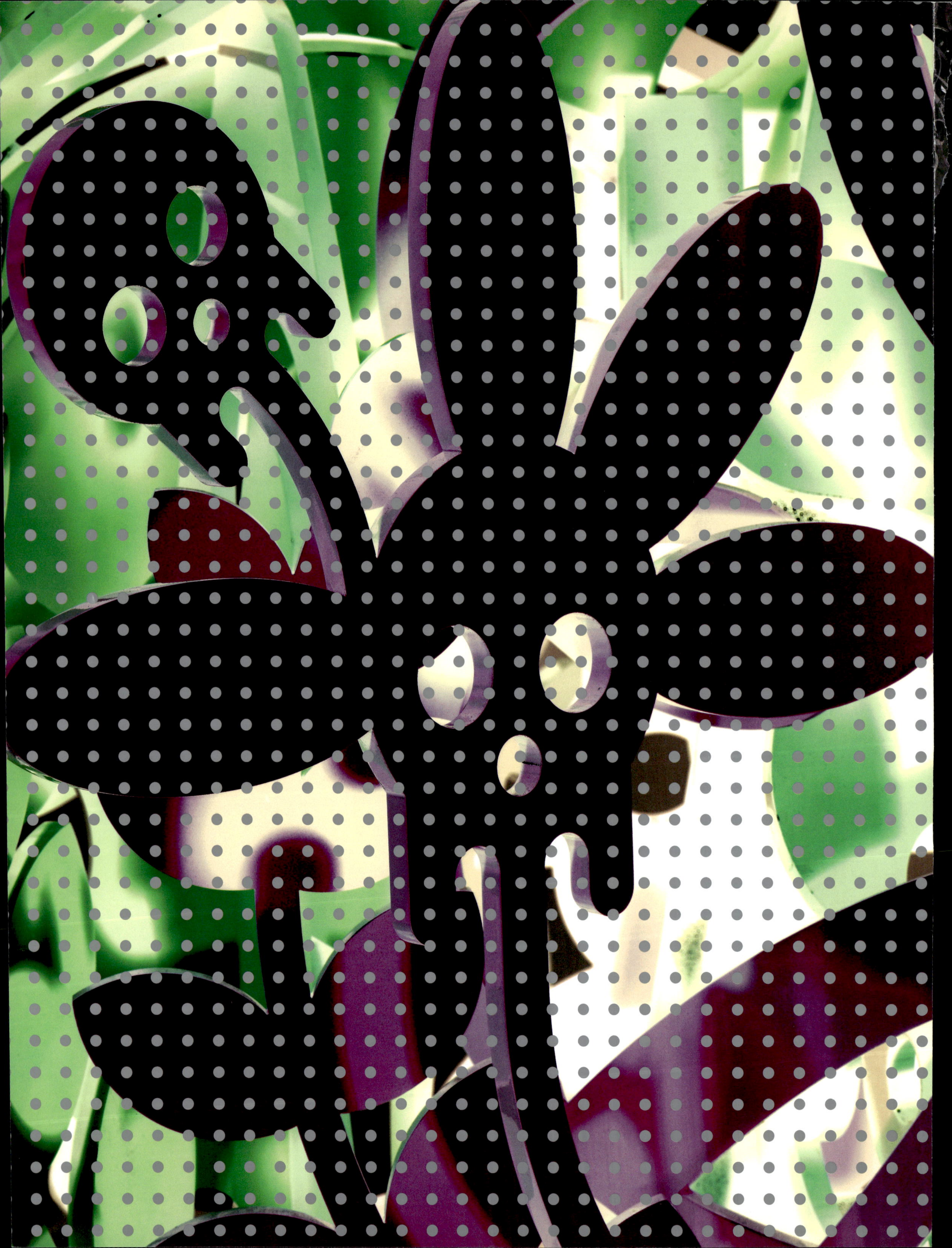

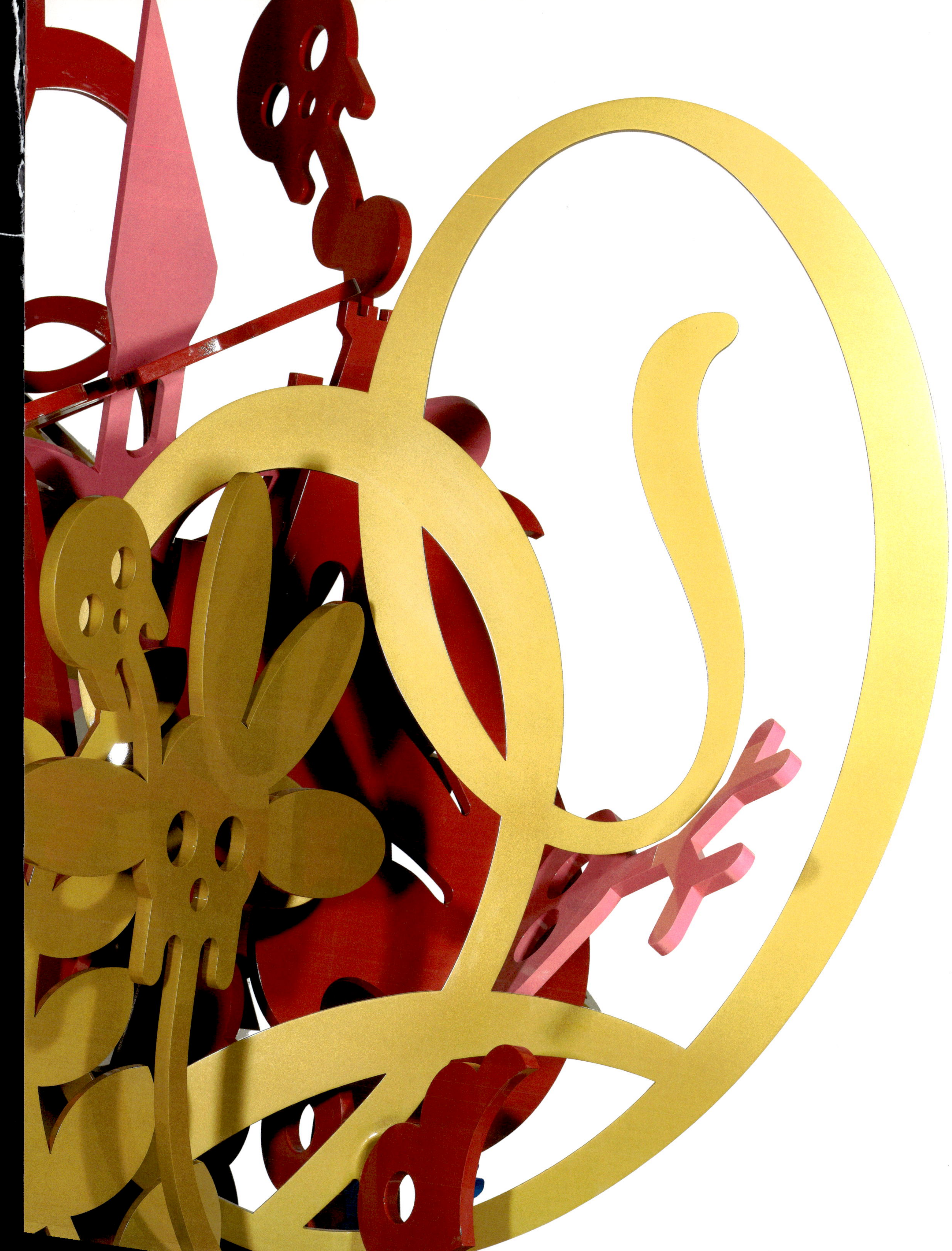

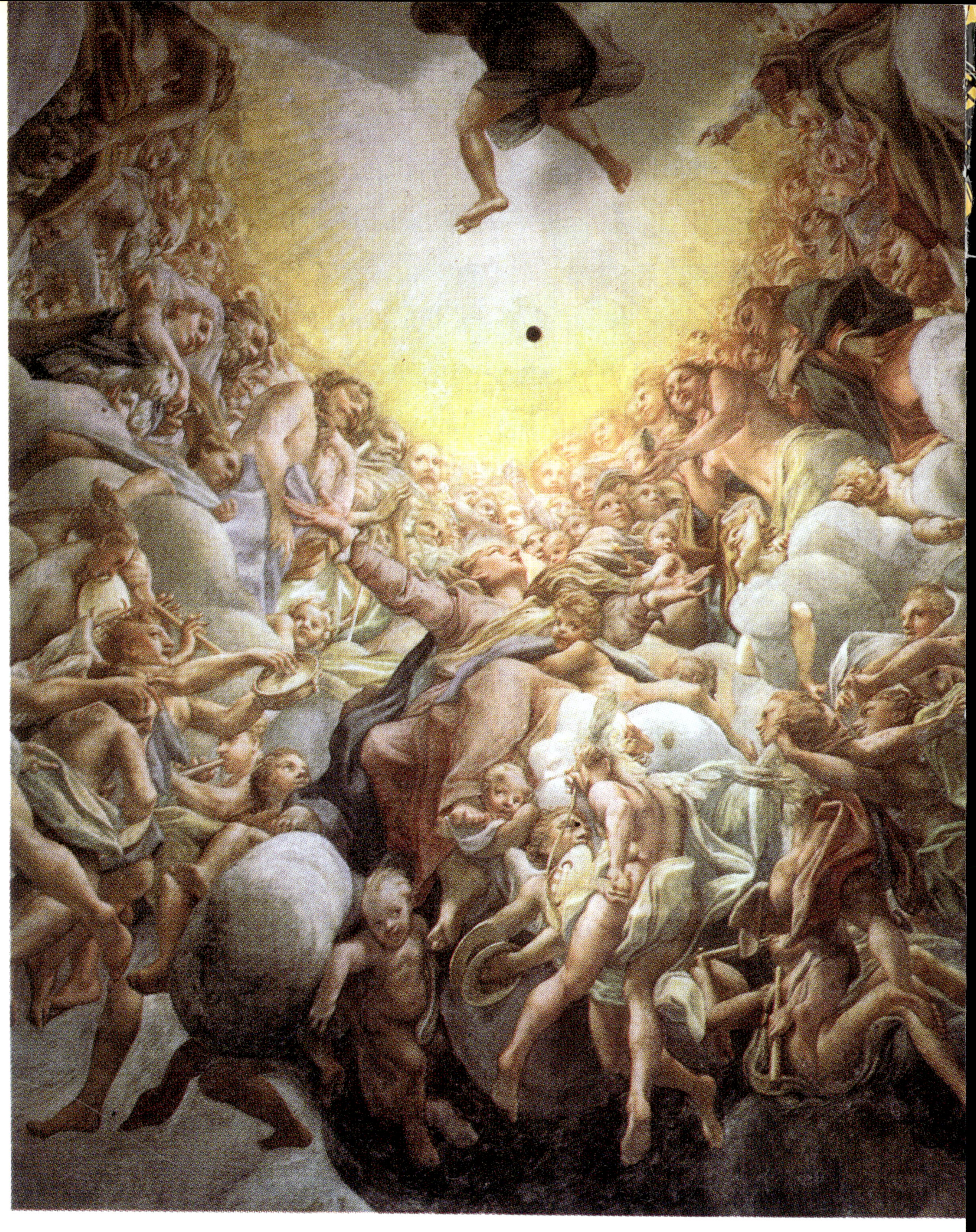

654. Correggio. *The Assumption of the Virgin* (portion). c. 1525. Fresco. Dome, Parma Cathedral

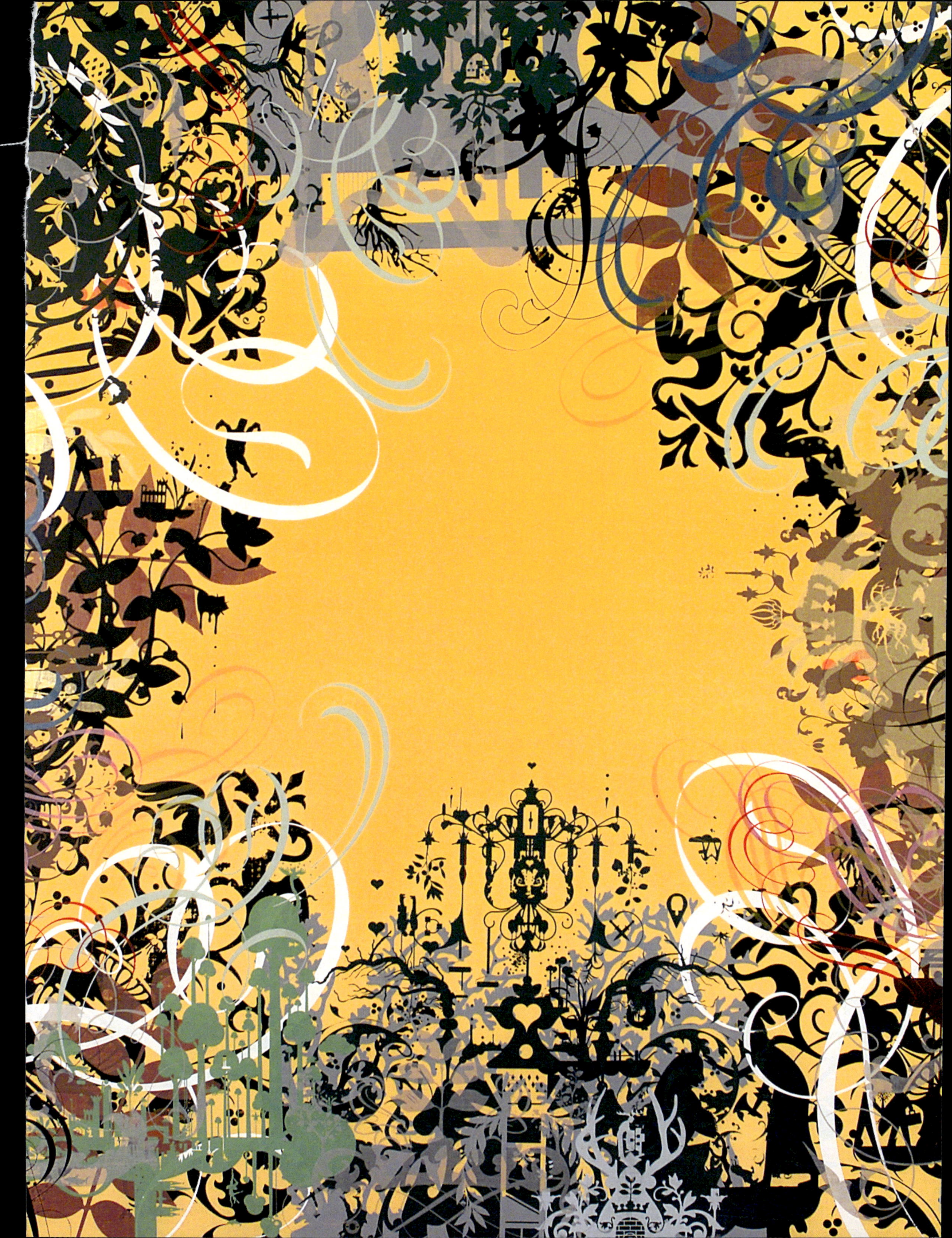

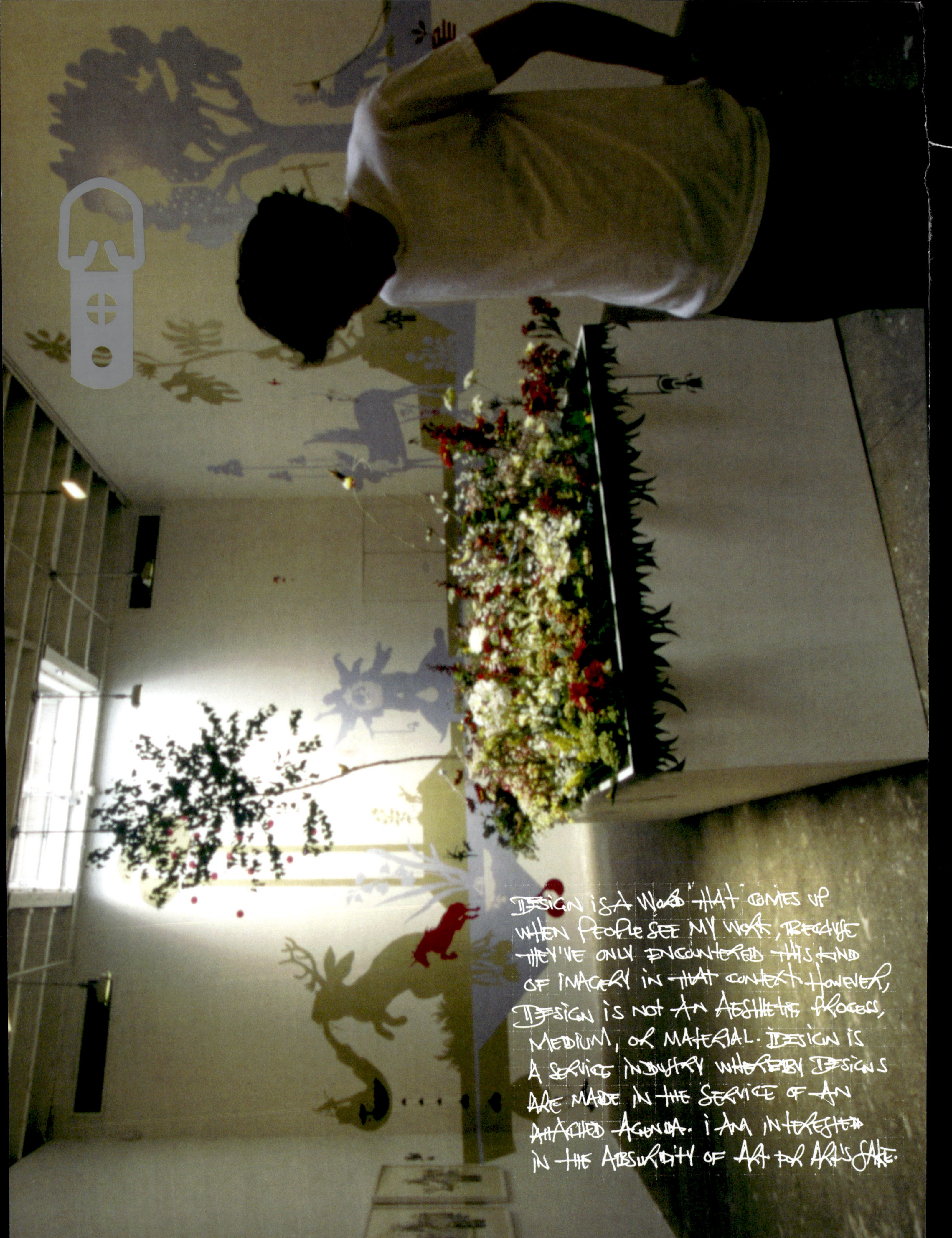

DESIGN IS A WORD THAT COMES UP WHEN PEOPLE SEE MY WORK, BECAUSE THEY'VE ONLY ENCOUNTERED THIS KIND OF IMAGERY IN THAT CONTEXT. HOWEVER, DESIGN IS NOT AN AESTHETIC PROCESS, MEDIUM, OR MATERIAL. DESIGN IS A SERVICE INDUSTRY WHEREBY DESIGNS ARE MADE IN THE SERVICE OF AN ATTACHED AGENDA. I AM INTERESTED IN THE ABSURDITY OF ART FOR ART'S SAKE.

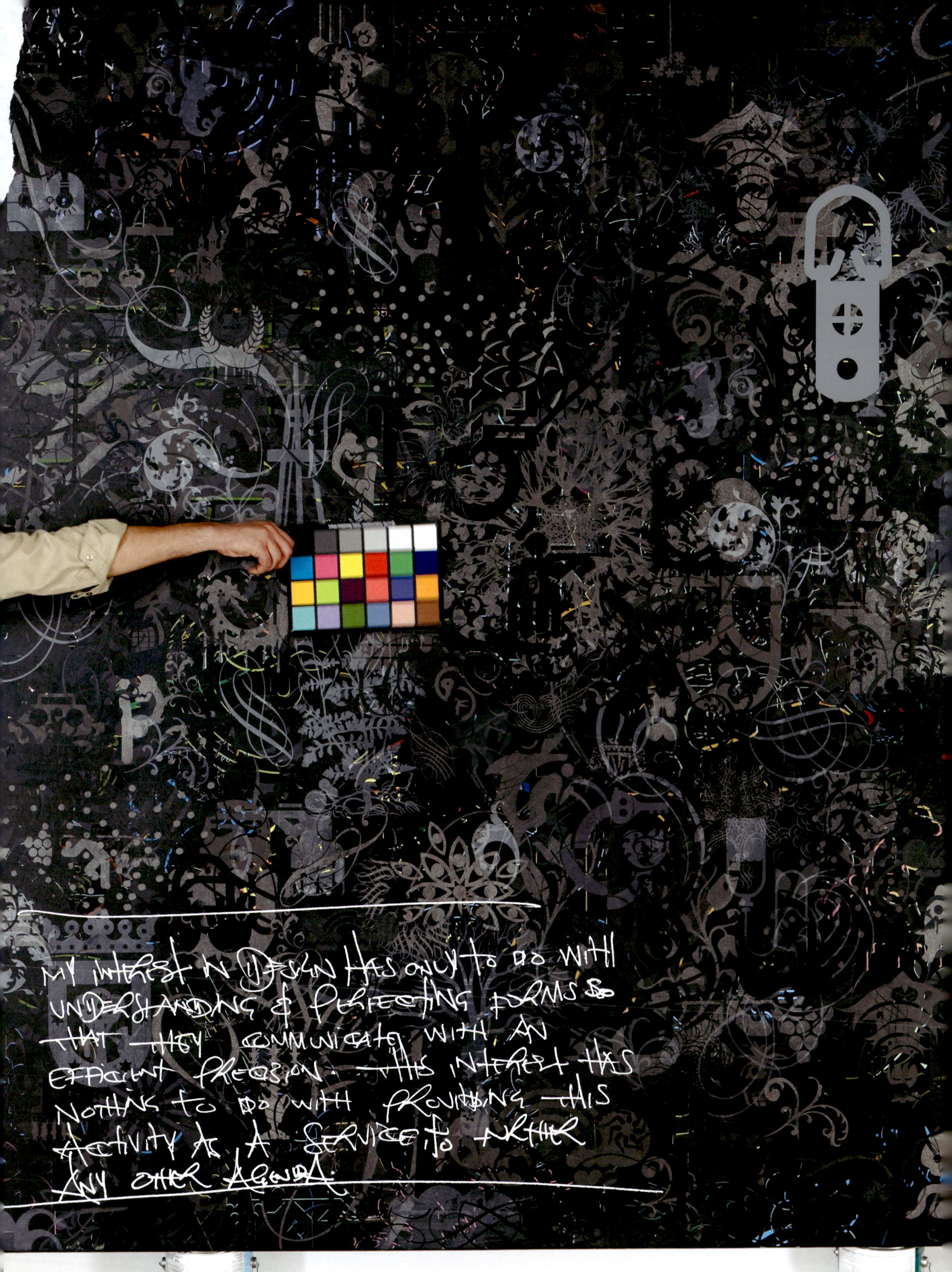
MY INTEREST IN DESIGN HAS ONLY TO DO WITH
UNDERSTANDING & PERFECTING FORMS SO
THAT THEY COMMUNICATE WITH AN
EFFICIENT PRECISION. THIS INTEREST HAS
NOTHING TO DO WITH PROVIDING THIS
ACTIVITY AS A SERVICE TO FURTHER
ANY OTHER AGENDA.

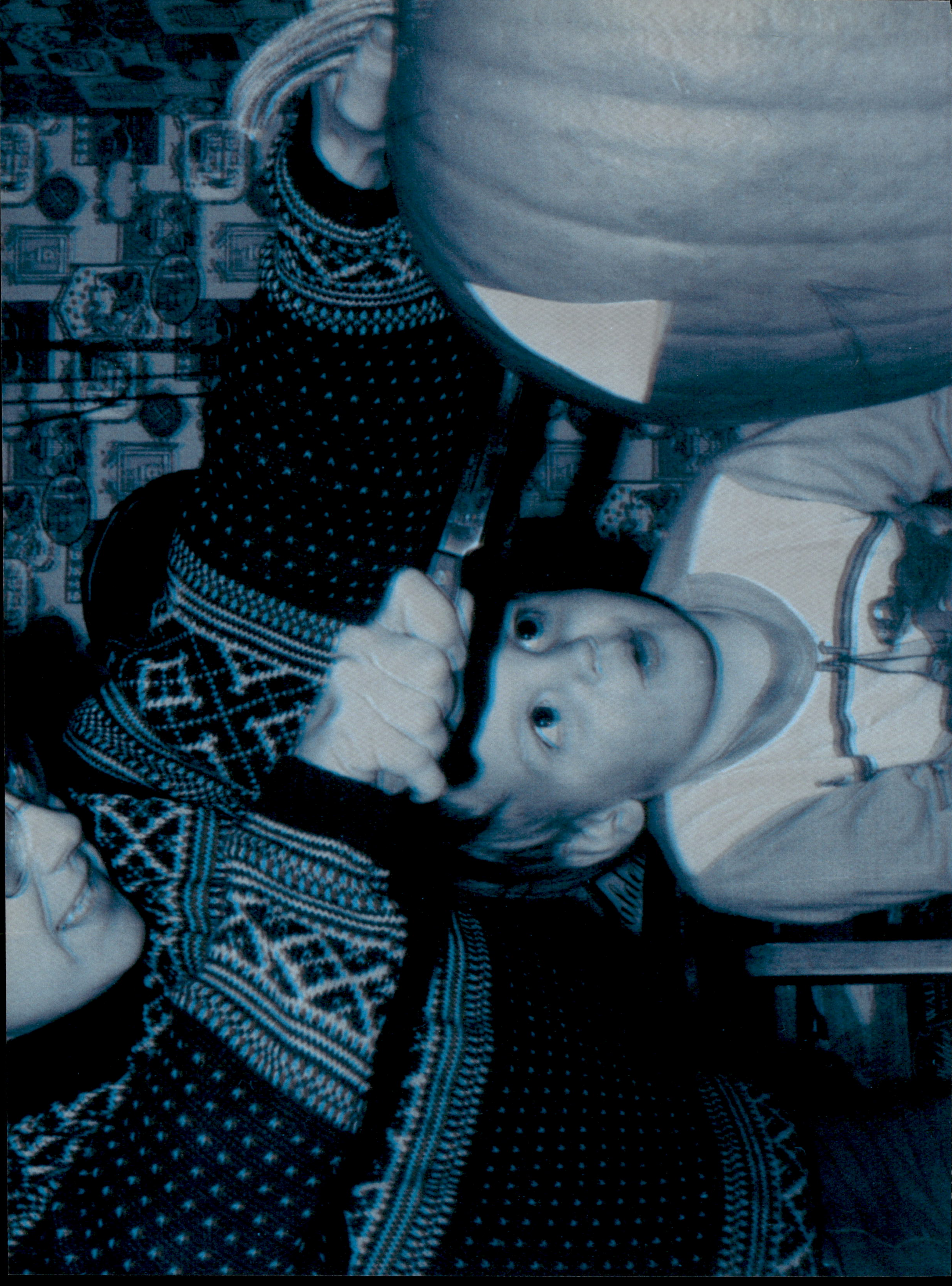

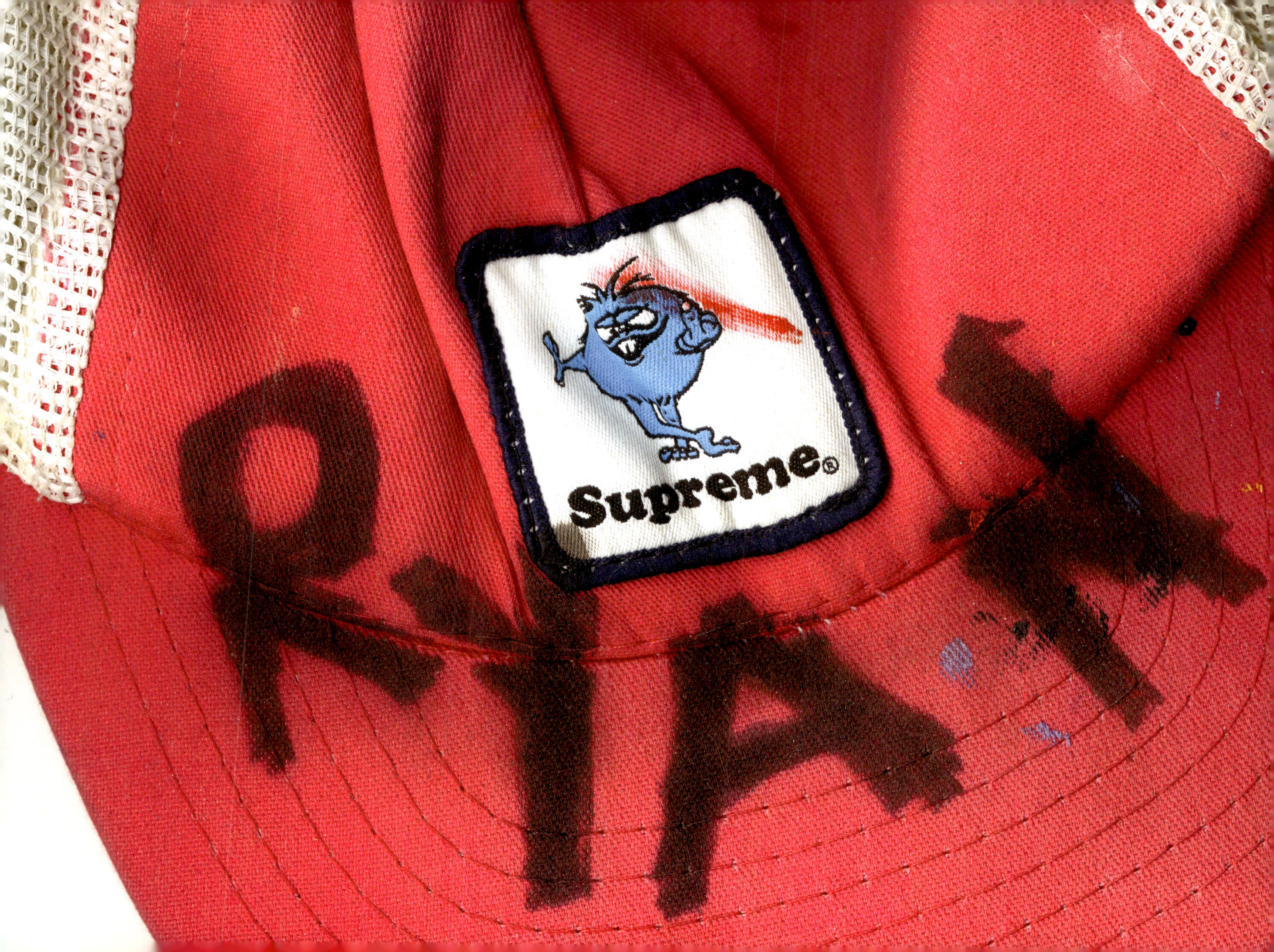
Supreme

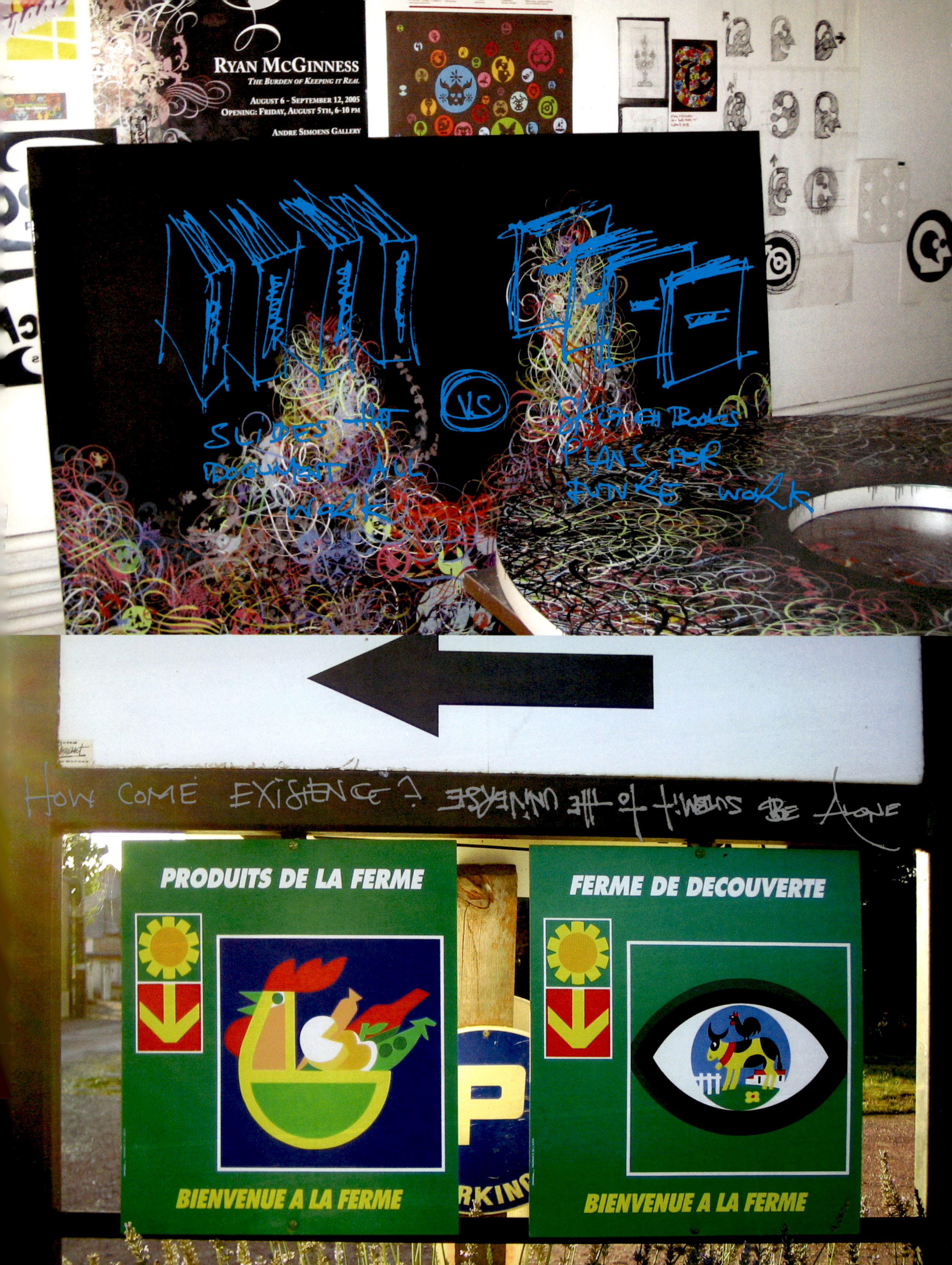
RYAN McGINNESS
THE BURDEN OF KEEPING IT REAL
AUGUST 6 - SEPTEMBER 12, 2005
OPENING: FRIDAY, AUGUST 5TH, 6-10 PM
ANDRE SIMOENS GALLERY
SLIDES THAT DOCUMENT ALL WORK
VS
SKETCHBOOKS PLANS FOR FUTURE WORK
HOW COME EXISTENCE?
BE ALONE
PRODUITS DE LA FERME
BIENVENUE A LA FERME
FERME DE DECOUVERTE
BIENVENUE A LA FERME

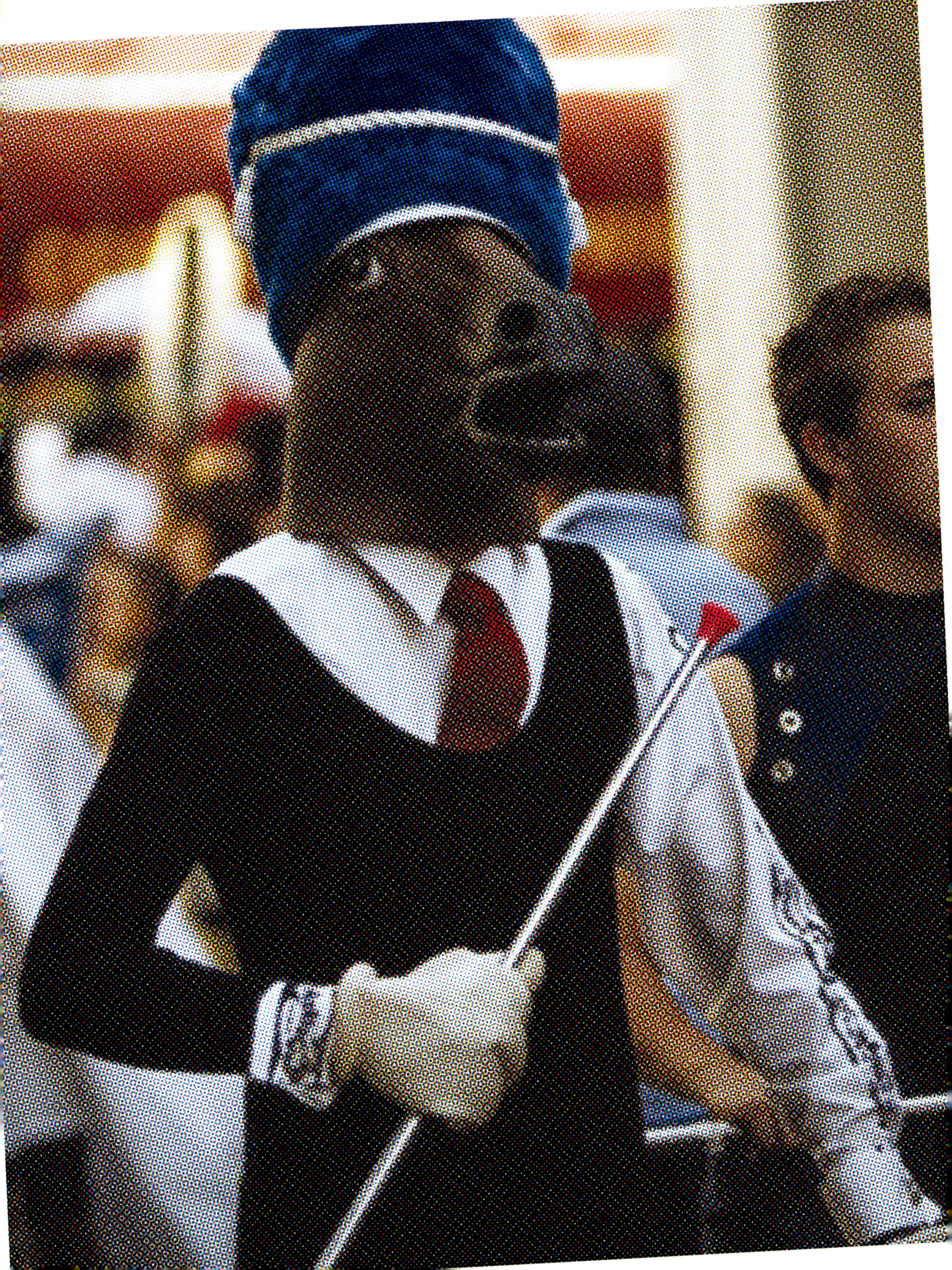

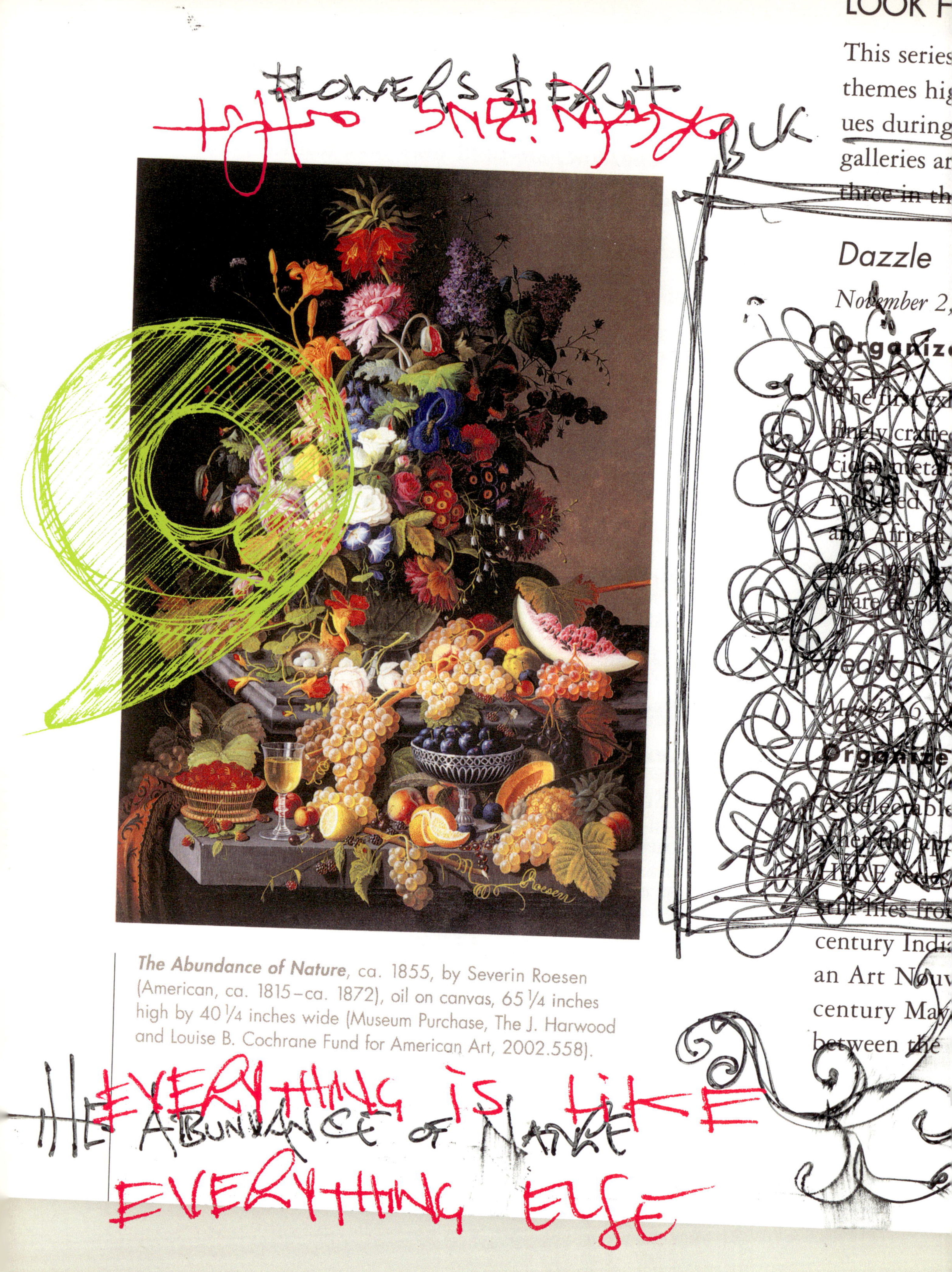

The Abundance of Nature, ca. 1855, by Severin Roesen (American, ca. 1815–ca. 1872), oil on canvas, 65 1/4 inches high by 40 1/4 inches wide (Museum Purchase, The J. Harwood and Louise B. Cochrane Fund for American Art, 2002.558).

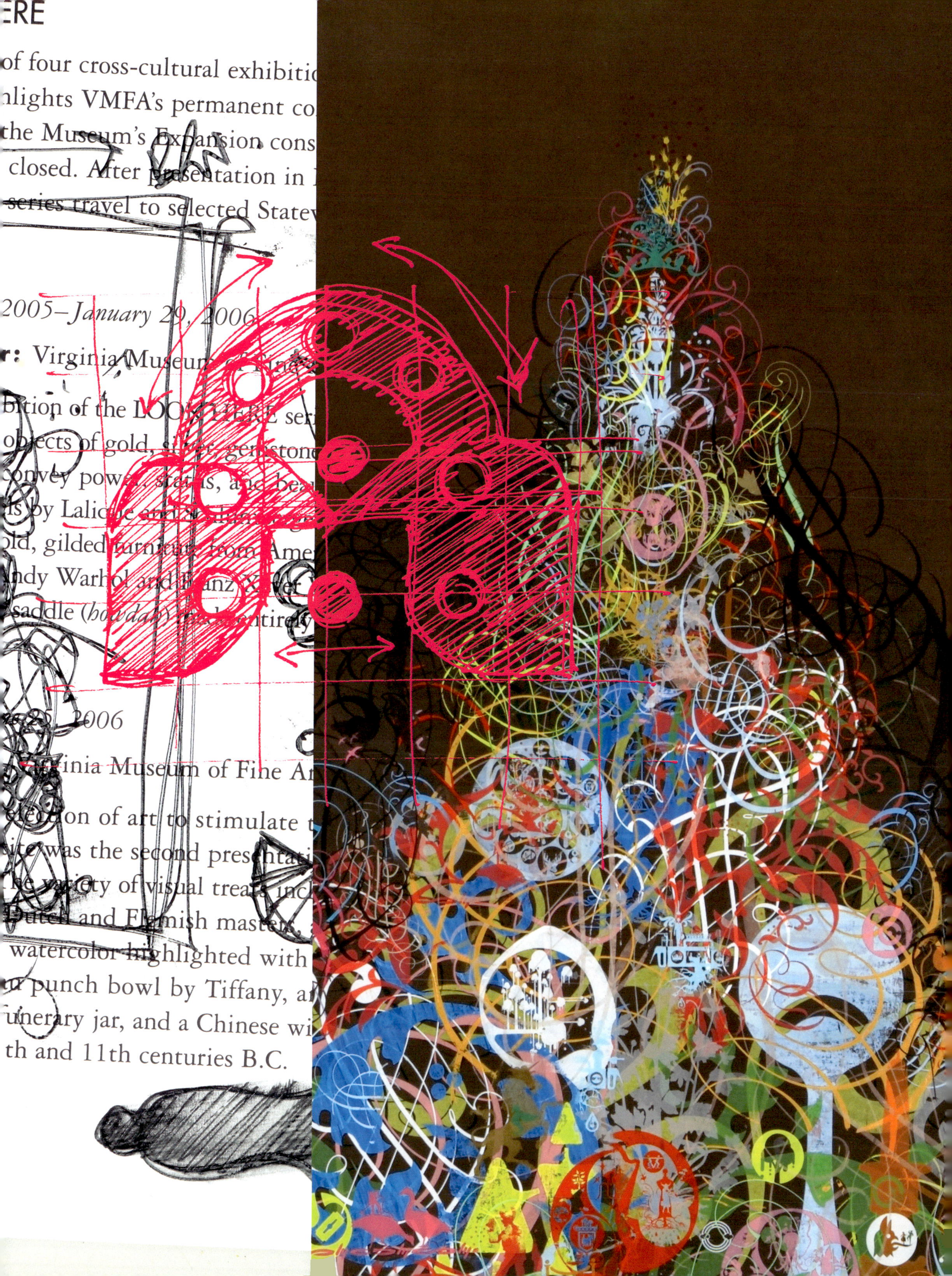
ERE
of four cross-cultural exhibitio
hlights VMFA's permanent co
the Museum's Expansion cons
closed. After presentation in
series travel to selected State
2005–January 29, 2006
r: Virginia Museum
objects of gold
convey pow
ld, gilded
ndy Warhol
saddle
2006
inia Museum of Fine Ar
on of art to stimulate
was the second pres
ty of visual trea
Dutch and Flemish mast
watercolor highlighted with
punch bowl by Tiffany, a
unerary jar, and a Chinese w
th and 11th centuries B.C.

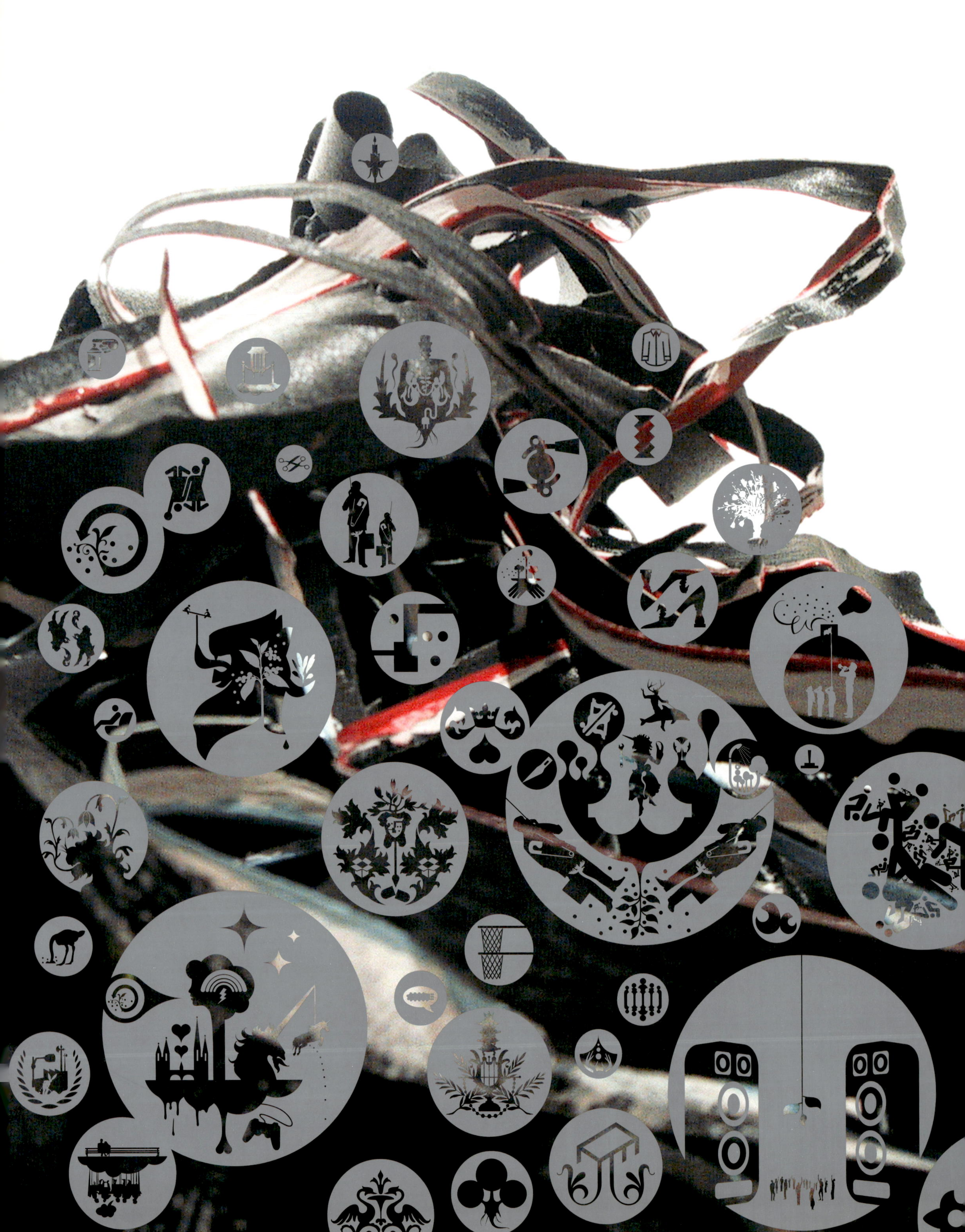

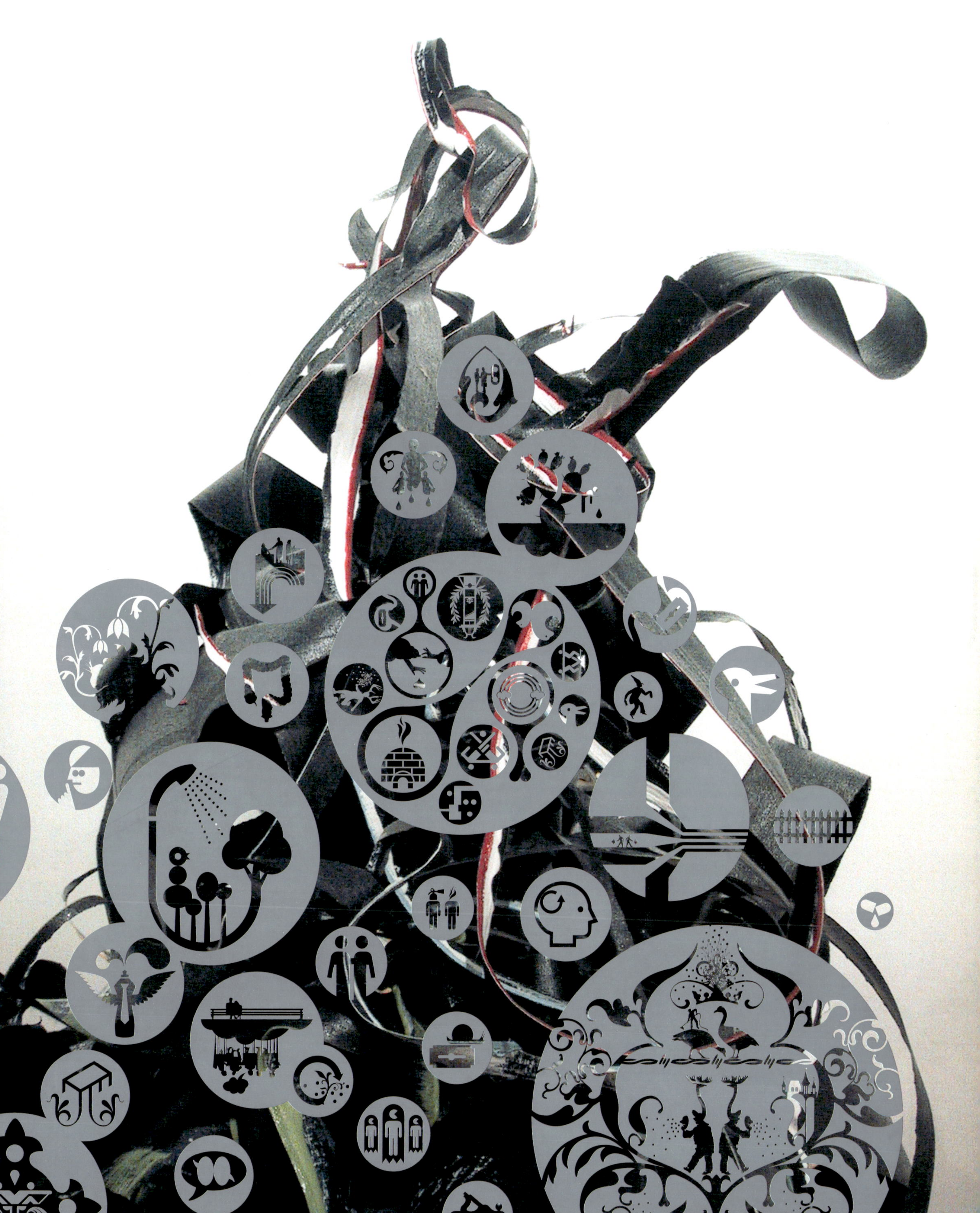

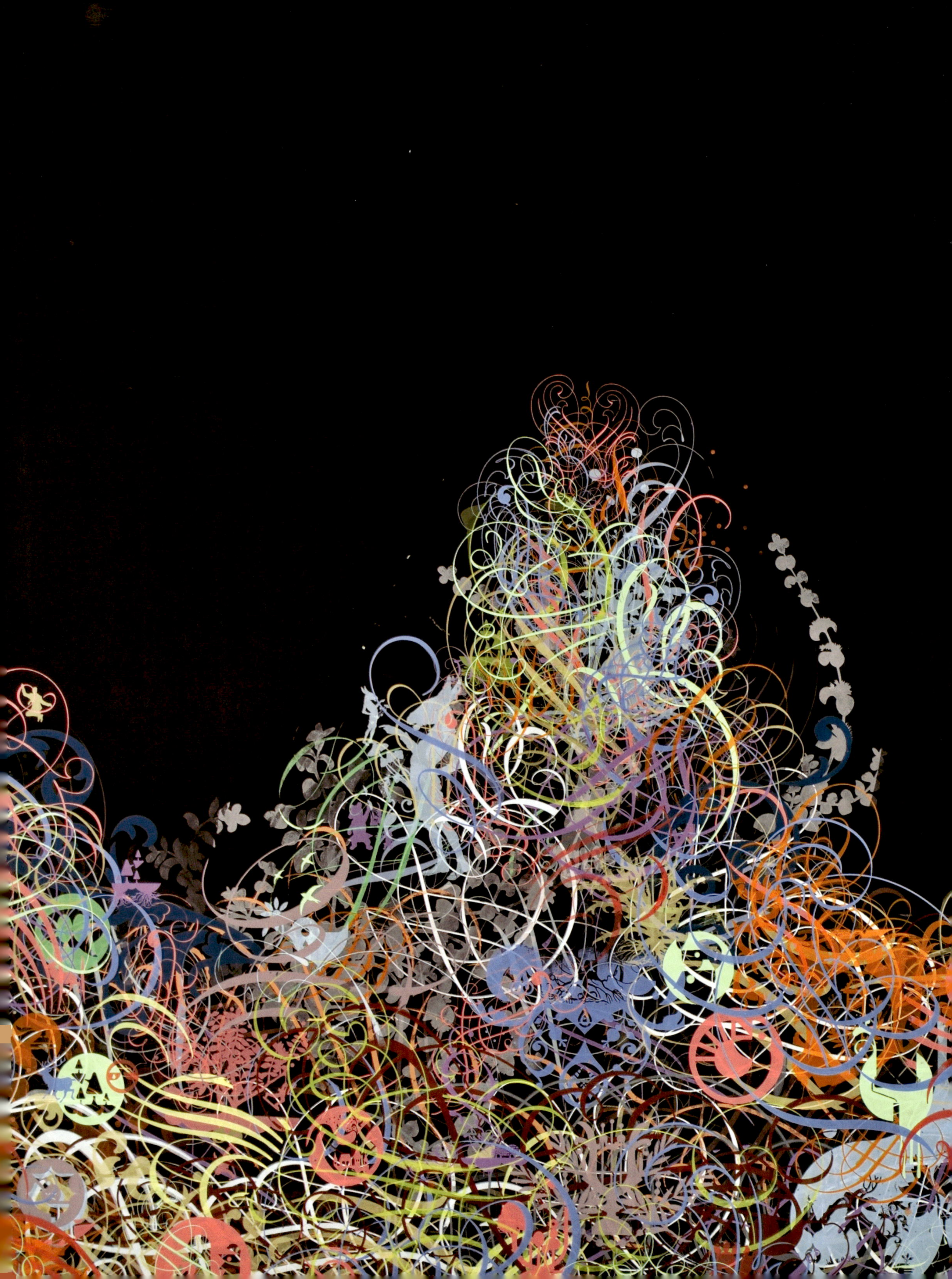

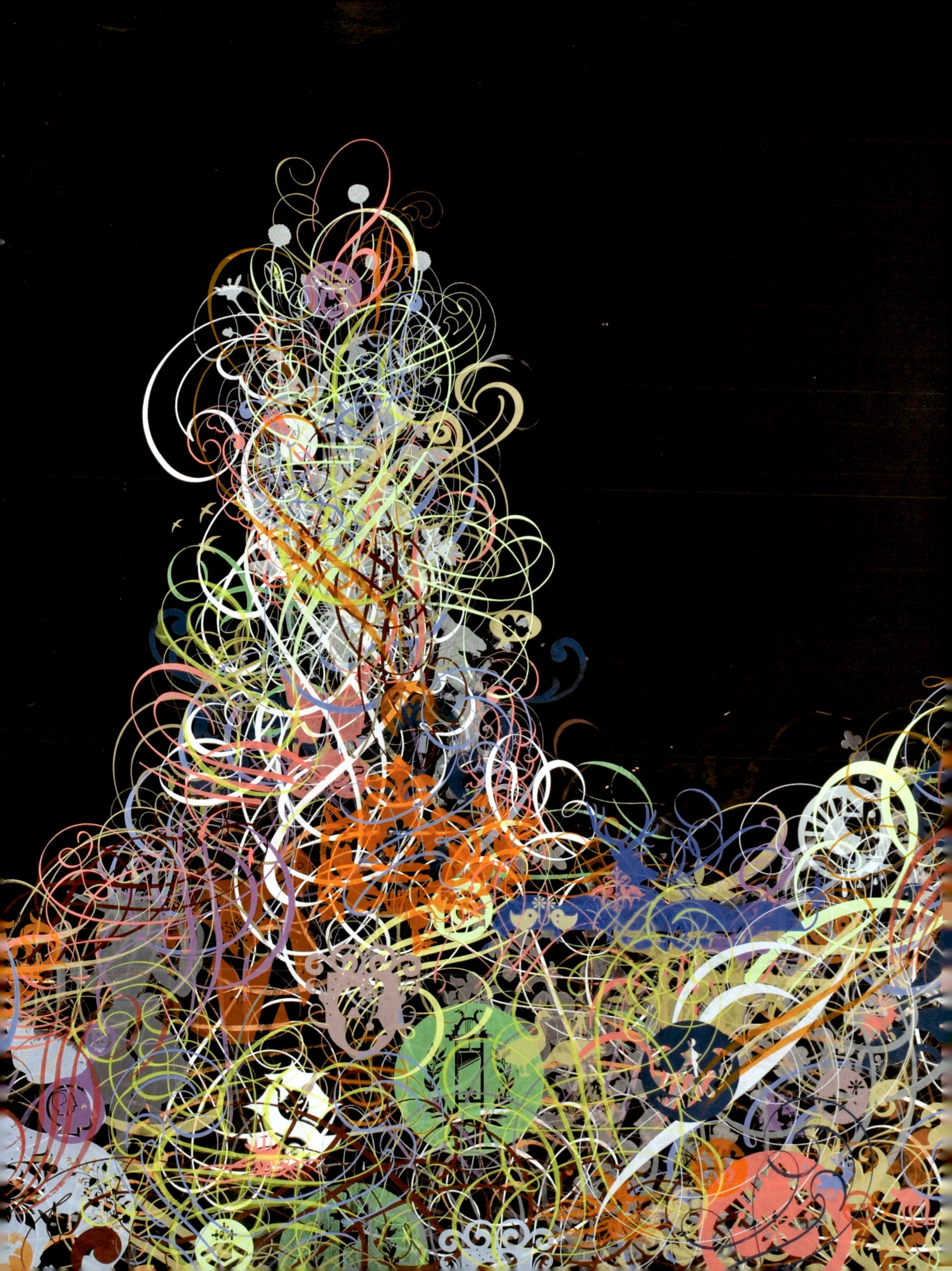

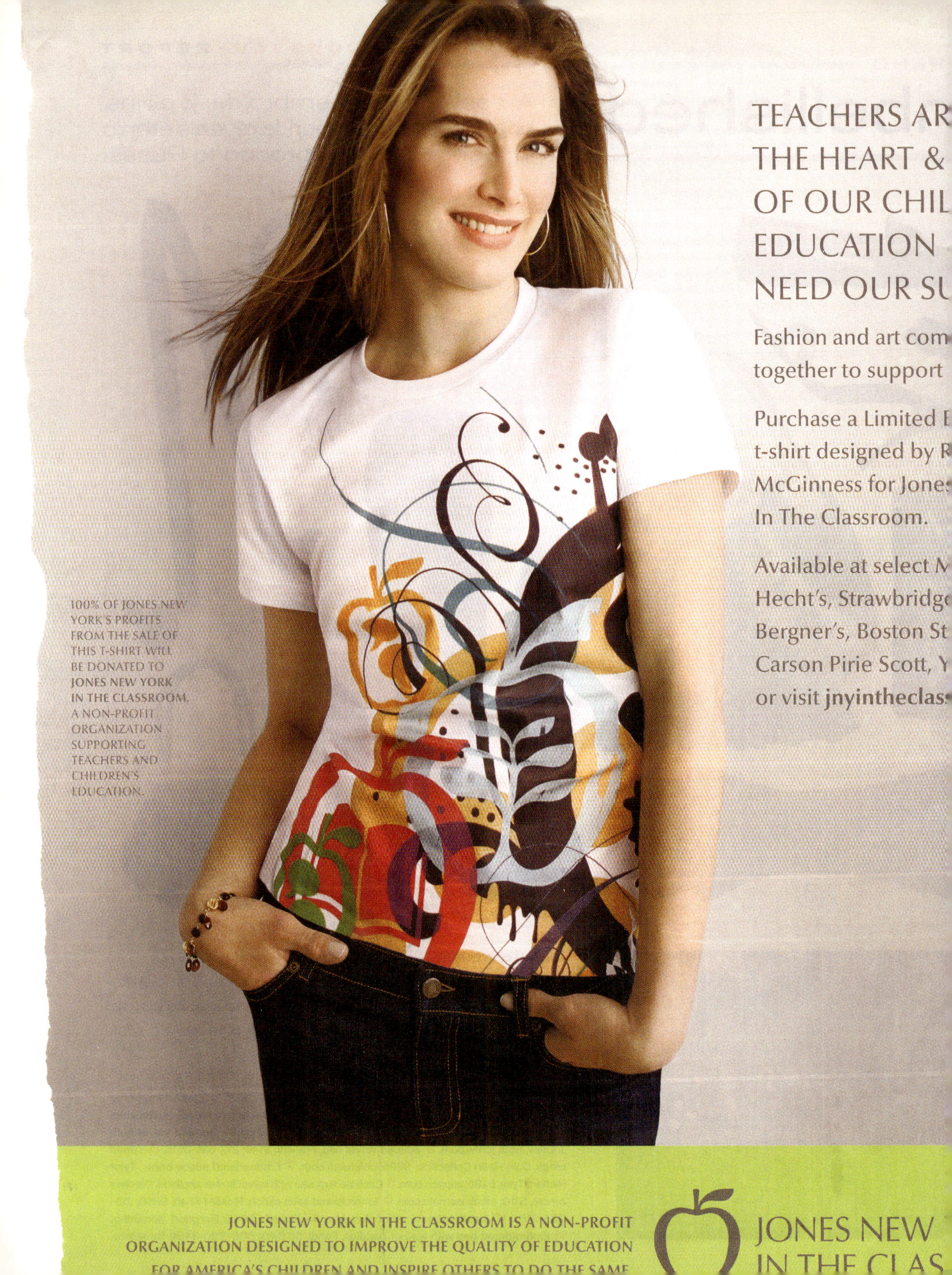

TEACHERS AR
THE HEART &
OF OUR CHIL
EDUCATION
NEED OUR SU

Fashion and art com
together to support

Purchase a Limited E
t-shirt designed by R
McGinness for Jones
In The Classroom.

Available at select M
Hecht's, Strawbridge
Bergner's, Boston St
Carson Pirie Scott, Y
or visit **jnyintheclass**

100% OF JONES NEW YORK'S PROFITS FROM THE SALE OF THIS T-SHIRT WILL BE DONATED TO JONES NEW YORK IN THE CLASSROOM, A NON-PROFIT ORGANIZATION SUPPORTING TEACHERS AND CHILDREN'S EDUCATION.

JONES NEW YORK IN THE CLASSROOM IS A NON-PROFIT ORGANIZATION DESIGNED TO IMPROVE THE QUALITY OF EDUCATION FOR AMERICA'S CHILDREN AND INSPIRE OTHERS TO DO THE SAME

JONES NEW
IN THE CLAS

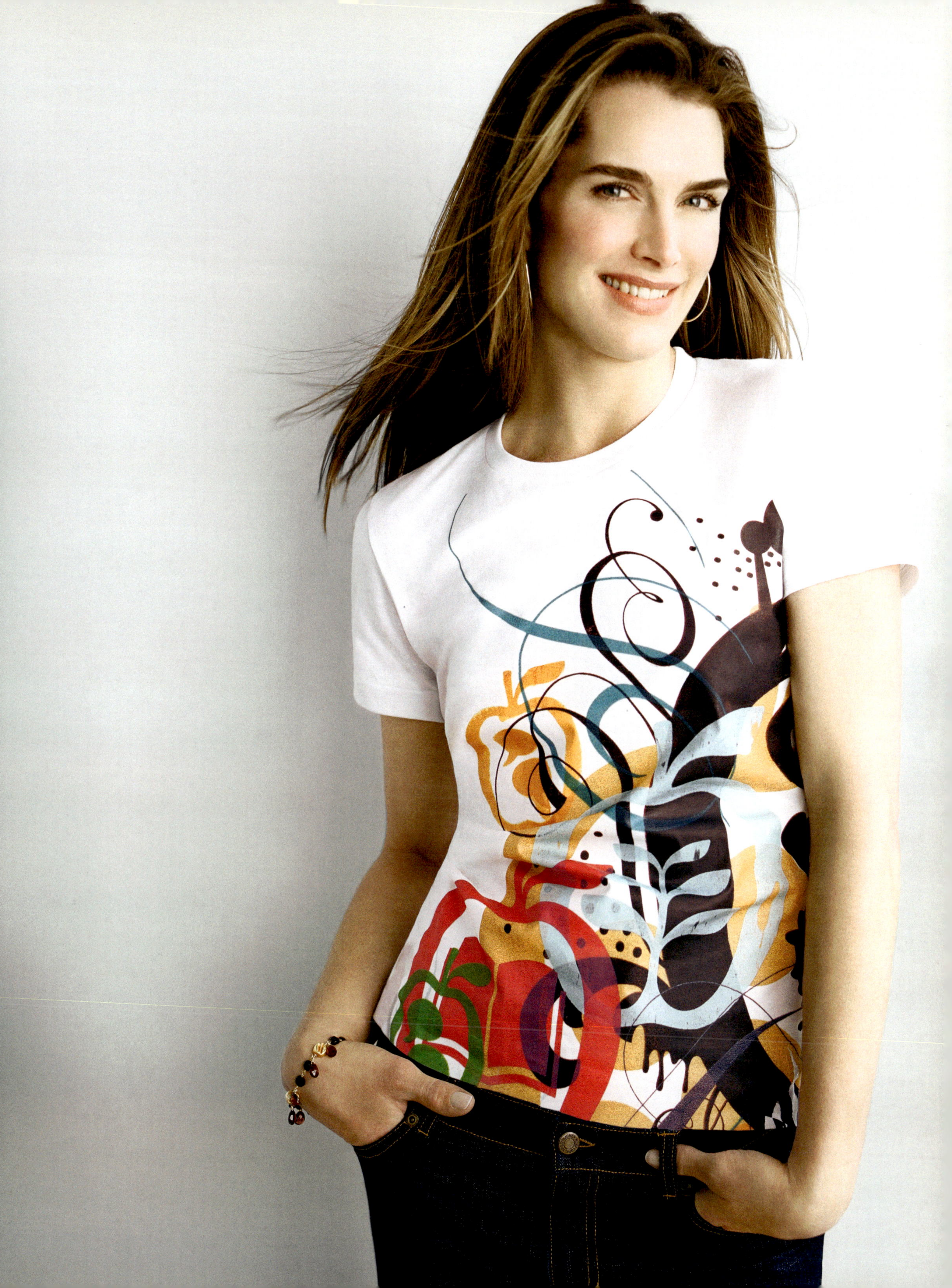

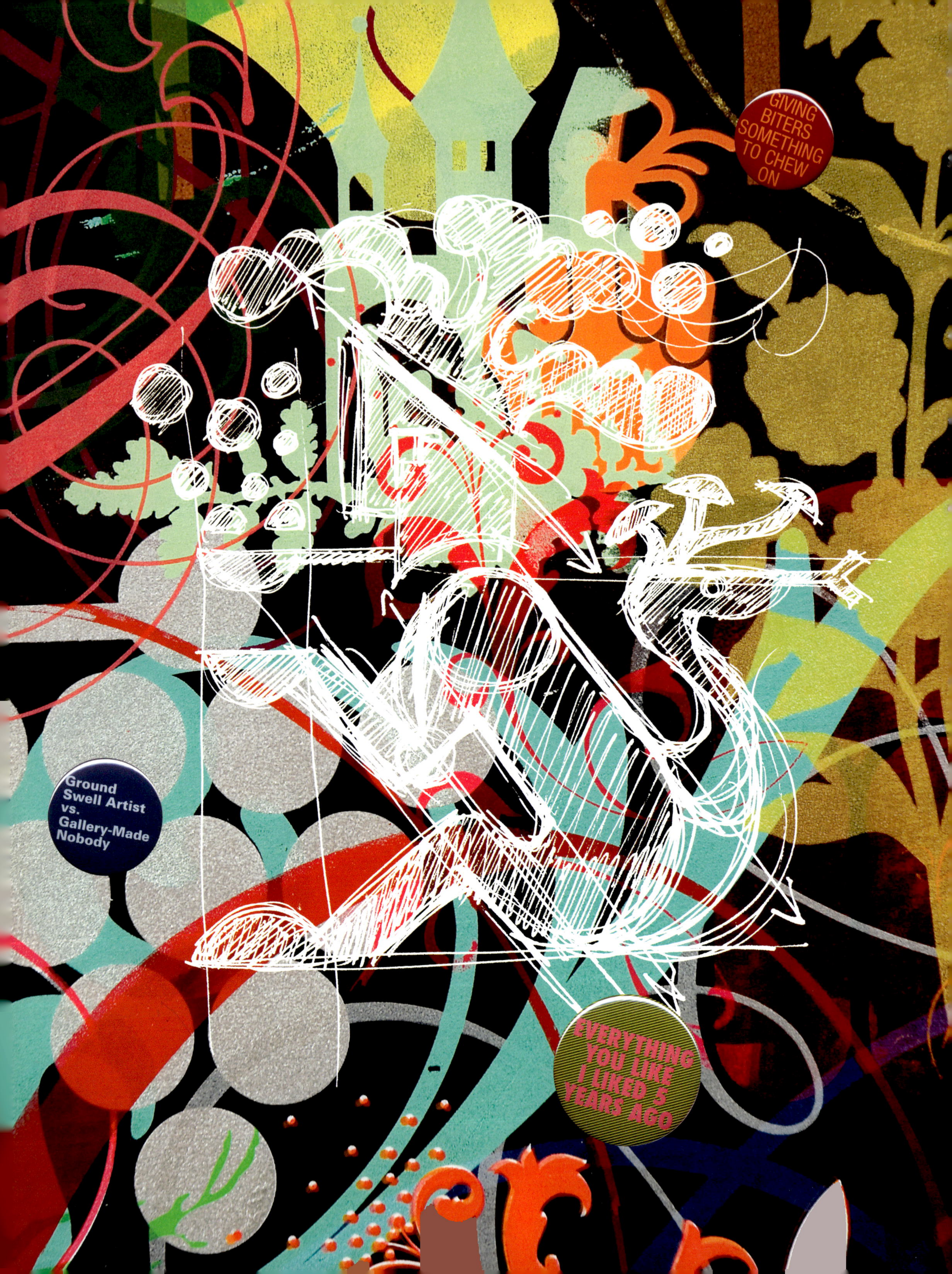
GIVING BITERS SOMETHING TO CHEW ON
Ground Swell Artist vs. Gallery-Made Nobody
EVERYTHING YOU LIKE I LIKED 5 YEARS AGO

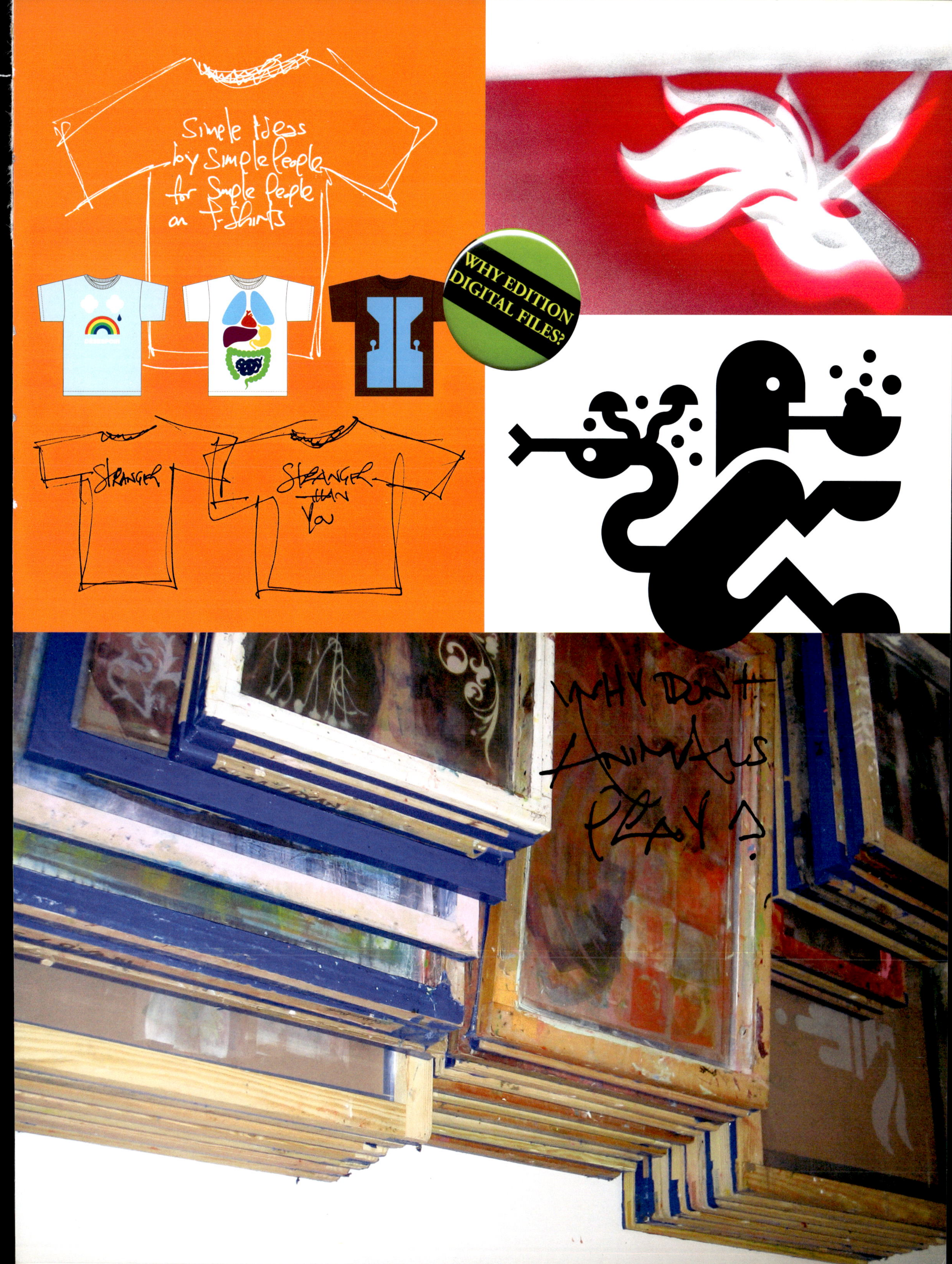
Simple Ideas
by Simple People
for Simple People
on T-Shirts
WHY EDITION
DIGITAL FILES?
STRANGER
STRANGER
THAN
YOU
WHY DON'T
ANIMALS
PLAY?

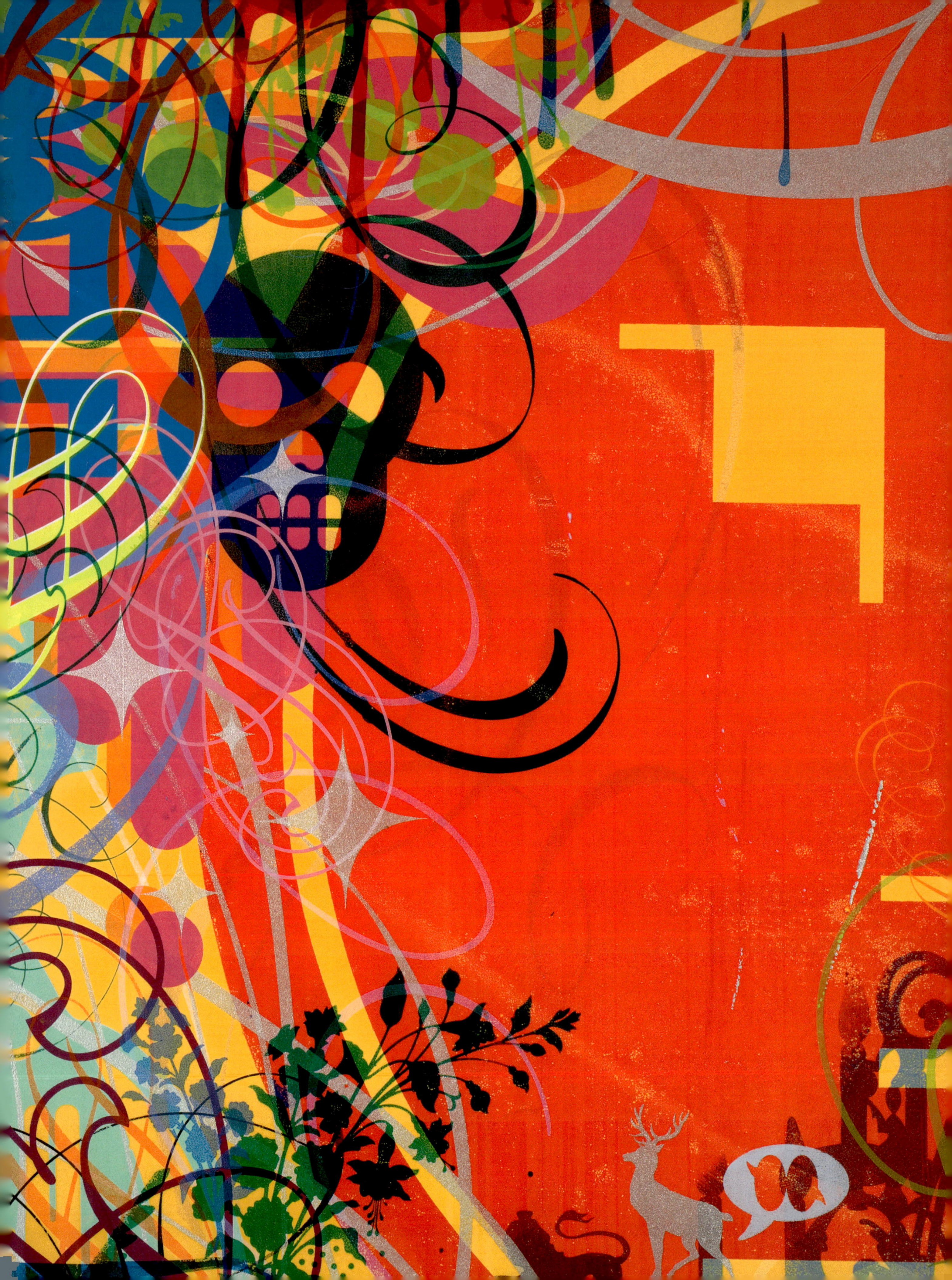

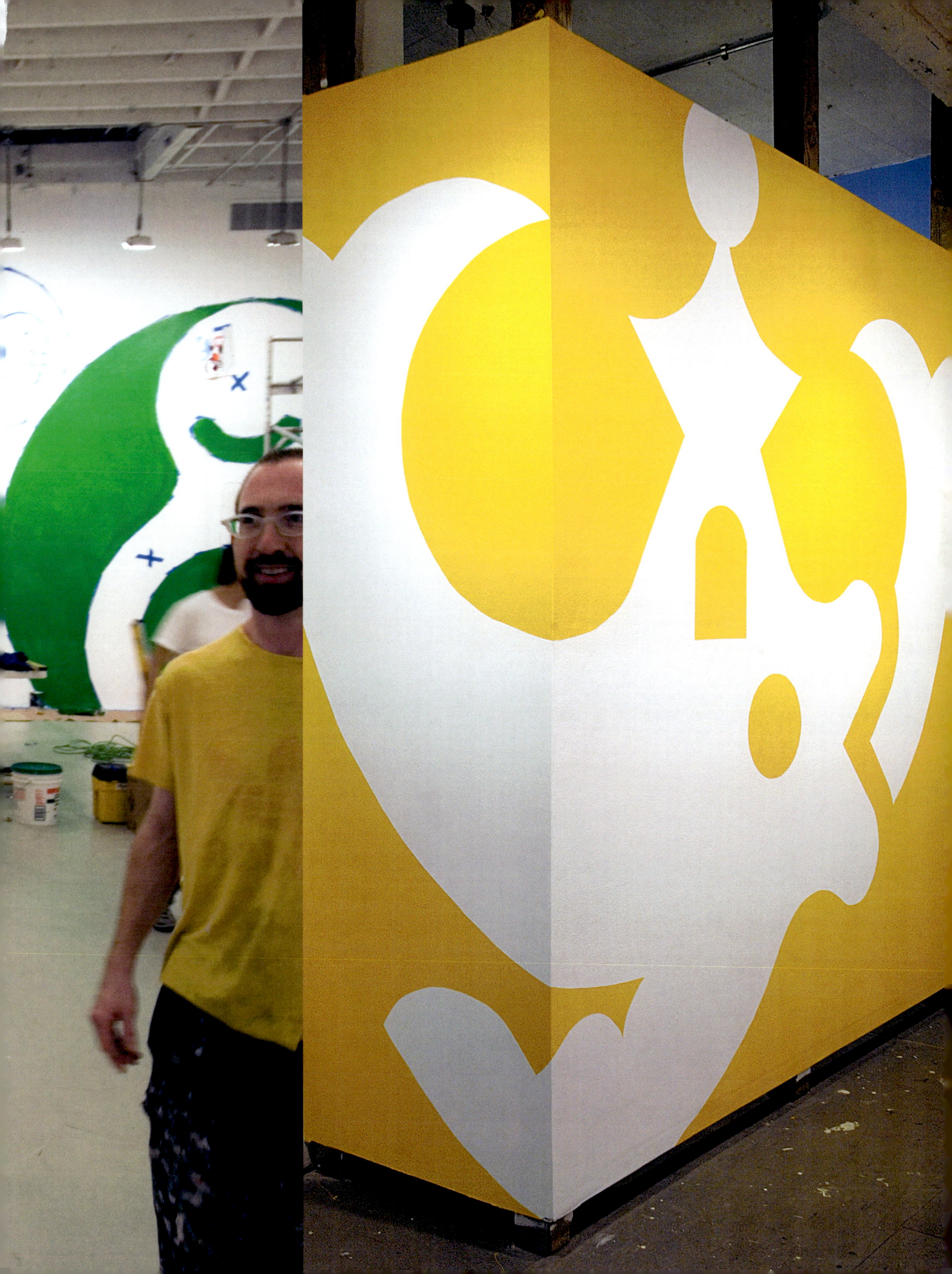

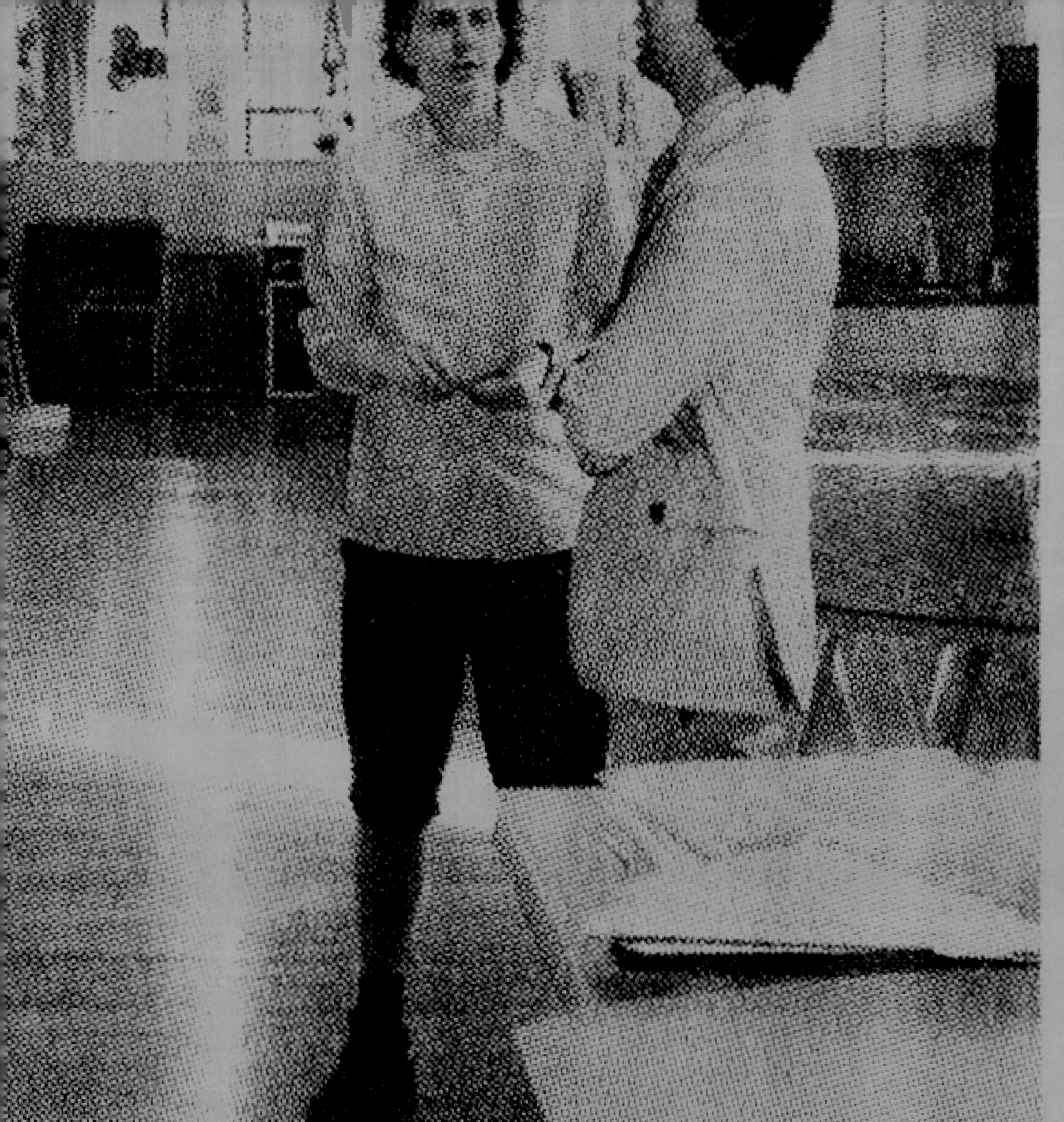

Ozier Muhammad/The New York Times

ft, at his Manhattan studio with
n the artist and delivered a coup.

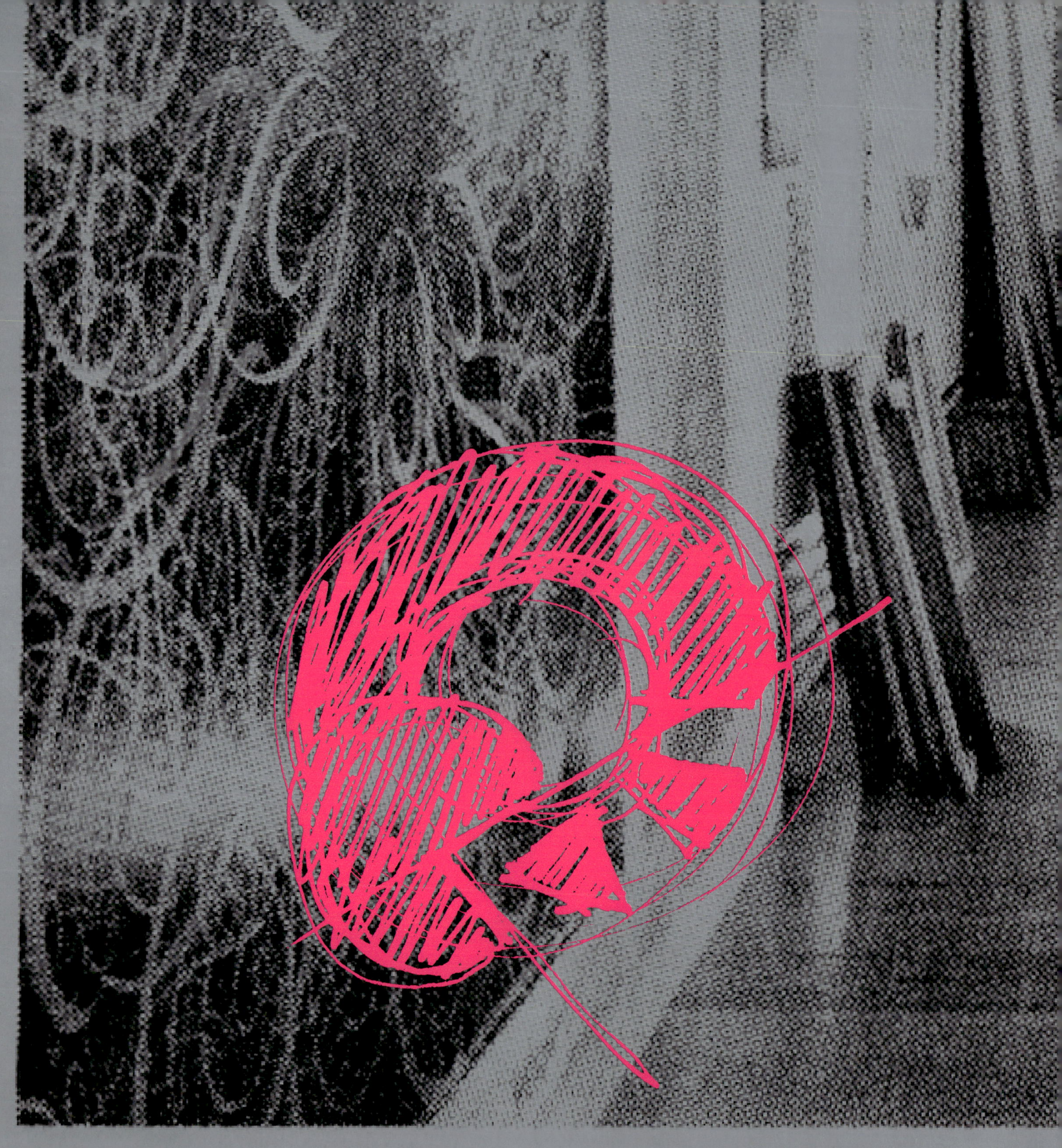

'COUNT ME IN' Ryan McGinness, le
Jacob Lewis, who set his sights o

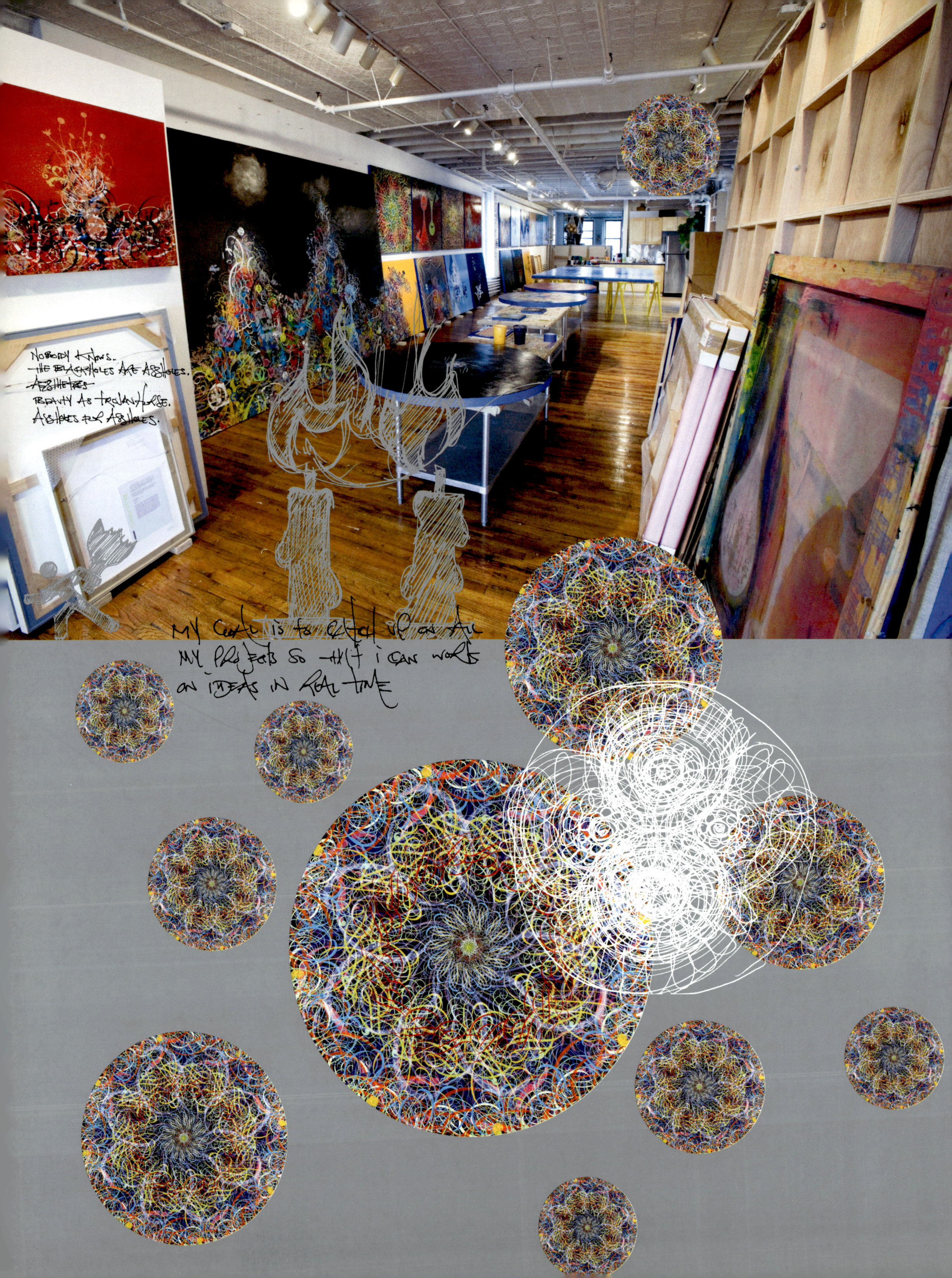
NOBODY KNOWS.
THE BLACKHOLES ARE ASSHOLES.
ASSHETICS
BEAUTY AS TROJAN HORSE.
ASSHOLES FOR ASSHOLES.
MY GOAL IS TO CATCH UP ON ALL
MY PROJECTS SO THAT I CAN WORK
ON IDEAS IN REAL TIME

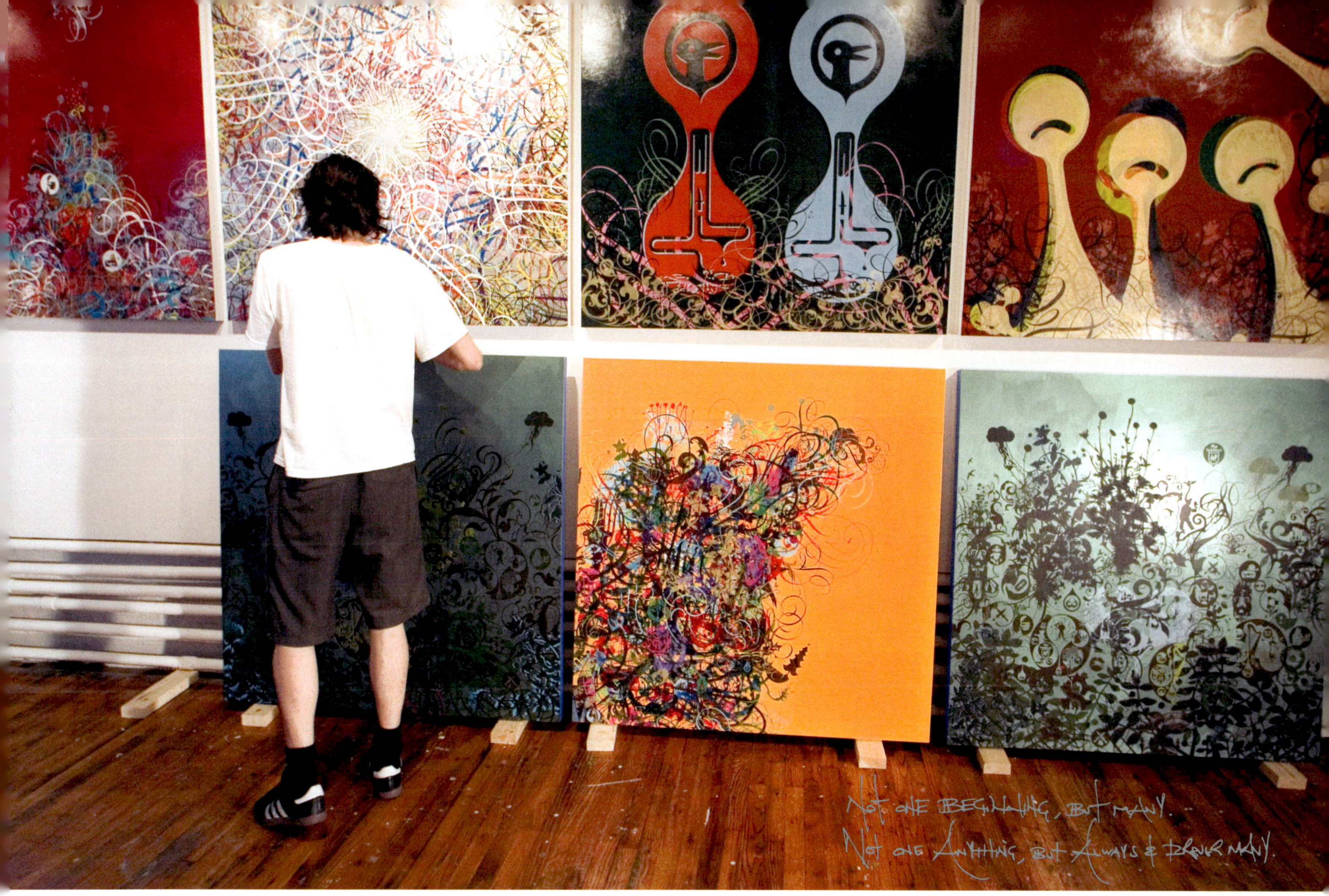

NOT ONE BEGINNING, BUT MANY.
NOT ONE ANYTHING, BUT ALWAYS & FOREVER MANY.

MANY BEGINNINGS.

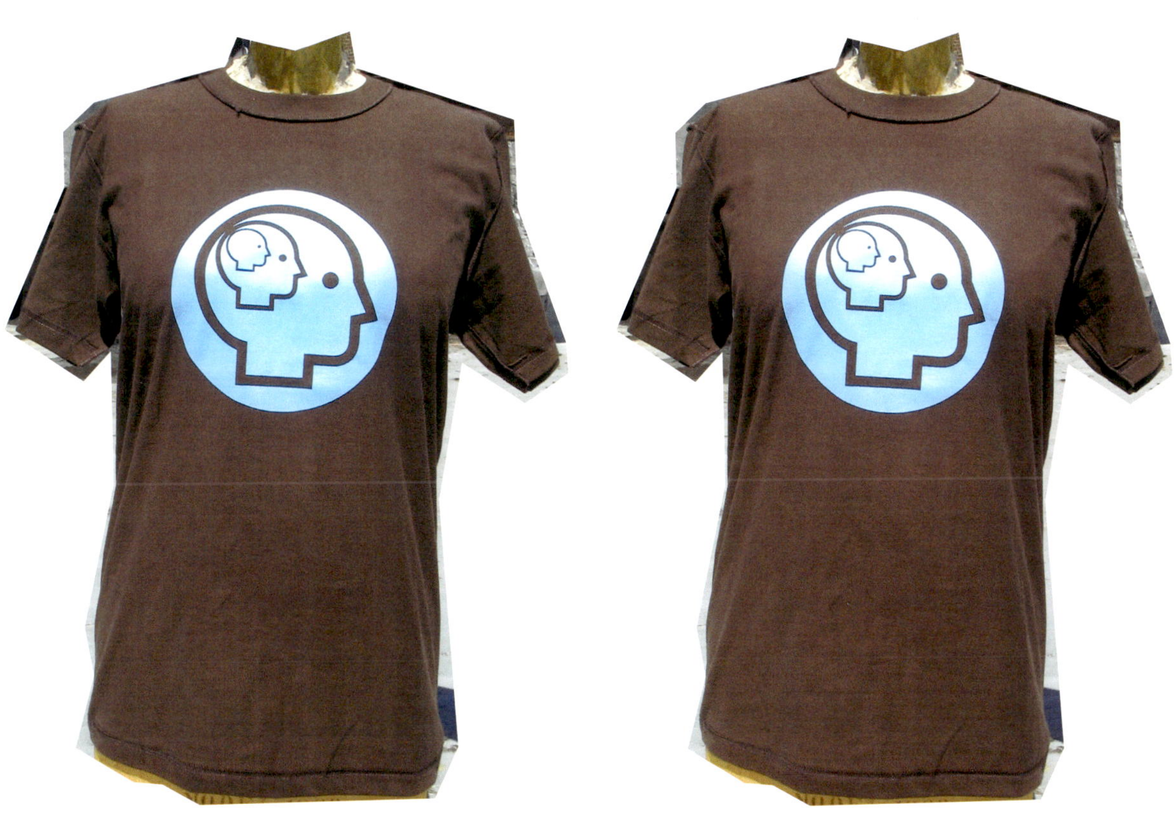

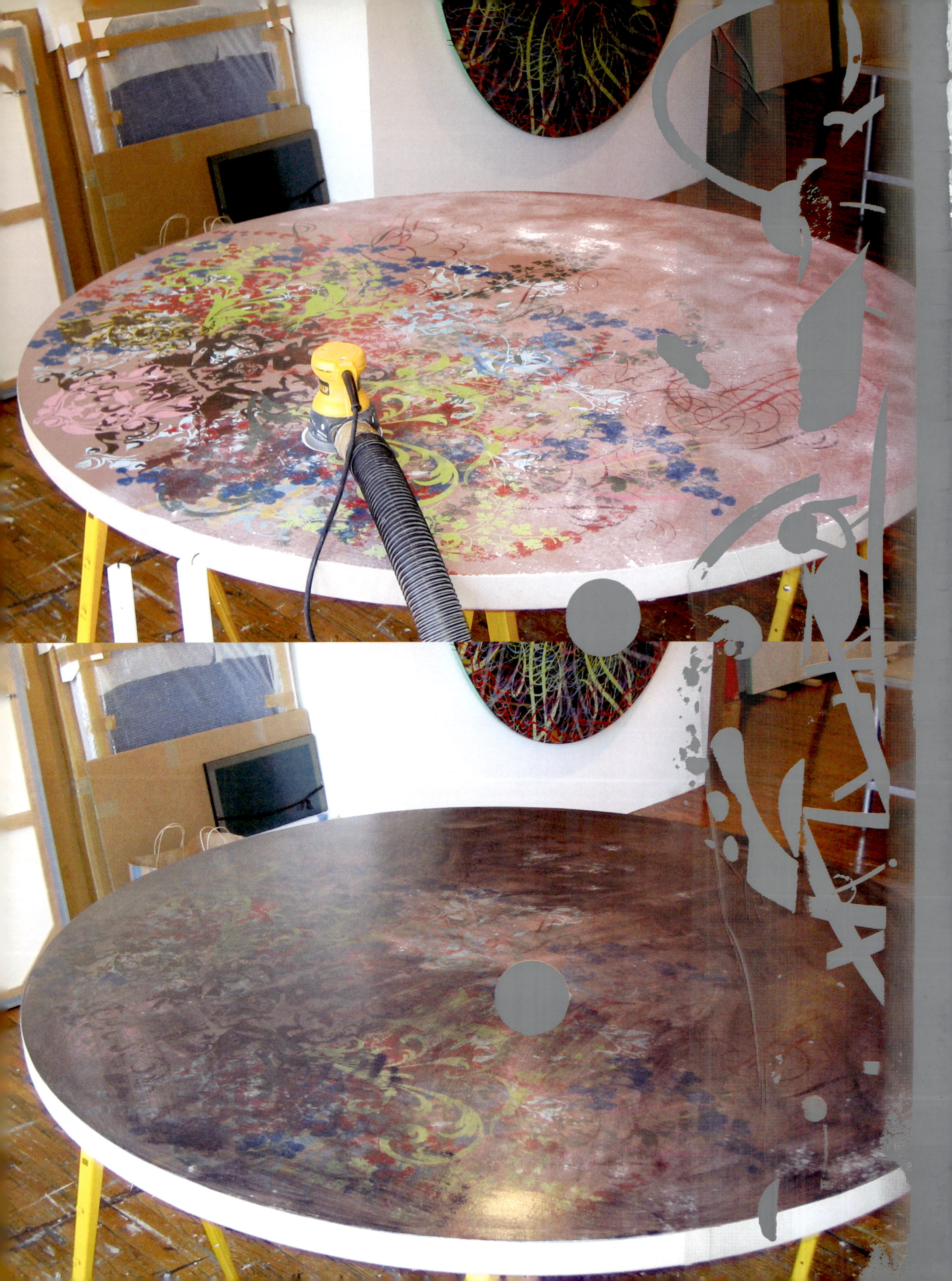

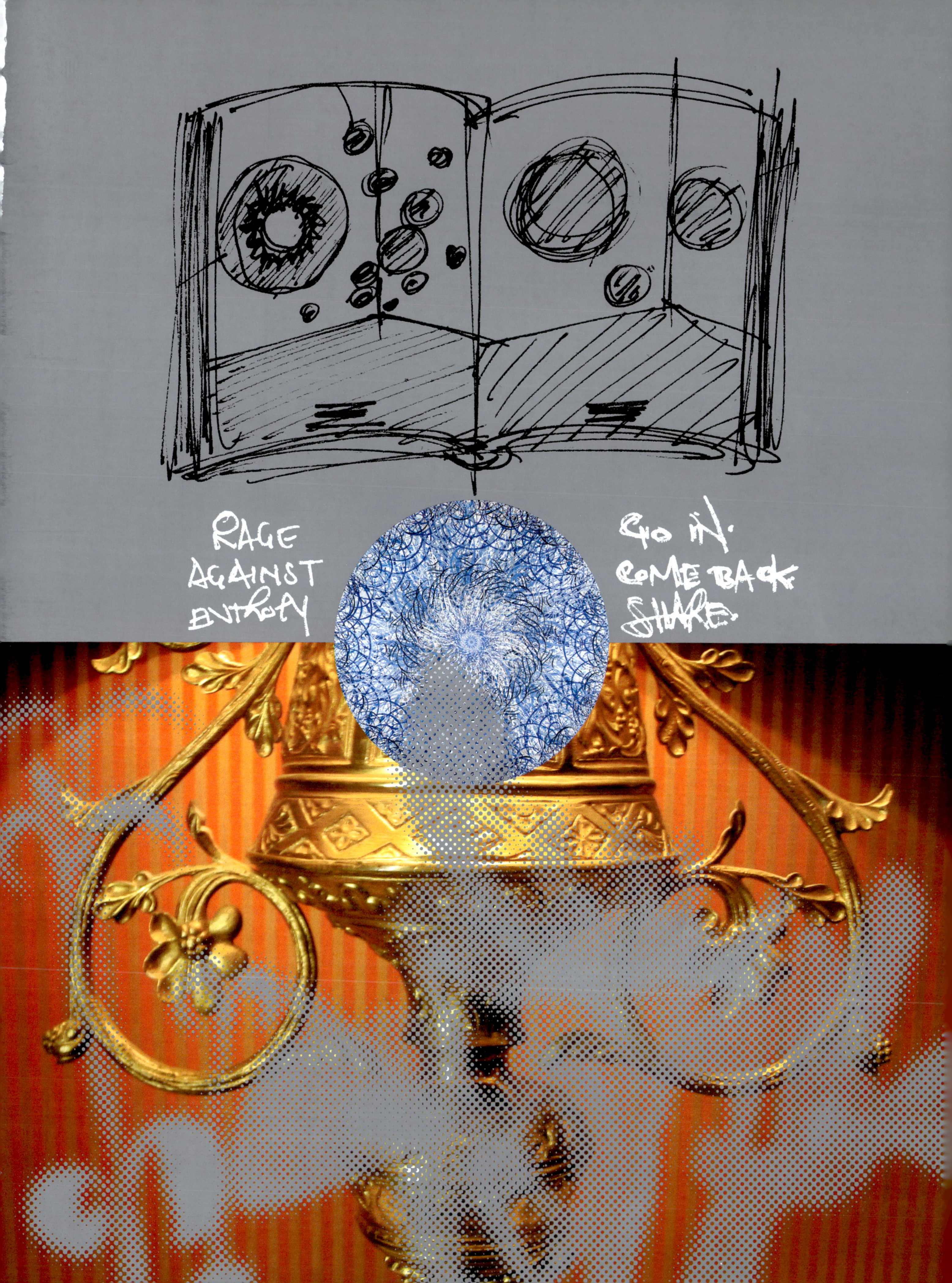
RAGE
AGAINST
ENTROPY
GO IN.
COME BACK.
SHARE.

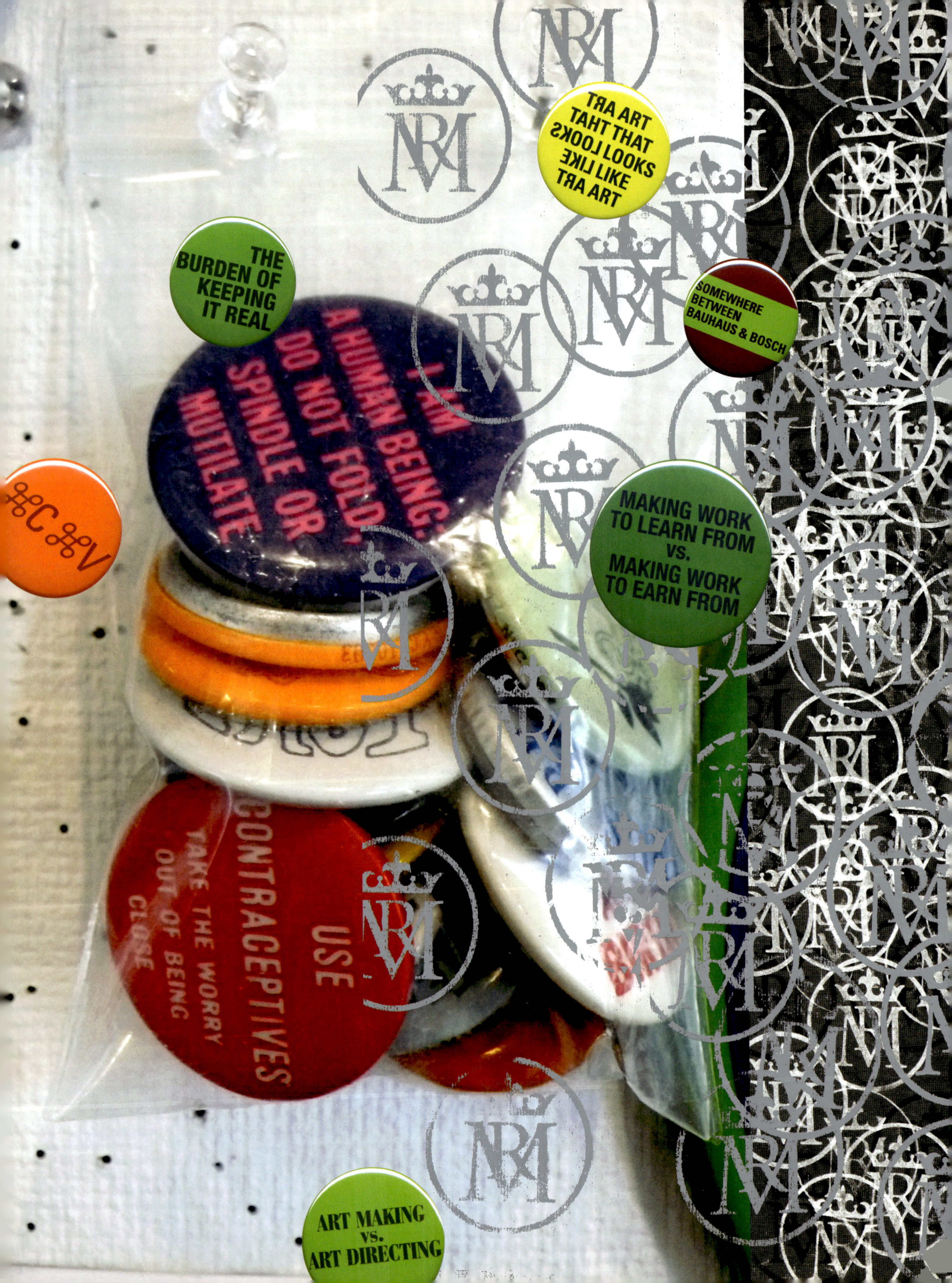
TRA ART
TAHT THAT
SKOOL LOOKS
EKIL LIKE
TRA ART
THE BURDEN OF KEEPING IT REAL
SOMEWHERE BETWEEN BAUHAUS & BOSCH
I AM A HUMAN BEING: DO NOT FOLD, SPINDLE OR MUTILATE
⌘C ⌘V
MAKING WORK TO LEARN FROM vs. MAKING WORK TO EARN FROM
USE CONTRACEPTIVES
TAKE THE WORRY OUT OF BEING CLOSE
ART MAKING vs. ART DIRECTING

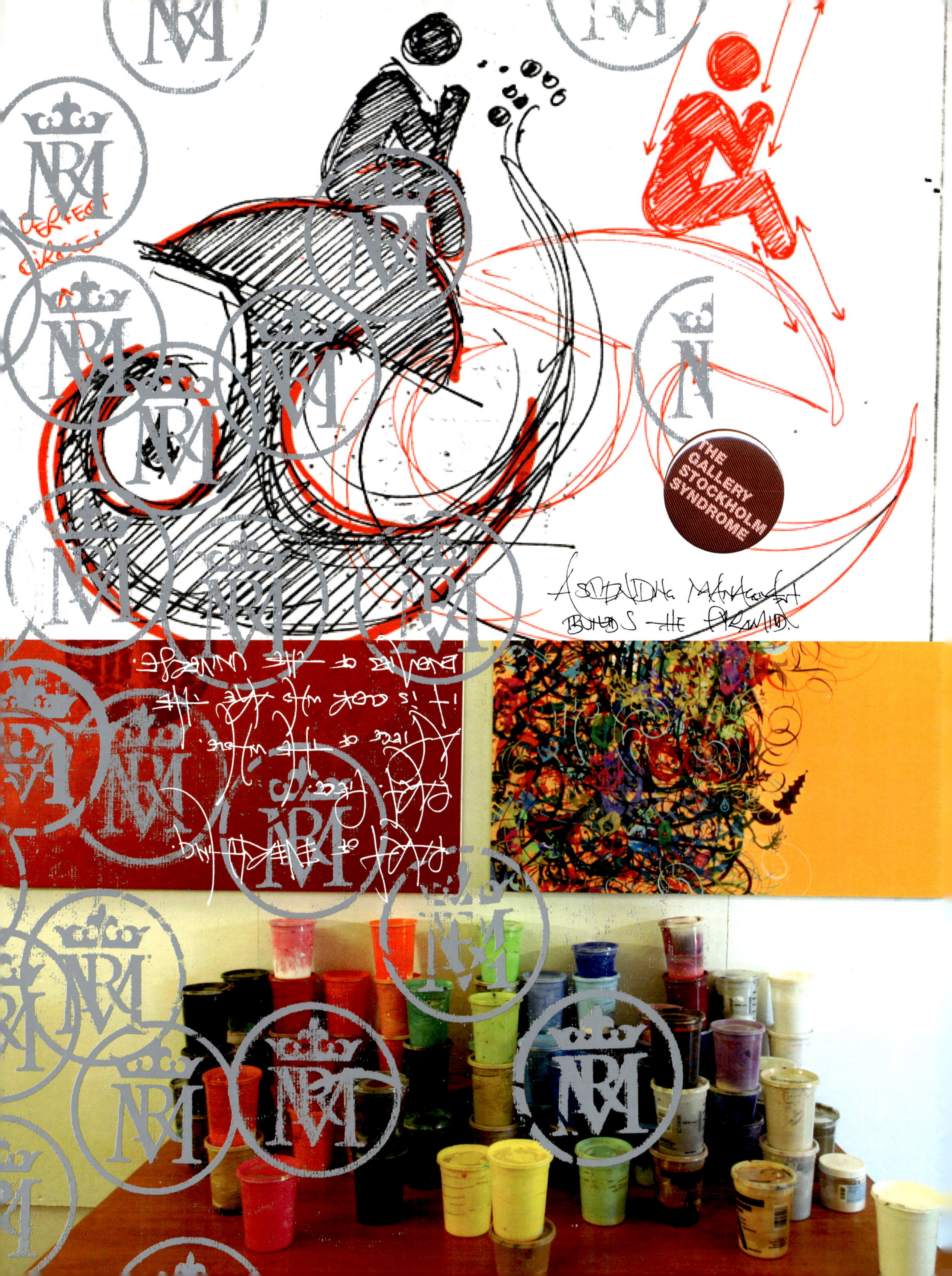
THE GALLERY STOCKHOLM SYNDROME
ASCENDING MANAGEMENT BUILDS THE PYRAMID.

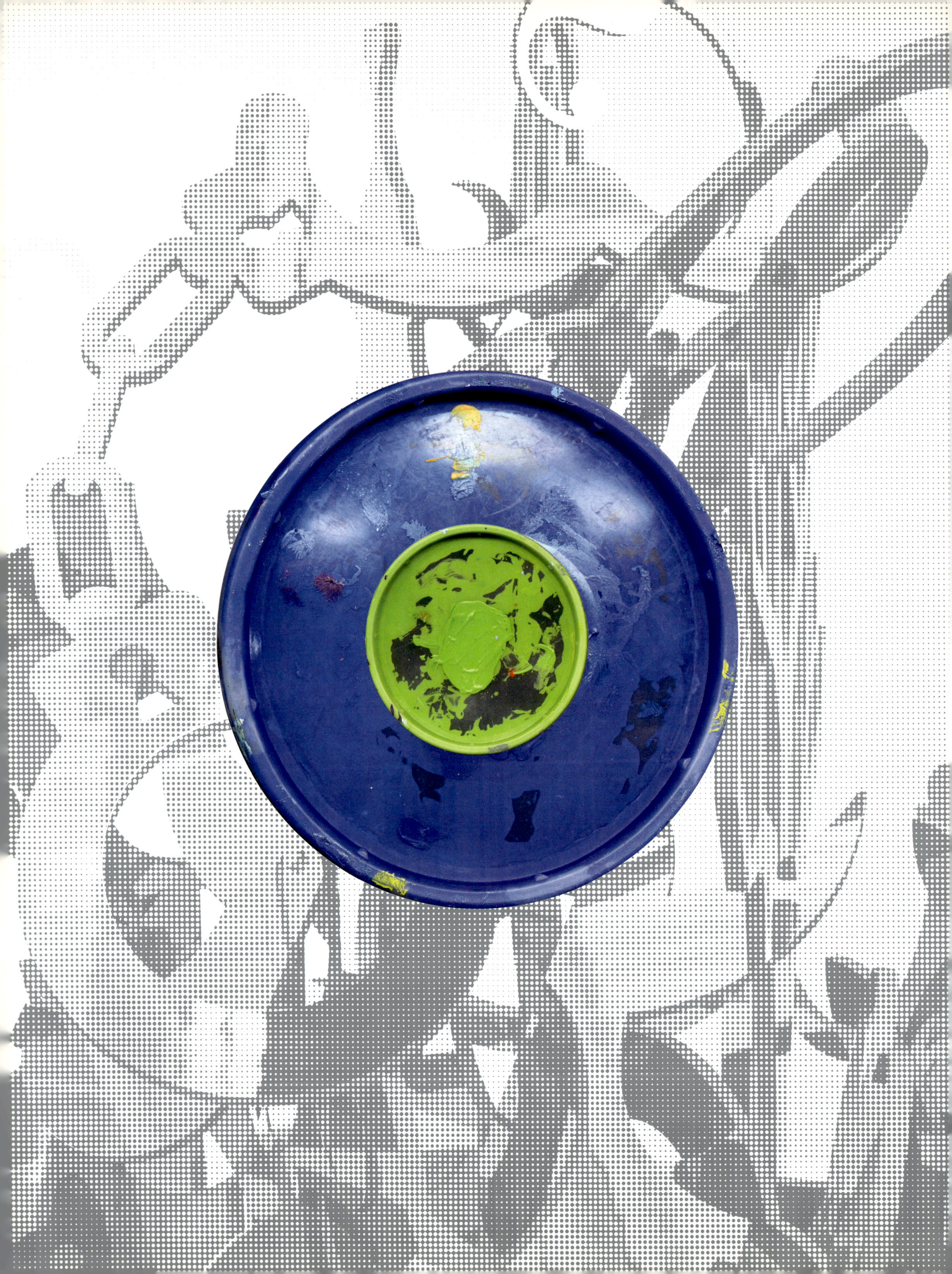

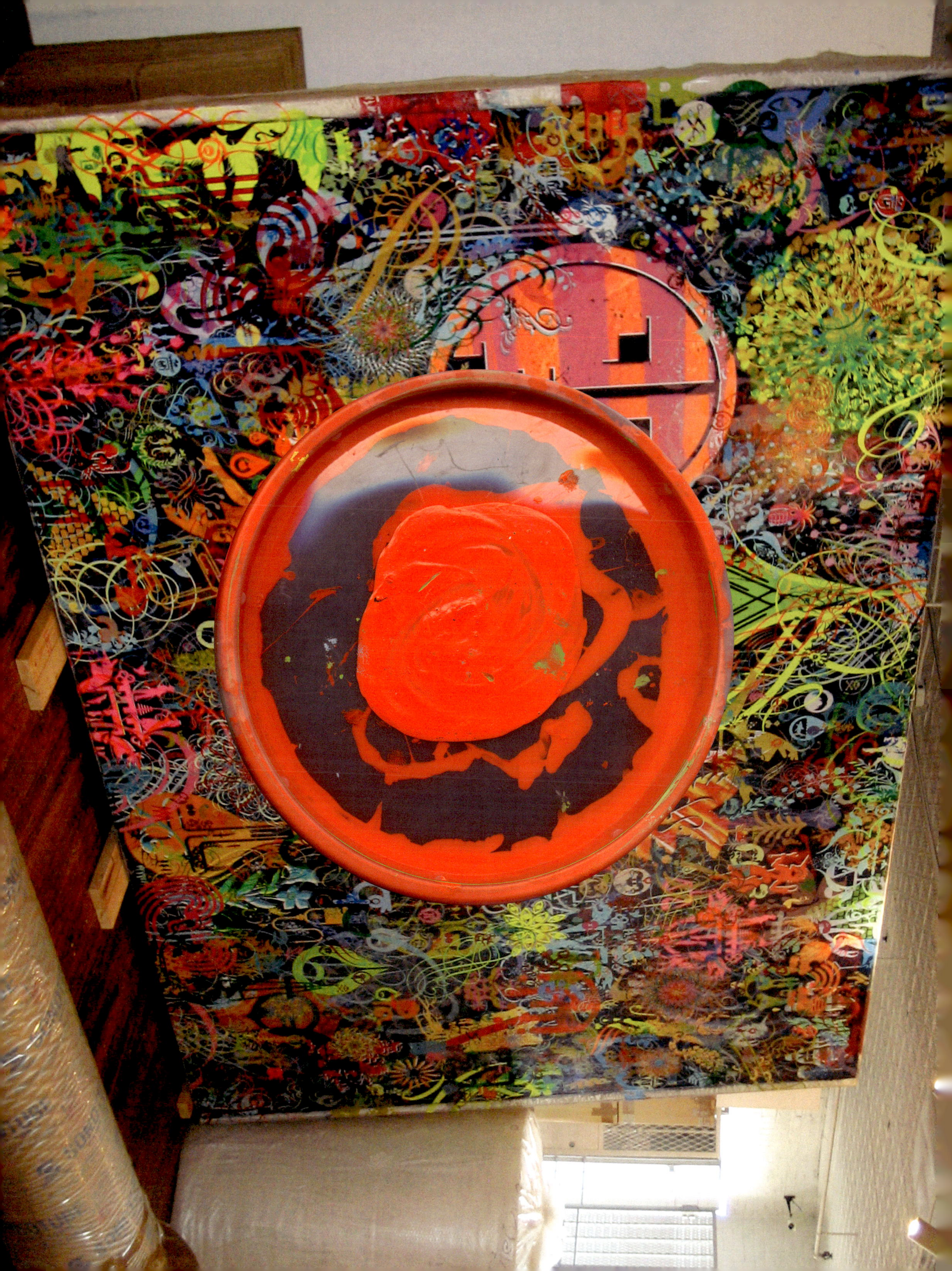

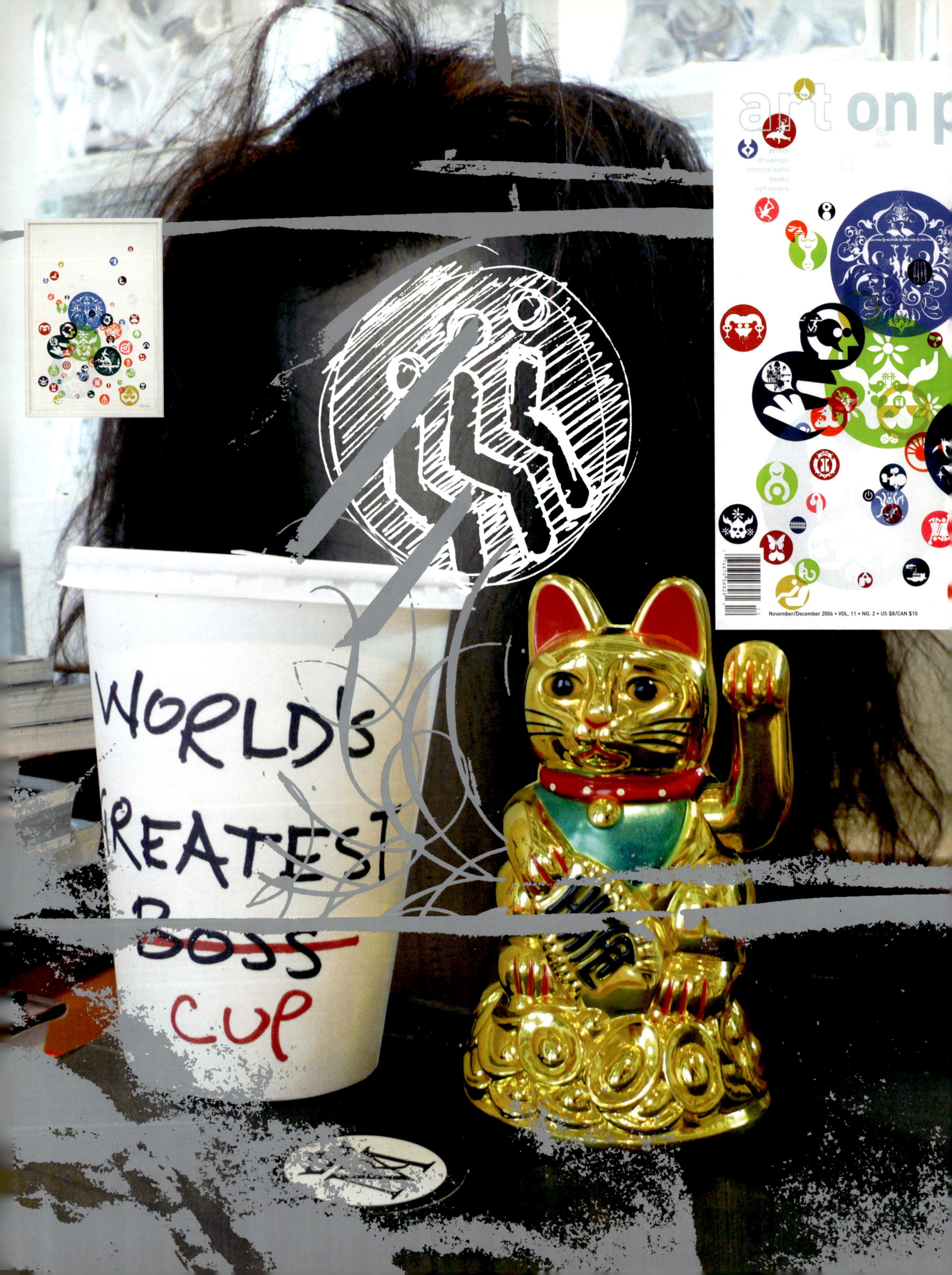
art on p
prints
drawings
photographs
books
ephemera
November/December 2006 • VOL. 11 • NO. 2 • US $8/CAN $10
WORLD'S
GREATEST
BOSS
CUP

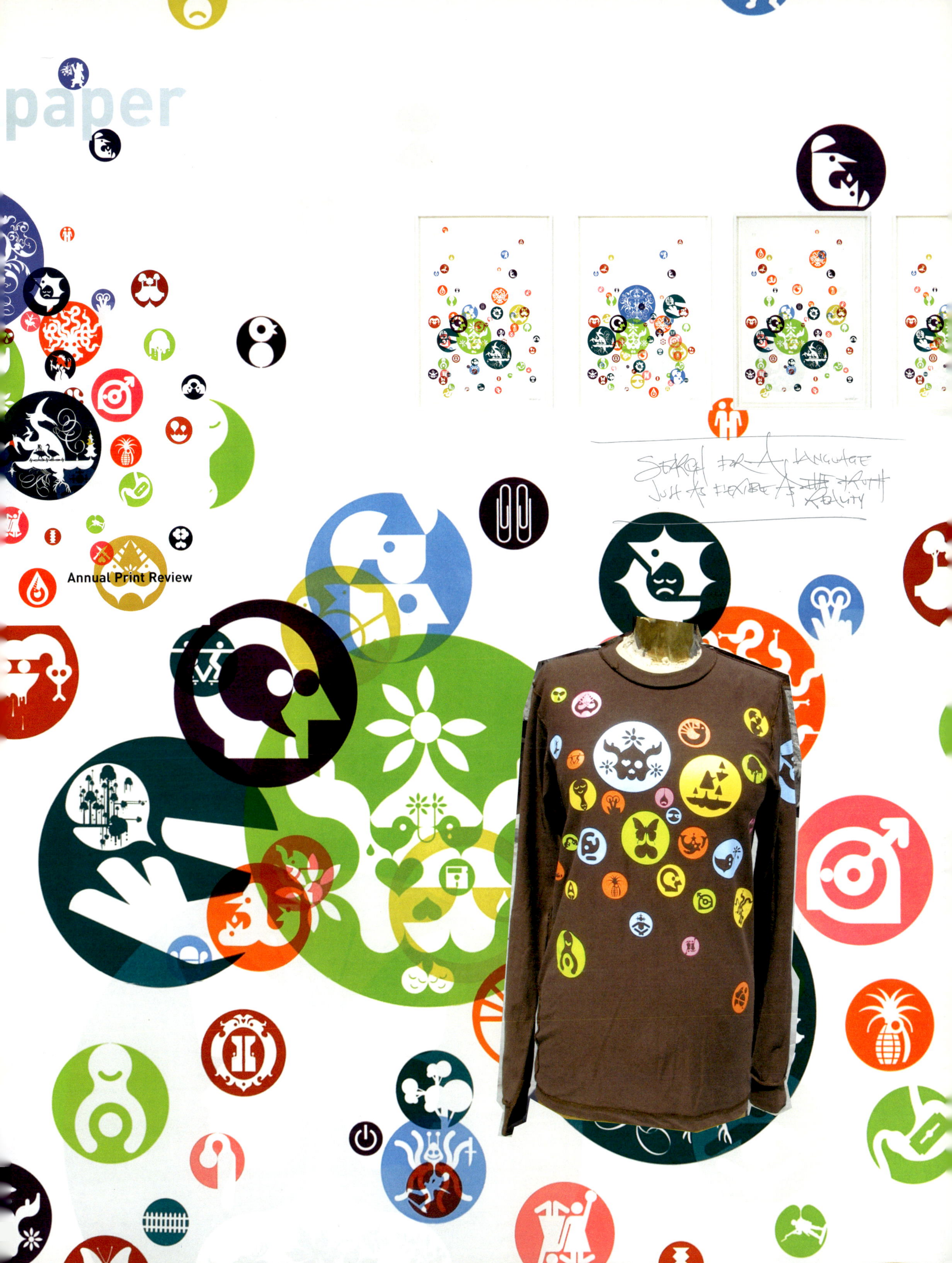
paper
Annual Print Review
SEARCH FOR A LANGUAGE
JUST AS FLEXIBLE AS THE TRUTH REALITY

Color Palette

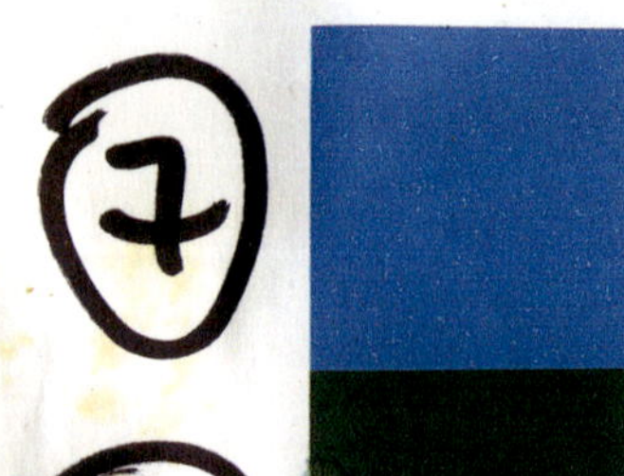
Bright Blue: Pantone 299

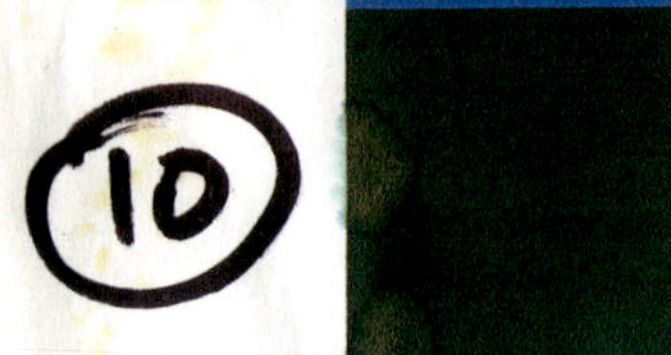
Dark Green: Pantone 343

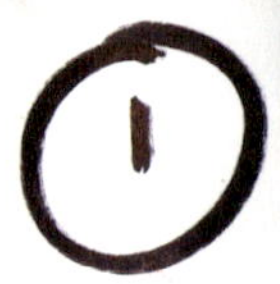
Light Blue: Pantone 277

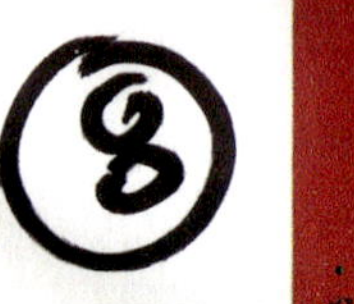
Maroon: Pantone 209

Lime Green: Pantone 382

Orange: Pantone 021

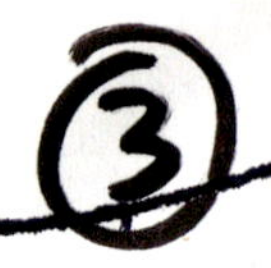
Hot Pink: Pantone 232

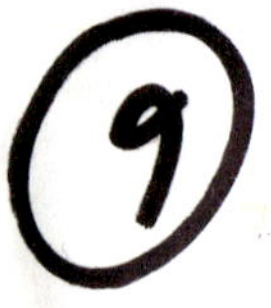
Purple: Pantone 266

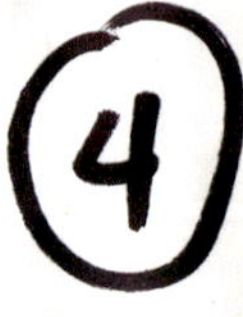
Dark Yellow: Pantone 110

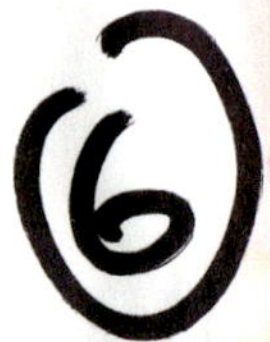
Red: Pantone 187

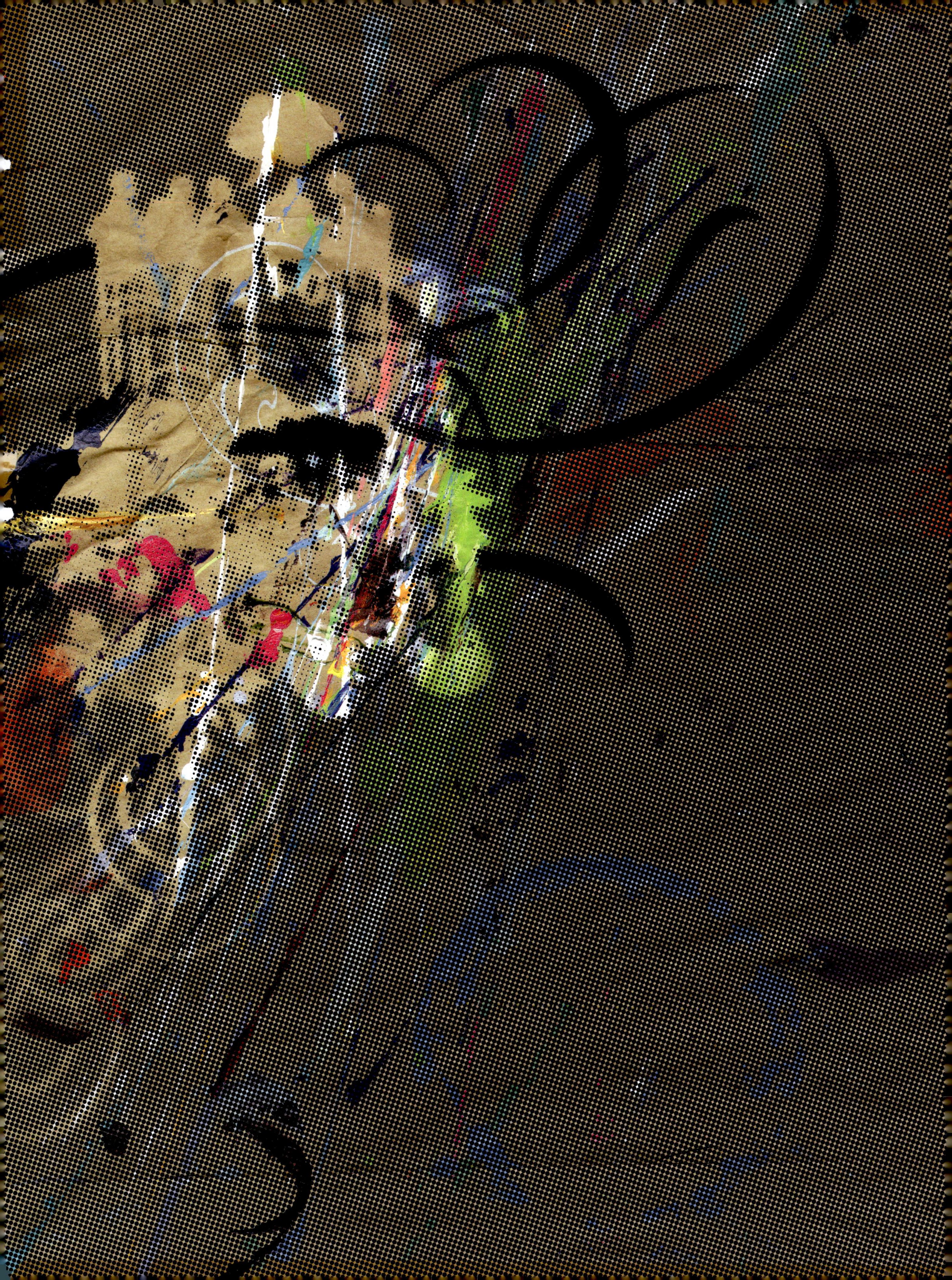

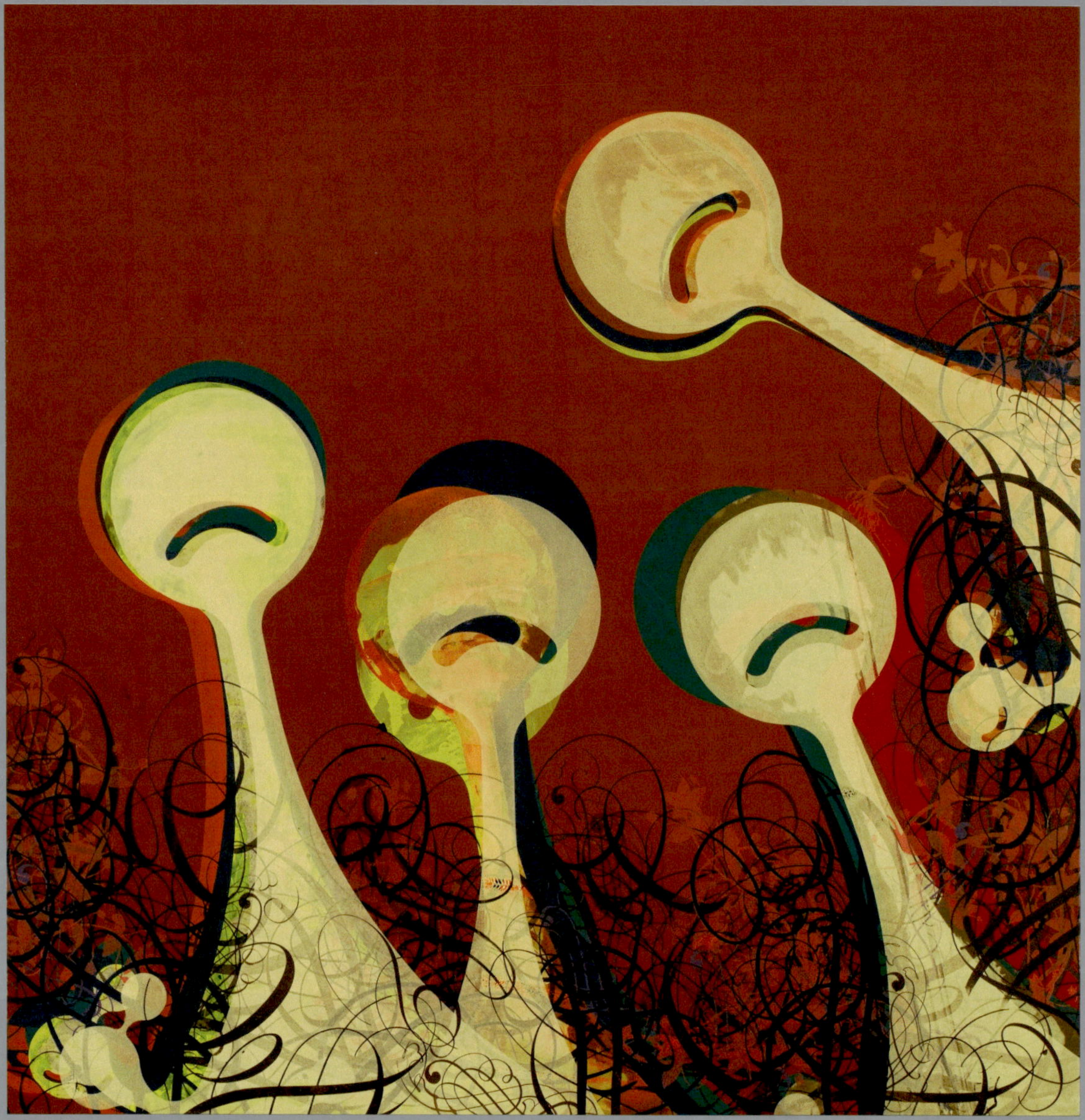

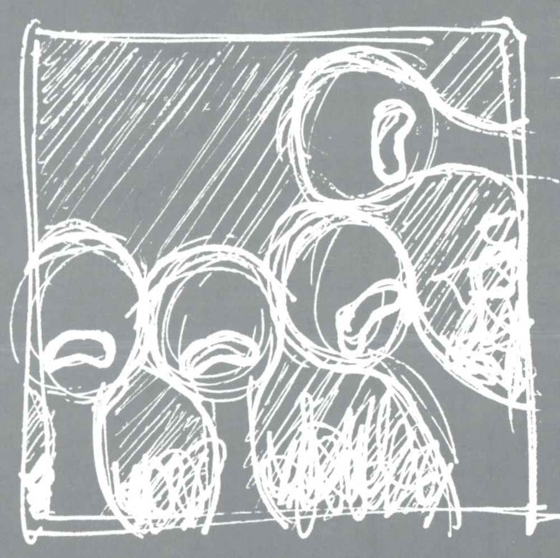

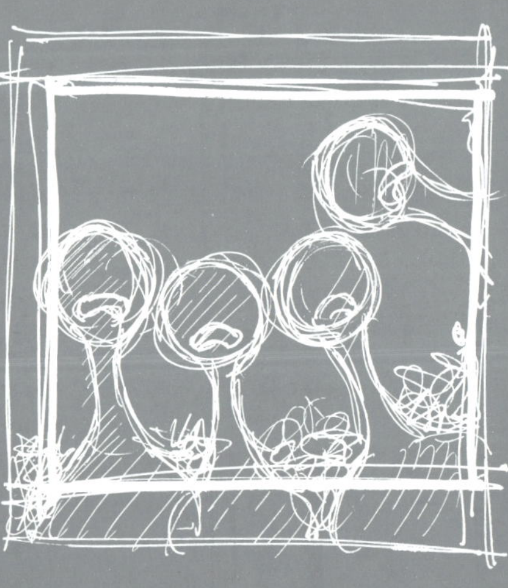

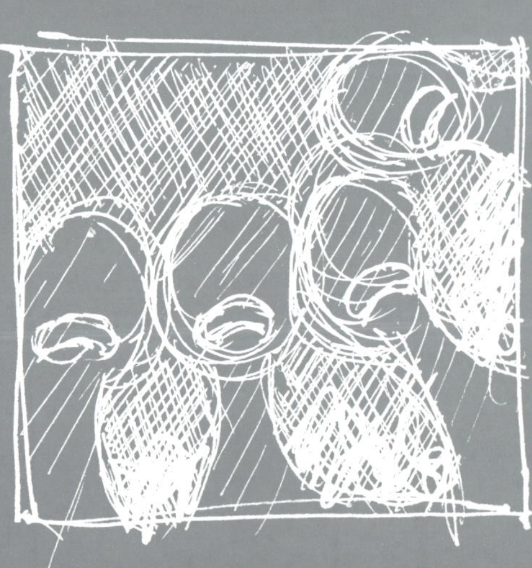

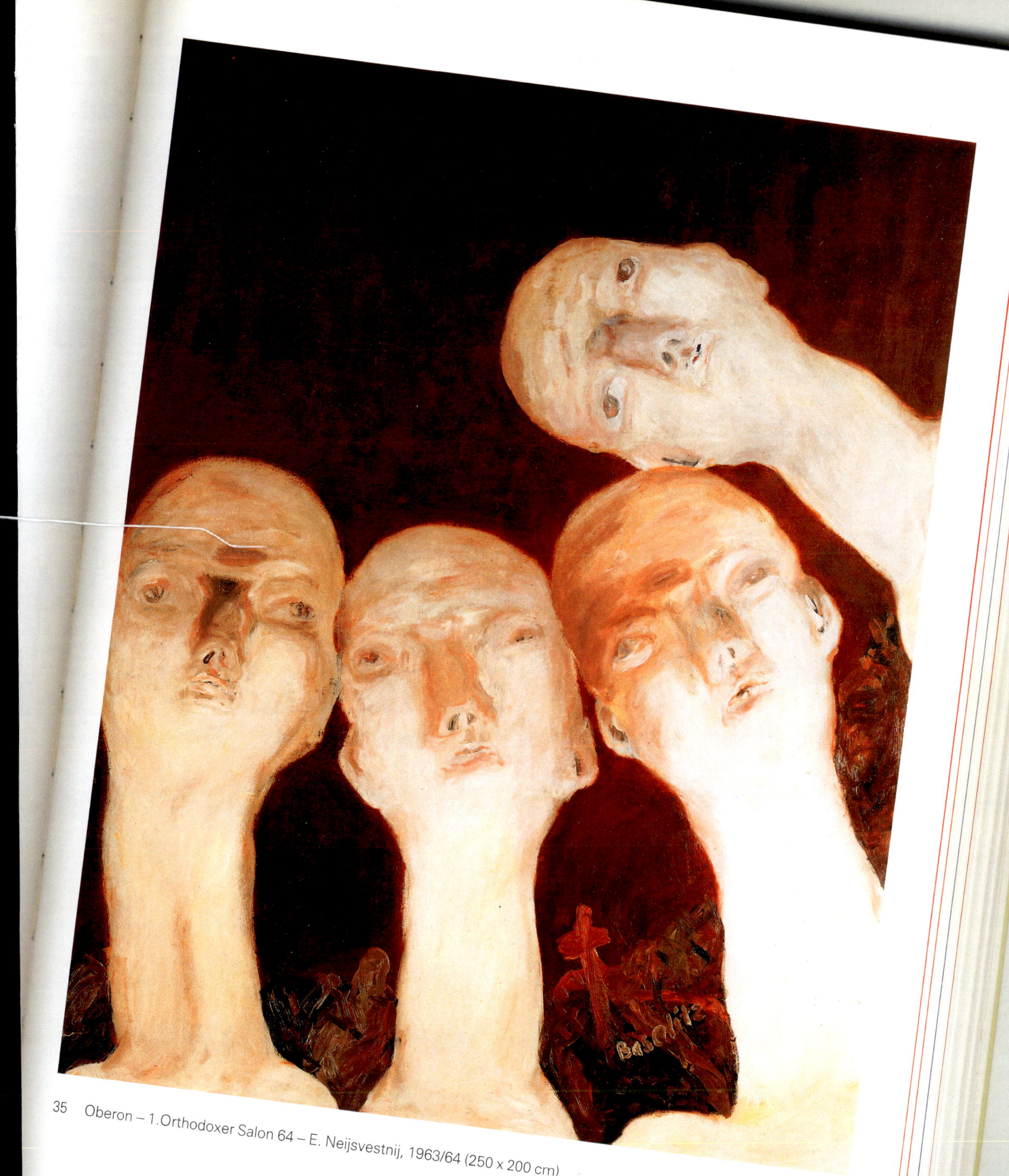

35 Oberon – 1.Orthodoxer Salon 64 – E. Neijsvestnij, 1963/64 (250 x 200 cm)

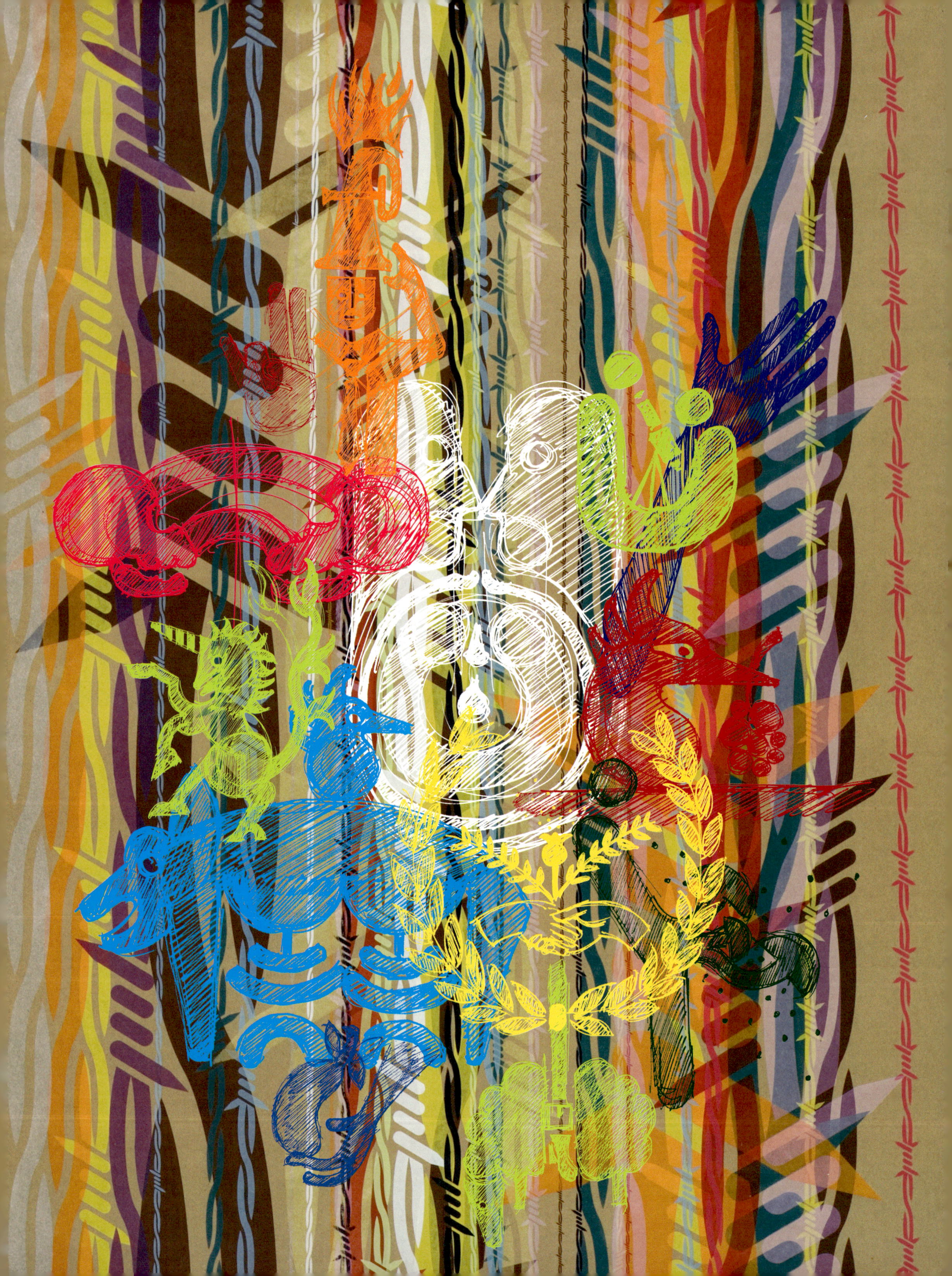

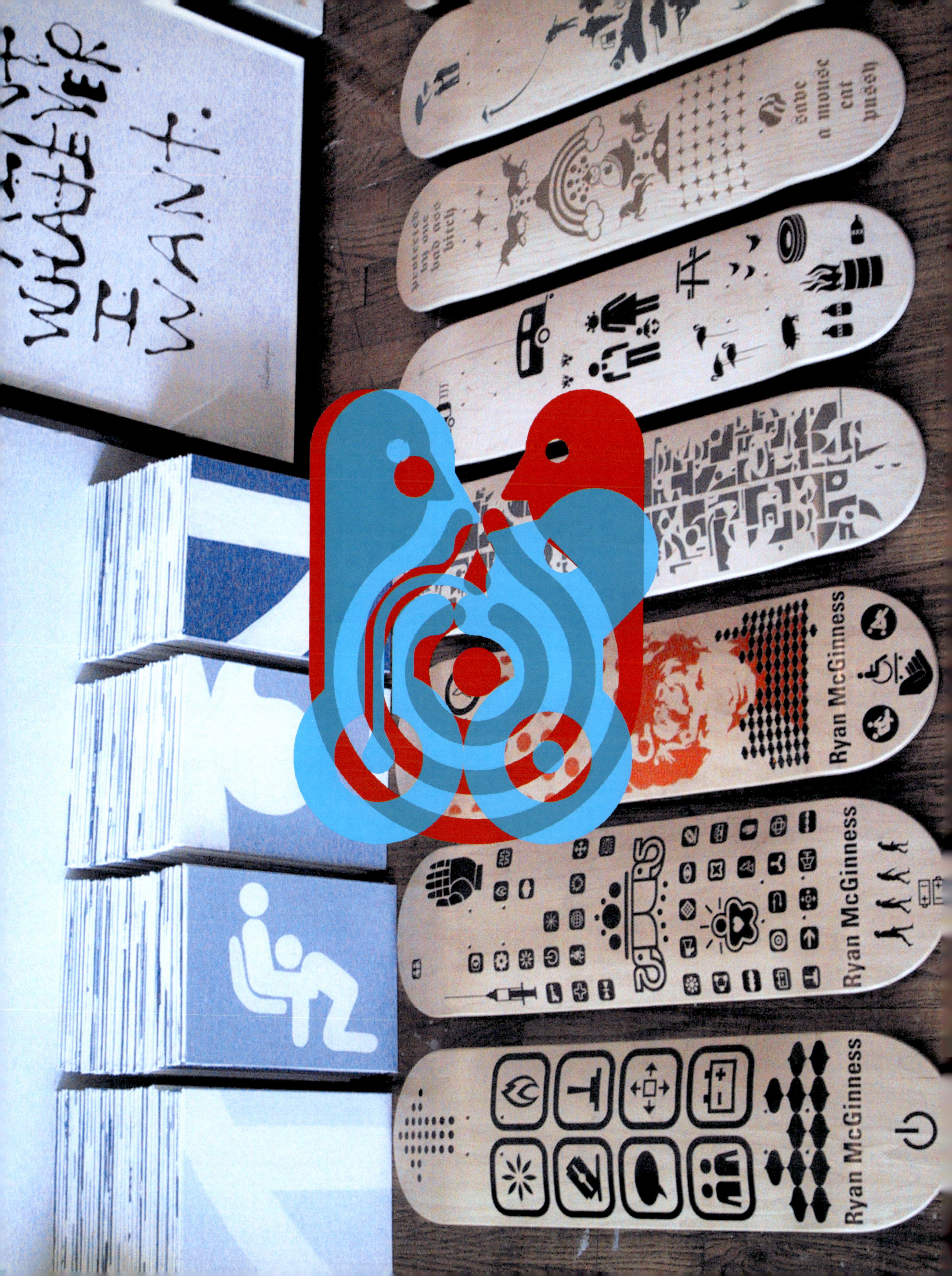
WHATEVER
I
WANT.
save
a mouse
eat
pussy
Ryan McGinness
Ryan McGinness
Ryan McGinness

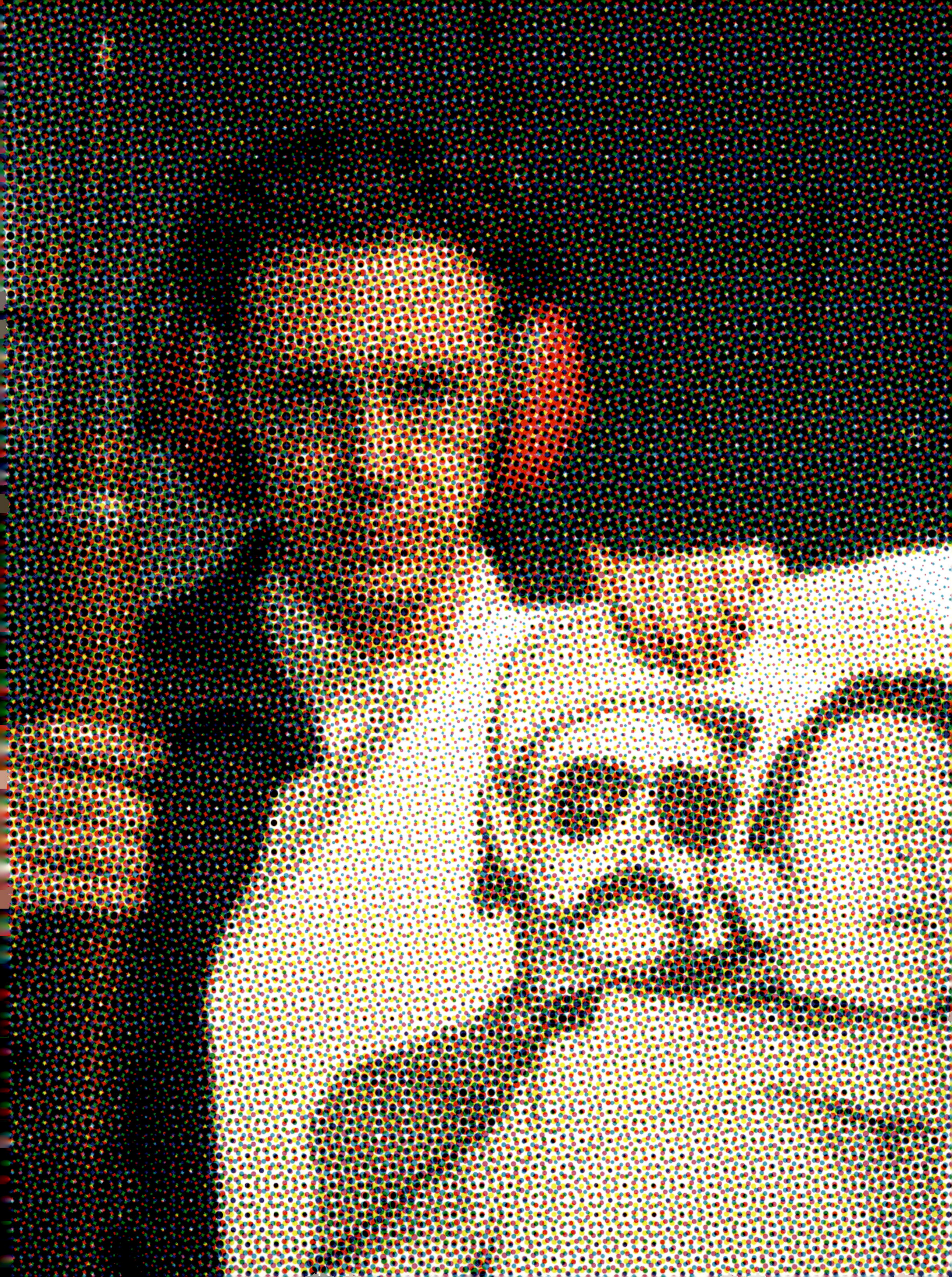

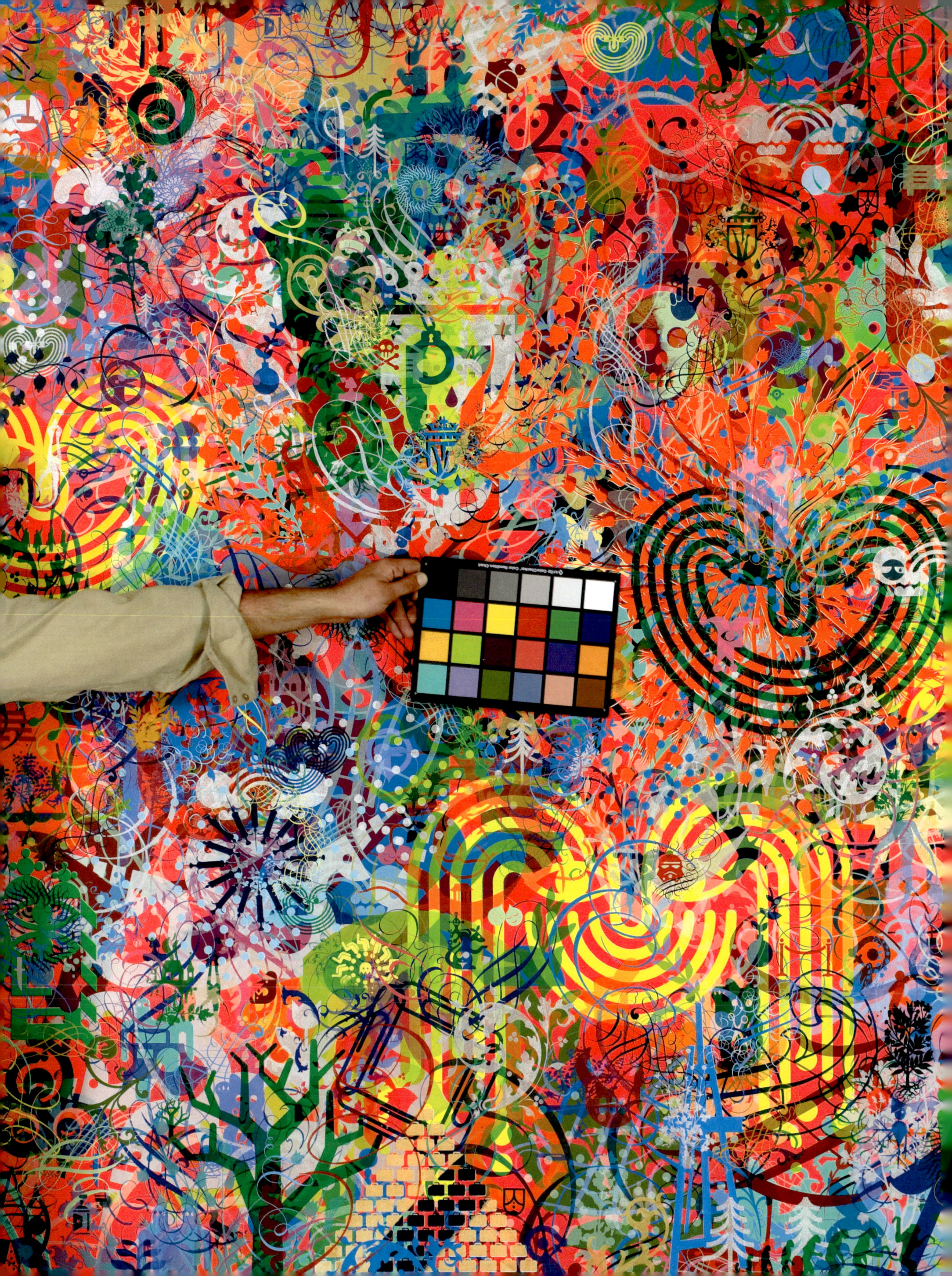

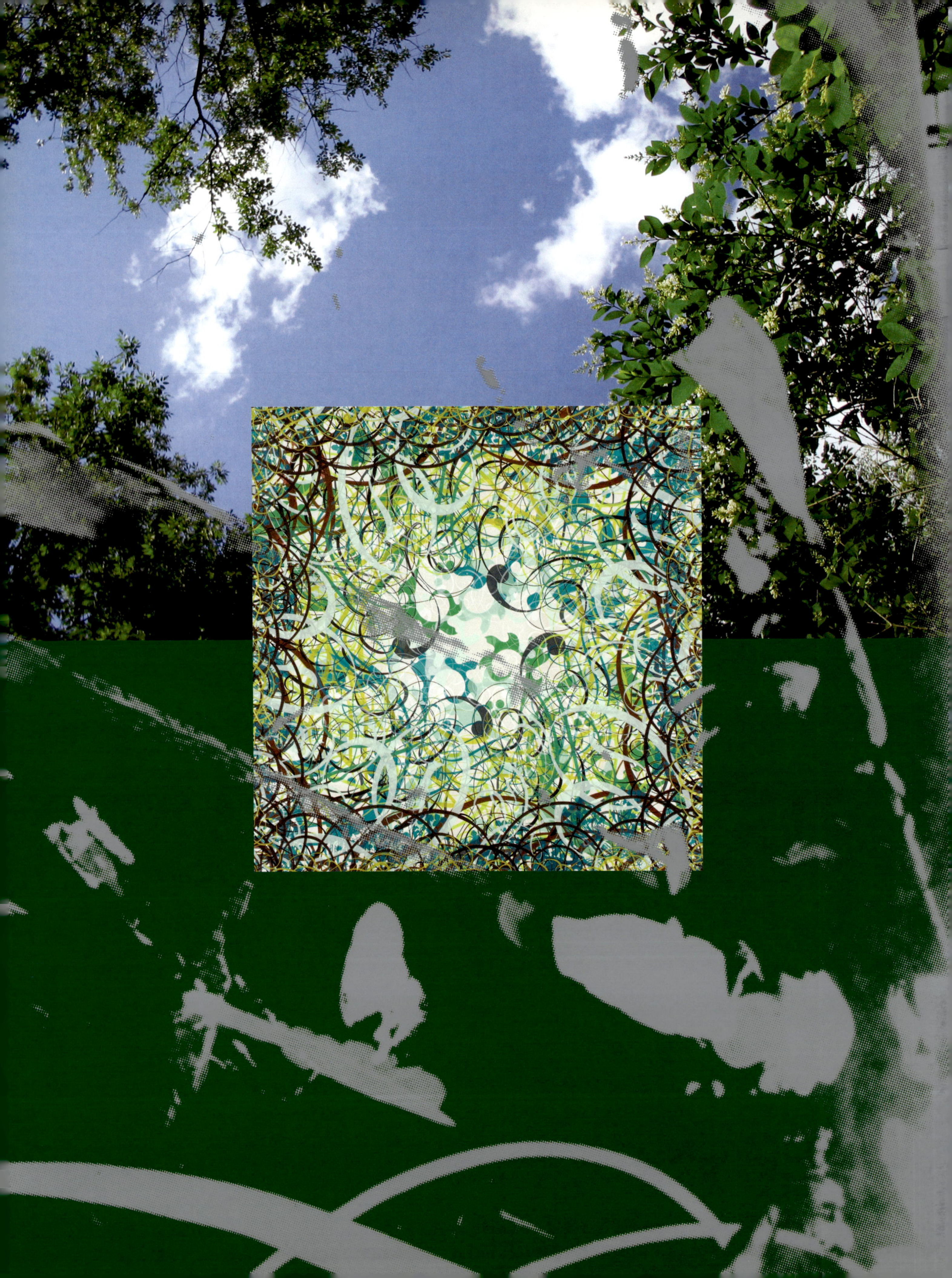

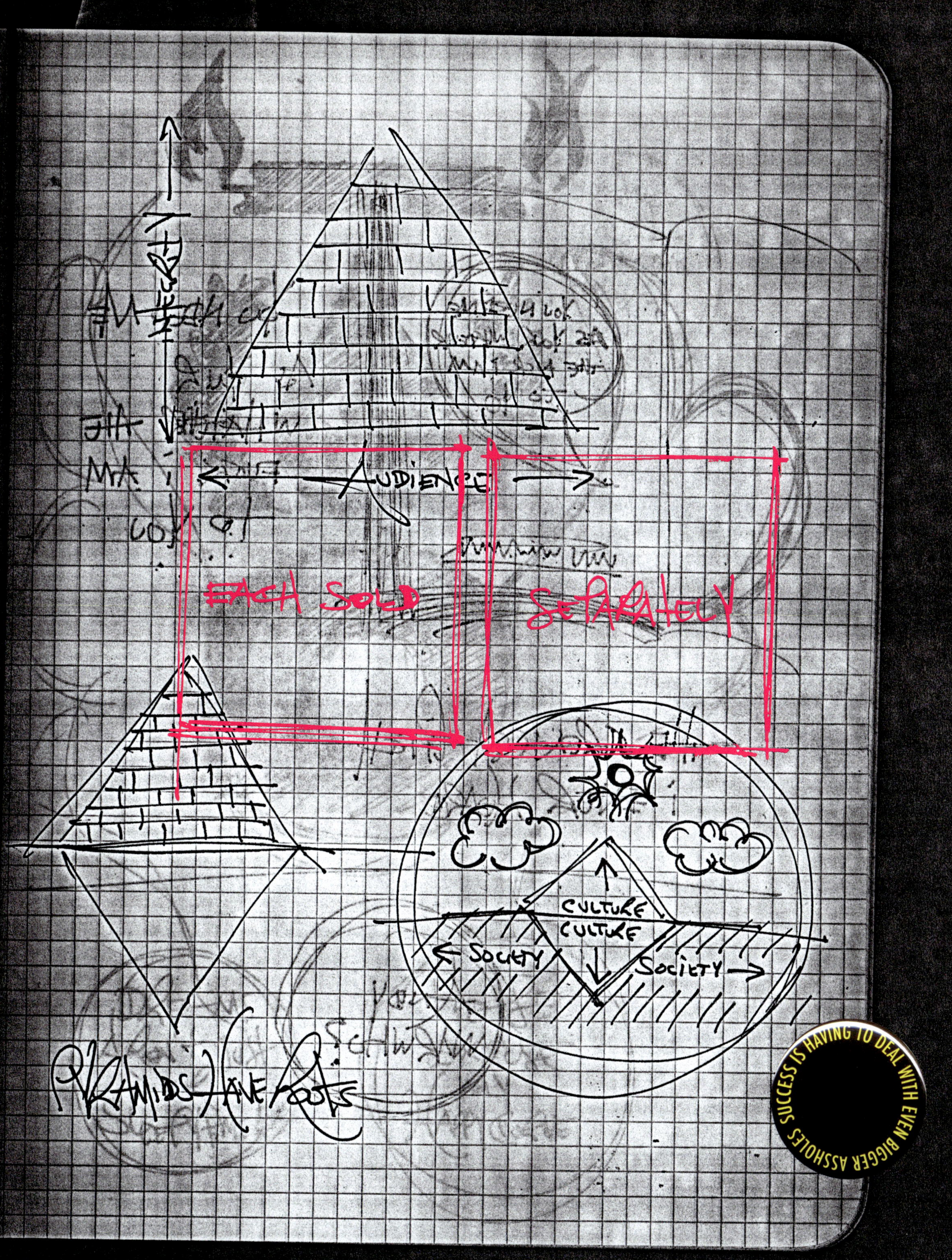
AUDIENCE
EACH SOLD
SEPARATELY
CULTURE
CULTURE
SOCIETY
SOCIETY
PYRAMIDS HAVE ROOTS
SUCCESS IS HAVING TO DEAL WITH EVEN BIGGER ASSHOLES

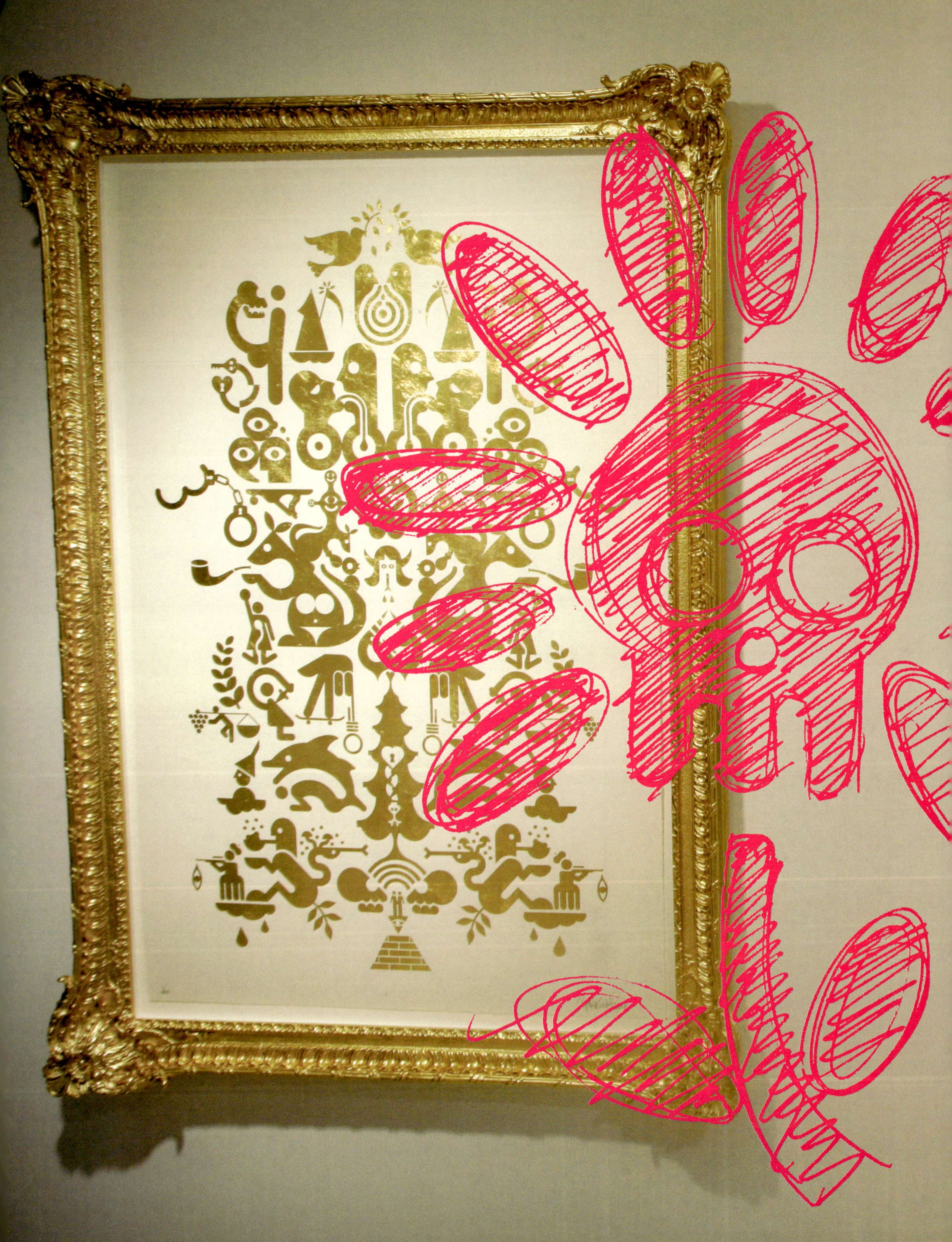

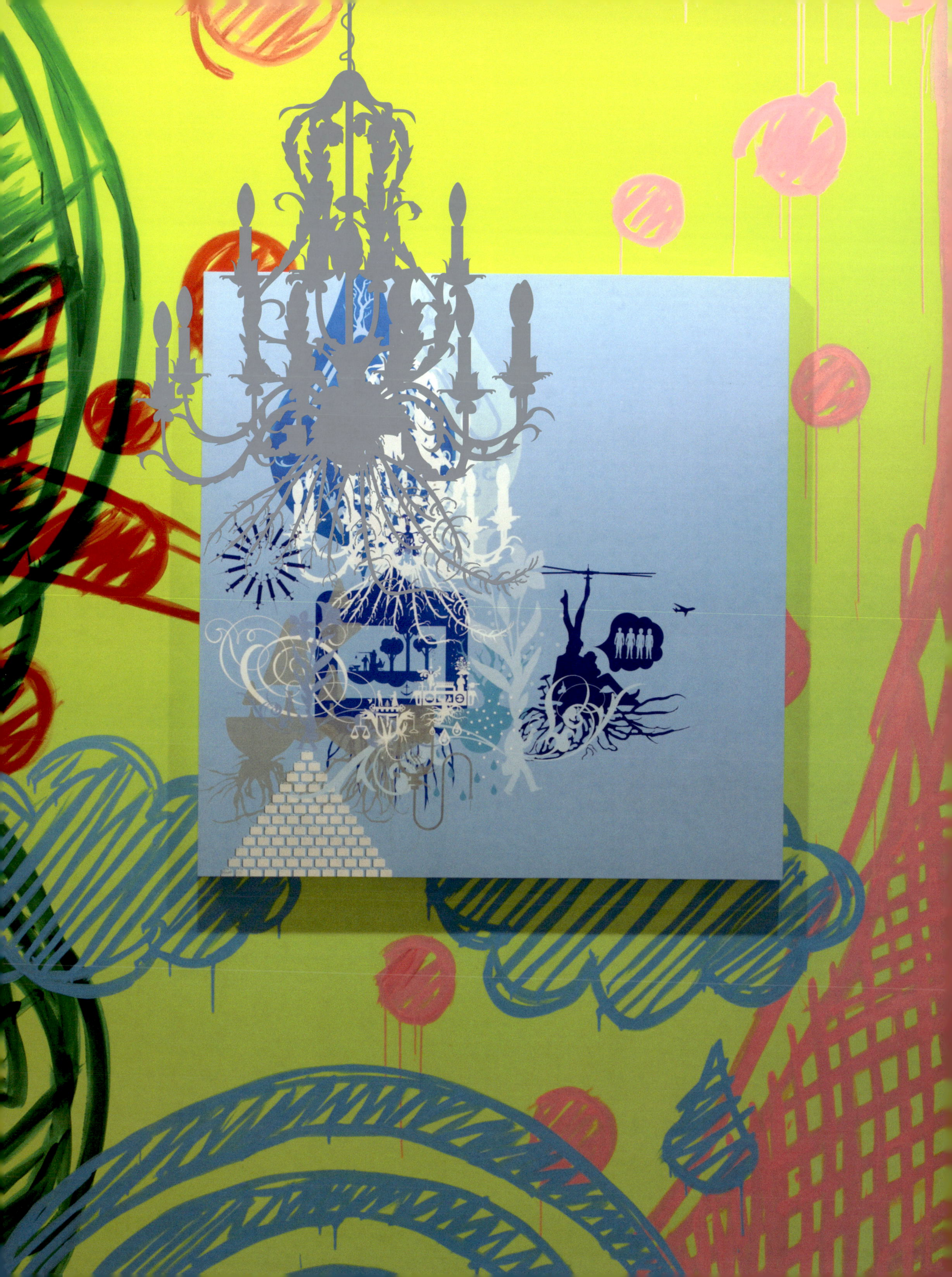

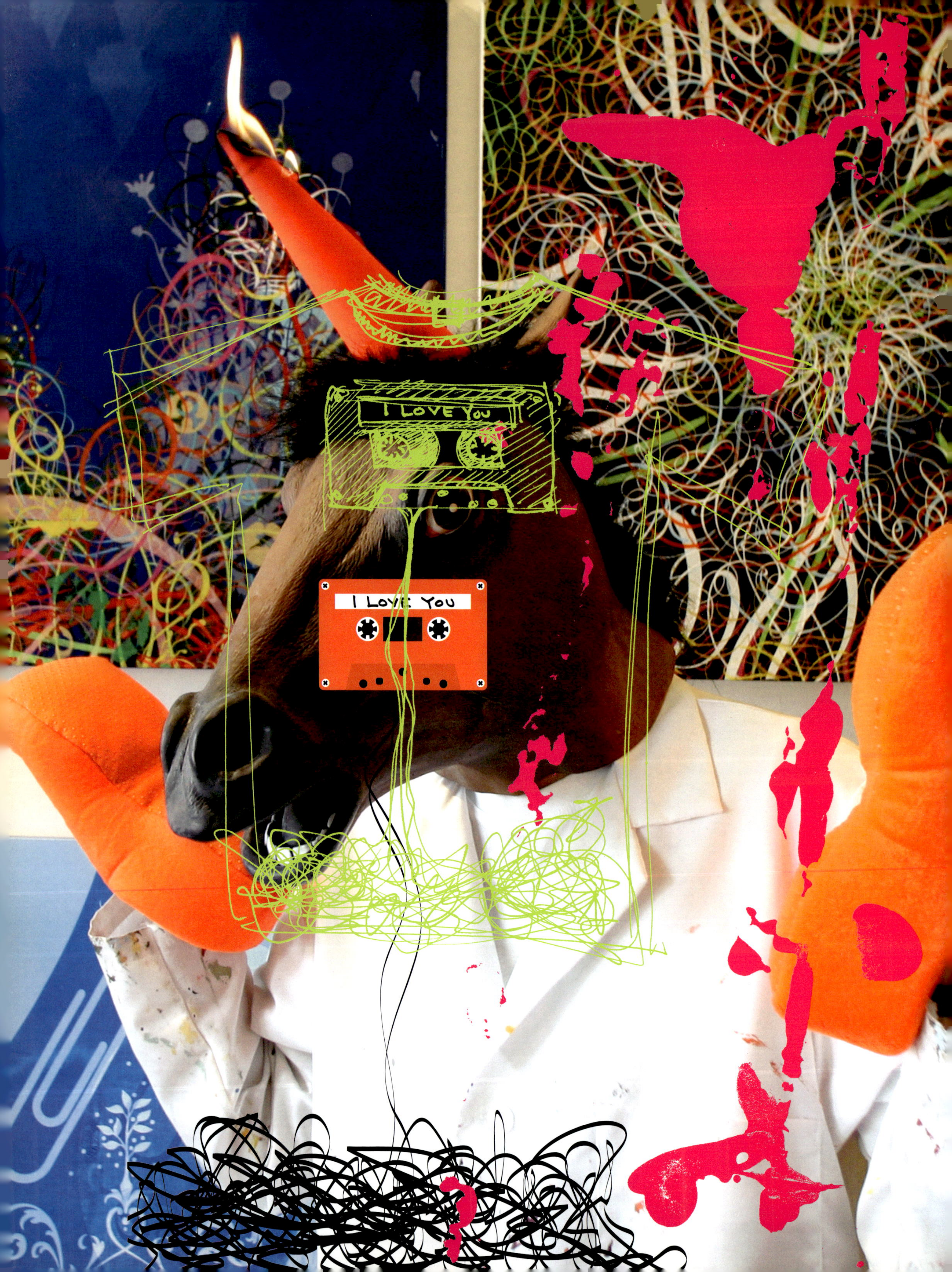
I LOVE YOU
I LOVE YOU

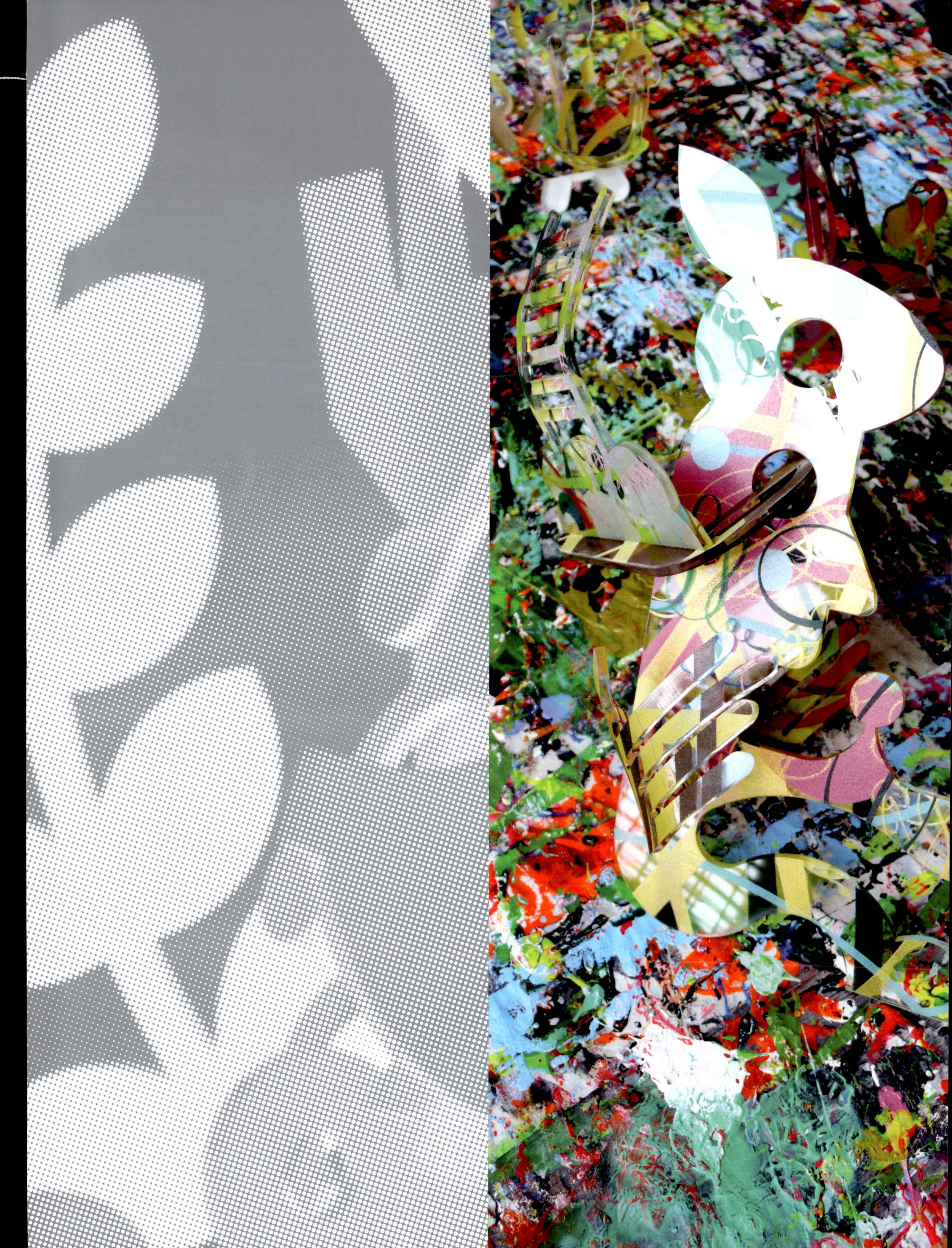

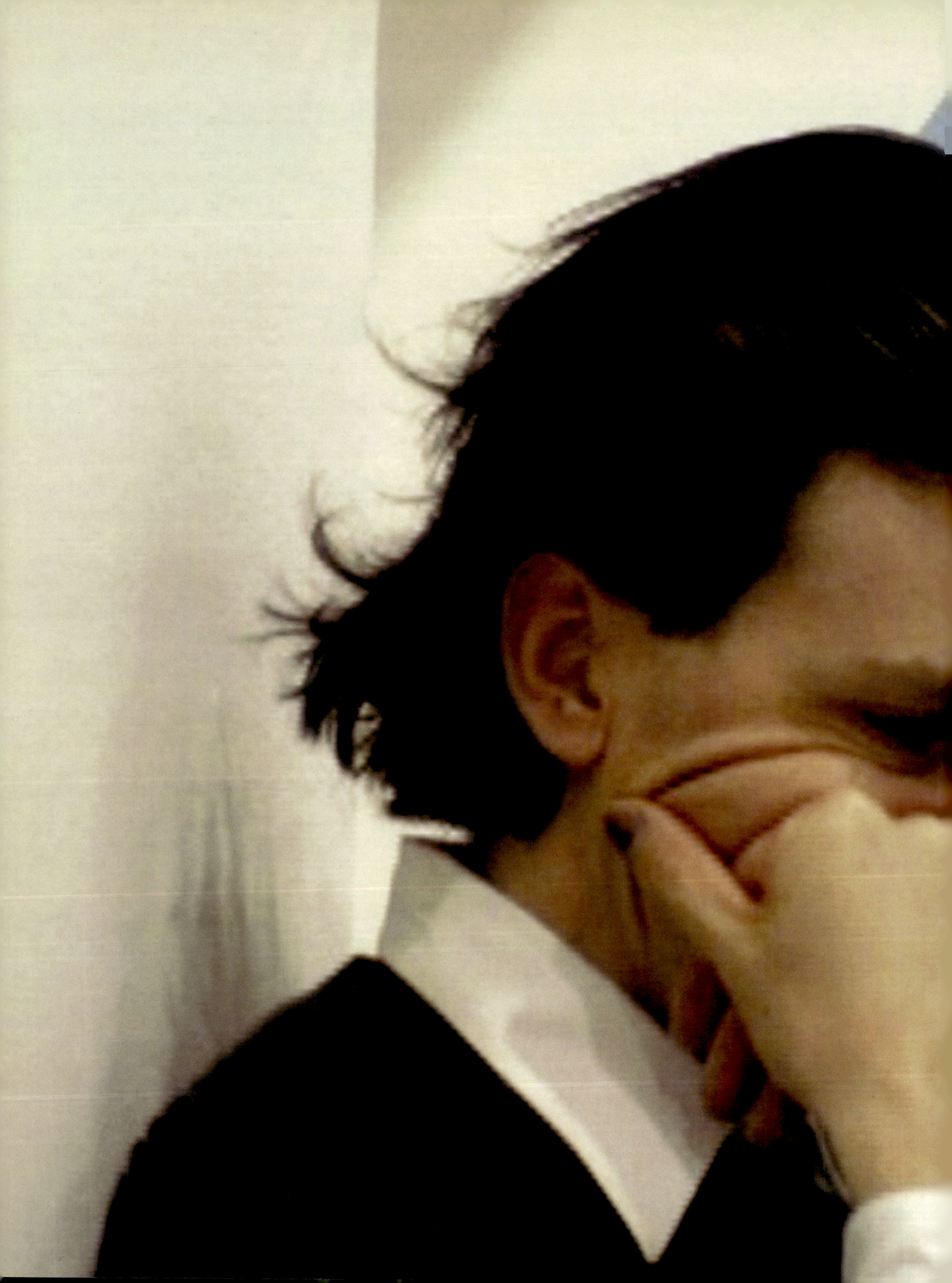

"The thumbnail process
sketches I make for each
drawing want to be folde
into the final work…I us
go through a process of
sketching, drawing, refi
tweaking, and that is no
starting to collapse.
I think it is the result
me not being able to get
drawings out of me fast
for my own satisfaction.
Perhaps McGinness is in
hurry after all.
Jonathan T. D. Neil

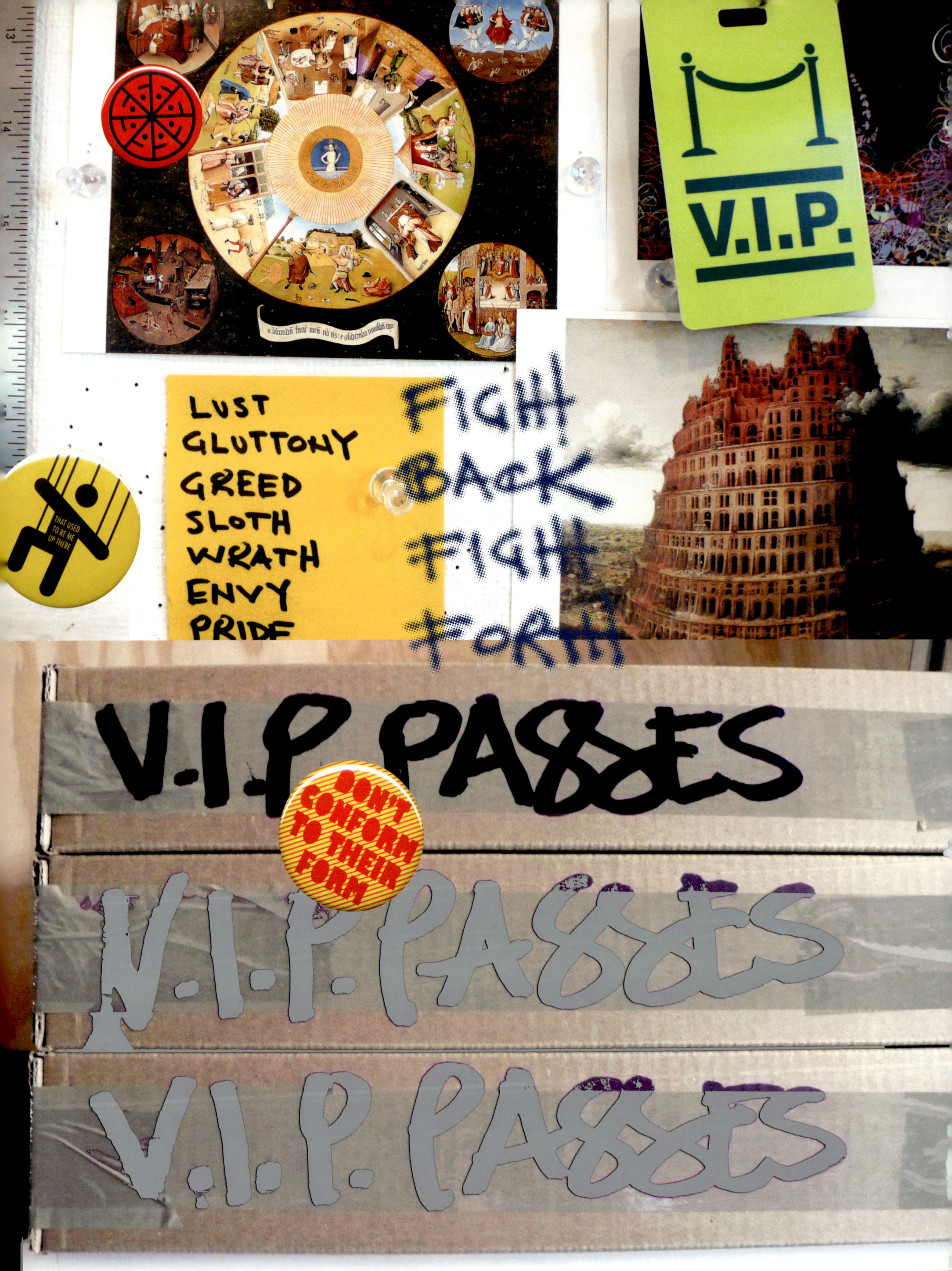
V.I.P.
LUST
GLUTTONY
GREED
SLOTH
WRATH
ENVY
PRIDE
FIGHT
BACK
FIGHT
FORM
THAT USED TO BE ME UP THERE
V.I.P. PASSES
DON'T CONFORM TO THEIR FORM
V.I.P. PASSES
V.I.P. PASSES

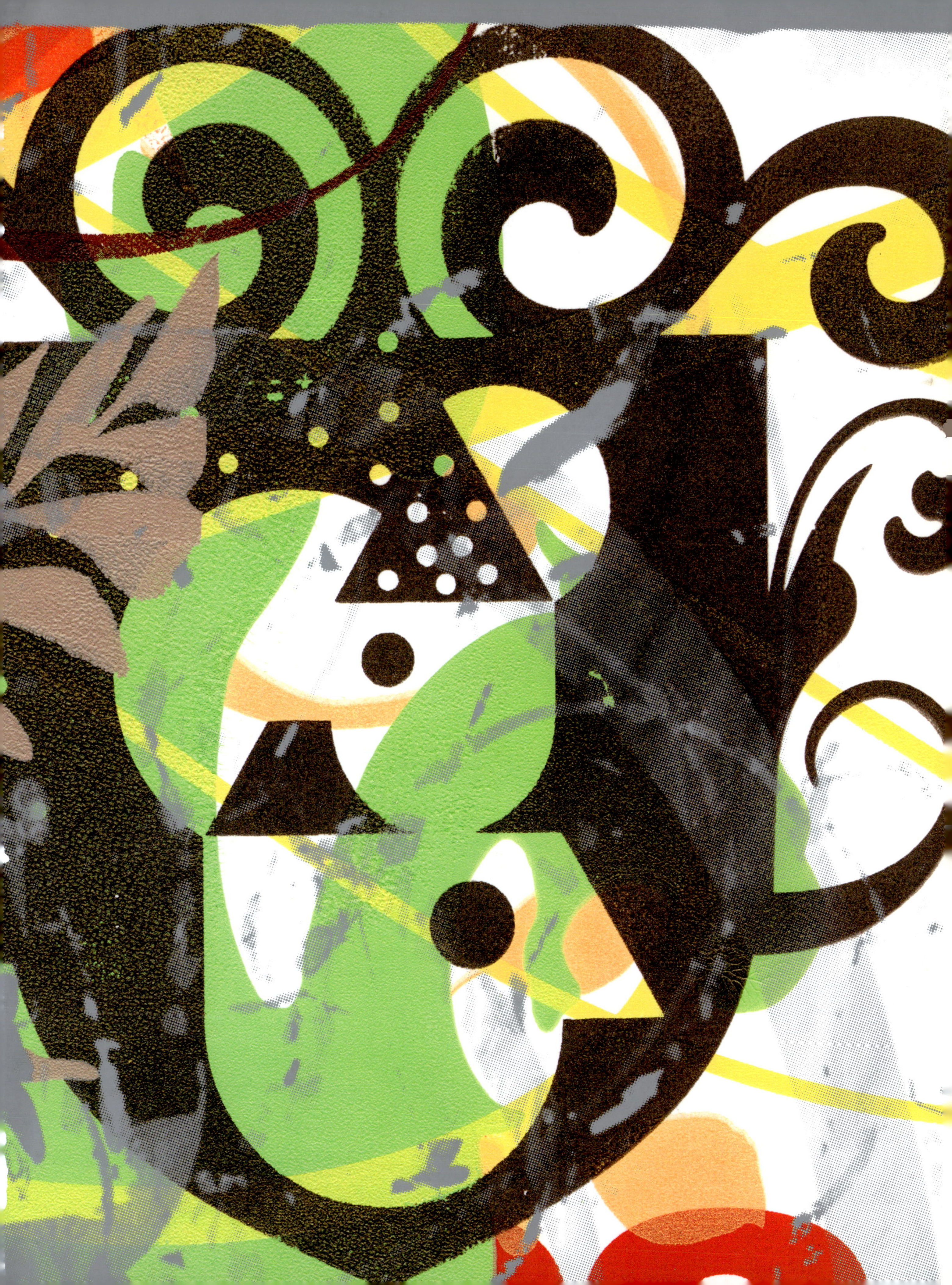

yan McGinness

hic Lush | 2004
nyl on painted aluminum panels
5 panels each 91.44 cm x 91.44 cm

yan McGinness, a highly prolific American artist who has
ad solo exhibitions around the world, has developed an
aborate visual language based on graphic icons. The
mbols for universal communication he manipulates derive
om recognizable slices of popular culture. Their layered
rganization on the slick, almost industrially manufactured
rfaces of his work offer open-ended narratives about
ontemporary consumer habits, values and appetites.
While some elements in this piece are taken directly
andardized visual language, such as the 'recycling
e round 'power on' emblem found on computers,
af symbol taken from this school's trademark, other
eated by the artist himself and suggest more complex, if
mbiguous, ideas. This work, sprinkled with graphic referen
business and Canadian culture, speaks about global issue
f diversity, environmental awareness and international
ommerce. These values are embraced by the Schulich Schoo
f Business for which the work was specially commissioned.

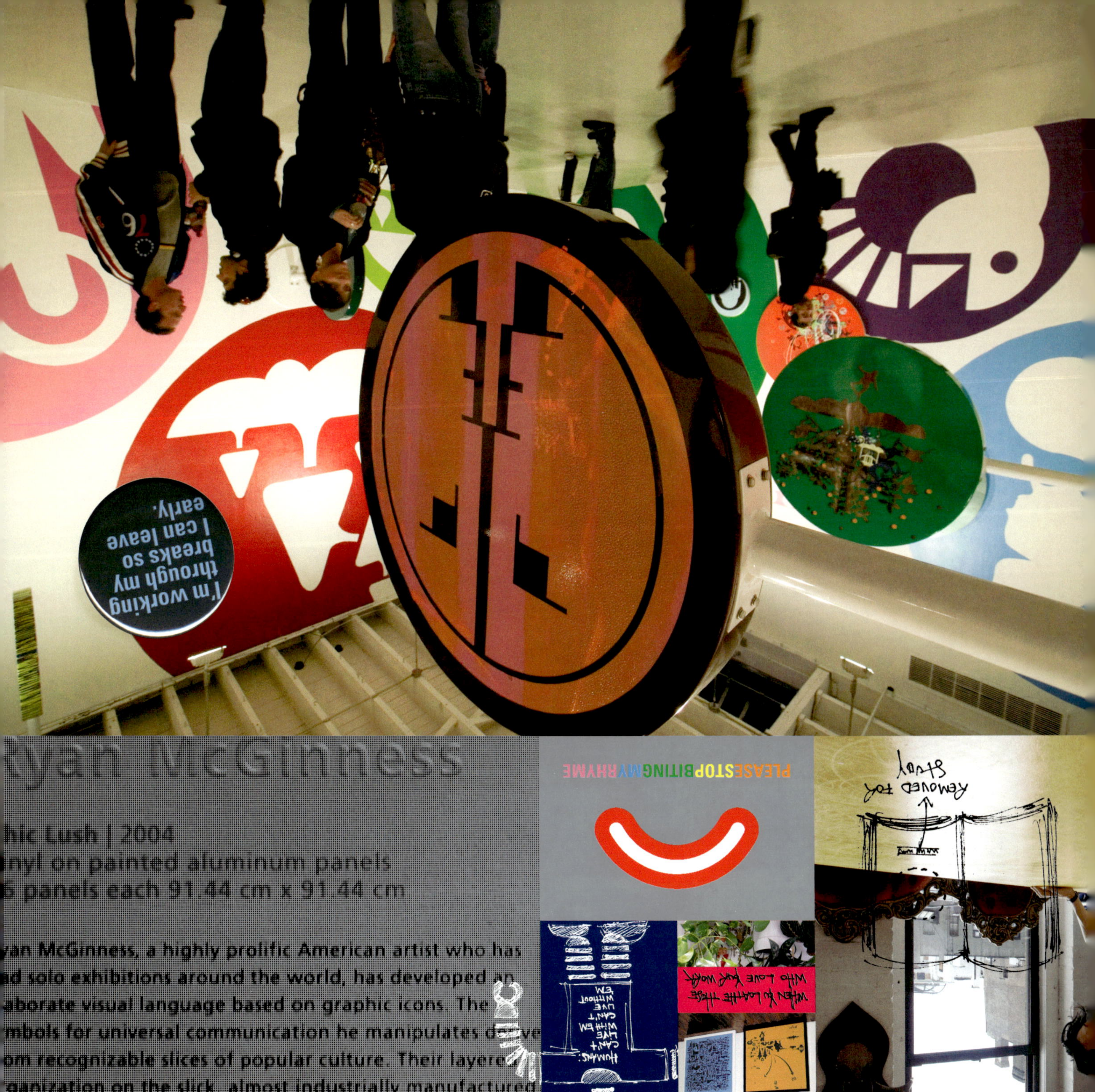

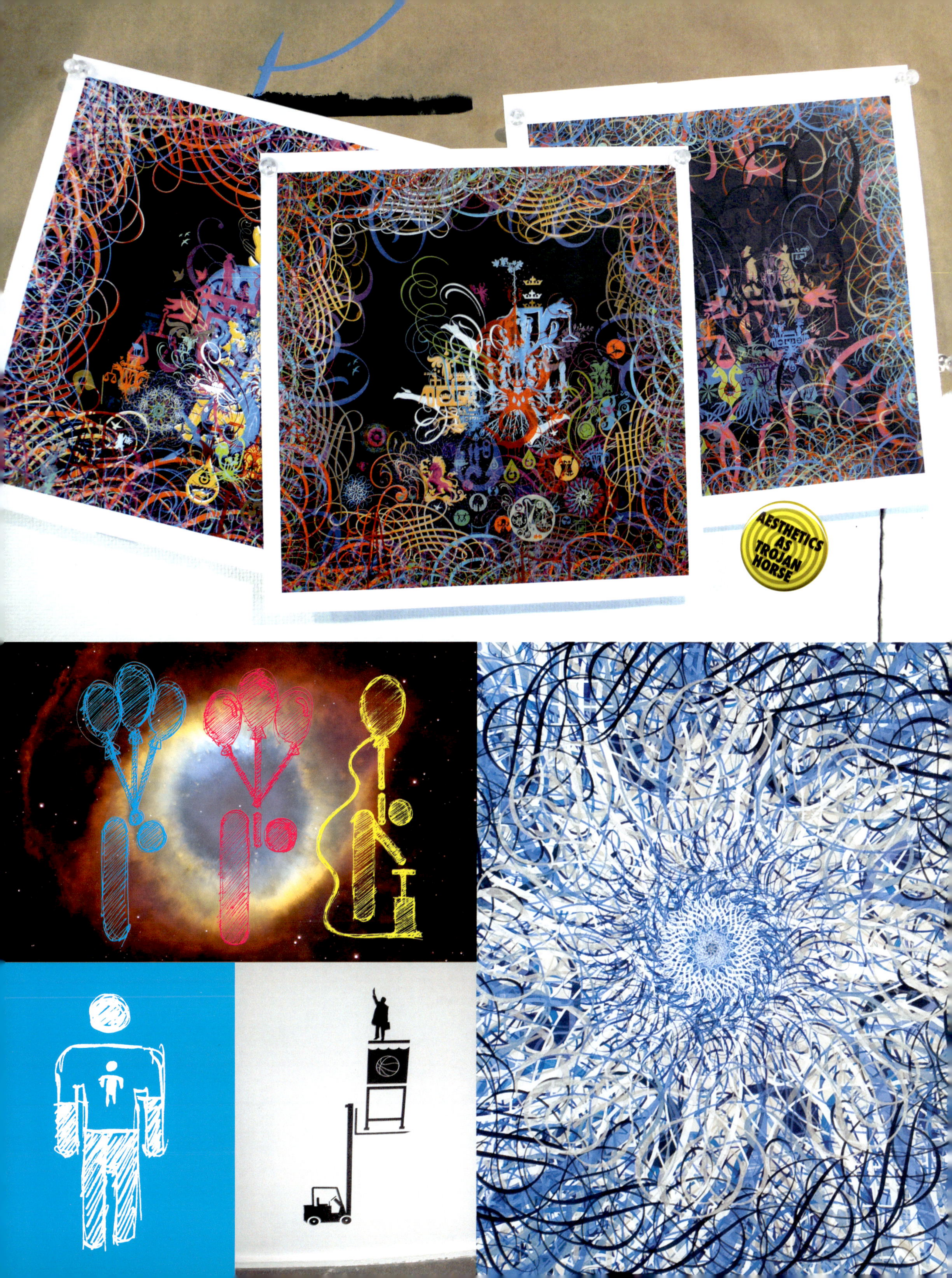
AESTHETICS
AS
TROJAN
HORSE

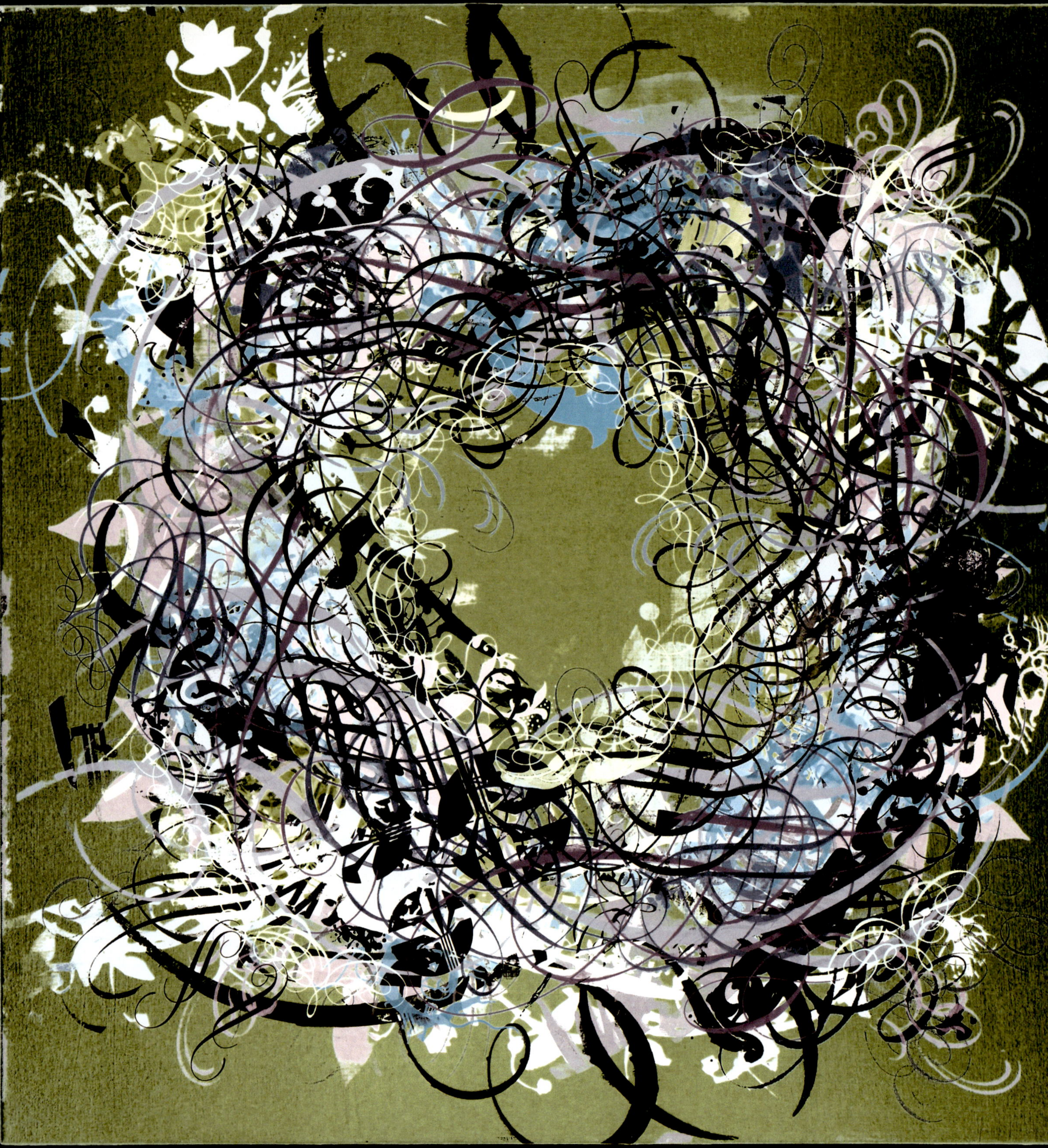

WHAT BUSINESS DOES SO-AND-SO HAVE DOING SUCH-AND-SUCH? I REALLY LIKE THE IDEA OF SOMEBODY NEEDING BUSINESS TO DO SOMETHING.

A GOOD PAINTING EXHIBITS SELF-EVIDENT REASONS FOR THE EXISTENCE OF EVERYTHING WITHIN ITS PICTURE PLANE

A GOOD PAINTING EXHIBITS SELF-EVIDENT REASONS FOR THE EXISTENCE OF EVERYTHING WITHIN ITS PICTURE PLANE

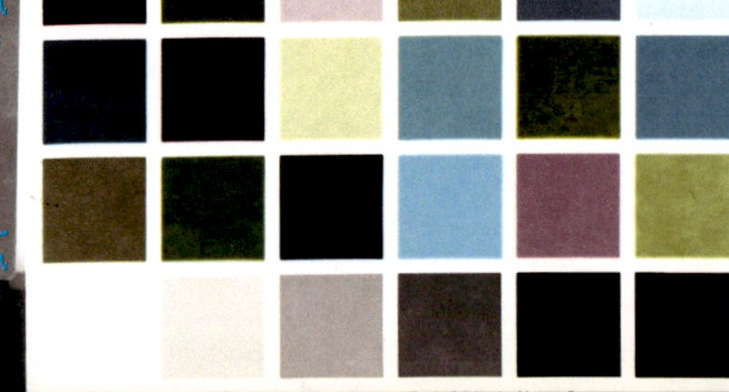

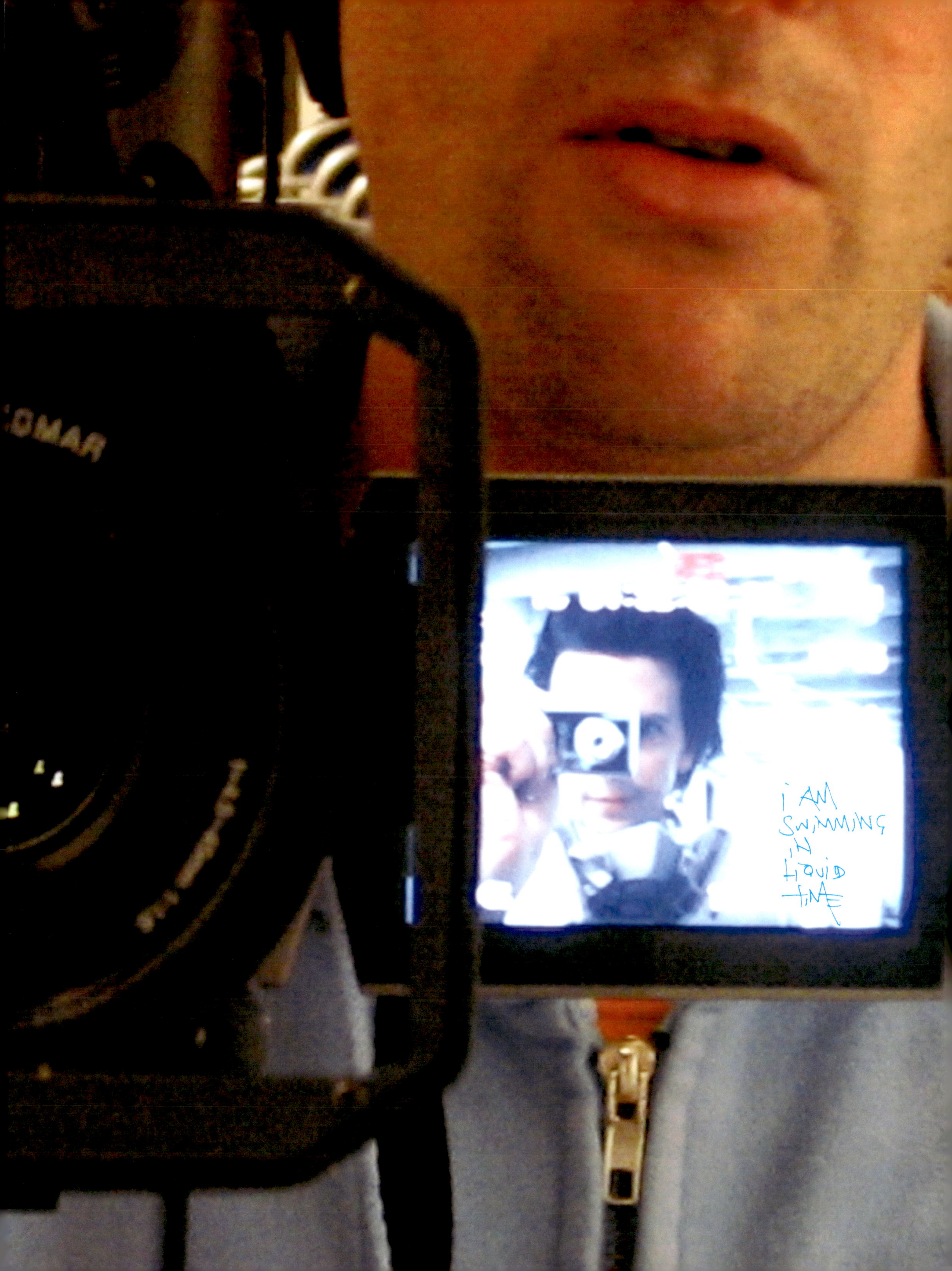
I AM
SWIMMING
IN
LIQUID
TIME

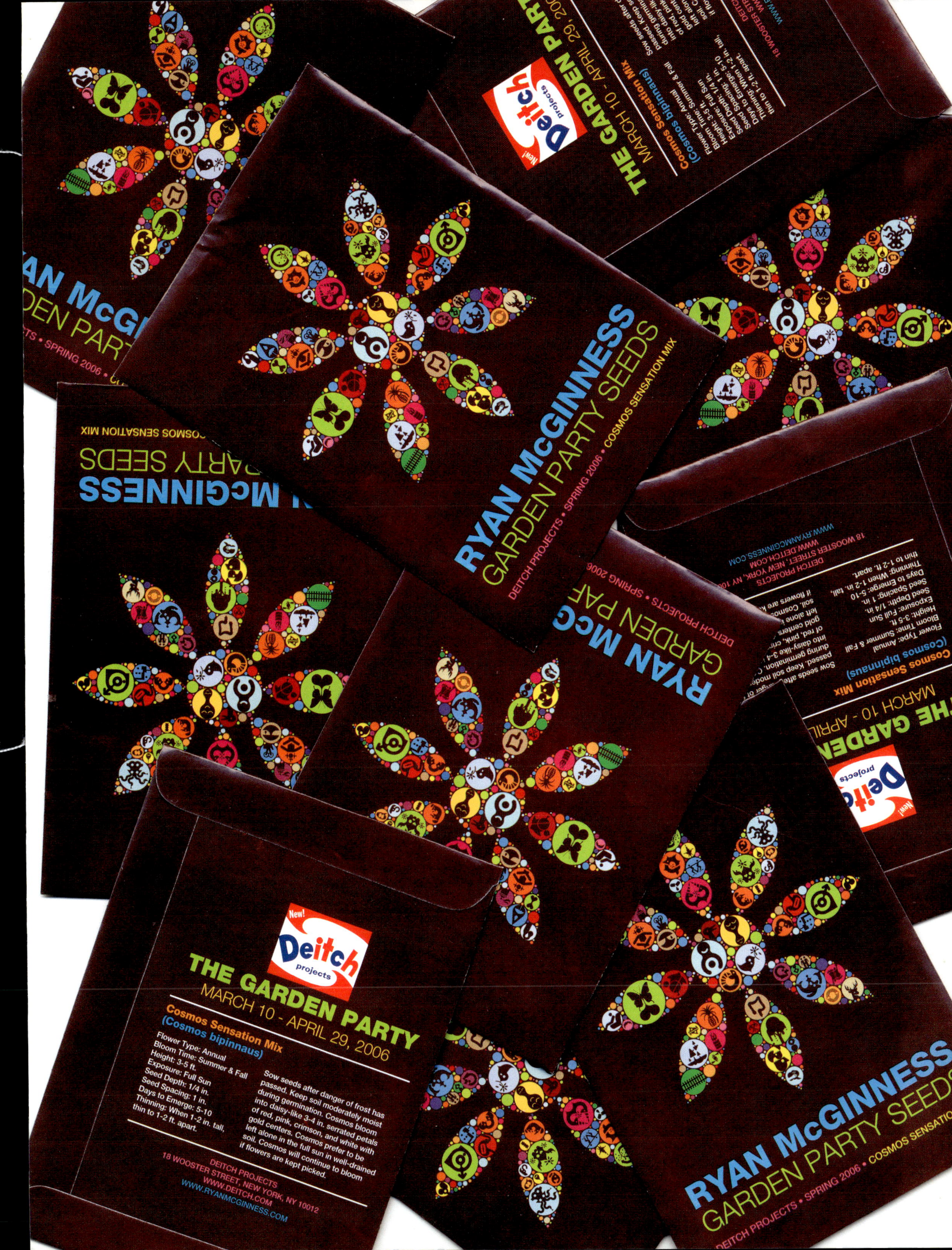

RYAN McGINNESS
GARDEN PARTY SEEDS
DEITCH PROJECTS • SPRING 2006 • COSMOS SENSATION MIX
New!
Deitch projects
THE GARDEN PARTY
MARCH 10 - APRIL 29, 2006
Cosmos Sensation Mix
(Cosmos bipinnaus)
Flower Type: Annual
Bloom Time: Summer & Fall
Height: 3-5 ft.
Exposure: Full Sun
Seed Depth: 1/4 in.
Seed Spacing: 1 in.
Days to Emerge: 5-10
Thinning: When 1-2 in. tall, thin to 1-2 ft. apart.
Sow seeds after danger of frost has passed. Keep soil moderately moist during germination. Cosmos bloom into daisy-like 3-4 in. serrated petals of red, pink, crimson, and white with gold centers. Cosmos prefer to be left alone in the full sun in well-drained soil. Cosmos will continue to bloom if flowers are kept picked.
DEITCH PROJECTS
18 WOOSTER STREET, NEW YORK, NY 10012
WWW.DEITCH.COM
WWW.RYANMCGINNESS.COM

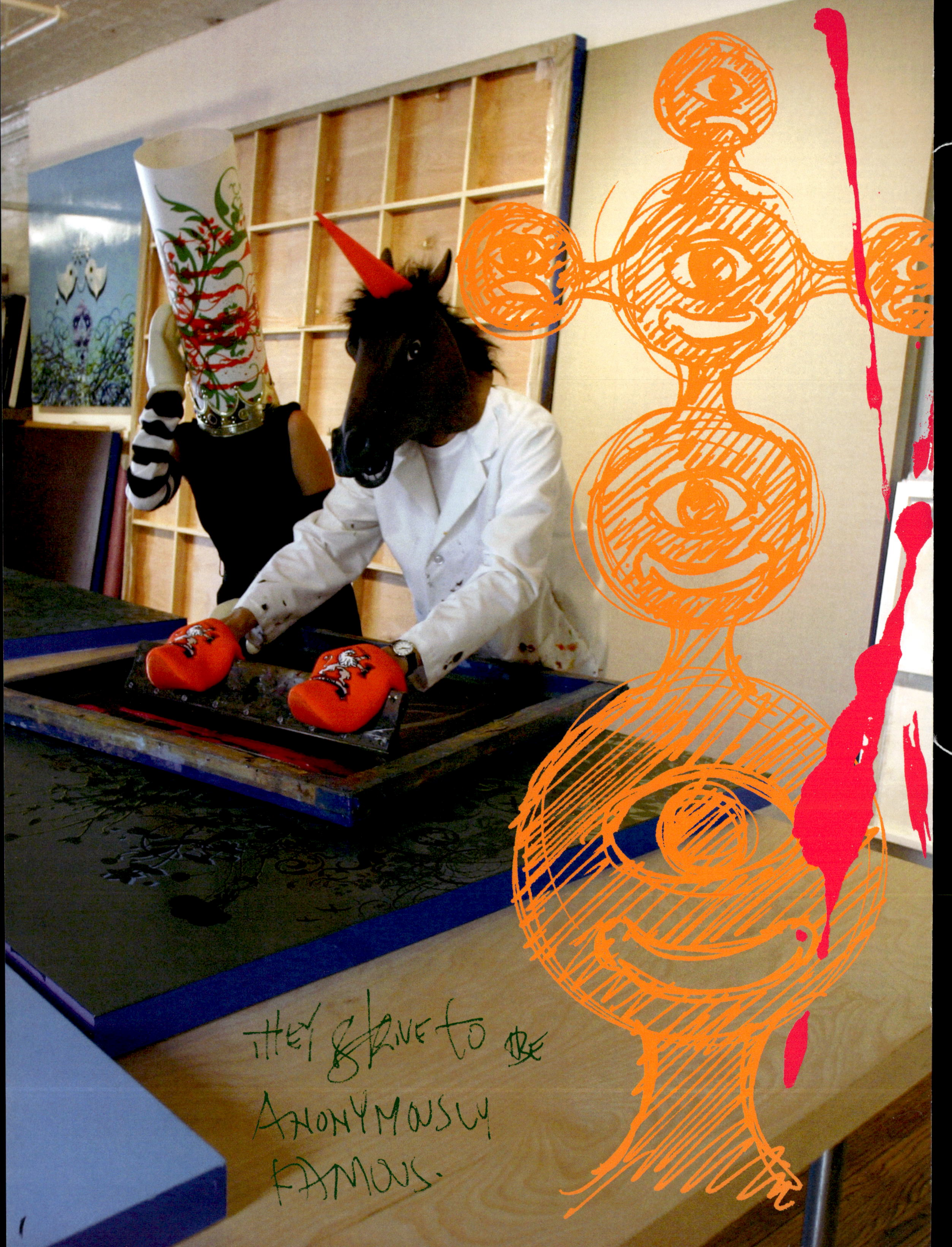
THEY STRIVE TO BE
ANONYMOUSLY
FAMOUS.

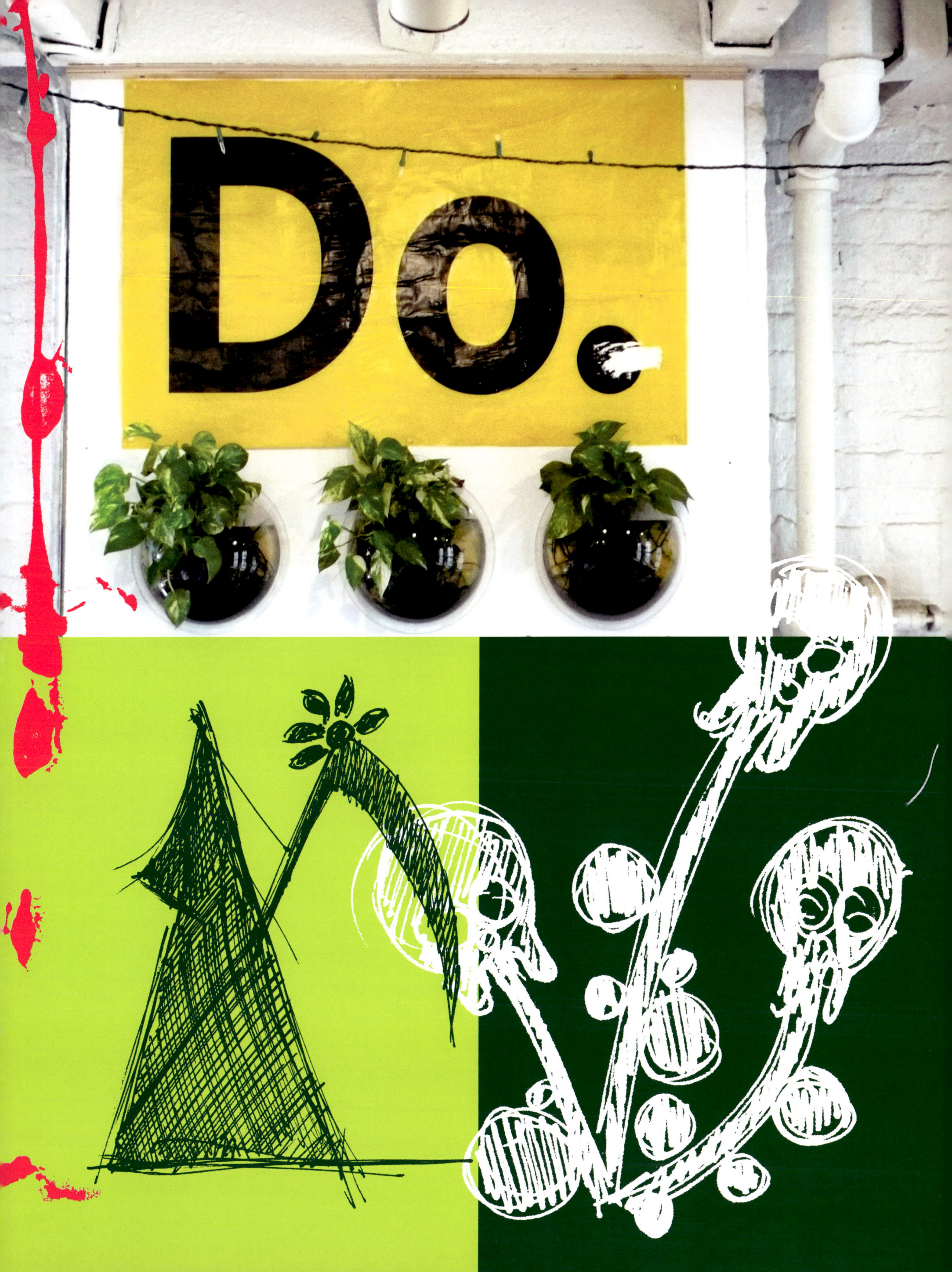
Do.

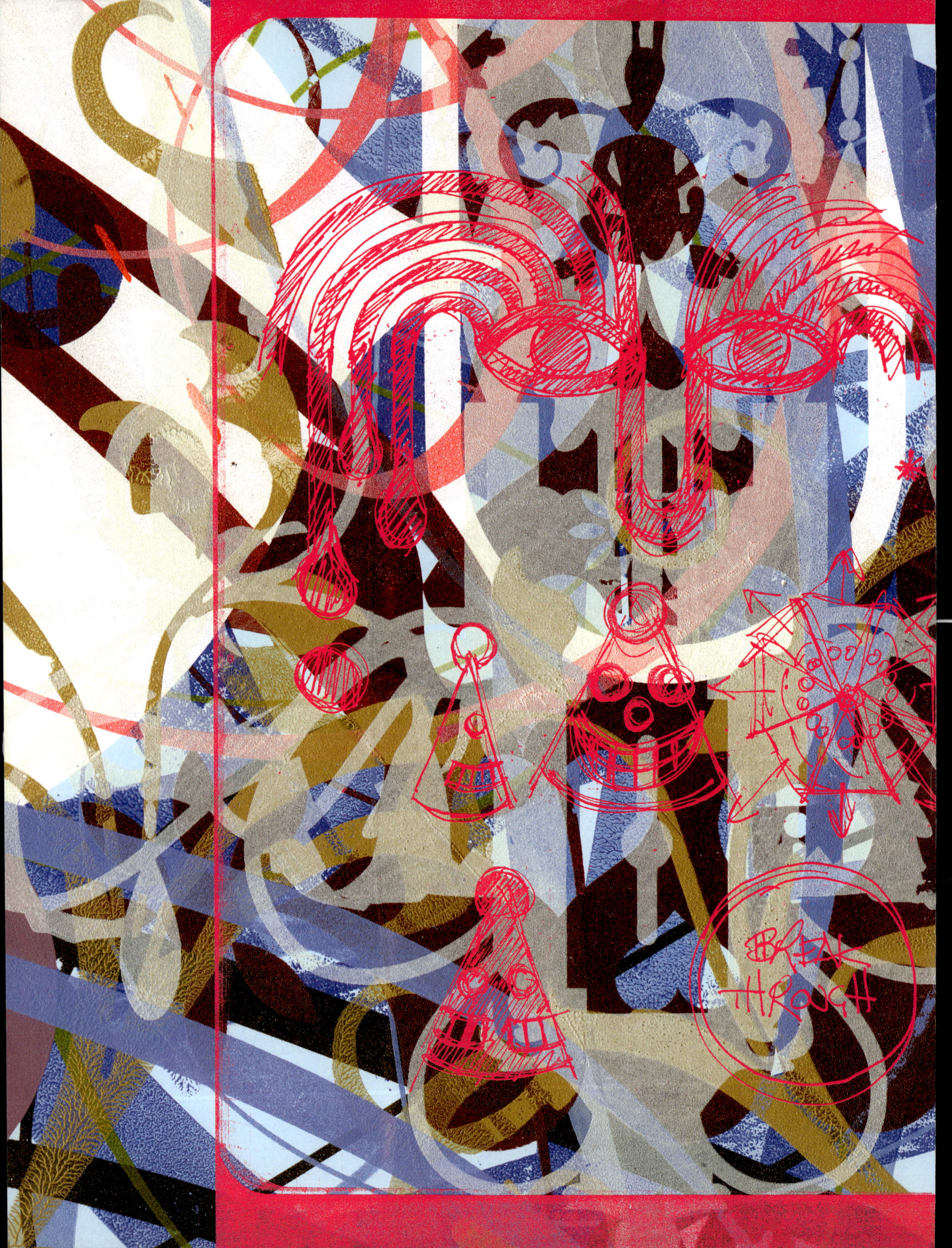
BREAK
THROUGH

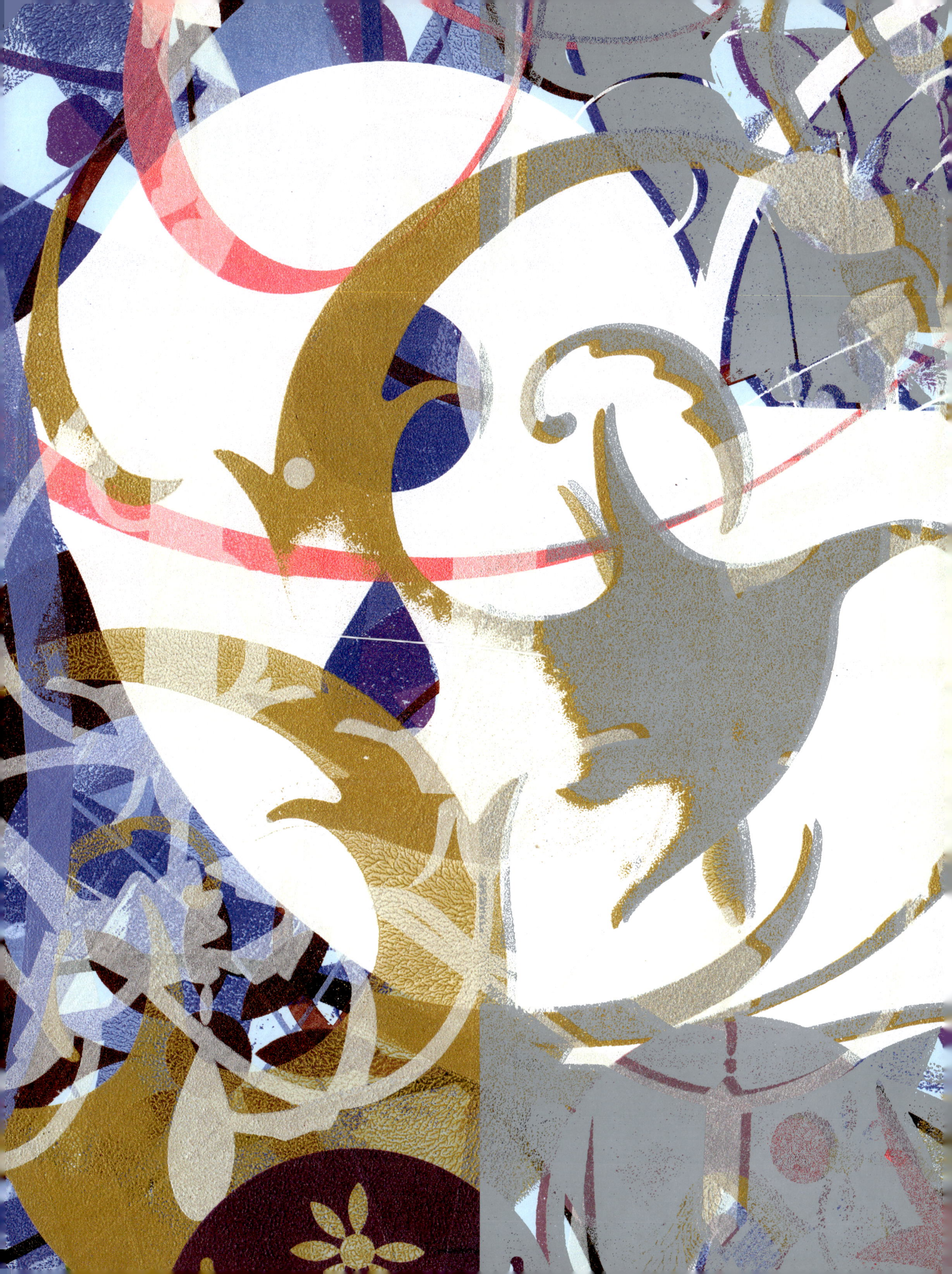

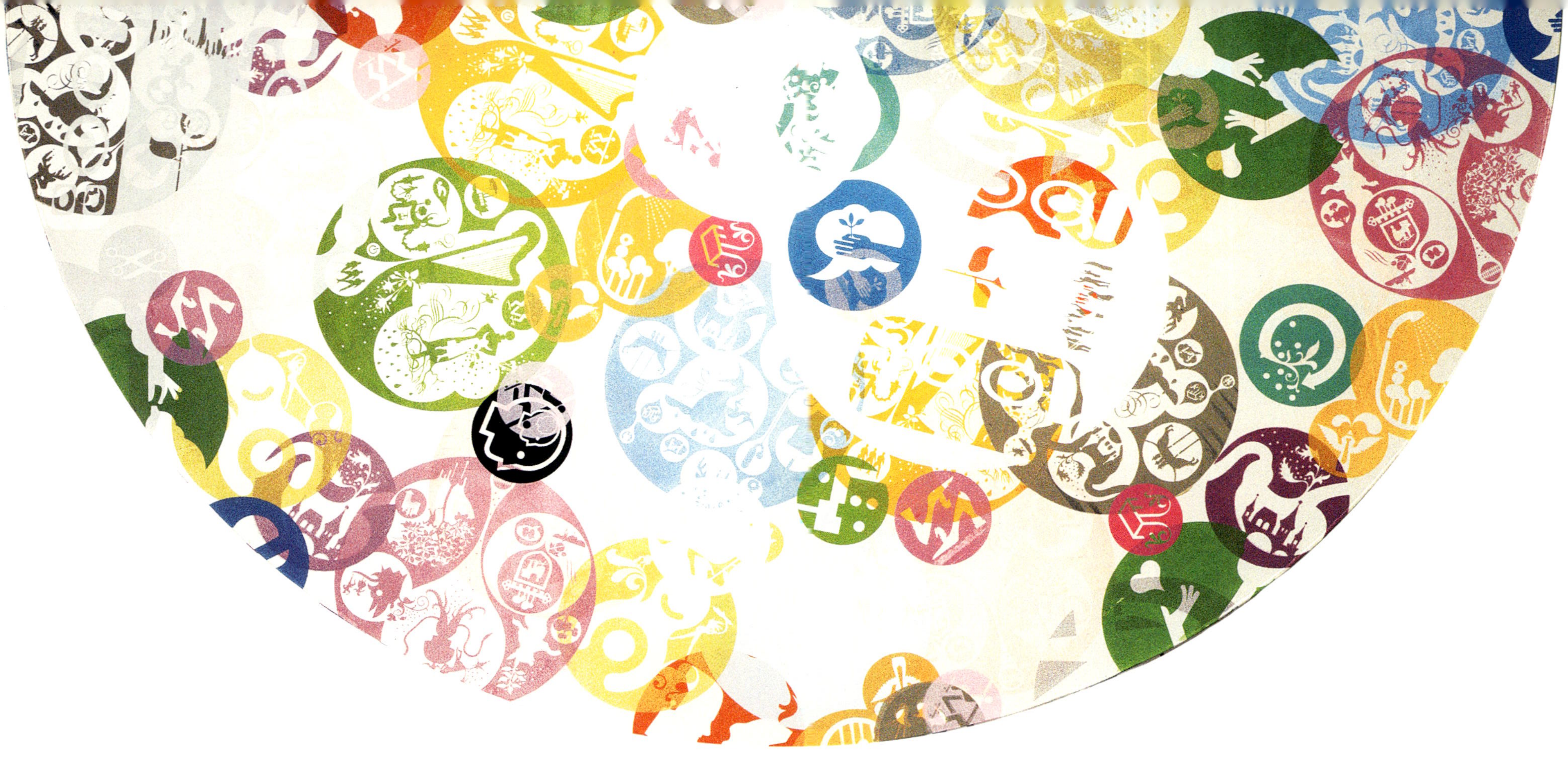

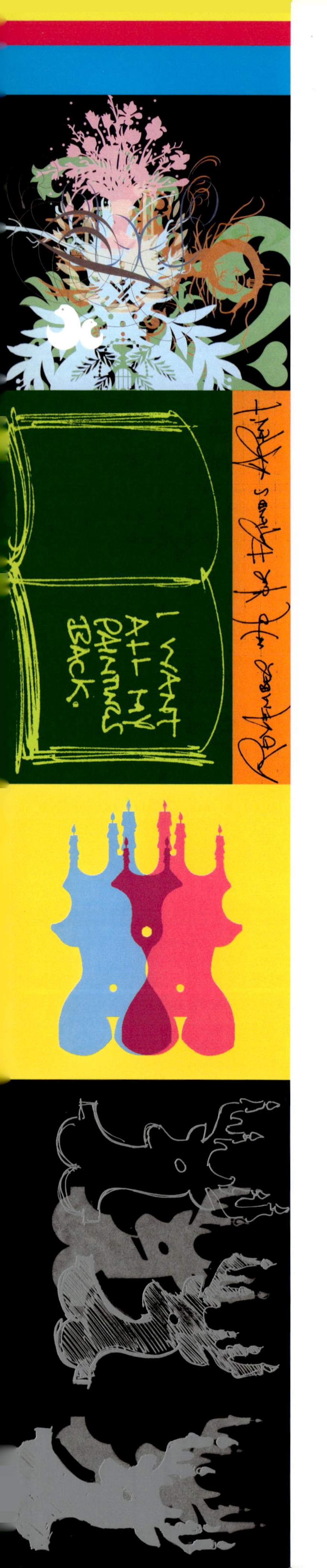
I WANT ALL MY PAINTINGS BACK.
REMEMBER WHO YOUR FRIENDS AREN'T

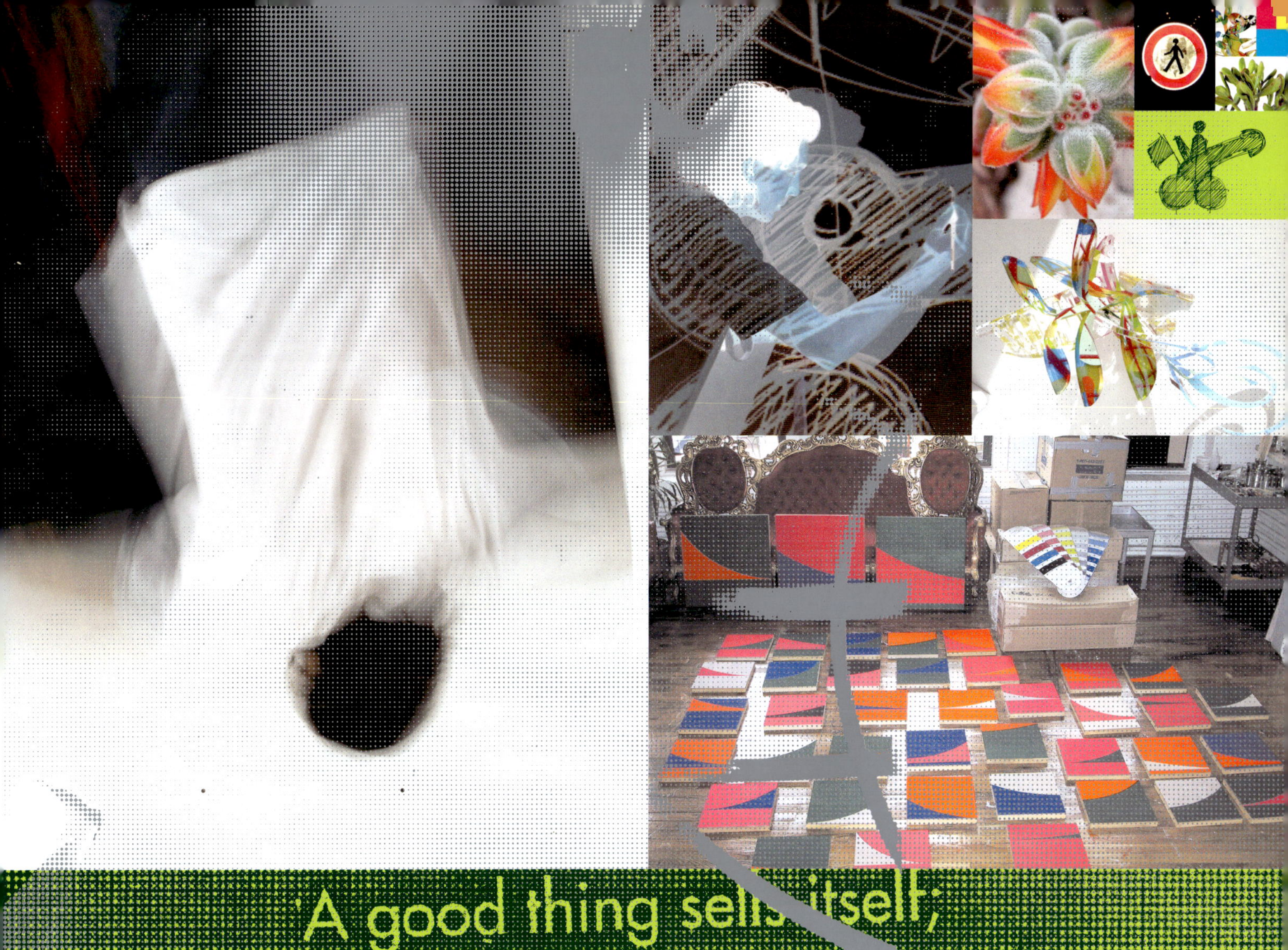

A good thing sells itself;
a bad thing advertises itself for sale.

—EAST AFRICAN PROVERB

Before you ask a man for clothes,
look at the clothes he is wearing.

—YORUBA PROVERB

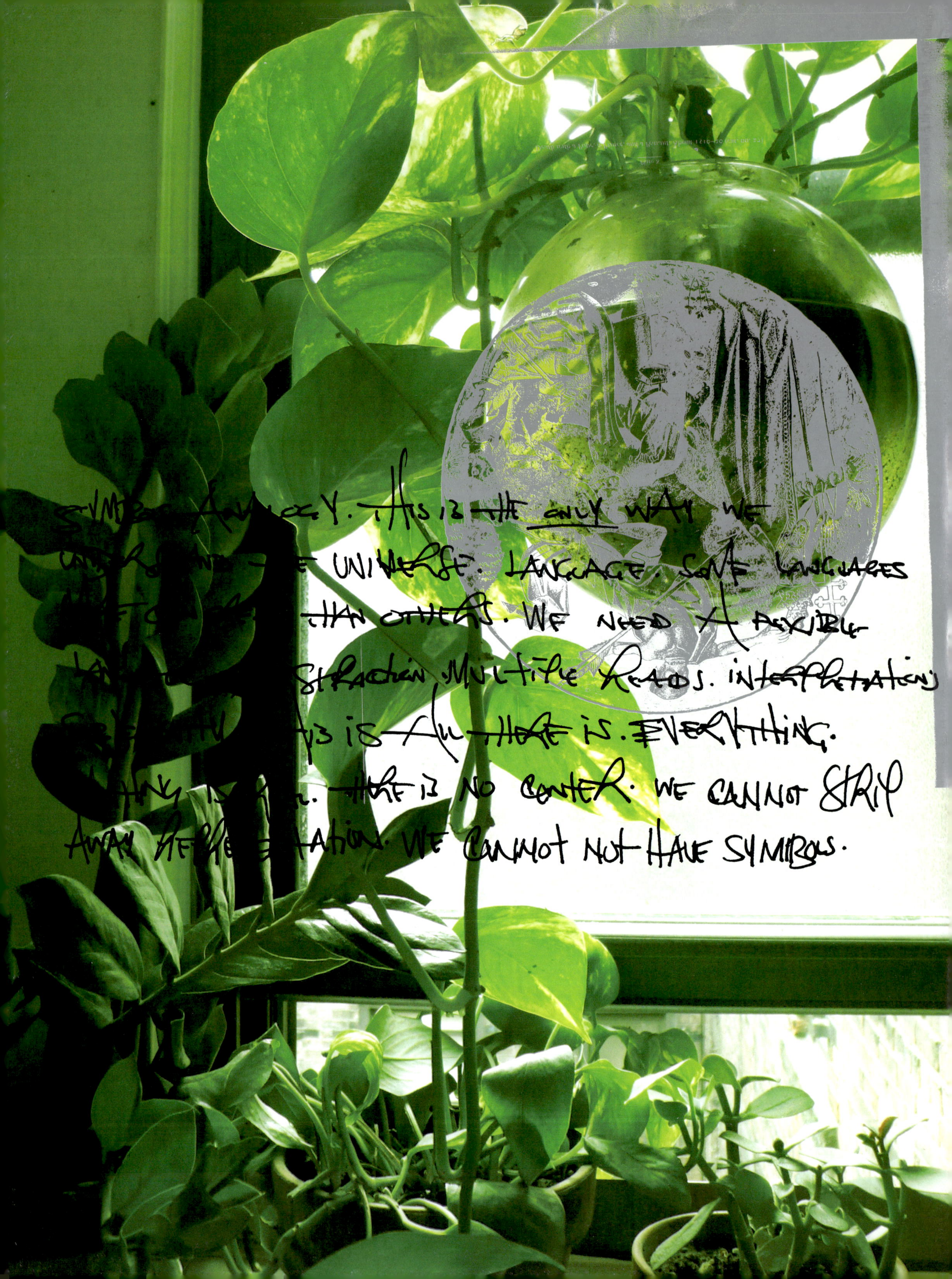
ANALOGY. THIS IS THE ONLY WAY WE
UNIVERSE. LANGUAGE. SOME LANGUAGES
THAN OTHERS. WE NEED A FLEXIBLE
MULTIPLE READS. INTERPRETATIONS
IS ALL THERE IS. EVERYTHING.
THERE IS NO CENTER. WE CANNOT STRIP
AWAY REPRESENTATION. WE CANNOT NOT HAVE SYMBOLS.

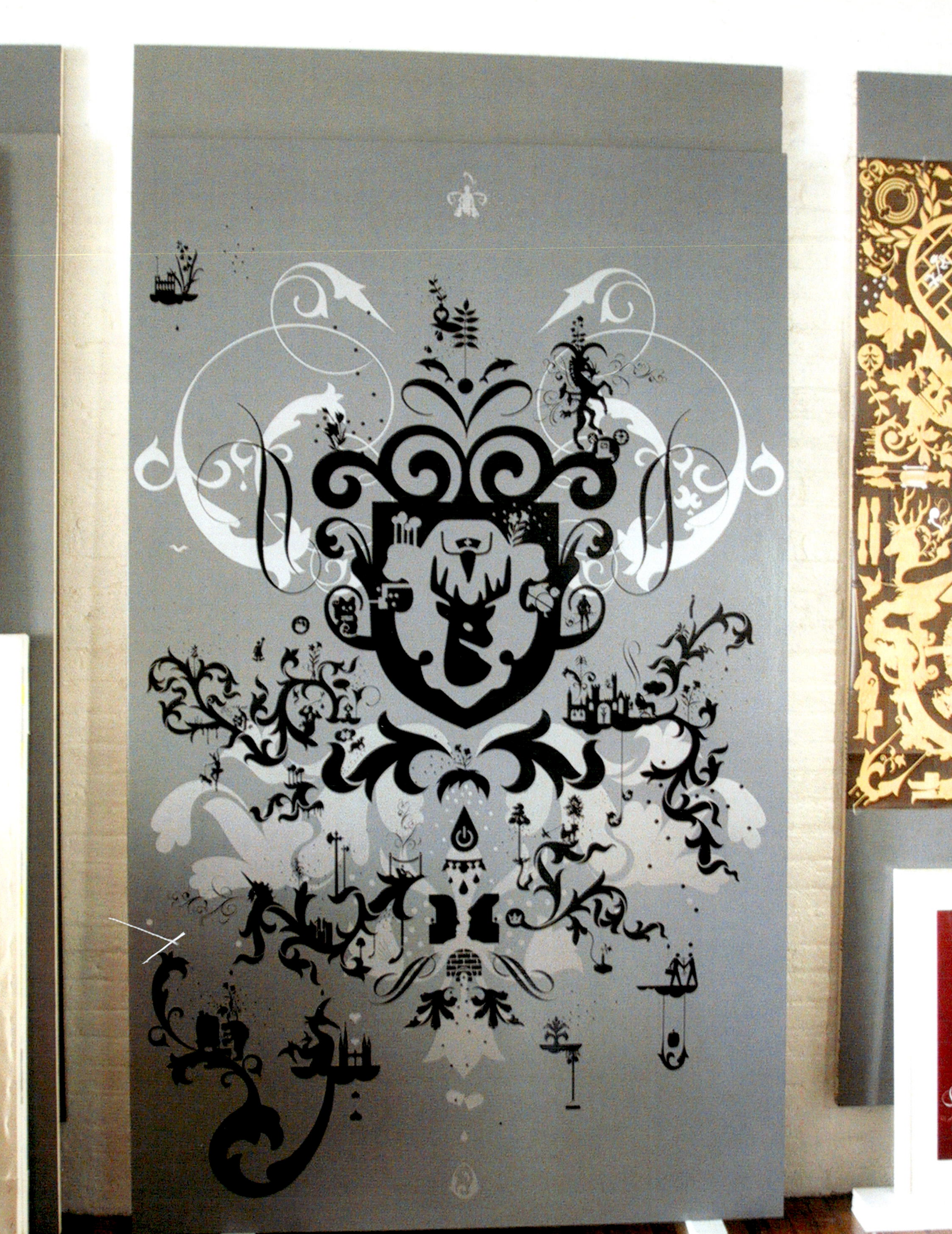

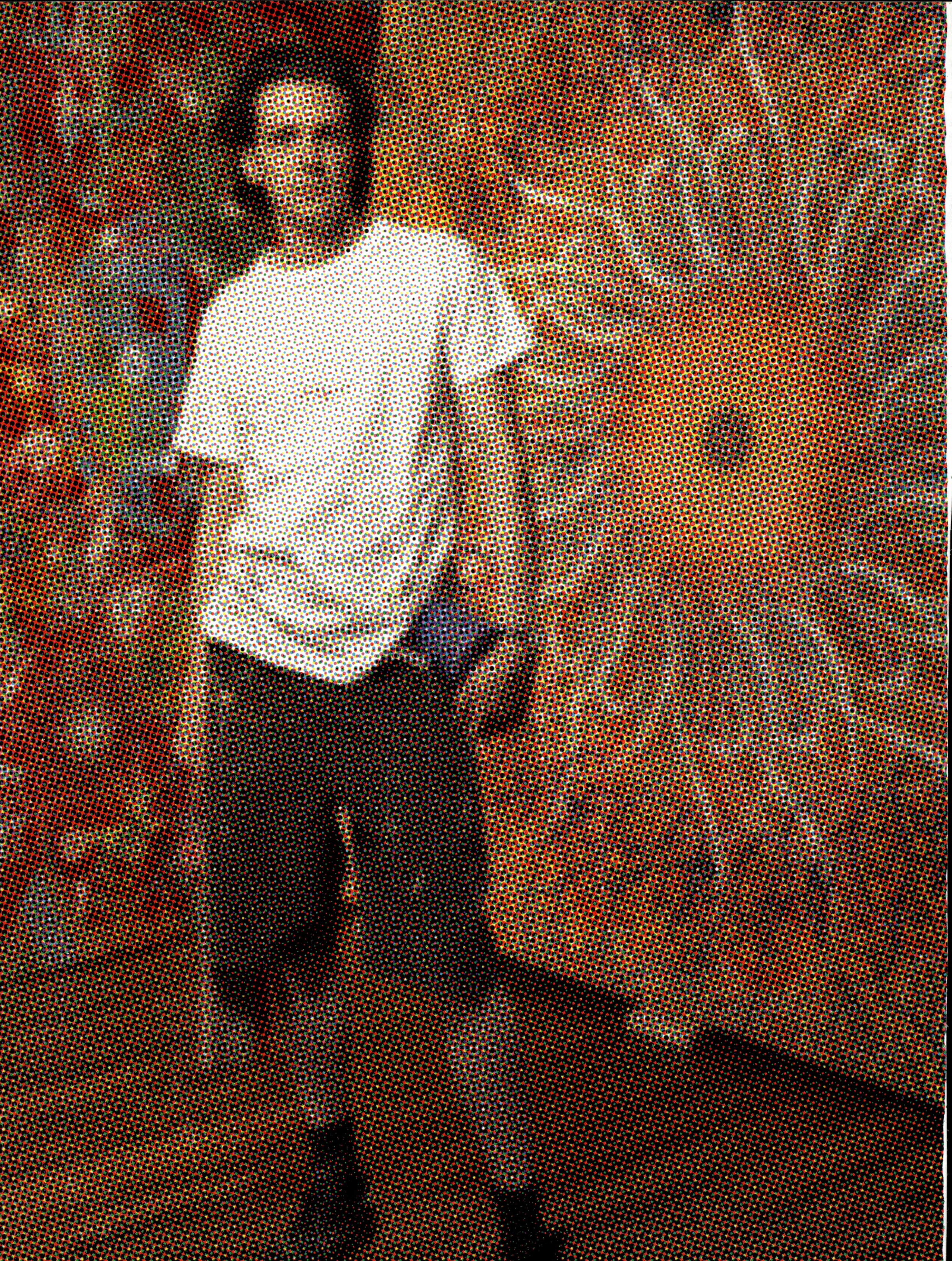

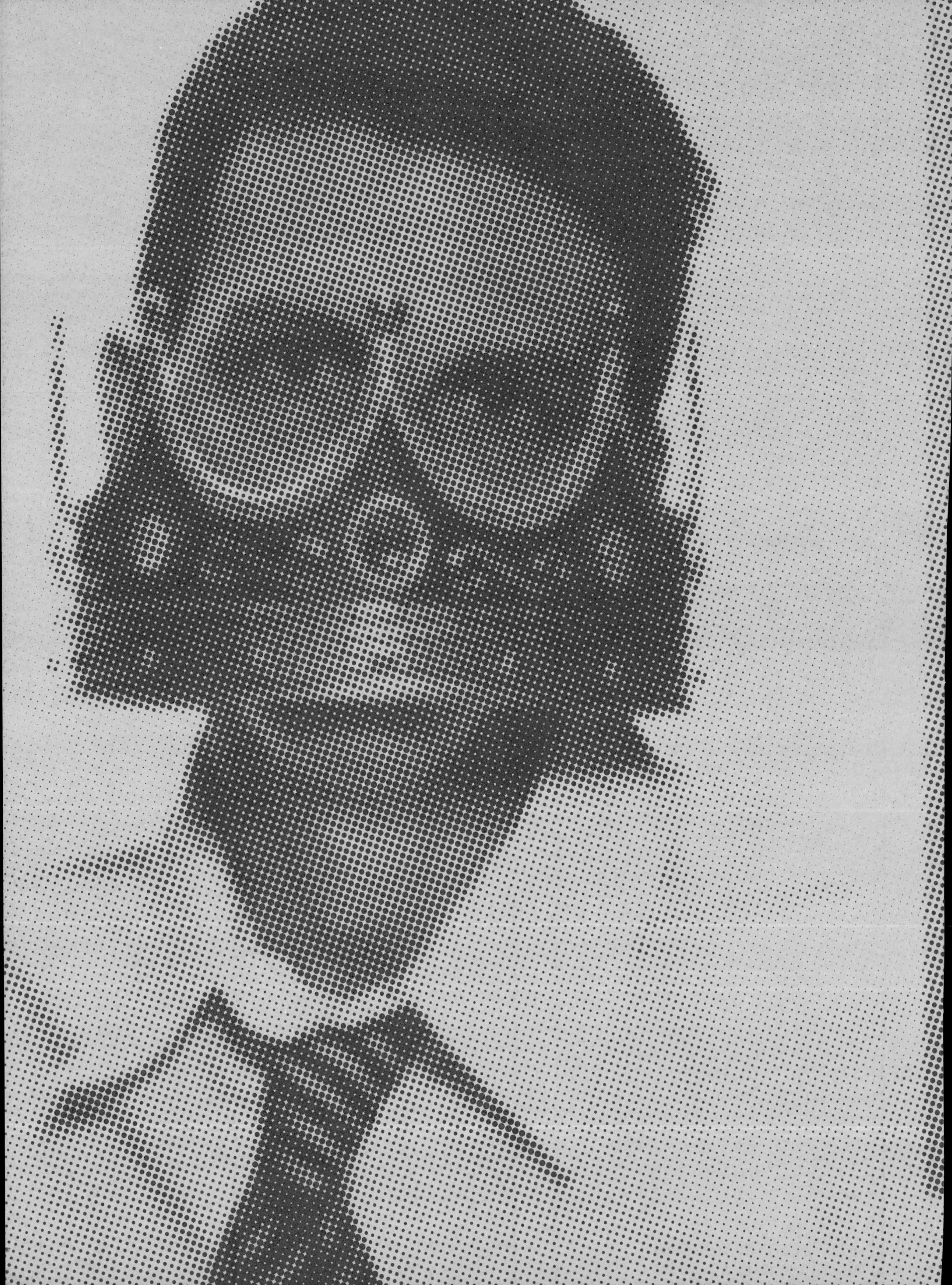